ANCIENT LETT

Ancient Letters

Classical and Late Antique Epistolography

Edited by

RUTH MORELLO AND A. D. MORRISON

OXFORD
UNIVERSITY PRESS

OXFORD
UNIVERSITY PRESS

Great Clarendon Street, Oxford, OX2 6DP,
United Kingdom

Oxford University Press is a department of the University of Oxford.
It furthers the University's objective of excellence in research, scholarship,
and education by publishing worldwide. Oxford is a registered trade mark of
Oxford University Press in the UK and in certain other countries

© Oxford University Press 2007

The moral rights of the author have been asserted

First published 2007

Published in the United States of America by Oxford University Press
198 Madison Avenue, New York, NY 10016, United States of America

British Library Cataloguing in Publication Data
Data available

Library of Congress Cataloging in Publication Data
Data available

ISBN 978-0-19-920395-6

Editors' Preface

WHY LETTERS?

Since the publication of Trapp's anthology of *Greek and Latin Letters* in 2003, we are more aware than ever of the dazzling variety of letters and letter types which have survived from the ancient world. Trapp has also usefully reminded us of the difficulties of defining and classifying the letter genre. Ancient theorists prescribe some guidelines about (for instance) the material, linguistic register, or length appropriate to the epistolary form, but even their prescriptions are notoriously broken by many of the most famous surviving corpora of letters. So, to take just one example, Demetrius tells us that one should avoid technical material in letters—the letter should not simply be a treatise with a greeting tacked on at the beginning and a farewell at the end—but (as Inwood and Langslow both point out in this volume) the longest and most technical of Seneca's *Epistulae Morales* or several ancient letters on medical topics cannot be excluded from a discussion of ancient letters simply because they break this 'rule'. Conversely, Cicero's *De Officiis* makes a claim to epistolarity which we must take seriously (see Gibson and Morrison's Introduction in this volume), and employs epistolary colour to situate itself within the tradition of letters of advice from father to son, but nevertheless seems an unlikely candidate for inclusion in the epistolary canon.

With this in mind, we adopt a generous and inclusive definition of the letter, the boundaries of which Gibson and Morrison explore in their introductory essay. One useful way, for example, of looking at the letter is to say, with Henderson, that it is a medium for creating 'shared virtual space' for communication (Henderson's good example being the 'private Republic' inside the letters exchanged between Cicero and his brother). Our spectrum ranges from 'documentary' letters on papyrus (Hutchinson), to the entirely artificial letters produced by writers of the Second Sophistic period (Hodkinson, König).

Moreover, our volume urges discussion of technical or philosophical letters alongside high-flown literary letters and suggests that we should consider differences between them to be matters of degree not of kind (Langslow). We look for 'epistolary colour'—anything which suggests to us that we are indeed reading letters in any given instance—and we investigate its effects and its functions within individual texts, across whole collections, and in the literary tradition.

Our primary question throughout this volume is not, then, 'What are letters?' (on which see Gibson and Morrison) but 'Why letters?' What purpose is served by casting any text in epistolary form and what epistolary features make the letter form especially attractive wherever another form might be available to the writer? Naturally we cannot, in a volume of this kind, aspire to comprehensiveness of treatment, but we share an interest in the following themes.

1. The utility and accessibility of epistolary writing

Although the linguistic register of letters varies widely, and, as Langslow points out, the style of a cover letter accompanying a medical treatise is sometimes more high-flown than the treatise itself, nevertheless, it remains generally true that the letter form is associated with a relatively simple communication style. Hoffer, for example, in his study of repeated marked expressions in Cicero's letters points to his often 'casual and improvisatory' style in this genre; König, too, remarks upon the tolerance of the letter genre for repetitiveness of a less specific kind. The 'intimate space' of letters (Henderson) fosters an apparently 'conversational' style (ancient theorists famously speak of the letter as 'one half of a dialogue'), which not only facilitates communication between writer and addressee, but also generates the sense in the external reader that s/he is 'eavesdropping' upon a private world and thus getting a privileged or unmediated glimpse of the writer's life and inner feelings—that s/he can 'track the writer's thoughts' (Hoffer).

That is not to say that letters are ever 'artless' or that our impression of being eavesdroppers is necessarily justified, particularly when we realize that many letters were intended for the eyes of someone other than the named addressee, and that the writer might deploy sophisticated rhetorical strategies for the benefit of that other intended reader (so, for example, Henderson suggests in this volume that Cicero's letters to his brother were written with Caesar in mind as the (more?) important addressee). Nevertheless, we should recognize this psychological phenomenon as part of the appeal of letters, an element of the invitation offered by a letter to all its readers (both its addressee(s) and the wider public) which may be exploited by the skilled epistolary communicator. Letters suggest frankness and openness and so are as well suited to skilful demonstrations and instantiations of a writer's chosen persona (Fitzgerald, Hutchinson), or of the characters of fictional epistolographers (König), as they are to the maintenance of friendships and the fostering of a community (see, for example, Freisenbruch on Fronto's manipulation of the arts of epistolary friendship or Morello on Pliny's campaign against *inuidia* in his literary circle).

However, the personal appeal of letters should not lead us to undervalue the rhetorical, literary, and intellectual advantages for a writer of choosing the epistolary form. As Inwood shows, we must not dismiss, for example, Seneca's decision to write letters in the latter part of a stunningly successful and varied literary career as merely 'weary personalism', nor should we be fooled into thinking that in these letters we see 'the man himself'. As he argues, our perception of Senecan stoicism has been skewed by our failure to realize that Seneca's decision to return to and renew the literary form used by Epicurus must have been the result of a deliberate choice in favour of letters as the most appropriate medium for discussion of ethical questions; ethics (as the study which asks every day, 'How must I behave?') naturally belongs in the accessible medium of letters (as Morrison also argues, in reference to Horace's *Epistles*) and to think that Senecan stoicism was not interested in logic or physics is to misread Seneca's creative observance of the generic requirements of his *epistulae morales*.

2. Power dynamics and role playing in letters

As Ebbeler points out in her analysis of two famous dysfunctional Christian correspondences, letter exchange advertises and negotiates social status. Certain types of relationship and of status differential (such as father/son or teacher/pupil) are particularly common in surviving letters; one of the borderline candidates for inclusion in the epistolary canon which are discussed by Gibson and Morrison in the Introduction to this volume—the *De Officiis*, addressed by Cicero to his son—takes its epistolary character partly from allusion to the tradition of earlier letters from parents to sons (by Cato, for example, or Cornelia). Even where there was no such paternal relationship, participants in a correspondence might choose to adopt epistolary roles which mimicked them, or to assert themselves by dwelling upon and magnifying the consequences of such role-playing (see e.g. Freisenbruch and Ebbeler). The differences in power, competence, or technical expertise which can be dramatized in such role-playing (see e.g. Langslow) make the letter form especially suited for the transmission of knowledge or of advice, and as we shall see, one of the strongest affinities of the epistle is with a variety of didactic traditions.

3. Special epistolary topics

Certain topics seem to gravitate towards the letter form. The example dwelt upon by several of our papers is the topic of health, which was particularly common in Latin letters. Here, of course, we point especially to Langslow's discussion of medical letters, in which he notes that medical prefatory letters had a particularly strong appeal in the Latin as opposed to the Greek traditions. Further, both Freisenbruch and Hoffer discuss the distinctive use of personal medical information or of medical metaphors in letters. In Fronto, for example, a letter itself could be presented as either infection or panacea, or as teaching aid *and* health tonic (Freisenbruch). Epistolary remedies are readily available for diseases and imbalances of the mind too. Seneca, whose model, Epicurus, favoured *hugiainein* ('be healthy') as the standard salutation at the beginning of letters, in place of the more common *chairein* (Inwood), plays upon the extension of this epistolary motif from physical to philosophical health in *Ep.* 15:

Mos antiquis fuit, usque ad meam seruatus aetatem, primis epistulae uerbis adicere 'si uales bene est, ego ualeo'. Recte nos dicimus 'si philosopharis, bene est.' Valere enim hoc demum est. Sine hoc aeger est animus;

corpus quoque, etiam si magnas habet uires, non aliter quam furiosi aut
frenetici ualidum est.

The ancients had a custom, which has been preserved right up to my own
lifetime, of adding to the opening words of a letter, 'if you are in good health
it is well; I am also in good health'. We say, rightly, 'if you are philosophizing,
it is well'. For this is, ultimately, 'being in good health'. Without this the mind
is ill; the body, too, even if it has great power, is no 'healthier' than that of a
man who is crazed or frantic.

The maintenance of physical health, as Pliny's letters on the daily
routines of Spurinna (3.1) or on his own summer habits (9.36)
suggest, requires daily attention, and the health of the mind calls
for similar ongoing effort. In *Ep.* 15, Seneca emphasizes the close
formal link between letters and health and ties it to the philosophical
work he is doing in his own letter corpus. Letters are particularly
suited to this kind of topic, partly because of the sense of development and change they afford (a series of letters, for example, can
report on changes in health from day to day) and partly because of
their natural association with current news and current projects—a
sense of urgency hangs about several surviving letters from the
ancient world (König, Hutchinson). As Morrison points out, for
example, the difference between a didactic text like the *De Rerum
Natura* and one like Horace's *Epistles* lies precisely in the sense of
urgent ongoing discussion and effort in the epistle, as well as its
open-endedness, as opposed to the body of knowledge presented to
the reader as a discrete unit for assimilation in Lucretius. As he says,
ethics needs to be done every day—hence letters. The two practices of
regular maintenance of epistolary relationships and daily care of the
body and mind are closely linked.

4. Letters as a didactic mode

A significant number of surviving papyrus letters contain specific
commands or instructions (Hutchinson), either about gifts which
they accompany, or about decisions that need to be made and
implemented by the writer or (more usually) the addressee. This
natural inclination towards the delivery of instructions, combined
with the relative simplicity of communication style, gives the

letter form an astonishing didactic utility and range of application, from the relatively mundane practical instructions discussed by Hutchinson to the specialized technicalities of the medical letters surveyed by Langslow. The lessons taught may define the community to which they are addressed: as Freisenbruch observes, letters teach people how to belong and this general lesson is specifically applied by, for example, Pliny's coherent and well-planned programme for teaching his addressees, in effect, how to function in literary and epistolary circles (Morello).

In pursuing a didactic agenda, the letter genre becomes remarkably elastic, adapting and adopting features from almost any other genre for best effect: for example, Horace adapts and alludes to Socratic dialogues and didactic poems as well as the Epicurean letter corpus in the service of his ethical agenda (Morrison), and Seneca's letters may be read *both* as philosophical treatises and as letters (Inwood). Finally, the writers of fictional letters can exploit the expectation that instructions belong in letters and the parallel awareness that such a fragile medium of communication may fail to achieve its goal, in order to show their letter writers tasting frustration and disappointment as epistolary wishes and hopes are repeatedly dashed and their world resists their attempts at control by letter (König).

5. The effect of collections of letters

Individual letters become an even more effective didactic medium when collected together, and several of our papers examine this and other functions of books of letters, a form which Hodkinson suggests might even be considered a separate genre in its own right. Several of the corpora we examine build a sense of community both among the addressees of individual letters and for the general reader; the letters of Epicurus maintained a scattered Epicurean community around the Mediterranean (and one might point also to the letters of the New Testament, which are not discussed in this volume). Moreover, deliberately gathering letters together in books allows a writer to demonstrate his social influence (see e.g. Rees on the effect of gathering Cicero's letters of recommendation together), or to suggest the wide applicability of the lessons taught in the letters by collecting letters to many addressees in a single volume (Morrison). Fronto and his imperial addressees acknowledge the role of epistles in defining and building a community, but adapt the motif to emphasize the unusual strength of their own affection, almost, as it were, outside the community's normal life (Freisenbruch). This feature of ancient letters may also lie behind the strength of the open letter in the ancient world: as Fear points out, in his study of St Patrick's letter excommunicating the followers of Coroticus, the open letter has not always been associated with a position of enraged weakness, since the letters with the most significant scope and impact in the world of the Roman empire, at least, were imperial rescripts (which might in certain circumstances be publicly inscribed), as well as the letters of the New Testament. Letters connect individuals with one another (see, for example, Rees on the 'triangulation' of relationships established in the formulaic letters of recommendation in Rome), and even medical letters may have successfully breached the injunction against 'technical' letters precisely because they were intended to have a broad appeal to a community of readers (Langslow). Collecting letters together makes them even more accessible, reinforces the epistolary character of individual items in the collection (see e.g. Morrison on the way in which some of Horace's less obviously 'epistolary' *Epistles* 'borrow' epistolary colour from their neighbours in the collection), and offers new literary possibilities.

6. The reader's expectations

Finally, many of our papers investigate the expectations generated in the reader by the writer's decision to use the letter form, and the results for the implicit dialogue between epistolographer and reader. These expectations can be as basic as the anticipation of particularly epistolary motifs, such as the separation of writer and addressee which typically 'gets the whole epistolary situation going' (Morrison), or the sense of privileged access to a private world which we have already mentioned above. On a more sophisticated level, letters can offer their own distinctive form of narrative and that phenomenon depends heavily upon the engagement of the reader with the writer's epistolary decisions. Both Hodkinson and König look at how the construction of new forms of epistolary narrative in fictional collections exploits the almost irresistible urge in the reader to make his or her own assumptions about the place of a letter in a story; letters expect reciprocity and follow-up (see Henderson and Ebbeler, among many others in this volume), and as readers we are caught up in that expectation and we will naturally and automatically conjure up in our minds some version of what might happen next. König demonstrates, in particular, how the inclusion of a response or pair to a letter can confound such assumptions and startle the reader, especially if that response is unexpectedly hostile. The result is a new story, quite unlike the one we had already begun to 'fill in' for ourselves on reading the first letter.

The sense of a uniquely epistolary version of the didactic 'plot' is also relevant to our understanding of the epistolographer's manipulation of a reader's expectations. Horace's *Epistles* encourage us to read them as a tale of the narrator's own progress (Morrison), while Fronto's correspondence presents a whole series of narratives about the evolving teacher–pupil contract contained within them (Freisenbruch). Meanwhile, Pliny's correspondence, like Cicero's, seems to tell the story of the narrator's life in the form of a tale full of gaps, repetitions, and (especially in the Ciceronian collections) temporal anomalies which force the reader to re-consider issues already raised several times before (including the status of a letter itself, as Fitzgerald points out). Finally, of course, such gaps and repetitions built into the fabric of a book of letters encourage *re-reading* and a process of contrasting individual letters with those which have gone before in the collection and remembering the earlier phases of the story.

The Editors would like to thank all those who spoke at and attended the Ancient Letters Conference in July 2004, from which this volume developed, as well as the old Victoria University of Manchester, its Research and Graduate Support Unit, Hulme Hall, and the Society for the Promotion of Hellenic Studies, for making it possible for the conference to be such a success. Thanks are due also to our colleagues in the Department of Classics and Ancient History at Manchester, to the anonymous readers for the Press, who were all full of good ideas, and to Hilary O'Shea for overseeing this book's passage into print.

Contents

List of Abbreviations

ANRW	*Aegyptische Urkunden aus den Königlichen (Staatlichen) Museen zu Berlin, Griechische Urkunden*, Berlin.
CPR	*Corpus Papyrorum Raineri*, Vienna.
D.-K.	= Diels-Kranz (H. Diels, W. Kranz (eds.) *Die Fragmente der Vorsokratiker*, 6ᵗʰ edn. (1951–2), Zurich)
EM	*Etymologicum magnum*, ed. T. Gaisford (1848), Oxford.
OLD	*Oxford Latin Dictionary*
PCG	*Poetae Comici Graeci*, eds. R. Kassel, C. Austin (1983–), Berlin and New York.
PL	*Philosophy and Literature*
SB	*Sammelbuch griechischer Urkunden aus Ägypten*
SEG	*Supplementum Epigraphicum Graecum* (1923–)
SGO	*Steinepigramme aus dem griechischen Osten*, eds. R. Merkelbach, J. Stauber (1998–), Stuttgart and Leipzig.
Suppl. Hell.	*Supplementum Hellenisticum*, eds. H. Lloyd-Jones, P. Parsons (1983), Berlin and New York.
TLL	*Thesaurus Linguae Latinae*

List of Contributors

JENNIFER EBBELER is Assistant Professor of Classics at the University of Texas, Austin, and author of several articles on ancient epistolography.

ANDREW FEAR is Lecturer in Ancient History at the University of Manchester and author of *Rome and Baetica: Urbanization in Southern Spain* (Oxford, 1996).

WILLIAM FITZGERALD is University Lecturer in Classics and Fellow of Gonville and Caius College Cambridge, and author of *Catullan Provocations* (California, 1999) and *Slavery and the Roman Literary Imagination* (Cambridge, 2000).

ANNELISE FREISENBRUCH completed her Ph.D. thesis at the University of Cambridge on 'The Correspondence of Marcus Cornelius Fronto' in 2003, and is now a freelance history researcher working in the media.

ROY GIBSON is Professor of Latin at the University of Manchester and author of *Ovid, Ars Amatoria Book 3* (Cambridge, 2003).

JOHN HENDERSON is Professor of Classics, University of Cambridge, and Fellow of King's College. He is the author of *Pliny's Statue: The Letters, Self Portraiture & Classical Art* (Exeter, 2003) and *Morals and Villas in Seneca's Letters: Places to Dwell* (Cambridge, 2005).

OWEN HODKINSON is currently completing his D.Phil. at The Queen's College Oxford.

STANLEY E. HOFFER is the author of *The Anxieties of Pliny the Younger* (Atlanta, 1999).

GREGORY HUTCHINSON is Professor of Greek and Latin Languages and Literature, University of Oxford, and Fellow of Exeter College. He is the author of *Latin Literature from Seneca to Juvenal* (Oxford, 1993) and *Cicero's Correspondence* (Oxford, 1998).

BRAD INWOOD is Professor of Classics and Canada Research Chair in Ancient Philosophy at the University of Toronto and author of *Reading Seneca: Stoic Philosophy at Rome* (Oxford, 2005).

JASON KÖNIG is Lecturer in Greek at the University of St Andrews and author of *Athletics and Literature in the Roman Empire* (Cambridge, 2005).

DAVID LANGSLOW is Professor of Classics at the University of Manchester and author of *Medical Latin in the Roman Empire* (Oxford, 2000).

RUTH MORELLO is Lecturer in Classics at the University of Manchester and joint editor with R. K. Gibson of *Re-Imagining Pliny the Younger* (Johns Hopkins, 2003).

ANDREW MORRISON is Lecturer in Classics at the University of Manchester and author of *The Narrator in Archaic Greek and Hellenistic Poetry* (Cambridge, 2007).

ROGER REES is Senior Lecturer in Classics at the University of Edinburgh and author of *Layers of Loyalty in Latin Panegyric AD 289–307* (Oxford, 2002) and *Diocletian and the Tetrarchy* (Edinburgh, 2004).

Introduction:
What is a Letter?

Roy K. Gibson and A. D. Morrison

LETTERS AND LITERATURE

The editors of this volume have speculated in general terms in the Preface about some of the general reasons why authors might use the letter form in preference to other forms, that is the purpose served by casting a document in epistolary form, and also about the invitation a reader receives on being asked to read a document under the rubric 'letter', that is the contract or code being offered to the reader in these circumstances. Various other particular reasons emerge from a number of the papers contained in this volume. But what, exactly, is a letter? The question is an important one both in relation to the ancient letter as a category, and within the context of the present collection. Indeed one might say that the question 'what is a letter?' is in some senses specifically a creation of volumes like the present one, which gathers together not only examples of the letter spread across a range of times and classical (or post-classical) cultures, but also letters of widely varying character, including documentary letters, fictional letters, letters in verse, philosophical letters, open letters, and letters meant only to be read by their recipient. Considered separately, each of these types might be acknowledged (to varying degrees) to be epistolary in character. But, once they are brought together, we are compelled to ask what, if anything, unites this diverse collection of documents as a type or category of writing worthy of separate study?[1]

---

[1] Cf. the expansion of Wilson (2001) 186 on the ' "epistolary"... as an inexact and slippery critical category'.

Asking for a definition of a letter is in some ways analogous to asking for the definition of various ancient literary genres, such as didactic or the ancient novel (both, notoriously, apparently discernible ancient forms with little or no correspondence to ancient critical categories).[2] The different strategies for defining or picking out such genres provide possible models for the definition of the letter. One might attempt for didactic, for example, to produce a list of necessary and sufficient conditions which a didactic poem has to satisfy to be categorized as 'didactic', as Volk has recently attempted:[3] explicit didactic intent; the 'teacher-student constellation'; poetic self-consciousness; 'poetic simultaneity', the creation of a dramatic illusion of a lesson under way as the poem progresses.[4] Toohey, on the other hand, has produced a more open-ended set of characteristics drawn from a wide range of poems normally thought of as 'didactic':[5]

(*a*) A didactic [poem] speaks with a single authorial voice and this is directed explicitly to an addressee, who may or may not be named.
(*b*) It is usually a serious literary form.
(*c*) Its subject matter is instructional, rather than merely hortatory.
(*d*) It may be, and often is, quite technical and detailed.
(*e*) Included within the narrative are normally a number of illustrative panels. These are often based upon mythological themes.
(*f*) The metre of didactic poetry is that of narrative epic, the hexameter.

Such a list, of course, depends on a prior classification of a certain set of poems as 'didactic'—the set from which the characteristics are observed. But how is such a set defined? If by the list of characteristics, then it seems impossible to avoid circularity. This may, however, only be an apparent problem—such lists of characteristics may in fact make explicit precisely those characteristics on which a classification of a poem as 'didactic' are made. The list itself is an

[2] See Selden (1994) on the ancient novel.   [3] See Volk (2002) 36–41.
[4] For some of the problems involved in this approach, see Sharrock (2003). Volk's definition excludes such figures as Parmenides from the category of didactic (though this might be a problem only with her definition, rather than any attempt to provide a list of necessary and sufficient conditions).
[5] From Toohey (1996) 4.

explanation of how and why we categorize certain poems as didactic (and, by extension, exclude others). Trapp has recently offered a similar 'phenomenology' of the letter, a list of 'contextual and formal characteristics', rather than a 'watertight definition' (i.e. something along the lines of Volk's necessary and sufficient conditions for didactic), which it is helpful to reproduce (with our own subdivisions) here. A letter is:[6]

(*a*) a written message from one person (or set of people) to another
(*b*) requiring to be set down in a tangible medium
(*c*) which itself is to be physically conveyed from sender(s) to recipient(s)
(*d*) overtly addressed from sender(s) to recipient(s), by the use at beginning and end of one of a limited set of conventional formulae of salutation (or some allusive variation on them) which specify both parties to the transaction
(*e*) [usually involving] two parties [who] are physically distant (separated) from one another, and so are unable to communicate by unmediated voice or gesture
(*f*) normally expected to be of relatively limited length.

Again, rather than seeing this as a circular set of characteristics depending on a prior definition of a set of texts as letters, we should see this rather as making explicit our typical criteria for deciding whether something counts as a letter. But even such a list leaves the boundary between what is a letter and what is not quite a letter unexplored, as Trapp himself acknowledges.[7] Some scholars have even suggested that the letter is in some sense the quintessentially literary form, that all literature is a kind of letter, for example, Derrida: 'Mixture is the letter, the epistle, which is not a genre but all genres, literature itself.'[8] Where are we to draw the boundary

[6] From Trapp (2003) 1.
[7] See Trapp (2003) 1 n. 3: 'The question where the boundary is to be set between "letters" and other pieces of writing that are in various ways comparable without qualifying as members of the family is not a trivial one, but lies beyond the scope of this introduction.'
[8] See Derrida (1987) 48, and also de Pretis (2002) 11–13 for a tentative expression of a similar view. Altman (1982) 212 argues that letters in one sense 'represent' literature as a whole, e.g. the (epistolary) relationship between author and addressee standing for the general (literary) relationship between author and reader.

between letters and non-letters? Or is there no boundary to be drawn? Are all the characteristics of letters shared by other genres, or all genres?

TWO THOUGHT-EXPERIMENTS—GREEK VERSE EPISTLES AND CICERO'S *DE OFFICIIS*

One way of deciding where the boundary between letters and other types of text lies, and whether this is a worthwhile question to pose, is to consider borderline cases. We shall look here at two such cases— the history of the classification as letters of various Greek poems, more recently thought not to qualify as letters, and Cicero's *De Officiis*.

Why are there no Greek verse epistles to compare with the Latin verse epistles of Horace or Ovid? Is this simply a matter of preservation? Not in the usual sense. A century ago, say, there were several poems which were regarded as verse epistles, as letters, such as Pindar's *Pythians* 2 and 3, and *Isthmian* 2, and Theocritus' *Idylls* 11, 13, and 28.[9] Why these were thought to be letters in the first place, and what happened to remove these poems from the category of the letter is a good way to think about what we mean when we talk about letters, particularly verse or fictional letters, what it is about them which makes them letters, and how they are related to other forms of poetry, particularly poems with prominent addressees.

The main reason for classifying such poems as *Pythians* 2 and 3, *Isthmian* 2, or *Idylls* 11, 13, and 28 as letters was straightforward: their clear resemblance to letters.[10] If we take again Trapp's list of

---

[9] See e.g. for Pindaric 'poetic epistles' Wilamowitz (1922) 285–93, 310 (*Pyth.* 2, 3, *Isthm.* 2), Farnell (1930) ii. 136 (*Pyth.* 3), and Bowra (1964) 124, 135 (*Pyth.* 2, 3, *Isthm.* 2), who cites Drachmann (1891) 189 for the same view on *Pyth.* 2 and 3. The view of these poems as poetic epistles was still widespread in the middle of the 20th cent.: see Harvey (1955) 160 (*Pyth.* 2, 3), Burton (1962) 78, Gantz (1978) 19 (*Pyth.* 3), and in general Young's survey of this view of *Pyth.* 3 (1983) 31–4. See Gow (1952) ii. 208 for Theoc. *Id.* 11 and 13 as letters. Haight (1948) 530 regards *Id.* 12 and 29 as letters and 11, 13, and 21 as 'semi-letters'.

[10] Often allied to a perception that these poems were somehow different, e.g. in tone or content, from comparable poems by the same poet. *Pyth.* 3, for example, lacks an explicit reference to an epinician occasion for its composition.

epistolary characteristics, we can see how close these poems get. *Pythian 3*, for example, certainly seems to be a written message from one person to another—it begins with a first-person wish by the narrator that Chiron were still alive,[11] and later addresses Hieron with what appears to be advice (εἰ δὲ λόγων συνέμεν κορυφάν, Ἱέρων, ὀρθὰν ἐπίστᾳ, μανθάνων οἶσθα προτέρων..., 'But, Hieron, if you can understand the true point of sayings, you know the lesson of former poets...' v. 80),[12] which parallels the common proverbial and paraenetic quality of many letters.[13] There is also considerable emphasis on the separation of narrator and addressee, e.g. καί κεν ἐν ναυσὶν μόλον Ἰονίαν τάμνων θάλασσαν | Ἀρέθοισαν ἐπὶ κράναν παρ' Αἰτναῖον ξένον, 'And I would have come, cleaving the Ionian sea in a ship, to the fountain of Arethusa and to my Aitnaian host...', vv. 67–8), which explains the need for this form of communication, and implies that the text itself has travelled, rather than the narrator. Moreover, at 115 lines, *Pythian 3* is of relatively restricted length.

Idyll 11, on the other hand, does not stress the separation of narrator (here 'Theocritus', a version of the historical author) and addressee, although the reference to the Cyclops as 'my countryman' (v. 7) and the fact that Nicias lives in Miletus in *Idyll 28* (v. 21), we might take as indicating that such a separation is meant to be read as standing behind the poem. *Idyll 11* begins with an elaborate address to the poem's recipient, which jokes about his profession:

Οὐδὲν ποττὸν ἔρωτα πεφύκει φάρμακον ἄλλο,
Νικία, οὔτ' ἔγχριστον, ἐμὶν δοκεῖ, οὔτ' ἐπίπαστον,
ἢ ταὶ Πιερίδες· κοῦφον δέ τι τοῦτο καὶ ἁδύ
γίνετ' ἐπ' ἀνθρώποις, εὑρεῖν δ' οὐ ῥᾴδιόν ἐστι.
γινώσκειν δ' οἶμαί τυ καλῶς ἰατρὸν ἐόντα
καὶ ταῖς ἐννέα δὴ πεφιλημένον ἔξοχα Μοίσαις.

There is no cure for love, Nicias, no lotion, no salve,
it seems to me, other than the Muses. This is something
painless and pleasant for men, but it is not easy to find.
I know you know this well, because you're a doctor,
and loved exceedingly by all nine Muses.   (vv. 1–6)

---

[11] We term the writer of a letter the 'narrator'.
[12] Translations of Pindar are taken from Race (1997).
[13] See e.g. Trapp (2003) 40–1.

This opening section sets *Idyll* 11 as a very personal communication between 'Theocritus' and Nicias, and introduces the *exemplum* of the Cyclops and Galatea. The poem is again brief (81 lines), and 'Theocritus' returns at the end to sign off the poem with another joke at Nicias the doctor's expense:

> Οὕτω τοι Πολύφαμος ἐποίμαινεν τὸν ἔρωτα
> μουσίσδων, ῥᾷον δὲ διᾶγ' ἢ εἰ χρυσὸν ἔδωκεν.

Thus Polyphemus shepherded his love
by singing, and fared better than if he'd spent gold.   (vv. 80–1)

This poem even seems to have been part of a two-way exchange between 'Theocritus' and Nicias, as the scholia quote a 'response':

> ἦν ἄρ' ἀληθὲς τοῦτο, Θεόκριτε· οἱ γὰρ Ἔρωτες
> ποιητὰς πολλοὺς ἐδίδαξαν τοὺς πρὶν ἀμούσους.

This then was true indeed, Theocritus: the instruction of the Loves turns many, who knew not the Muses before, into poets.

(*Suppl. Hell.* 566)[14]

There are several points of contact, then, between these poems and typical characteristics of letters. One obvious characteristic from Trapp's list which the poems above do not show, however, is 'the use at beginning and end of one of a limited set of conventional formulae of salutation (or some allusive variation on them)'. But it cannot only be the omission of the Greek equivalent of 'Dear So and So' which means these are not letters—after all, early examples of 'real' letters do not use such formulae,[15] and nor do many of the poems in Horace's *Epistles*. Why then should we omit poems with prominent addressees, on typical epistolary topics (*Pyth.* 3 on health/sickness, *Idyll* 11 on love and consolations for love), emphasizing or implying the separation of narrator and addressee, from the category of the letter?

Part of the explanation for deciding against the epistolary nature of these poems is, of course, our increased awareness of the context for the production of Greek poetry, which is particularly relevant in the case of Pindar's so-called epistles. For one thing the fact that Archaic and early Classical Greek literature is not straightforwardly

---

[14] Translation from Hunter (1999) 221.   [15] See Trapp (2003) 37.

written and read, but 'oral' (in this case composed to be performed
and *heard*) means positing that various poems are letters (written to
be read) is less attractive.[16] There is also now a much clearer sense of
the generic conventions of epinician poetry,[17] so that the critical
impetus to classify problematic examples as a different type of
poem has largely disappeared. Young, in particular, has convincingly
shown how *Pythian* 3 fits into the conventions of Pindaric encomi-
astic poetry,[18] so that we now understand much more clearly that
elements which appear 'epistolary', such as the separation of narrator
and addressee, are in fact typical of Pindar's epinicians.[19]

But the absence of Hellenistic Greek verse letters is more of a
puzzle. Letters were ubiquitous in Hellenistic Egypt, and we have an
extremely large number preserved on papyrus. Some even enclosed
epigrams, so that the letter was one vehicle for the dissemination of
poetry.[20] The answer to a riddle preserved from Antiphanes' fourth-
century comedy *Sappho*, on the letter, makes the point:

> The feminine being is a letter (ἐπιστολή), and the babies within her are the
> letters of the alphabet she carries around. Although they are voiceless, they
> talk to people far away if they wish . . . (fr. 194 *PCG*)[21]

Much like *Idylls* 11, 13, and 28 of Theocritus? Ultimately, the exclusion of poems like these *Idylls* from the category of the verse epistle
rests on a lack of parallels for such verse epistles in Greek. The
affinities with letters which the poems display are not enough to
overcome the lack of unambiguous further examples to point to. The

---

[16] See Carey (1981) 23–4. The awareness of the 'oral' nature of Archaic literature
began, of course, with the work of Parry and Lord.

[17] Starting with Bundy (1962).

[18] See Young (1968) 27–68, (1983).

[19] See Herington (1985) 190–1 for 'sending' the song in Pindar. There are still
some scholars who describe *Isthm.* 2 as a 'poetic epistle', such as Gentili (1988) 172.
This may be related to the very 'epistolary' close of the poem: 'Impart these words to
him, Nikasippos, when you visit my honorable host' (47–8). Letters, of course, often
play with the temporal disjunction between writing and reading the letter (e.g. the
Ciceronian Latin 'epistolary imperfect'). But the close of *Isthm.* 2 does not mean that
it was a letter: see Woodbury (1968) 540 n. 20. Such endings are, rather, part of a
wider play in Pindar's odes with the presentation of the time of composition and the
time of reception, and where the temporal 'point of view' of the ode is located, on
which see D'Alessio (2004) esp. 290 with n. 83.

[20] See Bing (2000) 146–8 on *Suppl. Hell.* 977.

[21] Translation from Rosenmeyer (2001a) 96.

fact that neither *Idylls* 11 nor 13 describe themselves as being 'sent', coupled with the absence of parallels, leads to their exclusion.[22] Rosenmeyer has recently argued for classing *Idyll* 28 as a verse epistle, on the basis of its similarity to the 'covering letter' type of epigram in the *Greek Anthology*, accompanying a gift.[23] But most of these epigrammatic 'epistles' are very similar to *Idylls* 11, 13, and 28 in sharing some epistolary characteristics, without being unambiguously letters. The exception is the 'love letter' at *Anth. Pal.* 5.9, by Rufinus, which Rosenmeyer also cites:

> Ῥουφῖνος τῇ 'μῇ γλυκερωτάτῃ Ἐλπίδι πολλὰ
>   χαίρειν, εἰ χαίρειν χωρὶς ἐμοῦ δύναται.
> οὐκέτι βαστάζω, μὰ τὰ σ' ὄμματα, τὴν φιλέρημον
>   καὶ τὴν μουνολεχῆ σεῖο διαζυγίην·
> ἀλλ' αἰεὶ δακρύοισι πεφυρμένος ἢ 'πὶ Κορησσὸν
>   ἔρχομαι ἢ μεγάλης νηὸν ἐς Ἀρτέμιδος.
> αὔριον ἀλλὰ πάτρη με δεδέξεται, ἐς δὲ σὸν ὄμμα
>   πτήσομαι, ἐρρῶσθαι μυρία σ' εὐχόμενος.

> I, Rufinus send many greetings to my sweetest Elpis,
> if she is able to flourish apart from me.
> I swear by your eyes, I can no longer support this desolation,
> nor separation from you in my lonely bed.
> But I visit the hill of Koressos or the shrine of great Artemis
> always drenched in tears.
> But tomorrow my own city will receive me again, and I will
> fly to your eyes, praying a thousand best wishes for you.[24]

Here we have clear play with a conventional epistolary opening and close. The beginning is closely modelled on the standard Greek for starting a letter ὁ δεῖνα τῷ δεῖνι χαίρειν ('X sends his greetings to Y'), which often appears with an intensifying adverb like πολλά ('many'), which we find here at the end of v. 1, while the end echoes the common Greek epistolary closing formula ἐρρῶσθαί σε εὔχομαι ('I pray you fare well').[25] This poem seems to have enough to stand as a verse epistle on its own, without the need for further parallels.

---

[22] See Hunter (1999) 261, who notes that we know nothing about the *Letters* of Aratus (*Suppl. Hell.* 106, 119).

[23] See Rosenmeyer (2001a) 100–10.

[24] Translation from Rosenmeyer (2001a) 107.

[25] On these opening and closing formulae in Greek see Trapp (2003) 34–5.

But this fact, that borderline epistolary poems need to be justified by parallel, or more explicit, examples is important, as it hints at the significance of the letter-collection. Should we be thinking about 'what is a letter?' not in terms of the individual letter, but entire collections, which themselves provide 'parallels' for interpreting them as letters?

It is time to try a different tack. One might try to answer the question of 'what is a letter?' as one might tackle questions such as 'what is a work of art?' Such a question might be answered in a totalizing manner, as John Carey has recently done: 'a work of art is anything that anyone has ever considered a work of art, though it may be a work of art only for that one person'.[26] But one might also appeal to the Humean concept of the competent judge:[27] 'art is anything a competent judge would judge as art', or perhaps, 'art is whatever one can persuade a competent judge to judge as art'. Taking the latter approach for the letter, that is 'anything one can persuade a competent judge is a letter', we shall engage on a second thought-experiment, and attempt to convince you that Cicero's *De Officiis* is a letter. This is not an arbitrary experiment. There was a well-established ancient literary tradition of treating philosophy in an epistolary format, beginning at least with Epicurus and projected back onto Plato and Aristotle through the corresponding pseudepi-graphic letters ascribed to them. Modern critics, in fact, routinely refer to the epistolary elements in, or the fundamentally epistolary character of, the *De Officiis*.[28] The work is explicitly addressed by Cicero as advice to his son Marcus, and at a number of points

---

[26] Carey (2005) 29; cf. op. cit. 30 'So far as I can see this is the only definition wide enough to take in, on the one hand the *Primavera* and the Mass in C, and, on the other, a can of human excrement and a child's blue-painted tie.' Compare also the similar definition of 'literature' offered at op. cit. 173–4 'My definition of literature is writing that I want to remember... Like all criticism of art or literature my judgements are camouflaged autobiography...'.

[27] See Hume (1757). For an aggressive critique of a very simplified version of this concept, see Carey (2005) 16–29.

[28] See (e.g.) MacKendrick (1989) 232 'the [*De Officiis*] is cast in the form of a letter', *Oxford Classical Dictionary*, 3rd edn. (1996) 1564 'Cicero's *De Officiis* was written in the form of a letter to his son in 44', Erskine (2003) 10 'it takes the form of a letter to his son Marcus', 12 'the character of the work, written as a letter to his son', and Ebbeler in this volume. Dyck (1996) is more neutral in his summarizing descriptions of the *De Officiis*: 'last extant communication with his son' (op. cit. 2), 'father–son communication' (op. cit. 13).

markedly approving reference is made by Cicero to famous letters of
instruction and warning written from fathers to sons, such as the
epistles of the elder Cato to his son, also called Marcus, (1.37) or
Philip to Alexander and Antigonus to Philip (2.48, 53). One possible
implication here is that the *De Officiis* is to be understood and read as
a work in the same mould.[29] On the other hand, the characterization
of the work as a 'letter' is apt to seem counter-intuitive or partial
when the three books of the *De Officiis* are read in full, and we are
perhaps more accustomed to think of it as a philosophical essay or
treatise. It is precisely this state of affairs which makes the work an
interesting test case.

We start by applying Trapp's categories, again, one by one to the
work. If (*a*) '[a letter is] a written message from one person (or set of
people) to another', then the *De Officiis* fulfils this first criterion
through being addressed by Cicero to his son Marcus (*Off.* 1.1, 2.1,
3.1: quoted below). The latter is in fact addressed in thirty-two
passages throughout the work.[30] The written 'message' to Marcus is
strongly marked: '[The *De Officiis*], from the very outset conceived
with young Marcus and his needs in mind, is deeply embedded in the
father–son relationship. It was meant as a call to order, an emphatic
reminder of his responsibilities to himself, his family, and his society'.[31] As for (*b*) 'requiring to be set down in a tangible medium', the
relative complexity of the 'message' of the *De Officiis* of course means
that it must be conveyed to Marcus in manuscript (rather than
verbal) form. A letter is also (*c*) 'itself to be physically conveyed from
sender(s) to recipient(s)': a circumstance, in fact, to which Cicero
explicitly draws the attention of his son—who is in Athens—in the
concluding paragraph of the *De Officiis* (3.121):

hi tres libri inter Cratippi commentarios tamquam hospites erunt reci-
piendi; sed, ut, si ipse uenissem Athenas...aliquando me quoque audires,
sic, quoniam his uoluminibus ad te profecta uox est mea, tribues iis temporis quantum poteris, poteris autem, quantum uoles.

---

[29] Cf. Griffin–Atkins (1991) xvii 'The literary inspiration for this "guidance and
advice" that young Cicero is to keep with his notes on Cratippus' lectures...is, in
fact, the Letter to a Son'. For Cicero's own comments in his correspondence with
Atticus on addressing the work to his son, cf. *Att.* 15.13a.2, also 16.11.4.

[30] See Dyck (1996) 60–1 on *Off.* 1.1 *Marce fili*.

[31] Dyck (1996) 12–13.

These three books should be accepted as fellow guests, as it were, among your lecture notes from Cratippus. If, however, I had come to Athens in person ... you would sometimes be hearing me also. In the same way, then, since now my voice reaches you in these volumes, may you give them as much time as you can; you can, of course, given them as much time as you wish.[32]

But it is not only physical conveyance which defines a letter, as letters usually carry some standard 'epistolary markers': (*d*) 'formally [a letter] is a piece of writing that is overtly addressed from sender(s) to recipient(s), by the use at beginning and end of one of a limited set of conventional formulae of salutation (or some allusive variation on them) which specify both parties to the transaction'. All three books of the *De Officiis* specify in their opening words that the son-recipient Marcus—who appears each time in the vocative—is being addressed directly by his father, and the whole work closes with a spoken farewell from father to son and an overt allusion to the written transaction between them:[33]

1.1 quamquam te, Marce fili, annum iam audientem Cratippum, idque Athenis...

Marcus, my son, you have been a pupil of Cratippus' for a year now, and that in Athens...

2.1 quemadmodum officia ducerentur ab honestate, Marce fili, atque ab omni genere uirtutis, satis explicatum arbitror libro superiore.

Marcus, my son, I think that in the preceding book I have explained well enough the way in which duties are based on what is honourable and on each particular type.

3.1 P. Scipionem, Marce fili, eum, qui primus Africanus appellatus est, dicere solitum scripsit Cato...

Marcus my son, Cato wrote that Publius Scipio, the one first surnamed Africanus, was accustomed to say...

3.121 habes a patre munus, Marce fili

Here you have a present, Marcus my son, from your father...

---

[32] All translations of Cicero taken or adapted from Griffin–Atkins (1991).

[33] On the high visibility of Marcus in the *De Officiis* (already alluded to), see further Dyck (1996) 10–16, esp. 13: 'As a father–son communication, *Off.* strikes an intimate tone unique among the extant *philosophica*. Thus though each of the three proems begins with the more formal mode of address *Marce fili*, this later melts to *mi Cicero* (1.1 and 3; 2.1 and 8; 3.1 and 5).'

... uale igitur, mi Cicero, tibique persuade esse te quidem mihi carissimum

Farewell, then, my dear Cicero, and be assured you are very dear indeed to
me...

The conditions in the *De Officiis* which satisfy the penultimate
criterion—whereby the need for a letter as a medium of transaction
normally arises because the 'two parties are physically distant (separated) from one another'—have already been alluded to. But it is
worth noting how Cicero explicitly draws the attention of the recipient in Athens to the physical distance from the sender in Italy (3.121,
partially quoted above):

si ipse uenissem Athenas (quod quidem esset factum, nisi me e medio cursu
clara uoce patria reuocasset)...

If I had come to Athens in person—as indeed I should had not my country
called me back in a loud voice in the middle of my journey...

The final criterion, that of 'relatively limited length', is the one most
obviously problematic for the status of the *De Officiis* as a letter. At three
hundred and seventy-two (modern) chapters long, this work does not
look much like a letter. Yet even here some mitigation may be offered.
One of the few ancient critics to discuss 'epistolary theory' in any detail is
Demetrius, who in his work *On Style* insists that moderate length is a
criterion by which good letter-writing should be judged (228):

The length of a letter... should be restricted. Those that are too long, not to
mention too inflated in style, are not in any true sense letters at all but
treatises with the heading 'Dear Sir'. This is true of many of Plato's *Letters*,
and that one of Thucydides. (Trans. D. C. Innes)

This stricture is revealing, because critically futile. The length of the
[pseudo-] Platonic letters—many times greater than the length of
the average epistle preserved on papyrus or in Cicero's own letter
collections—has proved no barrier to the reading and understanding
of these philosophical texts as in some important sense epistolary in
character. Why should we not allow some latitude here also to the *De
Officiis*?[34]

---

[34] One might add finally that the *De Officiis* possesses other epistolary markers in
addition to those cited, such as a repeated use of the second person form of address,
personal asides and remarks, an often dialogic or conversational style, and a distinctly
loose structure or style of treatment at various points; see Dyck (1996) 10–16, 49–52.

But, to conclude our thought experiment, why must our attempt to persuade you that the *De Officiis* is a letter fail? And what are the consequences, if any, of such failure? One reason it must (if only ultimately) fail is that Cicero himself never explicitly calls the *De Officiis* a letter, but refers instead to it as *tres libri* and *uolumina* fit to be placed beside the *commentarii* of Cratippus. Nevertheless, the treatise might well pass an epistolary version of an elementary test modelled on the minimal criterion for art set by John Carey ('[a letter] is anything that anyone has ever considered [a letter]') since a number of critics have commented on the epistolary character or form of the *De Officiis*. As for the second test, '[a letter] is whatever one can persuade a competent judge to judge as [a letter]', here our only really serious obstacle would be the criterion of length: this is a work substantial enough to require division into books. No other single letter from the Graeco-Roman world is divided up into three books. And yet, for all that, it could be argued that the *De Officiis* fits Trapp's phenomenology of the letter at least as well as Ovid's *Ars Amatoria* fits Toohey's phenomenology of didactic. The *Ars Amatoria* continues to be regarded—with whatever problems—as formally didactic despite the fact that it possesses neither the habitual serious-ness of the 'genre' nor, rather more importantly, the required didactic metre. In this context, need the (mere) length of the *De Officiis* pre-sent an insurmountable obstacle to an attempt to reclassify this work as a 'letter'?

But, rather than pursuing this possibly reductive and ultimately unfruitful line of argument, it seems more useful to reflect on the broader lessons which can be learnt from the near-fit of the *De Officiis* with an epistolary phenomenology. That is to say, rather than attempt-ing to construct either a more generous (or a more watertight) definition of the letter—one that might more firmly include (or exclude) the *De Officiis*—we could think of genre as a kind of spec-trum. Texts usually considered firmly within the category of letter can be seen to share core characteristics with marginal examples of the genre or even (as with the *De Officiis*) with quite different genres—and yet without doing damage to the idea of the letter as a useful category of literature. Here we turn to the idea of Wittgensteinian family resemblances.

CONNECTIONS AND COLLECTIONS

The Wittgensteinian idea of the 'family-resemblance concept' is often brought into discussions about genre, usually with regard to the internal connections between members of that genre. On the model of 'games' in the *Philosophical Investigations*,[35] different texts can share one or more characteristics with at least one other member, but there need be no one characteristic shared by all. Some poems might be in the same metre and language (e.g. the *De Rerum Natura* and the *Georgics*), while others might share only metre with these two examples (e.g. the *Works and Days*), or only the situation of a teacher educating someone with Hesiod's poem (e.g. the *Ars Amatoria*). But all might be classified as part of the same genre. Here the family-resemblance concept is doing much the same work as Trapp's and Toohey's lists above—making explicit (some of) the reasons we classify different things under the same category. It is as useful, however, to apply the idea of family resemblances 'between' genres, to use this as a way of thinking about the boundaries between different types of text. We can see that in many ways texts as diverse as *Pyth.* 3, *Idyll* 11, and the *De Officiis* do share several characteristics with letters, even if ultimately we don't find these sufficient to place them squarely within the category of the letter. But emphasizing these connections of letters to 'not quite epistolary' texts is also important. Letters are not the only 'code' for understanding texts which *do* qualify as letters, such as Horace's *Epistles*, which adapt a wide variety of texts including Socratic dialogues and didactic poems like the *De Rerum Natura*, as well as letters such as those of Epicurus.[36]

It is also important to see that the letter, even though it is a distinct type of text, with recognizable features such as those listed by Trapp, is also connected by some family-resemblances to other, non-epistolary types of text. This is not to say, however, that all literature is really or metaphorically epistolary, but to note that several texts can display characteristics similar to or reminiscent of letters. Such similarities can have a wide variety of effects on the reader, from drawing attention to

---

[35] See Wittgenstein (1967) §§ 65–71.   [36] See Morrison in this volume.

the imitation of or play with the letter-form, to directing the reader in the direction of a particular (epistolary) intertext. We should approach and interpret letters with full awareness both of the importance of their epistolary character, and their connections to other non-epistolary texts.

This brings us to the question of what the definition of a letter, the subject with which we began, is supposed to do. If such a definition is meant to divide off the letter, to make it a hermetically sealed conceptual category, clearly and definitively delineated from non-epistolary texts, then the futility of such a definition should be obvious. Letters cannot be separated in this manner from other texts, as the borderline cases we have studied show—a network of family resemblances, albeit less strong than those within the category of the letter, connect letters to texts and types of text 'outside' the letter. Such a definition, for example in the form of a set of necessary and sufficient conditions, is also problematic in that it may be used to exclude individual examples from the category of the letter and hence from the canon of texts to be read or criticized. This approach to letters shares some structural parallels with the making of aesthetic judgements. That is to say, asking the question 'what is a good poem?' inevitably leads to the question 'is *this* a good poem?'—which in turn all too often leads (in our experience) to the judgement 'this is not a good poem' and its inevitable if unintended corollary 'and therefore should not be read [much]'. Aesthetic judgements, whether or not the negative effect is intended, very often end up being used to 'exclude' from the canon.[37]

But it may be that one central problem in this approach to letters is the very act of asking 'is this a letter?', because often the epistolary character of an individual text is guaranteed by its place within a larger group of epistolary texts, such as in a letter-collection. A better question would be 'are *these* letters?' It is because of the title *Epistles*, and the occasional evocations of epistolary form, tone, and theme, that each of the poems in Horace's *Epistles* 1 'is' a letter.[38] Several individual 'letters', however, would no more satisfy all of Trapp's

[37] The negative effect of some aesthetic judgements does not mean, of course, that such judgements are impossible or incorrect. For the recent reintroduction of aesthetic judgements into the classical debate, see Martindale (2005).

[38] As Trapp (2003) 23 notes.

characteristics than Theoc. *Id.* 11 or Pind. *Pyth.* 3. The importance of
the letter-collection, then, to guiding the reader as to the need to read
its constituent texts as letters, cannot be underestimated.

We should also bear this function of the letter-collection in mind
as a central reason for the importance of paying attention to the
epistolary character of texts which are letters—much of the critical
violence done to letters such as Seneca's *Epistulae Morales* has been
the result of ignoring the epistolary character both of the collection
as a whole, and also the consequent epistolarity of each moral
epistle.[39] We can only achieve a full appreciation of such letter-
collections by taking seriously their claims to epistolarity, and by
remembering that the letter is not a type of text devoid of formal,
structural, and thematic connections with other types of text.

---

[39] See Inwood in this volume and Wilson (2001).

1

Down among the Documents: Criticism and Papyrus Letters

G. O. Hutchinson

Papyrus documents are rarely accorded much literary attention: sequestered from the general view, they live demurely, tended by experts. This critical neglect is particularly surprising with regard to letters, now the object of lively discussion. Despite changes over time, papyrus private letters as a mass offer a kind of starting-point from which may be seen to grow the more developed letters of Cicero and Pliny, and fictional and poetic extensions of the letter in Greek and Latin. These letters are not mediated by medieval manuscripts: we can look at the original handwriting and layout. We can look at drafts too. We can pursue types of letter and their relations with structures of class and culture across a much wider social range than the Roman elite. And the documents make us think about our categories of literature and the literary.[1]

Anyone who read *The Oxyrhynchus Papyri* vol. 18 from cover to cover might be excused for feeling a sense of bathos. The volume

I am very grateful to Dr N. Gonis for the benefit of his ready help and great knowledge of documents. The images were kindly supplied by Dr D. Obbink. The Cambridge literary seminar heard a version of these ideas, and made helpful comments; thanks especially to Dr W. Fitzgerald and Professor S. D. Goldhill.

[1] For a masterly introduction to documentary private letters, see Parsons (1980). Some desultory remarks on documentary letters: Hutchinson (1989) 358, (1998) 16. See also König in this volume. Funerary verse inscriptions form a striking example of a body of Greek material which as a whole should form the basis for considering the related Latin material even of the 1st cent. BC. There, though, we have to do with direct and extensive imitation; this will be illustrated elsewhere.

FIG. 1. *POxy.* 2190 (1st–2nd cent. AD)

opens with major new fragments of Aeschylus, Alcaeus, Callimachus, and Hipponax; it essentially ends with an account of bricks. And yet straightforward segregation of documents from literature may be too simple. Callimachus, *Iambus* 6 (in *POxy.* XVIII 2171) explores the relationship between dry numbers, poetry, and visual art. *POxy.* 2190, a letter from a student to his father, is not self-evidently more akin to the account of bricks (*POxy.* 2197) than to the poem in which Alcaeus laments his exile (*POxy.* 2165 fr. 1 col. ii 9–32 = Alc. fr. 130 b Voigt). It will be profitable to consider that letter more closely.[2]

The papyrus (Fig. 1) dates from around AD 100. The text has been much improved by John Rea; but there are so many uncertainties in the first column that a sparingly restored text is preferable.[3]

col. i

```
[   c.11   ]έωνι τῶι κυρίωι πατρὶ
[   c.11?  ] (vac.) χαίρειν
[   c.11   ]ης ἀθυμίας ἀπήλλαξας ῾ἡμᾶς᾿ δηλώσας ὡς
[   c.6  ἀδιά]φορα τὰ γενόμενα περὶ τοῦ θεάτρου,
[   c.9   φ]θάσας καταπλεῦσαι τυχεῖν λαμπρῶν           5
[   c.9   ἀ]ντὶ τῆς προθυμίας ἔπραξα. νῦν
[   c.10   ]. φιλόλογον, καὶ Χαιρήμονα τὸν καθη-
γητὴν καὶ Δίδ]υμον τὸν τοῦ Ἀριστοκλέο[υς], παρ᾿ οἷς
[   c.10   ]ετι κατορθῶσαι, οὐκέτι ἐν τ[ῆ]ι πόλει
[   c.9   ]αρματα, παρ᾿ οἷς τῆι εὐθείαι ὁδῶι χρη          10
[   c.9   ]ες διεφθόροσι. καὶ πρότερόν σοι ἔγρα-
[ψα  c.7  ] ἔγραψα τοῖς περὶ Φιλόξενον ἐπι
[   c.6   πρᾶ]γμα, καὶ ὑπ᾿ ἐκείνων τῶι εὐδοκιμοῦν-
[τι  c.7  ]αι παραιτησάμενον Θέωνα εὐθὺς
[     c.15     ] [ ] κ[α]ὐτὸς κατεγνωκὼς αὐτοῦ          15
[   c.13   ]ελως ἔ[χ]οντος τὴν ἕξιν. μεταδόν-
[   c.9   Φι]λοξένωι τὴν cὴν γνώμην, τὰ αὐτὰ μὲν
[   c.12   ]υτην μόνην τὴν τῶν σοφιστῶν ἀ-
```

---

[2] For Callim. fr. 196 Pf., see Hutchinson (1988) 26–7, Kerkhecker (1999) ch. 6, Acosta-Hughes (2002) 288–94; for Alc. fr. 130 b Voigt, Hutchinson (2001) 204–14, with lit. at 192 n. 6. Bricks are in fact of course an important subject...

[3] Rea (1993), the fundamental treatment. Further literature on and around *POxy.* XVIII 2190: Kleijwegt (1971) 116–23; Turner (1975) 5–9; McGing (1995) 53–4; Schubert (1995) 184–8; Cribiore (1996) 14, (2001) 56–9, 118–23; Gonis (1997) 48; Winter (2002) ch. 1; Heath (2004) 239. I have collated this papyrus from the original and inspected the originals of the other papyri principally discussed below.

.ο̣[ ].c̣υνπαθεῖν τῆι π[ό]λει φάσκων, καταπλε[ύς]α̣ν-
τα δὲ τὸν Δί{δι}δυμον, ὡς ἔ[ο]ικεν, φίλον ὄντα αὐτῶι καὶ   20
σχολὴν ἔχοντα, ἔλεγεν ἐπιμελήςεςθαι τῶν ἄλ-
λων· μᾶλλον καὶ τοὺς τοῦ Ἀπολλωνίου τοῦ τοῦ Ἡρώ-
δου παραβαλε[ῖν] ἔπειθεν αὐτῶι. καὐτοὶ γὰρ μ̣ε̣τ̣ὰ̣ τούτου δει[ ].......καθηγητὴν ἕως τοῦ νῦν ἐπιζητοῦ-
ϲιν, ἀποθανόντος φιλολόγου ὧι παρέβαλλον. εὐ̣-   25
ξάμενο[ϲ] δ' ἂν ἔγωγε, εἴπερ ἀξίους λόγου καθηγητὰς
εὗρον, μηδὲ ἐξ ἀπόπτου Δίδυμον ἰδεῖν, τοῦτο αὐ̣-
τὸ ἀθυμῶ, ὅτι ἔδοξεν εἰς ϲύνκριϲιν τοῖϲ ἄλλο[ι]ϲ
ἔρχεϲθα̣ι̣ οὗτο̣ϲ̣ ὃϲ ἐπὶ τῆϲ χώραϲ κ̣αθηγεῖτο.

col. ii

τοῦτο οὖν εἰδώϲ, ὅτι, πλὴν τοῦ μάτην μιϲθοὺϲ πλείοναϲ   30
τελεῖν, ἀπὸ καθηγητοῦ οὐδὲν ὄφελοϲ, ἀλλα ἀπ' ἐμαυτοῦ
ἔχω. ταχέωϲ ὅτι ἐάν ϲοι δοκῇ γράψον. ἔχω δὲ
τὸν Δίδυμον, ὡϲ καὶ Φιλόξενοϲ λέγει, ἀεί μοι προ[ϲ]ε̣υ-
καιροῦντα καὶ πᾶν ὅτι δύναται παρεχόμενον.[c. 5]
τῶν ἐπιδεικνυμένων ἀκροώμενοϲ, ὧν ἐϲτιν ὁ Πο-   35
ϲειδώνιοϲ, τάχα θεῶν θελόντων καλῶϲ πράξομαι.
ἡ δ' ἐπὶ τούτοιϲ ἀθυμία ἐϲτὶν ἡ ὀλιγωρεῖν τοῦ ϲώματοϲ
ἡμᾶϲ ἀναγκάζουϲα, ὡϲ οὐδ' ἐπιμελεῖϲθαι δέον αὐ̣τ̣ὼ̣ν̣
[τ]ο̣ὺϲ μήπω πράϲϲονταϲ, καὶ μάλιϲτα ὅτε οὐ̣δὲ οἱ
χαλκὸν εἰϲφέροντέϲ εἰϲιν. τότε μὲν γὰρ πρὸϲ ἡμέραϲ   40
ὁ χρήϲιμοϲ Ἡρακλᾶϲ κακὸϲ κακῶϲ ὀβολοὺϲ ἐπ̣[ε̣]ιϲ-
έφερεν· νῦν δὲ ἅμα τῷ δεθῆναι ὑπὸ Ἰϲιδώρου, ὥϲ[π]ε̣ρ
ἦν ἄξιον, ἔφυγεν, καὶ ἀνῆλθεν, ὡϲ δοκῶ, πρὸϲ ϲέ. ὃν
εὖ ἴϲθι μηδ' ἂν ὀκνήϲοντά ϲοί ποτε ἐπιβουλεῦϲαι.
οὐ γὰρ ᾐϲχύνετο πρὸ πάντων μετὰ χαρᾶϲ τὰ περὶ τοῦ   45
θεάτρου ἐν τῆι πόλει φημίζων, καὶ λαλῶν τὰ ψεύ-
δη ἃ οὐδ' ἂν κατήγοροϲ εἴποι, καὶ ταῦτα μηδὲν ἄξιον αὐτοῦ πάϲχων, ἀλλὰ λελυμένοϲ καὶ ὡϲ ἐλεύθε-
ροϲ πάντα ποιῶν. ἀλλ' ὅμωϲ δύνῃ, εἰ μὴ πέμπειϲ αὐτόν, παραδοῦναί γε τέκτονι. ἀκούω γὰρ ὅτι νεακί-   50
ϲκοϲ δύο δραχ{α}μὰϲ τῆϲ ἡμέραϲ ποιεῖ. ἢ ϲύνζευ-
ξον αὐτὸν ἄλλωι ἔργωι, ὅθεν πλείονα χαλκὸν λή-
ψεται, ἵνα τὸ μιϲθάριον αὐτοῦ ϲυνλεγόμενον
πέμπηται ἡμεῖν διὰ χρόνου. οἶδαϲ γὰρ ὅτι καὶ ὁ Δι-
ογᾶϲ γράμματα μανθάνει. ἐν ὧι τὸν μεικρὸν πέμ-   55
πειϲ, πλατύτερον ἐν οἰκίᾳ ἰδιωτικῇ τόπον ὀψόμεθα.
ἵνα γὰρ γειτνιεύϲωμεν Διονυϲίῳ, ἐν μεικρῶι λείαν

τόπωι γεγόναμεν. ἐκομιcάμεθα τὸν κόϊκα, πάντα α...
.[.]ϲ ὅϲα ἔγραψαϲ ἔχοντα, καὶ τὰ ἄγγη cὺν τῶι ἡμικαδίῳ·
ἐν οἷϲ εὕρομεν, ἀντὶ χοέων ι̅η̅, κ̅β̅. καὶ ὧν ἔγραψαϲ ἔπεμ-   60
ψα μετ᾽ ἐπιϲτολῆϲ ἑκάϲτωι ἡμικάδιον. τοῦ ὀλοφάκου
τὰ ἑξ μέ(τρα) ἔλαβον καὶ κῶον ὄξουϲ πλῆρεϲ καὶ ταριχηρὰ
κρέα ρ̅κ̅ϛ̅ καὶ τὰ ἐν τῶι κάδωι καὶ τὰ ὀπτὰ λ̅.
ἔρρωϲο. Χοιὰκ δ̅.

Back, downwards along fibres:

ἀρ]χιϲρεῖ Νείλου   65

11 lege διεφθόραϲι	44 l. ὀκνήϲαντα	50–1 l. νεανίϲκοϲ
55 l. μικρόν	57 l. μικρῶι λίαν	

Supplements *ed. pr.*

Translation, omitting excessively fragmentary or obscure parts.

From... greetings to his lord father... You rescued us from... despondency when you explained that what happened with regard to the theatre was of no importance... (5) sailing to Alexandria obtain fine... in return for my zeal I have fared[4]... scholar[5] and Chairemon the teacher and Didymus the son of Aristocles, with whom... succeed, no longer in the city... ,[6] with whom... (10) the straight road... have come unstuck. I wrote to you before... I wrote to Philoxenus... (15) having condemned him[7]... in ability. Having communicated your opinion to Philoxenus... saying that... of sophists alone he felt sorry for the city[8] (20) and that the rest would be taken care of by Didymus, who had apparently sailed to Alexandria: a friend of his and in charge of a school.[9] He was trying to get the sons of Apollonius son of Herodes to go to him too. They have been looking too up till now, with Philoxenus, for a...[10] teacher: (25) the scholar they used to go to has died.

[4] As question Rea, perhaps less plausibly.

[5] So Rea here and in 25; a proper name Philologus is also possible (cf. McGing (1995) 3–4).

[6] κα]θάρματα (Rea), 'rubbish', of the teachers: a very attractive supplement. Roberts's chariots (in the *ed. pr.*) do not obviously relate to the events in the theatre as he would wish, and his chronology seems unlikely.

[7] It is not clear that the father must be the subject (so Rea); the καί of κ[α]ὐτόϲ and the full recapitulation would then seem unlikely.

[8] ἀπορ[ία]ν, 'shortage', though it seems so promising, is hard to fit with the trace before the right-hand vertical of ν; to the left of that trace, there is ink which may be part of a letter.

[9] Probably not 'the other sons' (masc.): cf. 32–3.

[10] Rea reads δει[ν]ότερον 'higher-powered', but there does not seem to be enough space for the first ν. Roberts's δεξ[ι]ώτερον is not possible.

If I had found some decent teachers, I would pray, myself, never to see Didymus even from a distance. I'm dismayed at the very fact he has claimed comparison with the other teachers, when he used to teach outside Alexandria. (30) Knowing that there is no profit to be got from a teacher, apart from giving out more pay for nothing, I've got other resources, thanks to myself.[11] Hurry up and tell me what you think. I've got Didymus, who always has time for me, as Philoxenos says, and gives me all he can.... (35) By attending the performances of the rhetoricians, including Posidonius, perhaps I shall do well, if the gods will.

It's depression about this situation that forces us to neglect our bodies...[12] and especially when we don't (40) have people to earn us money. The really useful Heraclas...[13] was bringing obols in wretchedly, the wretch; but when Isidorus quite rightly tied him up, he escaped and has now travelled back to you, I think. You must realize he wouldn't hesitate to scheme against you one day. (45) He showed no shame, above all, in spreading word of the theatre events in the city with glee, or in speaking falsehoods which not even a prosecutor would utter—and all this when he was not treated as he deserved, but was unrestricted and could do anything, like a free person. But if you're not sending him to us, you could at least (50) employ him with a carpenter. I hear a young man earns two drachmas a day. Otherwise, get him fixed up with some other work that he can earn more money from, so that his pay can accumulate and be sent to us every so often. You know Diogas too (55) is studying. While you're sending the little one, we're going to seek out a larger place in a private house. For we've been in a place that's too small, so we could be next to Dionysius.

We received the basket; it's got... all the things you mentioned in your letter. We've also received the jars with the half-cadus; (60) we found 22 choes in them, not 18. I sent a half-cadus, with a letter, to each one of the people you said. I got the six measures of whole lentils, a jar full of vinegar, 126 pieces of salted meat, the things in the cadus, and the thirty pieces of roast meat. Best wishes. Choiak the 4th [30 November/1 December].

Back, downwards along the fibres: 'To... high priest of the Nile.'

---

[11] ἄλλα (Roberts) enables 30–2 to cohere as ἀλλά does not.

[12] The things which those who are not yet πράccοντεc ought not to be looking after should refer to τούτοιc (cf. also 21–2), not the body. For other doubts on Rea's interpretation (that students are allowed to be scruffy), see below. [τ]οὺc μήπω πράccοντας remains obscure.

[13] Gonis (1997) 48 raises significant objections to 'every few days' for πρὸc ἡμέραc. He suggests 'for a few days'; but here that perhaps seems unexpectedly short, when no earlier source of income has been mentioned (τότε μὲν γάρ suggests the preceding plural is generic).

The writer is probably in his later teens; he and at least two brothers are in Alexandria, where he himself has reached the stage of studying rhetoric. The family is well-off enough to send children there, and dispatch lots of food, though the support of the sons needs to be specifically arranged. The father may be high priest of the Nile. Other aspects of class are particularly significant for our purposes. The son spells well and composes fluently. The very fact of his rhetorical education implies a familiarity with persuasive strategies; his reference to a κατήγορος 'prosecutor' (46–7), in a highly oratorical sentence, shows explicitly the impact of his studies.[14]

In choosing the size of papyrus for his letter, the writer evidently planned a substantial piece. A single column is much commoner for private letters. The choice of more columns often indicates a letter with unusual designs: so the detailed narrative of *PMich.* X 679 (2nd cent. AD), originally in at least three columns, much thinner than these. As often, this letter closes with practicalities, and as often the lines are squeezed together to fit into the remaining space. But these are not the writer's main concern.

We can hardly avoid the question whether the writer had a strategy. The document clearly has a pragmatic function, which we need to relate to its form; and, as with oratory, any persuasive shaping of the text would scarcely be separable from the text itself. It is notable that the treatment of Heraclas' flight is delayed until after the narrative of attempts to find a teacher. This might be (*a*) because the writer had forgotten about Heraclas until the letter drifted round to him; (*b*) because the letter is pursuing a systematic exposition, starting with earlier events and proceeding to the present; (*c*) because it is most effective for the writer to establish an image of himself as seriously involved in his education before he confronts the awkward circumstances of Heraclas' departure. (*b*) and (*c*) are compatible, and both imply strategies, of different kinds. (*a*) seems improbable. First, the letter begins from gloom on the business in the theatre; with this Heraclas' flight seems connected, and on this Heraclas had had much

---

[14] For the age of students, cf. Kleijwegt (1971) 116–20, *SGO* 03/02/72. The presence of at least another brother besides Diogas is suggested by the late reminder in 54–5; 'us' in 38 is taken to be a true plural. For the social position of high priests of the Nile (Rea's attractive reading), cf. *PWisc.* I 9 (AD 183).

to say. Second, the loss of Heraclas cuts off the sons' one source
of income; its restoration, through Heraclas, is the letter's main
practical object. Third, Heraclas, to justify to the father his flight
and his abandonment of the sons, must have given a highly coloured
account of their behaviour (or be feared by the sons to have given
one). Despite the father's reassurances, it seems unlikely that
Heraclas' negative presentation is not a subtext from the start.
These points also indicate that (c) should be relevant as well as (b).
They are reinforced by further consideration of preceding events.[15]

The son seems in fact fairly clear that Heraclas is with the father
(43–4, 49–54). Yet ὡς δοκῶ 'as I think' 43 shows that the father has not
stated this explicitly. A runaway slave would not so obviously be bound
to return to his young masters' father that his doing so can be inferred
with assurance. It seems likely that in saying 'don't worry about the
theatre' the father has implied a knowledge of events which, the son
supposes, could only have come from Heraclas. It would follow that
the son has not previously given the father an account of the theatrical
incident. This is confirmed by the elaborate narrative of the search for
a teacher. 11–12 and 16–17 talk of earlier communication in both
directions; but the account implies that the father has not yet been
informed of Philoxenus' reaction to his views or of the mediocre
Didymus. All this will hardly postdate the evidently recent events in
the theatre and the flight of Heraclas (it would be strange not to
mention the loss of income earlier if it preceded and hence affected
the search with Philoxenus). Nor would the son be likely to have
reported on the theatre but omitted to mention his following up of
his father's letter. This letter, then, is the first for some time. It responds
to an indulgent letter, accompanied by much food, and instructions to
give some of it to others. It is written against a background of slander,
an awkward event, and a breakdown in the father's arrangements.

One notable consequence is that the son is seen to resist an obvious
temptation. Rather to our regret, he does not give his own account of
what happened in the theatre to counterbalance Heraclas'. He prefers to
concentrate on a matter which is much more creditable to him; the

---

[15] POxy. VI 930 (2nd–3rd cent. AD) well illustrates the difficulties of getting and
keeping good teachers. For sons wishing to show parents their dedication to study cf.
POxy. X 1296.5–8 (3rd cent. AD), 3862.13–14 (4th–5th cent. AD; Christian); father's
admonition, POxy. III 531.9–11 (cf. Ebbeler below on some aspects of fathers and
sons in letters).

father does not actually need to be placated on the goings-on (cf. 3–4). This shows shrewd rhetorical calculation. More calculation, and support for (*c*), is suggested by the delay of a reply on the report, presumably from Heraclas, that the sons are looking squalid (37–8 appear to imply the father's knowledge). This is turned into a common device in letters whereby neglect of one's self proves grief. It forms the climax of a structure stressing the sons' or son's ἀθυμία 'depression, dismay', first of all at fears of having distressed their father (1), then at Didymus' inadequacy to the Alexandrian scene (27–8). Clearly these both relate to the father's educational plans for his sons. The final ἀθυμία is centred on education (37), and the financial problems are seen not as their only true worry but as a further aspect of the problems in education. This motive is stressed again at the conclusion of the passage on Heraclas (54–5), through the needs of Diogas. The whole structure, and especially the narrative of the first column, brings out through its proportions the importance of education to the writer.[16]

This argument is not undermined by the hopeful note which immediately precedes 37. The structure in any case persists; and the hopes of success are carefully fenced round with phrases of uncertainty ('perhaps, if the gods will'). The writer of course wishes to give some sense that the project is not a catastrophe. But so abrupt a movement from 'I will do well' to 'dismay at these things' is unlikely to be accidental. The writer is manifesting, and presumably striving to manifest, a youthful mixture of touching optimism and touching despair. This is supported by the open opposition, perhaps in the same sentence, of recent ἀθυμία and earlier προθυμία 'zeal, enthusiasm' (3–6). The writer's youthfulness is an essential part of the image he creates of himself, seen in his zeal and his forthright opinions. This is set against, and fits neatly into, the depiction of the father's relaxed generosity; it also counteracts an implicit contrary image of youth, of the sons as frivolous layabouts.[17]

[16] Neglect of hygiene through grief: e.g. *PFlor.* III 332.11–13 (2nd cent. AD), *POxy.* III 528.9–10 (2nd cent. AD) ('this curious and amusing letter', write the first editors on this passionate document, with patrician disdain for those who cannot spell and do not wash). Cf. also *BGU* III 846.9–10 (2nd cent. AD) for squalor in a young man to arouse pathos. The notion that students need not dress smartly like working grown-ups appears anachronistic; artistic evidence for dress in Egypt does nothing to support such a differentiation. For ἀθυμία cf. e.g. *POslo* III 159.18 (3rd cent. AD).

[17] Cf. *POxy.* X 1296.5–8 (n. 15 above) for reassurance of the father, with a straightforward future καλῶς ἥμε[ῖ]ν ἔςται 'I'll be fine'.

The piece is emerging as an effective and strategic design. Without such a strategy, we could still observe local pieces of telling writing; with such a strategy, we are encouraged to explore the detail more carefully. In this letter the skill of the writing has a particular point: it elegantly reinforces the image of the writer as a serious student of writing and speaking, and as a talented young man. However, his use of language needs careful definition. Some of his expressions have been thought 'rather literary'. Their absence from other documentary papyri could be altered by new finds; in any case, wider usage needs to be investigated. Thus the phrase 'not to see even from a distance', μηδ' ἐξ ἀπόπτου ... ἰδεῖν (27) is twice used of exile in a way which suggests it is a technical or standard phrase in that context. It also occurs in Philodemus, a writer of circulated literature, but not particularly recherché in language. κακὸς κακῶς (41) 'a wretched man wretchedly' in fact appears in *PWarr*. 13.17–18; in *POxy*. 2190 especially, it departs from normal usage, in which it describes destruction or disaster. In any case, the type of phrase is not alien to the papyri: cf. e.g. *POxy*. XLVIII 3409.21 μωρὰ μωροῖς, 'foolish things for foolish people', again used in not quite the normal way. An ellipse, 'may that bad man perish badly!' would only suggest all the more a pre-packaged and familiar rather than an abstrusely literary phrase. φημίζω 'spread reports about' appears in papyri occasionally, and in Mark 1:45 (δια-) and a wide range of first- to second-century prose; it is often used in explaining other words. ἕξις (16), presumably a rhetorical term, 'developed ability' (Quint. *Inst*. 10.1.1), comes from the specialized language of rhetorical education freely employed in the letter. In his words and phrases, then, the writer does not seem to be using language that would seem strikingly unusual or out of place in a letter. He would rather seem to be writing within the epistolary register, but exploiting a wide range of vocabulary. This would make against any argument that the letter was moving out of epistolarity into literature.[18]

---

[18] 'Rather literary': Rea (1993) 75. μηδ' ἐξ ἀπόπτου ... ἰδεῖν: cf. Philo, *Quod Omnis Probus* 7, Ariston of Pella *FGrH* 201 F 1 (Hadrian's legislation), on exiles and Jews not able to see τὸ πατρῷον ἔδαφος 'their native soil'; Phld. *De Pietate* 1.2178–81 Obbink, on not perceiving Epicurus' views. φημίζω: PGiss. 19 *recto* 3–4 (2nd cent. AD), SB X 10566.21–2 (3rd cent. AD); for its use in glossing, etc., cf. e.g. Schol. Pind. *Ol*. 1.13b, Hdn. *Epimer*. p. 61 Boissonade.

More notable than language is style. An illustration of this is the phrase μετὰ χαρᾶς 'with joy' (45). The phrase itself occurs several times in the papyri and the New Testament, but in a straightforwardly positive fashion. Here it gives lurid colour to Heraclas' abuse of the family. οὐ γὰρ ᾐσχύνετο πρὸ πάντων μετὰ χαρᾶς τὰ περὶ τοῦ θεάτρου ἐν τῇι πόλει φημίζων, καὶ λαλῶν τὰ ψεύδη ἃ οὐδ' ἂν κατήγορος εἴποι, καὶ ταῦτα μηδὲν ἄξιον αὐτοῦ πάσχων, ἀλλὰ λελυμένος καὶ ὡς ἐλεύθερος πάντα ποιῶν (45–9) 'He showed no shame, above all, in spreading word of the theatre events in the city with glee, or in speaking falsehoods which not even a prosecutor would utter—and all this when he was not treated as he deserved, but was unrestricted and could do anything, like a free person.' The use of pairs in the sentence is notable: the two parallel participial clauses, one describing, one concealing; the double phrase on Heraclas' liberty. After the amplitude on Heraclas' actions, the sentence takes fresh impetus with καὶ ταῦτα 'and that when'. Not only the accuser, but the indignation about Heraclas' not getting his deserts, creates a markedly oratorical atmosphere. The whole sentence has a vigour and vehemence which would make it memorable in an Attic speech.

Related is the sentence on Didymus which happens to end the first column: εὐξάμενο[ς] δ' ἂν ἔγωγε, εἴπερ ἀξίους λόγου καθηγητὰς εὗρον, μηδὲ ἐξ ἀπόπτου Δίδυμον ἰδεῖν, τοῦτο αὐτὸ ἀθυμῶ, ὅτι ἔδοξεν εἰς σύνκρισιν τοῖς ἄλλο[ι]ς ἔρχεσθαι οὗτος ὃς ἐπὶ τῆς χώρας καθηγεῖτο 'If I had found some decent teachers, I would pray, myself, never to see Didymus even from a distance. I'm dismayed at the very fact he has claimed comparison with the other teachers, when he used to teach outside Alexandria.' It begins with an elaborate participial structure, in which the writer distinguishes himself from his brothers (contrast the 'us' added in the first line). It ends with a strong rhetorical climax, in which the teacher who started off outside Alexandria is haughtily scorned. The sentence puts the writer's outlook on display: he is utterly part of the Alexandrian world, and reacts to the second-rate with despair and assured contempt. The style supports the depiction.[19]

Our earlier argument makes it seem likely that the approach to Heraclas, via a plural, at another climactic close, shows not random

---

[19] The short space at the end of the first column might conceivably help to mark an effective close.

recall but a judicious transition: καὶ μάλιστα ὅτε οὐδὲ οἱ χαλκὸν εἰcφέροντέc εἰcιν (39–40) 'especially when we don't have people to earn us money'. The transition operates within an epistolary form of continuous utterance, not a formally signposted declamatory exposition. (Letters often mark out a new topic, but not usually as part of a unitary structure.) Whether or not the letter was drafted first, deliberation and address appear on a larger and a smaller scale. The writer is institutionally at the very foot of the rhetorical ladder, Cicero at and Pliny near the top; but he seems far from innocent of rhetorical skill.[20]

Yet effective manipulation of language need not be so close to the milieux of education and formal rhetoric. A pair of letters will illustrate some of the complexities here. *POxy.* XLVIII 3396–7 (4th cent. AD) form part of an archive of documents (3384–429) belonging to a family heavily engaged in financial affairs, and particularly in the collection of taxes. Ubiquitous misspelling, limited vocabulary, and unambitious sentence-structure indicate a considerable distance from the world of the previous writer. And yet the letters are rightly reckoned by the first editor 'vigorous, expressive Greek'. 3396 is from Papnuthis to his parents when he is alone in Alexandria, 3397 from Papnuthis to his brother when the collection of taxes lands him in urgent difficulties.[21]

The external appearance of the two letters differs, and shows the interest of having the original letters (Figs. 2 and 3). 3396 is written less swiftly and more closely. It is not that 3397 is penned with unusual haste, as 3398 confirms, but that 3396 is written at more leisure. The prolonged list of greetings to Papnuthis' distant family, which takes 11 lines and overflows into the margin, shows the writer with more time on his hands than is the case—or than he wishes to seem the case—in 3397. In 3397 the final ἐρρῶcθαί cαι εὔχομαι πολλοῖc χρόν(οιc) 'I pray you will be well for many years' is, in my view, dashed off by the same hand at high speed, whether from circumstances or to make an urgent impression.[22]

[20] The supposed absence of interest in rhetoric at Alexandria is well argued against by Schubert (1995).

[21] Vigour: *ed. pr.* 76 (Shelton).

[22] The initial ε particularly suggests the identity of hand. It would be hard to account for a change at this point, and to suppose all the letters in the earlier hand written by the same secretary, rather than Papnuthis. The striking absence of greetings in *POxy.* 2190, even to 'the little one', might add an appearance of youthful brusqueness.

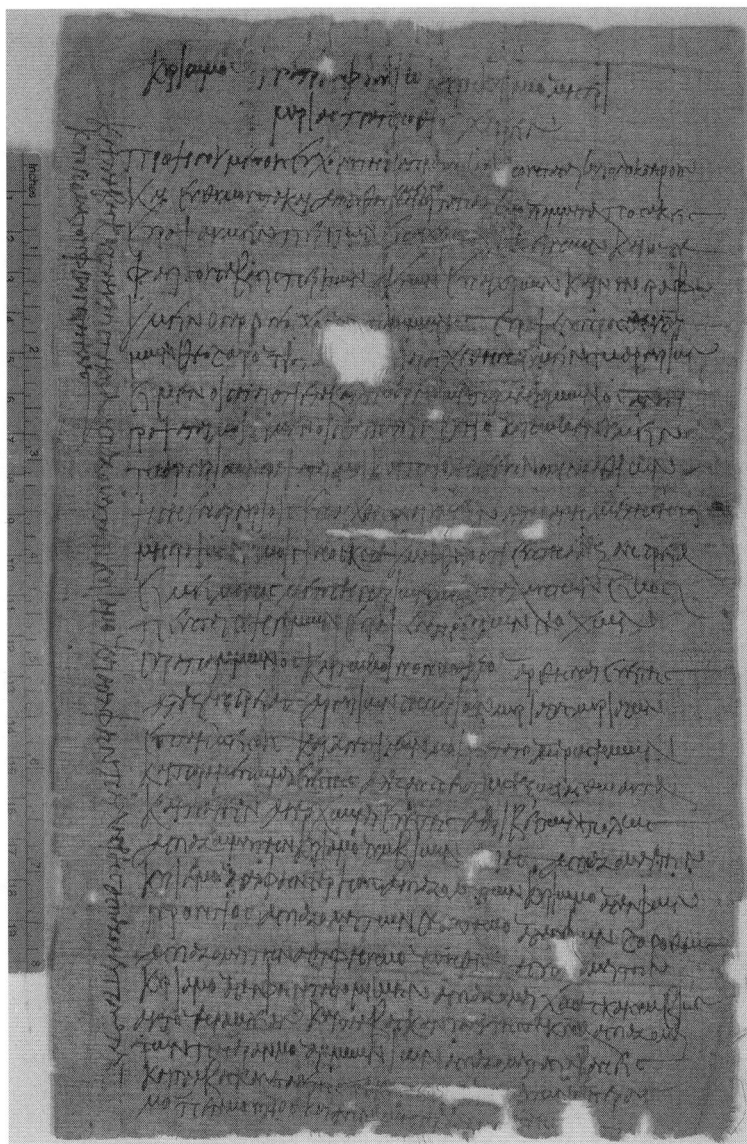

FIG. 2. *POxy.* 3396 (4th cent. AD)

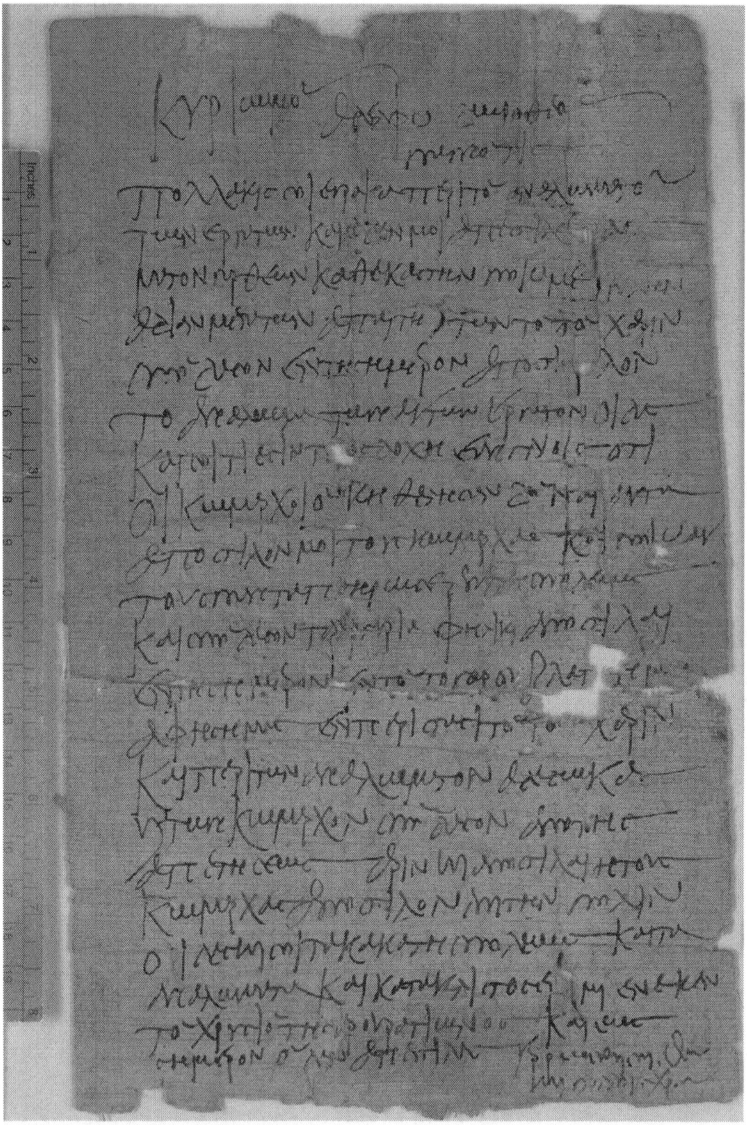

Fig. 3. *POxy.* 3397 (4th cent. AD)

Two moments from near the beginning of the letters may be compared: 3396.4–7 ποσάκεις ἔγραψα ὑμεῖν περὶ τῶν ἐναιχύρων ἐκείνων καὶ οὐδὲ φάcιc οὐδὲ βάcιc. περὶ τῶν αὐτῶν ἐναιχύρων καὶ νῦν γράφω ὑμεῖν, 'How often I've written to you about those pledges, and neither word nor move from you! Now too I'm writing to you about those same pledges.' 3397.3–4 πολλάκιc coι ἔγραψα περὶ τοῦ ἀναλώματοc τῶν ἐργατῶν καὶ οὐδέν μοι ἀπέcτιλαc 'I've often written to you about the cost of the workers, and you've sent me nothing.' We see the same rhetorical device, so to call it, in each. The opening ποσάκεις and πολλάκιc 'how many times, how often' leads to an indignant καί, 'and'. Similar phrases are common in papyrus letters; but it is apparent that they are still meant to carry weight, and they can be integrated effectively into the writer's discourse. The sentence in 3397 may be compared with the opening of the highly rhetorical 'letter of Philip' to the Athenians (not authentic in wording at least): [Dem.] 12.1 ἐπειδὴ πολλάκιc μου πρέcβειc ἀποcτείλαντοc . . . οὐδεμίαν ἐποιεῖcθ᾽ ἐπιcτροφήν, 'since I have often sent you envoys . . . and you have taken no notice . . .'. In 3396 the persuasive shaping is unmissable: the pithy οὐδὲ φάcιc οὐδὲ βάcιc 'neither word nor move' is itself subordinated to the emphatic picking up in the whole of the second sentence. There is little attempt to write in a different register for parents and for brother: the whole family, including the elderly mother (3403), enthusiastically belabour each other in such terms. On the other hand, the passage in 3396 does not immediately open the letter after the greeting: Papnuthis ostentatiously begins with a prayer for his parents' health. προηγουμένουc (= -ωc) εὔχομαι τῇ θίᾳ προνοίᾳ . . . 'to begin, I pray to divine providence . . .' (Cf. 3421.3.) Such a beginning would seem out of place in the extant letters between the two brothers: whether it is the situation or the relationship, some kind of differentiation is apparent in the writing. Such differentiation is frequently revealed by archives.[23]

The last sentence of 3397, before the rushed closing formula, raises intriguing questions. καὶ κατάκλιcτόc εἰμι ἕνεκεν τοῦ χρυcίου τῆc ἀρουρατίωνοc καὶ ἕωc cήμερον οὐδὲν ἀπέcτιλαc (21–3) 'and I have

---

[23] For similar sentences with 'often' cf. e.g. *POxy*. XIV 1766.3–5 (3rd cent. AD), *PLips*. I 110.10–12 (3rd–4th cent. AD). In [Dem.] 12 cf. also 15. *POxy*. XLII 3009 throws light on documents allegedly from Philip; perhaps this one should not be regarded too optimistically. For *POxy*. 3403 see Bagnall and Cribiore (2006) 212.

been imprisoned because of the land-based tax, and up to today you have sent nothing'. There is no break in the papyrus before this sentence; Papnuthis must be locked up while writing the rest. He could evidently contemplate an interview of recalcitrant comarchs; the confinement may be less overwhelming than we might think for a well-experienced tax-collector, who must often advance and reclaim sums himself. But the declaration remains climactic. It is saved for the end, and intensifies the indignant 'and' structure of the opening; the intervening letter has been particularly full of cπούδαcον 'make haste' and ἀπόcτιλον 'send' (cf. esp. 3408). The alternative that the imprisonment is metaphorical seems strained and unlikely to be grasped by the reader. But if it were metaphorical, the colour would add force to the close in a different way.[24]

The use of language to persuade is extremely evident in this group of letters. Though many phrases are standard, and the writing is less resourceful than in *POxy.* 2190, the writers plainly manipulate language to make an impact. Even without rhetorical education, a rhetorical impulse is apparent. Not that the only thread leading from *POxy.* 2190 is rhetorical: the use of language to build up a positive image of the writer can be pursued in regions far from urgent persuasion to a specific end, or from anything that seems connected to literature. We could look, for example, at how the words of letters shape and shade the impact of the gifts which often accompany or prompt them: so the father's and son's comments on the food which the father has sent (2190.58–64). The father's apparently practical mention of the amount, to ensure intact delivery, turns out to show his understated lavishness; father and son go through a nuanced and written ritual. We may note further that the son's letters to others will evidently add something to the presents, though these would seem a proof of benevolence in themselves. At the end of *POxy.* XXXIII 2680 (2nd–3rd cent. AD; Fig. 4), in an elegant hand, the probably affluent 'writer' declares herself willing to send her friend immediately anything she wants (a common turn). She then glosses her gift, mentioned earlier, of a jar of 'pickles' (pieces of salted meat or fish). Some pickles have sunk, so she has filled the jar further; this makes explicit

---

[24] Possible metaphor: *ed. pr.* 97.

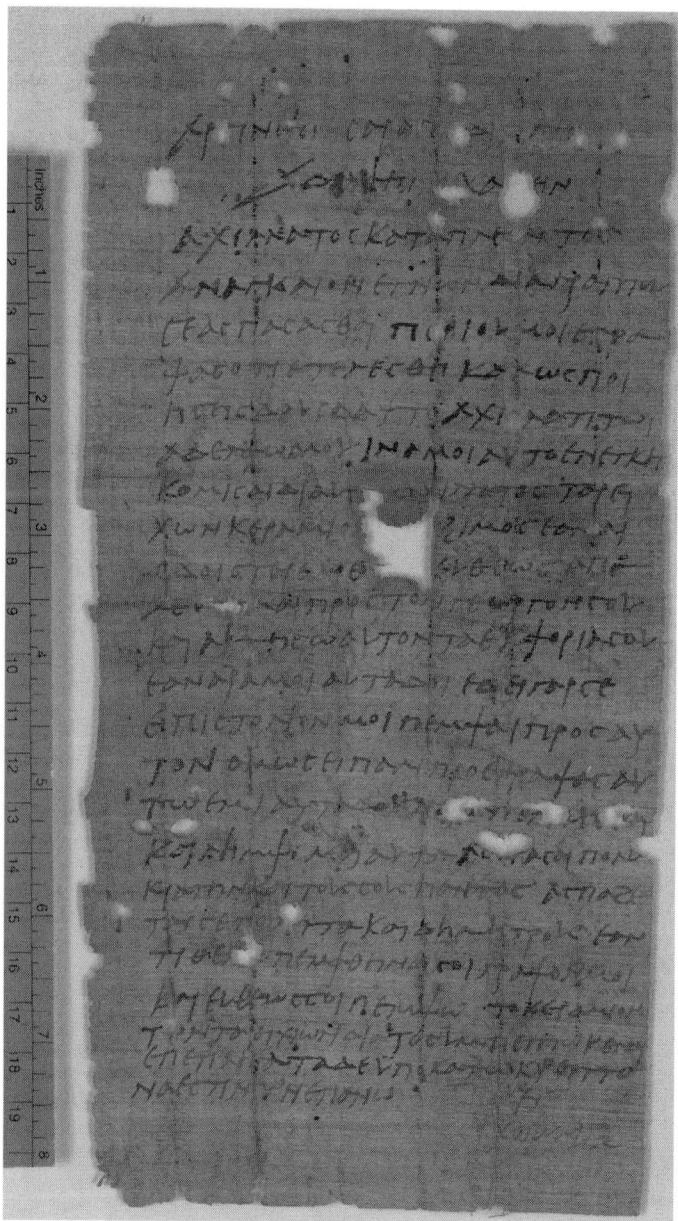

Fig. 4. *POxy.* 2680 (2nd–3rd cent. AD)

her thoughtfulness and generosity. But she gives a warning, so as to avert her friend's disappointment and display concern for her pleasure: the ones underneath are better than those on top. Even in such humdrum territory, we should be struck by the use of the specifically linguistic to create an impression and modulate a response.[25]

What, then, is the relationship between these private letters and literature, and what roles can critical analysis play? Two approaches could be envisaged, the first inadequate alone. First, then, the category of literature could be conceived in institutional terms: one might try distinguishing, say, between writing essentially for one reader and writing for readers or listeners beyond one's immediate circle. This would produce relatively firm broad divisions, even if there was much unclarity and complication on the borders. Handwriting, itself part of the division, provides illumination: one can make a broad distinction between the types of professional hand used for circulated literary works, and the documentary hands of letters—though there is considerable overlap in many specific cases. From this perspective, we could perform relatively obvious moves, observing features of real letters in epistolary literature, displaying drastic contrasts between mere documentary letters and literary productions, and tracing causal patterns. ('Literary' will be used in what follows in this institutional sense.) The ancient conventions and structures are of course important; such moves are useful, and may even turn out to be more complicated than expected.

Take one causal pattern, that of consolatory letters. Here the web of influence is intricate. Latin letters, eloquent and elaborate, are influenced by Greek philosophical treatises presenting themselves formally as consolatory letters to individuals. Greek letters are probably influenced by other letters and by model letters, which themselves will have been influenced by various traditions. (Specific model letters will be less relevant to teacher-hunting, tax-collecting, and pickles.) The Latin letters are probably influenced by Greek letters. Most Greek documentary examples spend only a few sentences on consolation; but the gap has been narrowed by the

---

[25] For *POxy.* XXXIII 2680 see Bagnall and Cribiore (2006) 300–1. On gifts in papyrus letters, cf. König in this volume.

appearance of a relatively extended consolatory letter on papyrus (*CPR* VI 81, 3rd–4th cent. AD), and by a model letter of consolation (*PHamb.* IV 254, 1st–2nd cent. AD). The story of this area of writing looks interesting, though the nature of the division between literary and non-literary seems ever less straightforward.[26]

The second approach, which should surely be added, would look beyond an institutional division. We could consider more broadly the shaping of language to affect a reader. Such an approach would leave us, not with a firmish division, but with an unlimited series of gradations. Critical scrutiny would not be simply switched off for documents. Analysis of linguistic manipulation and image-building could extend itself, without a need to show literary writing as completely different from non-literary, or to show all documents as alike in merit or the lack of it. Nor would the frequent recurrence of devices and expressions in documentary writing make them any less of interest: widely diffused tactics are as illuminating as idiosyncracies. Such an approach might be felt to diminish the importance of the literary. Yet more precise and informed discrimination need not have that consequence; and what the literary and the non-literary use of language share might be important too.

This line of thought has much in common with new historicism. But in practice new historicism often produces a brilliant display: the acknowledged literary masterpiece is juxtaposed with, and illuminated by, what had seemed low-quality or extraneous material. These spectacular leaps across apparent chasms do not quite fit the graded conception suggested here. More germane in some ways are the New

---

[26] For *CPR* VI 81 see Rea (1986), with a strikingly improved text; on consolation in papyri, see Chapa (1998), adding the model letter (privately produced?) *PHamb.* 254. Cf. also *PBon.* I 5 (*Corp. Pap. Lat.* 279) col. ii 26–vi 11 (consolation for disappointing legacies), with Trapp (2003) 275–7. For bibliography on consolation, regrettably excluding papyri, see Hutchinson (1998) 49 n. 1. The Ciceronian correspondence clearly shows the insufficiency of an institutional approach to literature; this is argued in Hutchinson (1998), and would appear generally to have been accepted. It might be possible to urge that letters by writers of published works form a special case; but the arguments of the present article do not depend on the Latin material. An institutional division based on the original act of writing is naturally complicated further when a letter written for one reader is subsequently circulated or published (generally circulated).

Rhetorics, and the extension of a rhetorical view of communication beyond literary contexts.[27]

It is hoped that this article may have done something to bring documents properly into the discussion of ancient letters, and to encourage the exploration of this abundant, relevant, and rewarding material. The documentary deeps are rich mines.

---

[27] For discussion of new historicism, cf. Thomas (1991); Hamilton (1996) 150–75; Gallagher and Greenblatt (2000); Schmitz (2002) ch. 10; Feeney (2004) 18–19; for rhetoric, cf. e.g. Moretti (1988) 2–9; Andrews (1992); Enos and Brown (1993). It considerably affects modern discussion of ancient epistolary writing that rhetoric remains less central and fiction more central for many modern conceptions of prose literature than for many ancient conceptions.

2

'…when who should walk into the room but…': Epistoliterarity in Cicero, *Ad Qfr.* 3.1

John Henderson

John Henderson

JOHN HENDERSON TO THE READER: GREETINGS

> I had nothing to do on this hot afternoon
> but to settle down and write you a line…
> 'You Wear it Well',
>
> > (Rod Stewart, *Never A Dull Moment*)

A. INTRODUCTION

A1. The three-book collection of (Marcus) Cicero's Letters to (Quintus) Cicero dramatizes the years of their writer's *tempora* ('crisis') between the fall-out from his consulate, through his banishment, return, and shift of alignment from unease with Pompey to investment in Caesar (60–54 BCE). Besides Marcus' own spell out in the cold (58; return in 57), they are occasioned by three periods of Qfr.'s absence from Italy, as praetorian proconsul of Asia (61–59; return in 58), and as legate, to Pompey in Sardinia (56–55), and to Caesar in Gaul (54). Their *epistoliterarity* spans the whole range from formal broadside through mimetic bulletin to keeping channels open. This essay 'explores by the bullet-point' the pulsating textuality of 3.1 (= *enucleate perscribere*,

3.3.1). A text and translation (D) follow the essay and conclusion (B–C), and a bibliographical note (E) is appended).

A2. *Ad Qfr.* ♥♥♥.♥

Dateline: dates through September 54 BCE.
From: properties in the country and Rome.
To: an encampment of Caesar's army in Furthest Gaul.

As ever, M is taking care of Qfr., iron fist in kid gloves. Later, this collection will run into a communicative jam when urgent letters must travel distances in rapid succession and at varying speeds, and depend on availability of suitable, or indeed any, postmen. The usual imperious disregard for the resources squandered in this elite's business of firing off volleys of the most flippant of momentaneous notes across pre-telegraphic miles and oceans wears especially thin as hermeneutic vulnerabilities are multiplied and heightened by a jumble of factors. Polemology and politics conspire to match (we must presume) life-and-death action narratives in the all-in fighting at one end, and make-or-break parliamentary shenanigans in the in-fighting at the other. Psychological 'soul-brother' interdependence is a lifeline that is non-recuperable once snapped; it demands non-stop grooming and thera-peutic preening; tautens whenever threatened, not least by prolonged separation, so textuality must signify tension *tout court.*

At the same time, express delivery would mean piggybacking on the commandant's offical mailtrain, yet that service exposed these same letters to associated security risks, limiting the parameters for expressive or off-the-record confidences. Privately conveyed messages would doubtless lag behind, forfeit topicality and impetus, besides the risk of attracting attention to smuggled deviousness, when the point in going so far was precisely to get closer than writing relations could come to said commandant, so that 'Cicero' could at all times both be with Caesar and never leave the helm of the Republic. *Caesar* will boss, feature, mention, come up, get dragged in somehow, for topic after topic, once the overture on Qfr.'s estates is done (3.1.8, 9 × 3, 10 × 2, 11 × 3, 13, 17, 18, 20, 25). *Caesar* is, in truth, the destination of this correspondence, 'Qfr.' the dummy address, holding mailbox and poste restante, and that is what he is at his post for, battling at the front. Whatever M commits to paper, know that he writes in full knowledge that this is for *Caesar*'s 'benefit', and as such carries no significant onus to inform; every word is in this sense 'aiming off', letting *Caesar* know, constantly, that the message is: M. Tullius is on board and (so he avers, and must keep re-affirming) committed to the cause, 'a second', political, 'brother' (18). Everything comes to Caesar, one way or another, no sweat (10):

de publicis negotiis *quae uis ad te Tironem scribere*, neglegentius ad te ante scribebam quod **omnia minima maxima ad Caesarem mitti sciebam**. rescripsi epistulae **maximae**.

On the political situation, *on which you want Tiro to write you*, I've been writing you before now a bit nonchalantly because **I've known that EVERY-THING, mini through maxi, gets sent Caesar**. I've answered the **mega-max** bulletin.

Such exchanges across a long and fraught time-lag between dispatch and delivery in the lap of the gods are going to pass in the night, miss, concertina, crash, pile up, hit the buffers. This will occur in spectacular style *intertextually* between the later communiqués of book 3, but a stunning internal variant, of *intratextual* multiple pile-up, has struck the anthologist as exactly the mood-setting extravaganza apt to lead out this final gathering. The texture of its writing is pure epistoliterarity: marked, pock-marked and post-marked as impromptu, improvisatory, sheer imperfection. In particular, the letter sports explicit rumination on the set of vagaries besetting epistolary temporality (3.1.8):

uenio nunc ad tuas litteras quas pluribus epistulis accepi dum sum in Arpinati; nam **mihi uno die tres sunt redditae et quidem, ut uidebatur, eodem abs te datae tempore**, una pluribus uerbis in qua primum erat quod *antiquior dies in tuis fuisset ascripta litteris quam in Caesaris*. id facit Oppius **nonnumquam necessario** ut, cum tabellarios constituerit mittere **litterasque a nobis acceperit, aliqua re noua** impediatur et **necessario serius** quam constituerat mittat neque nos **datis iam epistulis** diem commutari curamus.

Now I get to your letters, received them in quite a few bulletins while at the Arpinum place—you see, **3 were delivered to me on one day and actually, so it seems, your end they were sent same time**—No. 1 in quite a few words, in it point 1 being, *an older dateline was noted on your letter than on Caesar's*. This is Oppius' doing, **quite often it's necessity**: when he's planned sending off couriers **& got a letter from me**, gets tangled up in **some development** and... *it's necessity*, sends it off **later** than he planned, 'n' we don't bother getting date altered **once letter's handed over**.

Qfr.'s simultaneous triad don't strike the recipient as importantly sequential, and in any case, a fourth piece arrives later, though written, and dated, much earlier—before the others are answered (13). Then M adds, of his own output, that delay in the post can lead to shuffling in the order of arrival as well as staggering in the date of dispatch way past the attested date of completion. Uncertainty, misapprehension, sidetracking, *incuria* are (face it) systemic in high turnover postal relationships. (Carefully paraded epistolary *nonchalance* always deconstructs: *neque nos... curamus* ∼ *neglegentius... scribebam*, 10.) In 3.1, some forty-five items of information swarm, jostle, tack together in one multipart bulge of jotting; the component subunits were set down in order, but the boundaries, imbrication, and narrativity of these are fluid, complex, and progressively fraught as can be. From the recipient's end, it's all a question—the 'Oppius effect' again (8)—of *ifs and buts*, a fragile chain of tragedies round each corner; of dicing with *near-misses* at obliviation (13):

quarta epistula mihi reddita est Id. Sept. quam a. d. IIII Id. Sext. ex Britannia dederas. in ea nihil sane erat noui praeter *Erigonam* (quam **si** ab Oppio accepero, scribam ad te quid sentiam, nec dubito quin mihi placitura sit) et, **quod paene praeterii**, de eo quem scripsisti *de Milonis plausu scripsisse ad Caesarem*. ego uero facile patior ita Caesarem existimare illum quam maximum fuisse plausum. et prorsus ita fuit. et tamen ille plausus qui illi datur quodam modo nobis uidetur dari.

Bulletin No. 4. Reached me 13 Sept. Mailed from Britain 10 Aug. In it no news at all, bar *Erigone*—**if** once I get it from Oppy, I'll write you my take, no qualms 'case she won't get my vote; and—**nearly skipped him**—on the guy you wrote *as having written to Caesar about Milo's standing ovation*. Me, I'll easy let Caesar go think that ovation was big as it gets, and that's entirely how it was; & yet & still that ovation handed him looked at one way does seem handed *me*.

('But ifs': *neque... nisi*, 2, *spero... fore*, 2, *si uendere uellemus*, 3, *si tibi uidetur...*, *si... habuero*, 7, *si... minus*, 9, *si cui... petiero*, 10, *si... rescripsero...*, *siquid habebo*, 11, *si... accepero*, 13, *si... tenebo*, 13, *si quid... esset quod... uellem...*, *quod si... inciderit*, 21, *si quod inuenisset*, 23; 'nearly': *nihil ei restabat praeter...*, 1, *cum... iam...*

complicarem, 17, *paene par*, 18, *paene afflictus*, 24.) All a question...
of epistolary misinformation, conniving, projection, and counter-
transference.

It all gets out of hand. Letters are no autonomous singletons; they
are a *culture*—fungal teletechnology. By *his* end, the author is less
than happy with this fortnight's desultory collage. He is bound to be.
By the end, any end, the ageing paging of this albumtross is long past
its send-by date.

B. ESSAY

B1. Escape from the epic filmset of roasting Rome back to the womb
of Arpinum launches an organized, orderly, orbit, as M retraces his
whistle-stop tour through seemingly unannounced check-up visits to
spy on work in hand at Qfr.'s properties at Arcanum (10 Sept.),
Herus', and Manilius' (near Arpinum), then 'down Veal Broadway
to Fufidius' farm' (bought at Arpinum, and in its environs—the
'Babuleian district'), and so to Laterium (13 Sept.). The 'news out
of town' bulletin includes the inflammatory reminder that Qfr. is a
minimum of a couple of months away from any intervention, when
what 'they say you specify' doesn't 'get M's vote. ... Still if you feel
different write back asap' (2, *te scribere aiunt... mihi, ut est, magis
placebat. ...tu tamen si aliter sentis, rescribe quam primum*); and
features memos for chasing up when back in Rome. Once it has been
pronounced *good as done*, through-put on 'finishing touches in
Rome' is brisk, and M then wishes (*a*) that Q. Jr. may in future be
brought along out of town by his mother (it will need fixing by dad
responding to the present letter by writing a conjugal letter home to
ask nicely); and (*b*) that Jr. could've already been allowed out to
spend *this* getaway break rambling with uncle *at Arpinum* (1–7; 7):

de Cicerone...atque utinam **his diebus in Arpinati**, quod et ipse cupierat et
ego non minus, mecum fuisset.

On Cicero...In fact just **wish these days at the Arpinum place**, as (1) he
fancied and (2) I did, just as much, he'd been with me.

So much so far on the time and place of writing.

Now the journey continues, *across the page* (8, 12):

uenio nunc **ad** tuas litteras...
uenio **ad** tertiam....

First we negotiate a tricky sequence of actual letters received from
Qfr., 'in quite a few bulletins while at the Arpinum place'. To
be precise, *three* of 'em for the price of one arrived together on the
same day 'and actually, so it seems, they were posted at the same
time'. The itinerary as we work through the checklist of points raised
by these letters doubles up with the journey just completed, both in
the sense that the writing is, we presume, still coming out of Arpinum and in that their writer worked to-and-fro from Arpinum as his
base in-between items—first *loca*, on location, now *loci*, from passage
to passage. First, 'no. 1', 'the mega-max bulletin', then 'the tiddler',
and so we get to 'letter 3' (8–10, 12). *Not sorted by sequence of writing*,
then. (Can we listen in to catch Cicero's brain or notes going for the
treble in alphabetizing *Trebatium- Trebonium- de tribunatu*, 10–11?)
And not clear, either, at what point these replies have been penned,
though we shall find they are none of them corrected, glossed, or
further *referred to*, in what lies ahead. But we are not yet home and
dry: a certain 'Bulletin' ordained for future reference as 'No. 4' has
also arrived, we gather at or outside Arpinum before or during or
after that visit to Laterium, on that very day of 13 Sept. 'Mailed from
Britain 10 Aug.' (13). 'In it no news at all, except' a couple of bits and
bobs: i.e., we are left to wonder, 'nothing he didn't know before this
flying visit to Arpinum', or, more particularly, 'nothing new' to
Cicero *now he has read letters 1 to 3*, **because** he has read them? If
we ask, did these correspondences only ever write each item just the
once (usually? even in such extraordinary circumstances as this tour
of duty at the frontier?) ...?, then of course even this puzzle must beg
the basic epistolary question of what constitutes such a news 'item' (a
latest development in the context of a 'news story' already established, or the appearance of a 'new departure' starting from cold?).
And 'no news': is a letter minus news (at most) a cipher, self-
confuting contradiction in terms? How close is M to acknowledging,
when it comes to Qfr.'s internecine post, that all news becomes a dead

letter once pre-empted? Any letter will empty into vacuity if sat on too long. 'Nearly skipped' *that.*

More pressing grammatological considerations are raised by the next entry or so (14):

reddita etiam mihi est peruetus epistula, **sed sero allata**, in qua de ... item de ... Romam cum uenissem a. d. XIII Kal. Oct. ... Cicero noster dum ego absum non cessauit ...

Again, reached me, extra, real ancient bulletin. **Delivery late in day though.** In it, on ... Likewise on ... Rome, upon my getting here 18 Sept., ... Our Cicero while I was away no slacking ...

'Late in day'. (Too) Late for what? At what point *in his story* did the writer writing these words leave Arpinum, *and get back here to Rome*? Did the bundle of 'recent' letters arrive at Rome, thence to be fast forwarded express to Arpinum, and their reply penned there, only to be fetched back to Rome unposted, there 'to be continued'...? And has the present instalment kicked in at the late arrival of what happens now to figure as 'No. 4', displaced down the line of reception entirely through the contingency of time taken in transit, in its intersection with the scheduled movements of the addressee...? Wrecked by happenstance, outflanked by wiring ahead. That earlier promise to follow up on leads 'once back in Rome', including the remark that one wanted man 'is *at time of writing* in Rome', tends to strengthen the view that *the place of writing* for the inspector's account was not Rome, so must've been in or near Arpinum territory (4):

... quem ego **Romae** aggrediar et, ut arbitror, commouebo et simul M. Taurum, quem tibi audio promisisse, **qui nunc Romae erat**, de aqua per fundum eius ducenda rogabo.

... I'll get after him **in Rome** and (I bet) I'll get his skates on, + in one go M. Taurus (**he's currently at Rome**), I'm told he promised you, I'll chase up on question of putting water through his farm.

Or have we got it all wrong, reading over Qfr.'s shoulder, and both our travel-narratives so far were put on paper after the round trip was a thing of the past, to be recollected and now merged into new information acquired since return to town? After all, it emerges, we were betting heavily on the apparent location of the point of narration as pin-pointed by that complex of deictic shifters, 'In fact just wish *these days spent at the Arpinum place,* as (1) he fancied and (2) I did, just as much, he'd been [t/here?]*with me*' (7). And (paradoxically?) it was natural for us so to do, when M just noted those 'finishing touches in Rome' in the terms he chose (6):

... sed **etiam ipse crebro interuiso,** quod est facile factu. quam ob rem ea te cura liberatum uolo.

... but, again, **I frequently run an eye over too,** easy done, so you be carefree on that score, just for me.

Especially as we notice how this blurs into the reply to 'Letter 4': 'In it, on Earth Shrine/Catulus colonnade: your memo. Both happening full tilt. Fact, at Earth's I've sited the statue of you' (14, *in qua de aede Telluris et de porticu Catuli me admones. fit utrumque diligenter. ad Telluris quidem etiam tuam statuam locaui*). Which keeps it elusive whether (*a*) we are reading mental or drafted notes or written accounts of the Arpinum episode(s) produced on site(s), and have also traversed replies to the batch of letters read and answered *then* and *there*, up to No. 3, before proceeding to catch up with No. 4, and thereupon, or thereafter, process more copy appended back at Rome...; or (*b*) M has set out to write Qfr. a survey of his affairs on the home front, involving a circuit of visits in, out, and then back in the capital, and written as he went, by instalments, as it came, and all along made sure the final report would seamlessly achieve a panoramic synchronicity (or synchronicity-*effect*). Or even (*c*): has M written all of it *up* this way, in Rome, on Sept. 18?

B2. At any point, especially given the nature of the business conducted by M in Qfr.'s affairs, on his own initiative, it could prove *essential* to Qfr. (so to M, too) to be sure on which day it could truthfully be claimed that, on M's written testimony as first-person witness, each specific state of affairs obtained, on what date, exactly, any particular contractual arrangement was formulated and agreed in his name, and to what point where through the month all the simultaneous projects on the books had progressed with quite what prospects, estimates, and outlook. Making an overview look like a snapshot when it was spread over a week in the calendar had its temptations, and its risks, its drawbacks; then again, there again, it has its advantages, if the overall picture is top priority, energetic vigilance in minute-by-minute monitoring of the desired effect, and if reassurance is the targeted affect.

Yet in tension with this, there is the raw responsibility to make these urbane letters from home a pleasure to receive and to polish off, welcoming us into an *intimate* space where we'll nest snug and safe ('back with best beloved river, refitted myself..., running real purty,... fuller yield', 1, 'never a spot shadier..., water welling... good and full..., stunning sweetie', 3, 'nothing so cool, nothing so mossy', 5, 'an estate's worth of pleasure', 14). 'Back to paradise' makes a reliable entrée to textual privacy (so 3.1 begs to play 'prologue': cf. e.g. *De Legibus* 1.1–5, esp. 2.4–6, 5 fr. 3), away from unpleasant worlds beyond the correspondents' control ('temperatures way up high..., height of drought', 1, 'them wells are gasping', 11; 'a drag', 10, 21 × 2), off to a comforting space with 'room to breathe' (unlike Rome, 7: 'tarnished nadir, no-show', 15, 'a massive hate demo... Nowt more tarnished', 24; cf. 16). Yes, in letterland, writing partners call it as they see it, in cahoots; they decide what matters, what matters to *them*—the weather and the vibe, building extensions and home design, holdings and investments, those family tensions and what-about-the-boy...(1–7, 14, 19); and that 'statue of you' (14). 'When's life gonna begin?' (12)—The Cicerones live in each other's letters, feeding on their topics and cannibalizing everyone else's (8–14, 16–18, 20–3, 25)—they harp and haver on epistoliterarity (8, 11, 21, 23, 25).

Summertime and, on paper, the living is 'easy' (*facile*, 3, 6, 10 × 3, 13), the shackles off, at a stroke of the pen (*quod mihi erit curae*, 1, *curat... qui mecum fuit*, 2, *te cura liberatum uolo*, 6, *te... libero*, 9), it can all be so *nice*, sweetening even what's *nasty* (*recte erat-politae-concinnum-recte fieri*, 1, *honestae-boni-ampla-perfectum*, 2, *mirifica suauitate*, 3, *summo in nos amore-grata est-summo meo dolore et desiderio tamen ex parte gaudeo-te... quotidie plus diligo, immortaliter gaudeo-pergaudeo*, 9, *nec quod metuamus nec quod gaudeamus*, 10, *pergratum perque iucundum*, 12, *absolutum-honeste*, 14, *dolui... suauissimis..., suauiores-grauiorem dolorem*, 17, *suauem et grauem... suauius*, 19, *pergratae-gratum-humanissime*, 20, *amabiles*, 22, *satis commodas*, 25). Fit for a consul *or two* (*summam dignitatem*, 1: cf. 2.14.1). There's a 'place' for us (*quo loco-loci-locum-loco-collocauerat*, 2, *eo loco-locum-locis*, 3, *eo loco*, 4, *non est locus*, 7, *spati*, 11, *locaui*, 14), nowhere nicer, not ever (*uidi numquam... nusquam melius*, 3 ∼ *non enim meminimus maiores*, 1), where the brothers can set the world to rights, and election hassle, courtroom scandal, will lie down and stay put as written (15–18, 24)—finessed (10), ignored (11), or let slip (13). And this literary place is *it*—'nearly' (24).

For familiar letters are the wilful preserve of *arbitrariness*—opinionated assertion, 'likes' and 'dislikes', rule OK, ready or not (*mihi ualde placuit-non probaui*, 1, *magis placebat-ualde probaui*, 2, *affirmo-praestabo*, 3, *ita placuit*, 4, *sane probaui-ualde placet-laudaui*, 5, *probo-tibi placere*, 10, *placitura sit*, 13, *non placuerat tibi-praestare*, 14, *uehementer exspecto*, 15, *uehementer... ut arbitror-ualde obligaui*, 16, *probo*, 17, *non placuerat*, 18). So let's brag a bit ('(I bet)', 4). Ham up the politesse ('I don't mind, but you too please don't you mind my not backing down', 7). Indulge flights of fancy ('sort of like a mantra', 5, 'sort of DoS', 19). Crack the odd joke ('Those characters [sc. statues] look like they're doing the gardening—and pushing their ivy', 5, sc. having this *poet's* corner dress the part!). Let rip into raptures (*amore sum incensus*, 18, *ualde mehercule... admodum delectatus... delectauerunt*, 19; cf. *delectabit*, 5, *delectari-delectauit*, 22). This prima donna acting up is one's *duty*, off-duty (esp. *cetera eius suscipio*, 14, cf. *crebro interviso... ea cura*, 6, *et tu fouebis et nos quibus cumque poterimus rebus augebimus...*, *facio diligenter et faciam quod mones*, 9, *uehementer satis facio rebus omnibus... multa iam feci quae uoluit quaeque a me petiuit.... ualde obligaui*, 16, *uideor id iudicio facere, iam enim debeo*, 18, *quod et curares de se diligenter et tamen consilio se uerissimo iuuares... te sibi gratum fecisse quod... humanissime diligentissimeque locutus esses*, 20; perverted in *munus fundi... exspectet*, 9). All these textual palpitations stamp their textural palpation onto this hug of words between soulmate inseparables. Franked 'ego altering'.

So there is the epistolary perk and prerogative of *informality*, most effortlessly achieved by cultivated variety, miscellaneity, and by spottiness; and characteristically realized by affected nonchalance in stitching (hopping?) to and fro between focused precision and chilled-out mulling. Here, textuality is all about interweaving these

asymptotic temporalities with those incongruent temperamen-
talities: 'these days at the Arpinum place' when the head of house
was feverishly auditing the family piles, were *also* both (*a*) 'these'
daydreamy 'days at the Arpinum place' when darling nephew
shoulda been there (7, **his diebus in Arpinati**), and, again, (*b*)
'these' lazy hazy 'days' when (for all the prose diarrhoea) the man
of letters finds it just as impossible to cut it, to get the *poetic* juices
flowing in paradise as it 'is' (or at any rate 'was', last time of asking,
and of hearing back: '**right now**—who knows?') in any forsaken
marécage (11):

libros meos omnis quos exspectas incohaui sed conficere non **possum his
diebus**. orationes efflagitatas *pro Scauro* et *pro Plancio* absolui. poema *ad
Caesarem*, quod composueram, **incidi**. tibi quod rogas, **quoniam ipsi fontes
iam sitiunt**, siquid habebo spati, scribam.

All my books you're hanging on for, I've made a start but can't manage to
knock on head, not **these days**. *For Scaurus* and *For Plancius* speeches I've
wrapped up after the badgering. *To Caesar* poem I got organized, **I've put on
hold**. *For Qfr.* thing you ask for, **given the actual wells are gasping right now**,
if I've got any legroom, I'll write it.

At any rate, a certain uncertain seamlessness between Arpinum
and Rome projects onto the mail-merge which has elicited, so as
now to continue to elicit, the composite tale of M's escape from, and
re-entry to, the orbit of hothouse Rome, where 'Gabinius' steals the
headlines (15–16):

Gabinium tres **adhuc** factiones postulant,... Lentulus... iam de maiestate
postulauit... ad urbem accessit a. d. XII Kal. Oct.... quod Cato non ualebat,
adhuc de pecuniis repetundis non erat postulatus. Pompeius a me ualde
contendit de reditu in gratiam sed **adhuc** nihil profecit nec, si ullam partem
libertatis tenebo, proficiet.

tuas litteras uehementer exspecto. quod scribis *te audisse in candidatorum
consularium coitione me interfuisse*, id falsum est.... **adhuc** erat ualde incertum et quando comitia et qui consules futuri essent.

Gabinius. **To date** 3 syndicates are after seeing him in court... Lentulus... has
already charged him... He (= G.) marched up to Rome 19 Sept.... As Cato
was unwell, **to date** not yet been charged on a count of extortion. Pompey's
really pushing for return to my good books, but **to date** not got anywhere, and
if I hang on to any %age of freedom, he'll get nowhere.

I'm waiting and waiting on a letter from you. Your writing that *you heard I was in on the candidates for consul pact*: no truth in it. . . . To date it's really not clear (i) when elections will come (ii) who'll be consuls.

Surely cut-above-the-rest M timed his breather and his return flight, he said, to escape 'holiday fortnight' (1, *ludorum diebus*; plus his obligations to visitors). He knew he wasn't going to miss the (low-key? skulking?) *reditus* of Gabinius to Rome, not while he had the chance to make sure word was: a debacle; he had to be there: to spread the news, and mock the afflicted. The *ludi Romani* ran 5–19 Sept.: in 54 BCE, anyone could dread a repeat of Pompey's grossed-out games at the inauguration of his Theatre of the year before (*In Pisonem* 65). For his part, ghoulish M saw he was back ringside on 18th, Gabinius knocking at the door on 19th. No, no coincidence.

Rather, the dénouement destined for this epistle.

At least (if it had not been so designed from that first, recreational, sentence) so it appeared to the writer, whether as composer or as ~~composer~~, to have worked, to have *fallen*, out.

For it is at just this juncture that the seams are, more than showing, they bulge sensationally; and split. They tell us we just got to 'the end'. *Here and now* for this script have, precisely, been the very day after the non-event that drew us back to base in time to be on time for the non-show (17):

cum hanc iam epistulam complicarem, tabellarii a uobis uenerunt a. d. XI Kal. septimo uicesimo die.

I'm just folding this bulletin, when couriers from you lot got here, on 20th (day 27).

'Just' when the fourth plonking 'to date' in a row (*adhuc*) has thudded onto the notepad, just when we dangle in suspended animation over the (electoral) fate of the nation (*adhuc erat ualde incertum et . . . et . . .*, 16, Qfr. to crystal ball: 'who will be consul when? *To date* it's really not clear'), enter il postino, with a bombshell, or two. I expect you literary sophisticates read for epistoliterary licence, in which case this 'just, now, in the act' (*iam*) emergency will soon downgrade from portentous coincidence to rhetorical coup? True, the to-all-intents completed letter *may* only have been drying for a few heartbeats, still awaiting the quietus of valediction before folding, sealing, and consigning to a package; but, as we have seen, supplementation by silent or but faintly waymarked continuation is definitely an option for this telecommunication correspondence, so the letter *may* well have been there overnight already, and perfectly likely to gather dust on the writing-desk, for days (?), pending a satisfactory courier. 'To hand' → 'On your hands' (24):

multos dies epistulam **in manibus** habui propter commorationem tabellariorum...

I had the bulletin **on my hands** day after day on a/c of courier delay,...

It's just *too* drama-queen perfect that it should be under these scriptoral circumstances that searing pain should rip into the letter-format, declaredly tearing compositional protocols asunder in order to express, enact, and mirror the pain of bereavement, one *paterfamilias* to another (17):

o me sollicitum. quantum ego dolui in Caesaris suauissimis litteris. sed quo erant suauiores, eo maiorem dolorem illius ille casus afferebat.

Wow I'm—I'm so cut up. All the pain I felt over Caesar's sweet, sweet letter—sweeter it is, greater the pain that calamity of his brought along...

Virtually in one sweep of the pen, pain yields to brave appreciation for writerly bravery: such Schadenfreude! Matched now by such (eminently quotable) sensitivity to epistolary style and sensibility. 'Calamity...chance' (*casus*) have intervened to dis-compose the inkslinger: Pompey's wife, Caesar's daughter, Julia is dead. As we know, but Cicero did not, this will undo the Republic in fratricidal civil war, one maxi unhappy family. Just when the humdrum details of personal portfolio and political charades were a wrap.

B3. Nonetheless, M means to be perfectly clear that he has made quite sure to take stock before extending his incremental 'Autumn diary' of a running commentary splurge for a soldier brother far from home. Lets us know almost at once that the first words he wrote on receiving the fateful joint package of letters from Caesar and Qfr. were *not* this *o me miserum*. This time the trek across the page to 'get to yr letter' (17, *sed ad tuas uenio litteras*) announces itself a hysteron proteron. First M deals with Qfr.'s 'point (i)' and (ii), matched as positive to negative (*etiam atque etiam probo*..., *miror*...; *mihi enim*

non placuerat, 17–18, 'I approve, again and again' ∼ 'I'm amazed…
did *not* get *my* vote'). But then we read on down the page to find that
he has read further down the page, and run smack into a second blow
for his composure (18):

quod inferiore epistula scribis, *me Id. Sept. Pompeio legatum iri*, id ego non
audiui…

Your writing, lower down bulletin, *I shall be made lieutenant to Pompey 13
Sept.*, first I've heard of it…

A second Cicero to play the generalissimo's legate (this time in
Spain)…and the commission commencing *a week since*…! The
shock to the system is too much, and the reflex has been to
telegram (18):

…non audiui **scripsique ad Caesarem** *neque Vibullium Caesaris mandata
de mea mansione ad Pompeium pertulisse nec Oppium.*

…first I've heard of it, **and I've written Caesar** to say (i) *Vibullius brought
no instructions to Pompey about my staying put*, (ii) *& neither did Oppius.*

'Written to Caesar', then—but not yet posted? How soon to intrude on
Caesar's sweet grief? At least Qfr. will know, when this letter-and-a-half
gets to him, what to tell Caesar to expect or, given a shared mailbag,
what Caesar's just then reading from M. And in the event that he should
find himself underwhelmed by insensitively timed and politically misguided yelping from M, Qfr. will have to hand the jolly ammunition
needed for the charm offensive that will sweet-talk him round (18):

ego uero nullas δευτέρας φροντίδας habere possum in Caesaris rebus. ille mihi
secundum te et liberos nostros ita est, ut sit **paene par.** uideor id iudicio
facere, iam enim debeo, sed tamen amore sum incensus.

In fact, I can have no *deuxièmes-pensées* in the Caesar dept., for me he comes
close second to you and our kid*s*… **nearly joint equal.** In my eyes I'm doing
this judiciously (time I did now, a must)—but still I AM ablaze, passionately
ablaze.

So scribble to Caesar, *then* cobble onto Qfr.'s special-number invol-
untary cries of pained sympathy mixed in with sincerest compliments
on the bliss of felicitously communicated pain; *then* settle to item-by-
item replies working down Qfr.'s brand-new offering, featuring as an
aside the news that, *quite some distance in,* one detail had interrupted

the task enough to demand instant diversion to fire off, in anger, a bullet-point or two in Caesar's direction. Nor does he resume his task, but instead works up an erotogenic lather of devotion to Caesar in a climax of simultaneous confession-cum-profession. What is more, now that M and we get right down to 'the bottom' of this M's missive (19, *haec infima*), we are set to discover, again after the fact, in retrospect, that this switchback passage bracketed between twin peaks of emotion has been privileged as the orgasmic finale, marked *ex post facto* by the authentic signature of Ciceronian authenticity on the page, his mark (19):

cum scripsissem haec infima quae sunt mea manu, uenit ad
nos Cicero tuus ad cenam, cum Pomponia foris cenaret.

**When I'd written these bottom bits, the last ones in my own
hand,** your Cicero got over to us for dinner, as Pomponia's
dining out.

B4. The epistoliterary medium was never more the massage than here, where amatory arson blazed in aposiopesis, and then 'in waltzed' (*uenit*) the living image of loving-lovely love in Ciceroland. Enter, right on cue, an irresistible irruption and therefore excrescence (again: this 'when' both is and is not graphematically immediate: *could* Caesar's '—but still I AM ablaze, passionately ablaze' have the last word *Ad Qfr.*? The ultimate envoi for *Ad Qfr.* 3.1 SAYS NOT). Just mention *amore... incensus*, and what should mooch over, but Qfr. Jr.? Self-reflexively playing the self-reflexive part of postie in a script for posting (19):

dedit mihi epistulam legendam tuam, quam paulo ante
acceperat, Aristophaneo modo ualde mehercule et **suauem**
et grauem; **qua sum admodum delectatus.**
    dedit etiam alteram illam mihi, qua iubes eum *mihi
esse affixum tamquam magistro.* quam illum epistulae
illae **delectarunt,** quam me. **nihil puero illo suauius,
nihil nostri amantius.** *hoc inter cenam Tironi dictaui,
ne mirere alia manu esse.*

He gave me your bulletin to read, a short while after he
received it, in the Aristophanes mood, real **sweet** 'n'
serious both, by crikey, **I was pretty well delighted.**
    Also gave me 2nd letter where you tell him *to staple
himself to me for DoS.* These bulletins so **delighted** him.
Me, too. **Nowt sweeter than that lad. Nowt loves me more.**

(This dictated over dinner to Tiro, so don't puzzle over the change of hand.)

No need to *imagine* this sympotic scene, *à deux* whether or not *nos* literally means 'just Marcus' (no Pomponia; Tiro and the staff don't count; and anyhow, only eyes for each another): heaven is so written into this joyous hug of uncle and nephew, 'nailed to one another' over dinner as spoudaiogeloiously didactic as this twinset of 'Aristophanic' and 'Ciceronian' funster paragraphs, the atmosphere is more graphically bottled in beloved Tiro's loving hand than if M had broken the spell to scribble it in Qfr's direction himself...

M's rule of writing to his brother in his own hand, only dictating to (a) Tiro when he says so (here: over dinner), permits this epistoliterary *jeu*, whereby there appears before the writer and (therefore, at time of reception) the addressee, a surreal mimetic double-whammy of a carbon copy of himself realized as correspondent: Qfr. Jr. brings Qfr. into M's presence bodily, for the embrace denied by epistolary absence; and, as acting postman, he brings with him a hot letter from his original, 'a short while after he received it' (quam paulo ante acceperat). Presumably from the same mail-train shipment that just brought Caesar's bad news and Qfr.'s latest to M, and fetched round the moment that mother wasn't looking, this letter instantly occasions a dreamscape *locus amoenus* of an insert: here, serendipitously, correspondence and correspondents correspond and co-respond through correspondents and co-respondents. Cicero and Cicero are literally, literarily, letterally, brought together, close as any two Romen could ever get, uncle for second dad, nephew for kid brother, melting triangular distance through metonymic relations realized by delivering on shared postal contact. Qfr. had to go to the ends of the earth and Caesar to lose his only begotten child so that back home the clan seat should witness the coming together of *paterfamilias* and *his* replica, when the elder brothers in both generations celebrate their twosome equivalence through metaphoric relatedness to Qfr. as realized by delivering the heart(h)-warming scene of symphysis to this single paragraph for the post.

And look! no hands: written when the writer's arms were both occupied with an armful, this breathless entr'acte simultaneously fulfils that (sneaky) request from Qfr. '*you want Tiro to write to you*'

(10), and makes that avuncular wish from two instalments on Qfr. Jr. back already come true, that '*Pomponia*... *fetch the boy out.* I'll cause a sensation if I have him with me when I'm on vacation' (7; cf. 14). True, Tiro writes 'on the' *personal* 'political situation' of the clan; and writes without deviating one jot or iota from his master's voice; this wondersome graphological dub implants writing *sans* author: ventriloquism *per litteras*. But the wish-fulfilment is, several times over, an epistolary accident waiting to happen, once a letter goes the distance and (inevitably) starts lapping itself at the run-in. All fairy godmother Pomponia knew of it was that she'd 'gone out to dinner'. All Qfr. knew of M's wish was that he only learned of it in this letter, a few paragraphs back, and yet the letter that asked him to send a letter has worked, hey presto!, without his ever sending or penning it, or knowing he should. Magic—one less letter to write to the trouble and strife! One less, selfless, chore to sort to big brother's satisfaction.

This marathon epistle will now be hauling itself back in, run its lead(s) down, for the duration. But this—this has been a special moment, when epistoliterarity conjures up pure writing, disappearing the secondariness of representation through the alienation device of substitution, the dummy scribe *in loco auctoris*; all so this wizz page will fetch the family itself, not more sentences about the family, all the way to the one who is cementing the family togetherness, both for now and through to the next generation, by embracing selfless deprivation in the lonesome wastes of a hostile back of beyond... If there was carry-over from penned Valentine for Caesar to mystic writing-pad for The Boy, the shift from manual to automatic writing separates the hype of polite noises from real postman's knock jouissance, past words. Holy grammatology.

B5. And still this multi-storey stack-up of a letter is not yet done. That self-enacting intensive phrase *etiam atque etiam* (17, 'I approve, again and again') will finally prove to set the definitive seal on the tectonics when the specially apt 'farewell' formula repeats it over again (25):

te oro **etiam atque etiam**, mi frater, ut ualeas.

I ask you, and ask **again and again**, brother mio, do see you fare well.

'Again' and 'again' the tic studs the shopping list, pulsating down the page (besides the doublets at 17 and 25, cf. *sed etiam*..., 6, *reddita etiam* and *etiam tuam statuam*, 14, *etiam alteram*, 19, *etiam. Gabinium*, 24; besides *etiam Oppio*, 10, and *etiam Memmio*, 16 and *non modo...sed etiam*, 10, 23. Add 'additions' to plant: *adiuncta cubicula et eiusmodi membra*, 2, *piscina et salientibus additis*, 3, *multa addidisse ad opus...*, *illa...addere*, *illud additum*, 5). The anti-compositional quality of this additive poetic will come to M's attention before he is done (23):

quod multos dies epistulam in manibus habui propter commorationem tabellariorum, **ideo multa coniecta sunt, aliud alio tempore uelut hoc:**

Because I had the bulletin on my hands **day after day** on a/c of courier delay, **that's why item after item has got bunged in together, each at a different time, e.g. this:**

And he will then, one second to last time, ham up the deplorable mechanics of the 'late extra' addendum (24):

quid praeterea? quid? **etiam....**

What...else? Umm. **Again—**

So this is bitty as any journal, and the last page will trade under this disclaimer, too, filled with annoyance, pique, vindictiveness, before the saving grace of 'second thoughts' on, precisely, Caesar bring these tottering unorganic proceedings to a resoundingly hypernatural conclusion after all. Before we get there, the final layer in this plum cake first off gently lowers the intensity, after passion for Caesar and high jinks for Qfr. Junior, with another couple of positive responses to epistolarity, both of them in fact second-hand notices of *superlatively* good vibrations from satisfied customers (20):

Annali **pergratae litterae** tuae fuerunt, quod *et curares de se* **diligenter** *et tamen consilio se* **uerissimo** *iuuares.*

P. Seruilius pater ex litteris, quas *sibi a Caesare missas esse* dicebat, significat ualde *te sibi* **gratum** *fecisse quod de sua uoluntate erga Caesarem* **humanissime diligentissimeque** *locutus esses.*

Annalis **much obliged** by your **letter**, *as (i) you're so* **focused** *looking after him, (ii) but also helping him with the* **sincerest** *advice going.*

P. Servilius Sr., on the basis of *letter sent him* he says *by Caesar*, indicates that *you really did* **oblige** *him in having spoken on his good will toward Caesar in* THE *most civilized,* THE *most* focused, *terms going.*

This coolant roll-call of relayed epistolary commendation for Qfr. has a third to bung in as next item but one—the thoughts must be what count, since M knocks the compliments off too cursorily for anyone to glean whether this curtseying is as bland noodling and canoodling as the quotes say, and just add a spot of tone to the general picture, or whether they represent milestones, long-coveted scalps or incipient campaigns, promising conversions or consolatory straws . . . (22):

T. Pinarius amabiles ad me de te litteras mittit; *se **maxime** litteris, sermonibus, cenis denique tuis **delectari**.* is homo semper me **delectauit** fraterque eius mecum est multum. qua re, uti instituisti, complectere adulescentem.

Titus Pinarius sends me lovely letter about you, *how **extremely delighted** he is by yr writing, conversation, and esp.* YOUR DINNERS. This hombre always has been a **delight** to me, his brother's with me loads. So: the way you've begun—keep the lad in your clutches.

This one clearly bridges back to a rehash of the avuncular scene in Rome, though here the understudy siblings standing in for Qfr. and M are part of the extended family of friends (*familiares*) and the hugs are at Caesar's end in Gaul, and grace *every* dinner party Qfr. throws there for the well-mannered lads of the younger generation on their best behaviour. (No surprise late arrivals, à la Alcibiades at Agathon's *Symposium*, there.) It reads very much that M ran out of stuff to say right here, if this is what prompts, as well as precedes, the outburst excusing/accusing this dreadful letter of being a hodgepodge of a tombola (23). On the other hand, *all* of the performance after his own hand resumes from Tiro looks to be a uniformly grudging and tetchy assortment of grumbles interspersed with (limp? token?) feel-good one-liners for Qfr.'s 'benefit'.

B6. The first pair of makeweight pleasantries put up a cheery façade ('so focused; the sincerest advice going; THE most civilized, THE most focused, terms going'). But feel M casting around for a re-entry that both chimes in with the new moment of writing and yet belongs in the same envelope as the album of material already recorded—he has palpably gone back to Arpinum to remind himself of all he's written above, and in retracing his account of the return to s(t)eamy Rome he is brought face to face with the latest episodes in two of the irritable sub-plots that figured in his first sallies (21–4 ∼ 9, 14–15):

cum Romam ex Arpinati reuertissem, dictum mihi est *Hippodamum ad te profectum esse.* non possum scribere *me miratum esse illum tam inhumaniter fecisse ut sine meis litteris **ad te** proficisceretur;* illud scribo, *mihi **molestum** fuisse.* iam enim diu cogitaueram ex eo quod tu ad me scripseras *ut, si quid esset quod ad te diligentius perferri uellem, illi darem,* quod mehercule hisce litteris, quas uulgo ad te mitto, nihil fere scribo, quod si in alicuius manus inciderit, **moleste** ferendum sit. Minucio me et Saluio et Labieno reseruabam. Labeo aut tarde proficiscetur aut hic manebit. **Hippodamus** *ne numquid uellem quidem* rogauit...

...T. Anicius mihi saepe iam dixit *sese tibi **suburbanum** si quod inuenisset non dubitaturum esse emere.* in eius sermone ego utrumque soleo admirari, et te de **suburbano** emendo cum ad illum scribas non modo ad me non scribere sed etiam aliam in sententiam de suburbano scribere, et cum ad illum scribas nihil te recordari de se de epistulis illis quas in Tusculano eius tu mihi ostendisti, nihil de praeceptis Epicharmi: Γνῶθι πῶς ἄλλῳ κέχρηται, totum denique uultum, sermonem, animum eius, quemadmodum conicio, quasi... sed haec tu uideris. de **suburbano** cura ut sciam quid uelis, et simul ne quid ille turbet uide. quid praeterea? quid? etiam.

Gabinius a. d. IIII Kal. Oct. noctu in urbem introierat et hodie hora VIII, cum edicto C. Alfi **de maiestate eum adesse oporteret,** concursu magno et odio uniuersi populi paene afflictus est. **nihil illo turpius.**...

When I got back from the Arpinum place to Rome it was told me **Hippodamus'd started out bound for you.** I can't write down *I was amazed at him behaving so uncivilized:* **starting out for** *you minus letter from me.* But I am writing this down, *it was a **drag** for me.* See, I'd been reckoning, long since, that arising from what you wrote me *any item I might want delivered to you with extra special care, I'd give it him,* 'cos crikey in these letters I send you run-of-the-mill, I write pretty well nowt, should it fall into anybody else's hands, it'd be a **drag** to put up with. Minucius, Salvius, Labeo—I'm saving myself up for them. Labeo'll either **start out** late or else stay here. **Hippodamus**—didn't even ask me for any wants....

...T. Anicius has by now told me often *he'd not bat an eyelid about buying you **a place outside Rome**.* In his talk, both things I keep finding amazing, (i) you on buying **a place outside Rome**, while you write him, you not only don't write me but even write in a different vein, (ii) while you write him you remember nowt of him, his letters you showed me at the Tusculum place, nowt on Epicharmus' commandment,

> *Reconnaissance!*
> *Regarde comment*
> *On traite les gens,*

in short, his entire face-talk-thinking, my best guess, you sorta...But that's yours to see to. On **the place outside Rome** take care I know your wants + meantime see he doesn't mess up at all. What...else? Umm.

Also—**Gabinius** on 27 Oct made his entry **to the City** & 2 p.m. today when **he had to attend, under public interest,** by order of Gaius Alfius, in massive hate demo of the united citizens of Rome he NEARLY got squashed. **Nowt more tarnished**...

~

in Hippodamo et nonnullis aliis arcessendis quid cogites non intellego. nemo istorum est quin abs te munus fundi **suburbani** instar exspectet....
Romam cum uenissem a. d. XIII Kal. Oct....
...**Gabinium** tres adhuc factiones postulant, L. Lentulus, flaminis filius, qui **iam de maiestate postulauit,** Ti. Nero cum bonis subscriptoribus, C. Memmius tribunus pl. cum L. Capitone. ad **urbem** accessit **a. d. XII Kal. Oct. nihil turpius** nec desertius. sed his iudiciis nihil audeo confidere. quod Cato non ualebat, adhuc de pecuniis repetundis non erat postulatus.

In having Hippodamus + a good no. of others sent for, I don't get your thinking. Nary a one of that lot don't anticipate a gift from you the size of **a farm outside Rome.**...
...**Rome, upon getting here 18 Sept.**...
...**Gabinius.** To date 3 syndicates are after seeing him in court: L. Lentulus, the *Flamen*'s son, he's **already charged him under public interest;** Tib. Nero + back-up team of worthies; C. Memmius, *Tribune* + L. Capito. He marched up **to Rome 19 Sept.: tarnished nadir,** no-show. But THESE courts, don't dare trust 'em an inch. As Cato was unwell, to date not yet been charged on a count of extortion.

In *this* version recapping Cicero's *reditus* from Arpinum on arrival in Rome, he finds in the summons to Gaul of the specially disliked envoy, 'Hippodamus' the horse-taming hero, bent on earning himself an out-of-town studfarm, exactly the cue for a barely transposed grouch at having this ever more unwieldy screed on his hands. If it hadn't been for Qfr.'s credulous, estate-risking, trust in this messenger from hell, M would've speeded up production, and written freely and frankly, at that, instead of serving up all this certified harmless pap and drivel. Like the present gripe about having missed the boat through the courier's premature malice, for example, which is itself one more, unpleasantly grim, way to spoil an already non(en)viable epustule. To get back at Qfr. for getting them both into this hole, Qfr.

will now have to wait still longer, and will only find out late in the day
that he's been kept waiting *because* M was kept waiting *because* the
dratted so-called favourite messenger dashed off north too soon
because Qfr. told him to. In fact, he will read and learn that, at time
of writing at least this section of the final sequence, M is holding out
for his own selected go-betweens to become available. And, tantaliz-
ingly, his last word on this meta-discursive wrangle over postality
leaves us with one candidate for delivering this letter undecidably
ruled in or out, as the case may turn out to have been: 'either late or
never'! (21) Qfr. knows this is the sort of thing that happens if M is
treated as if he doesn't count ('didn't even ask me for any wants',
indeed, 21). Now he's left to read that his brother may well have got
his retaliation in first by not sending him the giant news round-up
that he is reading, and to do so has chosen to tell him so . . .

B7. To rein in the bile, M tries more buttering up with saccharine
nothings to pass on to Qfr. (22: copied in from a pile of such notes
kept ready for spoonfeeding and jollying along?). But it doesn't work:
this letter that started so brightly with recreation in the fresh air of
home out in the Italian countryside has become a dustbin full of
refuse he's 'bunged in there, *item after item* has, each at a different
time', and all strictly 'because I had the bulletin on my hands *day after
day* on a/c of courier delay' (23). It's Qfr.'s fault, how it's gone to the
bad, just feel how he's souring every last word, even before it is
written (24): 'e.g. this:' (*uelut hoc.*). So to the second bone of con-
tention dug up from before, that Anicius hammering on about 'a
place outside Rome . . . a place outside Rome . . . a bloody place outside Rome' (23). Qfr. may have always had a short epistolary memory
('you remember nowt of him, his letters you showed me at the
Tusculum place, nowt on Epicharmus' commandment': steam pour-
ing out of the combination of anaphora, asyndeton, pronominal
pile-up, *nihil de epistulis illis . . . eius tu mihi, nihil de praeceptis*), but
M remembers telling him earlier about Hippodamus and co angling
for 'a place outside Rome to farm', and shoves before us the rhetorical
linkage that makes the connection of these two sore points in his own
mind palpable ('I can't write down that *I was amazed*' at Hippodamus, 21, *me* miratum esse ∼ 'both things I keep finding amazing', 23,
soleo admirari; cf. 14, de hortis).

Now that M has roundly spluttered at Qfr. through the flimsy screen of two-faced Anicius, who cops a sinister custard-pie in the form of a ('Mr Malice') quote from his finger-wagging alias Epicharmus, before hectoring M in his own right matches the Greek menace in his aposiopesis with one of his own, even as he 'bungs in' an untidy conjectural pun on 'bunging' (*coniecta* ∼ *conicio*; 23):

... totum denique uultum, sermonem, animum eius, quemadmodum conicio, quasi ... sed haec tu uideris. de **suburbano** cura ut sciam quid uelis, et simul ne quid ille turbet uide.

... in short, his entire face-talk-thinking, my best guess, you sorta ... But that's yours to see to. On **the goddam place outside Rome** take care I know your wants + meantime see he doesn't mess up at all.

The *Abbruchsformel*, naturally, marks the spot where disgust and ennui, suppressed rage and aesthetic revulsion at his own writing, combine to smudge this rotten Roman letter into an open display of in-ya-face rudeness slung straight at Qfr. (*Γνῶθι-tu uideris-uide*), who is good as dismissed from the letter with an abusive parody of *Aufwiedersehenformel* (*cura ut ... et simul ... uide*). This loathsome censorious Latin is out to disfigure all of *its own* 'entire face-talk-thinking', driven by *self*-loathing 'to see it *does* mess up'—and mess up good while it's at it (*et simul ... turbet*). And a touch of sarcasm echoes through 'take care I know your wants', after Hippodamus 'didn't even ask me for my wants', *cura ut sciam quid uelis*, 23 ∼ *ne numquid uellem quidem rogauit*, 21). Tully now chucks in his hand—throws in the towel.

B8. The guttiform drivelling onto the page clots, the kerfuffle on file crashes. Slanguage breakdown. One para- too far. ~~Paragraph~~ → *Paranoia* (24):

quid **praeterea**? quid?
    etiam.

What ... **else**? Umm.
    Again—

M has been toying with us ... for how long? This pesky stillicidal letter has been working up to this rhetorical coup ... at some point since he started back scribbling. Qfr.'s mailshot came in on 20 Sept. (17), after which postscripts were added (after that instant query for

Caesar was drafted, 17–18), and then Qfr. Jr. dropped in for feeding (19). How many bouts of postpostscripta are involved in the resumptive finale (20–5)? *non liquet.* That complaint of having 'had the **bulletin on my hands day after day** on a/c of courier delay, that's why item after item has got bunged in together, each at a different time' (23, **multos dies epistulam in manibus habui**) implies festering in the in-tray from delay *before* the renewed obligation to respond arrived on 20th, compounded by further frustration since then, as days queue and (claims M) entries cumulate. But the latest we shall learn will tell us M is laying it on pretty thick (25):

ex Britannia Caesar ad me Kal. Sept. dedit **litteras quas ego accepi a. d. IIII Kal. Oct.**....

From Britain Caesar mailed me a **letter** on 1 Sept., **received 27 Sept.**...

And we almost know, with startling precision, the final *here and now* for the whole formless amalgam, and for its last 'surprise' accretion, from the very apoplectic entry that he has been building up to, while elaborately throwing us off the scent (24):

etiam. **Gabinius a. d. IIII Kal. Oct. noctu in urbem introierat et hodie hora VIII**, cum edicto C. Alfi de maiestate eum adesse oporteret...

Again—**Gabinius on 27 Oct made his entry to the City & 2 p.m. today** when he had to attend, under public interest, by order of Gaius Alfius...

'This very day'. Maybe another day has dawned, but it's hard to envisage M keeping this long-awaited day for his *bête noire*'s utter public humiliation from gloating recapitulation on the page 'hour' after hour, let alone 'day after day'. In which case, everything since his handwriting took over again got transcribed between 20th and 28th Sept. (= *multos dies* ∼ 20–5). This letter opened with such an agreeably open-hearted survey of *its* construction-site good-as-ready for embellishment and finish, and now it is wrapping up with a paroxysm of poison pen malice deliberately dissembled as compositional hiccoughs caused by *facteurs de vérité*. M has been mentally preparing himself all through this holiday period for the return of Gabinius to Rome. All through the tour and his own entry to the city, M has been sharpening his nib against this day—this dyad of days: 19 Sept.: 15; 27 Sept.: 24). Readied to transcribe his enemy's comeuppance, *his way*, and steeled to tell it his way no matter what, our epistolary director unleashes an army of extras from the wings, filling his filmset with a riot (24):

concursu magno et odio uniuersi populi paene afflictus est.

in massive hate demo of the united citizens of Rome he NEARLY got squashed.

All through the adventure of writing what became this letter, from its faded preliminaries to its bitter end ... that peremptory *day in court* was set to welcome Gabinius back with open arms (24, **cum edicto C. Alfi de maiestate eum adesse oporteret**; cf. 14, *Lentulus ... qui iam de maiestate postulauit*).

If the hate-filled vendetta misfired in the huffing-and-puffing of triumviral Rome, M has a trick or two up his sleeve. In their private Republic, the brothers can enjoy venting epistolary spleen. And this can be their stage for contemplating the release onto an unsuspecting universe of a judicial system where villains do get their deserts, and no 'nearly' about it. Poets like these two know how to play god on paper, their stock in trade is to use textual stand-ins to re-run reality to suit themselves. Whereas the letter staggers on from session to session, so that an 'entr'acte' such as the Tironian note that records, by recounting, Qfr. Jr.'s intervention on the scene graphically flags up compositional fracture (19), writers in genres where drafting and revision are axiomatic, including interpolation of 'second thoughts', could count on disappearing all trace of the dramas and traumas of the process of composition. In an epic, a poet *could* cook up an extra episode and introduce it seamlessly into an already finished *opus*, and (hey presto) the fictional world would be whole again, and still again. (Much like a country mansion, in fact.) The fiend M sees how to condense Roman Law-and-Poetry into a surefire reception party for his foe that will *not* go off half-cocked. At the flick of a wrist, almighty Tully nails his man, and then some; two pesky birds of a feather with one majestic stone, in fact (24):

nihil illo turpius. proximus est tamen Piso. itaque **mirificum** ἐμβόλιον **cogito in secundum librum** Meorum Temporum **includere**, dicentem Apollinem in concilio deorum, *qualis reditus* **duorum** *imperatorum futurus esset; quorum* **alter** *exercitum perdidisset,* **alter** *uendidisset.*

Nowt more tarnished, though close second is Piso. **So it is I'm thinking of amazement-factor** *entr'acte* **to hypertext into** Cicero, In Time of Crisis,

Book II, Apollo's bubble at the gods' assembly saying *what kind of home-coming the **brace** of generalissimos are going to have, when 1 from 2 lost, and 2 of 2 sold, his army.*

The consular duo of 'Gabinius + Piso' (= 58 BCE) both enjoyed *imperium infinitum* out East and were cemented as one forever by their *Lex Gabinia Calpurnia* in aid of Apollo's Delos: *uos, geminae uoragines scopulique reipublicae, In Pis.* 41, *alter... alter,* 20, 44 (cf. 46–8, *amitteretus exercitum... exercitum uendidit*), *De Domo* 60, 62 (cf. 70, *par illud simile*), *De Prov. Cons.* 7 (cf. 2, *duo reipublicae portenta ac paene funera*). When (Pro)consular Piso first appeared in the letter, he was smuggled in under his special Ciceronian *Spott-name* 'Calventius Marius' (at war with himself, as Insubrian Gaul by (maternal) descent + hammer of transalpine barbarians hailing from Arpinum; 11). There, he was in tandem with *Clodius,* once respon-sible for Cicero's removal 'and so' for *his* (celebrated) *reditus* (and, currently/recently, disturbingly thick, M learns, with Caesar's agent Oppius, 11, 18):

...primum est de Clodi ad Caesarem litteris. in quo Caesaris consilium probo, quod tibi amantissime petenti ueniam non dedit uti ullum ad illam furiam uerbum rescriberet.

alterum est de Caluenti Mari oratione. quod scribis, miror, *tibi placere me ad eam rescribere,* praesertim cum illam nemo lecturus sit si ego nihil rescripsero, meam in illum pueri omnes tamquam dictata perdiscant.

... 1st point being on Clodius' letter to Caesar, and in this I approve Caesar's strategy, not giving in to you 'n' yr lobbying out of deepest love by writing back to that demon, not one single word.

No. 2/2 is on Calventius Marius' speech. You writing that *my writing back*—you amaze me—*gets your vote*—specially as nobody'll read THAT if I write no reply, whereas mine is getting swotted up by all the boys like a homework assignment.

Looming behind this correspondence where no Roman could miss them, however, was *the* Big 2 of these *Tempora* (whence Piso's barb that M 'goes for the ones he despises, not those he should be enraged with—and everyone knows who you mean', *In Pis.* 75). It showed earlier (9):

scribis de **Caesaris summo in nos amore.** hunc et tu fouebis et nos quibus-cumque poterimus rebus augebimus.

de **Pompeio** et facio diligenter et faciam quod mones.

You write of *Caesar*'s *deepest love for us*—you'll tend it and, whatever's in my power, I'll grow it.

On **Pompey**, I'm studiously doing and will do as you advise.

The brothers' agreed nostrum was precisely to conspire to stop treating this couple as a pair: they were now with Caesar, and no 'second thoughts' (18). There would be no 'return' for Pompey, so help M, not into *these* good books (15):

Pompeius a me ualde contendit de **reditu** in gratiam sed adhuc nihil profecit nec, si ullam partem libertatis tenebo, proficiet.

Pompey's really pushing for **return** to my good books, but to date not got anywhere, and if I hang on to any %age of freedom, he'll get nowhere.

Hence consternation, and knee-jerk reaction, at the exasperating 'news' that M has already for a week now officially been repeating the tour of duty already served by Qfr. in 56 BCE (legate to Pompey in Sardinia, *Ad Qfr.* 2.1–6), before Plan B took him off to be legate of Caesar in 54, in Gaul, 18):

quod inferiore epistula scribis, *me Id. Sept. Pompeio legatum iri*, id ego non audiui scripsique ad Caesarem *neque Vibullium Caesaris mandata de mea mansione ad Pompeium pertulisse nec Oppium.* quo consilio? quamquam Oppium ego tenui quod priores partes Vibulli erant; cum eo enim coram Caesar egerat, ad Oppium scripserat.

Your writing, lower down bulletin, *I shall be made lieutenant to Pompey 13 Sept.*, first I've heard of it, and I've written Caesar to say (i) Vibullius brought no instructions to Pompey about my staying put, (ii) & neither did Oppius. The thinking? Though I did put Opp. on hold, as the lead role was Vib.'s (you see Caesar's dealings with him were in person—he WROTE to Oppy) . . .

Talk of 'permission to stay on' inevitably brings Qfr. into the frame (*permissio mansionis tuae*, 9; *tuam remansionem etiam atque etiam probo*, 18). The pipe-dream-ticket bought by these tours of duty had been meant first to get M back in from the cold, then to oblige the Godfathers to back Qfr.'s own *reditus* to Rome, there to follow that yellow brick road already trodden by the likes of Gabinius and Piso, exactly as promised by his newly refitted mansion, in the bag, warrants M, from copper-bottom to new look top (1):

*propterea quod **summam dignitatem** pauimentata porticus habebat....*
pauimenta recte fieri uidebantur. cameras quidem non probaui, mutarique
iussi.

because flooring brings colonnade **top-notch class.** . . . Flooring seems going
fine; some ceilings I've flunked & ordered alterations.

B9. In inexorable turn, thought of Qfr. in Gaul brings *the* Big Cheese
Caesar into the frame, looming over this correspondence where no
Roman could miss him (25):

ex Britannia Caesar ad me Kal. Sept. dedit litteras quas ego accepi a. d. IIII
Kal. Oct., **satis commodas de Britannicis rebus**, quibus, ne admirer quod a
te nullas acceperim, scribit *se sine te fuisse cum ad mare accesserit.* ad eas ego
ei litteras nihil rescripsi, ne gratulandi quidem causa, propter eius luctum.

From Britain Caesar mailed me a letter on 1 Sept., received it 27 Sept., **plenty
agreeable on the Britain front**, writing in it so I don't get fazed at receiving
no mail from you *he was minus you when he reached the sea.* I've written
nothing by way of letter back to him, not even by way of congratulations.
Because he's in mourning.

The terms for this decade's *tempora* were initially set by Pompey the
Great's *reditus*; whatever became of third man in the IIIviratus
Crassus, just setting about the Parthians, the writing on the Roman
wall was the impending *reditus* of *magni Caesaris* back from Darkest
Britain (cf. Catullus 11: extremist unction of a far-out ultimatum).
Anticipation of this moment monopolized all the Cicerones' joint
thinking, not least in denial. We saw M give notice of the masterful
(Caesarian + Ciceronian) strategy of dealing with challenges from
opponents with withering silence whilst continuing to broadcast
initiatives of his own (11), and now he copes, over again, just the
way he did before, by steadfastly refusing to betray the slightest
interest in swashbuckling episodes of *Bellum Gallicum*):

de Britannicis rebus, cognoui ex tuis litteris **nihil esse nec quod metuamus
nec quod gaudeamus.**

On the Britain front, I realize from yr letter there's **nada, no call for fright,
no call for joy.**

Whatever tales may have filled Qfr.'s bulletins, whatever panic and
relief these brought M, their deal is that he will *not* be impressed by
world-conquest (big deal), not between the two of them (∼ *Ad Att.*

4.15.10, 18.5, and 4.17.6, *Britannicum bellum*; Trebatius' *Britannicae Litterae*: *Ad Fam.* 7.8.2 = 7.6–17). Instead, this correspondence rates Qfr.'s tour a(nother) campaign to capture political ingratiation. (Foreign policy election-driven: a superpower.) M writes that the bitter-sweet price is painful severance, but he *means* their double act will pay off big time (9, 17; 15):

tuas litteras uehementer exspecto.

I'm waiting and waiting on a letter from you.

All told, all goes according to plan, by the book, but nothing's going to plan, as he folds the letter once for all. For M resorts again to retaliation to written challenge with dignified silence (25):

quod a te **nullas acceperim**...ad eas ego ei litteras nihil **rescripsi**, ne gratulandi quidem causa, propter eius luctum.

at receiving **no mail from you**...I've written **nothing by way of letter back to him**, not even by way of congratulations. Because he's in mourning.

B10. This last shift closes the communiqué down, with a double block on communication, hitting out at the conquistador where it hurts, on M's stamping ground, the ego-swelling department of encomium, with the perfect alibi of silence in the face of the loss of a child. This to knock on the head the threat to the entire *Ad Qfr.* programme represented by the physical uncoupling of Qfr. from Caesar (25):

se **sine te** *fuisse cum ad mare accesserit.*

he was **minus you** *when he reached the sea.*

After the catalogue of togethernesses that selfless Qfr. has missed out on, this unspeakable severance takes M's biscuit (*Mescidium cum Philoxeno*...*uidi*...; *offendi Diphilum*, 1, *Caesius qui tum mecum fuit,* 2, *Mescidium mecum habui. is sese*... *tecum transegisse dicebat*, 3, *de qua mecum locutus esses*, 5, *utinam*...*mecum fuisset,*...*eat nobiscum*..., *si eum mecum habuero*, 7, *Balbum*...*mecum*...*assidere usque ad Id. Mai. futurum*, 12, *uenit ad nos Cicero tuus*, 19, *frater*... *eius mecum est multum*, 22; contrast *Hippodamum*...*tam inhumaniter fecisse ut sine meis litteris ad te proficisceretur*, 21). His epistolary strategy of creating a world to inhabit which at one end filters the unpleasantnesses associated with Piso...Gabinius...Clodius...Pompey, and at the other whites out the bloodcurdling carnage of Caesar and the Gallic hordes, ultimately justifies itself within the untidy ambit of this September round-up. For plunging into the microcosm of Arpinum & hinterland swamped and displaced all vistas outside M's purview. Put *everything* into perspective. All those legions of pygmies—Philotimus, Philoxenus, Mescidius, Diphilus, Caesius, Cillo, Nicephorus, Cincius (1–6)—gave him a sideshow to boss, and a role to strut, in Qfr.'s place (*ad litteram*). Here, urgent, vigilant, detailed, accurate accountancy would drown out cross-channel histrionics—and meet flair, imagination, and business acumen, in these testing times (esp. *offendi... tardiorem...*, *non probaui*, 1, *probaui*, 2, *quod melius intellego...*, *mihi plus uisum est*, 3, *perspexi*, 4, *probaui*, 5, *ipse crebro interuiso*, 6, *offendi*, 14). Eat your heart out, world-beaters, in these parts expert/amateur inspection of properties leads, 'straight' down the road (*recta Vitularia uia*, 3), to inspection *of* the road, utilities, and roadside amenities (4), while polishing Qfr's standing as major stakeholder in the Republic served to revitalize his curator, himself on the long road to full recovery. 'Changes are made (and *un*made)' (*mutari... iussi*, 1, *ut est, magis placebat...* ; *assa... promoui,... columnas... demolietur*, 2), the designer of decor(um) 'straightens out' ceilings and pillars (*cameras quidem non probaui*, 1; *columnas neque rectas neque e regione... demolietur, perpendiculo et linea discet uti*, 2), applies rhetoricized techniques of finish (*politae,... tectorium ut concinnum sit*, 1, *absolutum... in aedibus tuis tectum*, 14), builds into his creation the requisite modesties (*neque enim satis... atriolo neque fere solet nisi... in quibus est atrium maius*, 2, *non placuerat tibi esse multorum fastigiorum,... nunc honeste uergit in tectum inferioris porticus*, 14).

The whole scam always *was* a screen, naturally. In this customized landscape, M uses his cover of understudy for Qfr. to continue the fight to put 'the whole lot of them' in their place, and re-establish *himself* (if only in Ciceronian eyes) as the self-made 'architect' of Ciceronian éminence in Rome (1):

Ego... me refeci.

I... refitted myself.

(Cf. *Ad Att.* 4.2.5–7, *illi... qui mihi pinnas inciderant nolunt easdem renasci. sed... iam renascuntur...*, *domus aedificatur...*, *reficitur Formianum...*, 10.1, *litteris... recreor.*) Hitching a ride with the other Cicero handed him, not least, a vantage point for spraying consolatory satire on all and sultry (5):

ea uilla... tamquam philosopha uidetur esse, **quae obiurget ceterarum uillarum insaniam.**

that house... seems sort of like a mantra there **to put to scorn the mania of rest of houses.**

(Compare the wince at Caesar's ?mock?-sarcasm: *de tribunatu quod scribis, ego uero nominatim petiui Curtio et mihi ipse Caesar nominatim Curtio paratum esse rescripsit meamque in rogando uerecundiam* **obiur-gauit,** 10, 'On the tribunate, in your write, well I did lobby for Curtius, by name, & Caesar did write back that *it was waiting for Curtius, by name* + **put me to scorn** for *my shamefacedness in lobbying.*')

To be sure, no other letter 'to Qfr' begins by writing the word 'I'. The lasting word. (*Ego* × 19: *ego-me-mihi-mihi-mihi,* 1, *mihi-tu-mecum,* 2, *tibi-ego-te-te-te-nos-mecum-tecum-mihi,* 3, *mihi-tu-ego-tibi,* 4, *tuum-mihi-te-mihi-te-te,* 5, *te,* 6, *me-tibi-tu-mihi-tibi-ego-meum-tibi-nobiscum-mecum-me-tibi-mihi-te,* 7, *tuas-mihi-te-tuis-nobis-nos,* 8, *nos-tu-nos-tibi-ego-meum-ego-mihi-te-te-meum-te-te,* 9, *ego-mihi-meam-mihi-mihi-me-ego-tuo-tuis-te,* 10, *tibi-tibi-me-ego-tibi,* 11, *mihi-me,* 12, *mihi-te-mihi-ego-nobis,* 13, *mihi-me-tuam-me-mihi-tuis-tibi-noster-ego-ego-me,* 14, *me-tuas,* 15, *te-me-mihi-me,* 16, *uobis-me-ego-tuas-tuam,* 17, *mihi-me-ego-mea-ego-ego-mihi-te,* 18, *mea-nos-tuus-mihi-mihi-mihi-me,* 19, *tuae-te,* 20, *mihi-te-me-meus-te-mihi-tu-me-te-mehercule-te-me,* 21, *me-te-tuis-me-mecum,* 22, *mihi-tibi-ego-te-me-te-tu-mihi,* 23, *tu*-Meorum, 24, *me-ego-te-te-ego-te-mi,* 25. *Tu* starts only the expostulatory letter 2.9: 'You? "Interrupt"? Me?').

C. CONCLUSION

C1. The year and the correspondence will end shortly (Dec. 54 BCE) with no regrets over the Gabinius fiasco, premonitions over Milo's dreamticket for the consulate (antidote to Clodius), and indiscreetly discretionary blurting on the imperative need not to blurt from the time-expired statesman (3.7.3):

de motu temporum uenientis anni, nihil te intellegere uolueram domestici timoris sed **de communi rei publicae salute,** in quo etiam si nihil procuro, tamen nihil curare uix possum.

quam autem te uelim cautum esse in scribendo ex hoc conicito quod ego ad te ne haec quidem scribo quae palam in re publica turbantur, ne cuiusquam animum meae litterae interceptae offendant.

On the volatility of the coming year 53 BCE crisis, I didn't want you to understand anything to do with worries in our clan. **On the survival of Republican society,** though: yes. There's a topic where even though I'm *carrying* no responsibility, still I'm scarcely capable of not *caring*.

Now, just how careful I want you to be in what you write can be figured out from my not even writing to you all this messy Republican politicking out in the open, in case my letters fall into the wrong hands and put anyone's nose out of joint.

Instead, this dispirited old warhorse is out of it, he just made sure to tell any snoopers and Qfr., 'these people, this crisis..., no satisfaction possible, so what boots spleen?' (2):

litterae me et studia nostra et otium uillaeque delectant, maximeque pueri nostri.

It's **letterature** for me. Our studies, retirement, homes in the country, there's the joy, and most of all, our boys.

Start over here, with 'M at peace' (he trumpets: 3, *ego quiesco*), running through one last checklist from Qfr.: *'on your promise of slaves...; on Vatinius' laughable letter to Caesar,* as to your urging me to get it finished, that epic for Caesar, I have it finished—just need a trusty postman so it doesn't have the same accident as your *Erigone,* which [in M's eminently quotable *bon mot*] has had the distinction of being the only thing not safe on the highway from Gaul during Caesar's term as supremo; *on Qfr.'s Arcanum estate; on Felix's will;* and, last but not least, Q. Cicero, Jr., (4–9). Truly:

rescripsi ad omnia, mi suauissime et optime frater. uale.

I've replied to ABSOLUTELY EVERYTHING, my perfect brother, scrumptious and true. See you fare well.

C2. The editor of a correspondence can only work with what they have, but did the Cicerones really send each other no more pages between the turn-off in 54 and their joint proscription in 43 BCE? Was—is—it best to bring down this curtain just as consular Marcus slinks into the shadows, now his 'return' has gone sour and his comeback stalled; just as praetorian Qfr. faced standing in his brother's shadow for good, while lieutenant Cicero played war hero against onslaught from the Nervii nation, ill, besieged, holding out against 60,000 braves, 90% casualties, till Caesar, sending on ahead the year 54 BCE's prize letter, written in Greek, attached to a throwing-spear's thong, and launched into Qfr.'s stockade, only to stick in a timber turret for 2 days before it was noticed on the 3rd, came in the nick of time to save the day (exactly as the genius says he'd promised; Caesar, *De Bello Gallico* 5.40–52)? ... Maybe none of this registers on Marcus' radar because it's still in the offing (*late* in 54). Perhaps, too, more letters home, from that ominously looming cliffhanger of a year (53: no picnic), could have elided all mention of Quiffer's own comeuppance, when the bloody own goal he scored by *incuria* when left in charge of camp for another spell earned him a dreaded black mark from Julius, and that (conceivably) good as finished *his* epic off (ibid. 6.36–42; still in charge of some winter quarters at 7.90, but that's it—until M, finally winkled out of Rome to run a province, needed him by his side to help run nowhereland Cilicia in 51). Either way, on both sides now, our three books *Ad Qfr.* relate these ante-bellum *tempora* far enough—sparing us the consequences of Caesar's heroic mourning, and of *his reditus* to Rome, and self-vindication through invasion: brother set against brother, scarring that would never heal ... (The sibling anthology *Ad Atticum* leaps straight from 4.19 at the end of 54 into 51 at 5.1.)

It's an anthological mercy to stop history in its tracks, and imply: *fratres floruerunt.*

D. TEXT AND TRANSLATION OF CICERO, *AD QFR.* 3.1

Marcus Quinto Fratri Salutem

1 ego ex magnis caloribus (non enim meminimus maiores) in Arpinati summa cum amoenitate fluminis me refeci ludorum diebus, Philotimo tribulibus commendatis.

in Arcano a. d. IIII Id. Sept. fui. ibi Mescidium cum Philoxeno aquamque, quam ii ducebant non longe a uilla, belle sane fluentem uidi, praesertim maxima siccitate, *uberioremque aliquanto sese collecturos esse* dicebant.

apud Herum recte erat.

in Manliano offendi Diphilum Diphilo tardiorem; sed tamen nihil ei restabat praeter balnearia et ambulationem et auiarium. uilla mihi ualde placuit propterea quod summam dignitatem pauimentata porticus habebat, quod mihi nunc denique apparuit, posteaquam et ipsa tota patet et columnae politae sunt. totum in eo est (quod mihi erit curae), tectorium ut concinnum sit. pauimenta recte fieri uidebantur. cameras quidem non probaui, mutarique iussi.

2 quo loco in porticu te scribere aiunt ut *atriolum fiat,* mihi, ut est, magis placebat. neque enim satis loci uidebatur esse atriolo neque fere solet nisi in iis aedificiis fieri in quibus est atrium maius nec habere poterat adiuncta cubicula et eiusmodi membra. nunc hoc uel honestae testudinis, uel ualde boni aestiui locum obtinebit. tu tamen si aliter sentis, rescribe quam primum. in balneariis assa in alterum apodyteri angulum promoui propterea quod ita erant posita ut eorum uaporarium, ex quo ignis erumpit, esset subiectum cubiculis. subgrande cubiculum autem et hibernum altum ualde probaui quod et ampla erant et loco posita ambulationis uno latere, eo quod est proximum balneariis. columnas neque rectas neque e regione Diphilus collocarat. eas scilicet demolietur. aliquando perpendiculo et linea discet uti. omnino spero paucis mensibus opus Diphili perfectum fore; curat enim diligentissime Caesius, qui tum mecum fuit.

3 ex eo loco recta Vitularia uia profecti sumus **in Fufidianum fundum,** quam tibi proximis nundinis Arpini de Fufidio HS CCCIↃↃↃCIↃ emeramus. ego locum aestate umbrosiorem uidi numquam, permultis locis aquam profluentem et eam uberem. quid quaeris? *iugera L prati* Caesius *irrigaturum facile te* arbitrabatur. equidem hoc quod melius intellego affirmo, *mirifica suauitate te uillam habiturum piscina et salientibus additis, palaestra et silua uiridicata. fundum* audio *te hunc Babuleianum uelle retinere.* de eo quid uideatur ipse constitues. Caesius aiebat, *aqua dempta, et eius aquae iure constituto, et seruitute fundo illi imposita, tamen nos pretium seruare posse, si uendere uellemus.* Mescidium mecum habui. is *sese ternis nummis in pedem tecum transegisse*

dicebat, *sese* autem *mensum pedibus* aiebat *passuum* IIICIↃ. mihi plus
uisum est, sed praestabo sumptum nusquam melius posse poni. Cillo-
nem arcessieram Venafro, sed eo ipso die quattuor eius conseruos et
discipulos Venafri cuniculus oppresserat.

4 Id. Sept. **in Laterio** fui. uiam perspexi, quae mihi ita placuit ut opus
publicum uideretur esse, praeter CL passuum (sum enim ipse men-
sus) ab eo ponticulo qui est ad Furinae, Satricum uersus. eo loco
puluis non glarea iniecta est (id mutabitur) et ea uiae pars ualde
accliuis est, sed intellexi aliter duci non potuisse, praesertim cum tu
neque per Lucustae neque per Varronis uelles ducere. Varro uiam
ante suum fundum probe munierat; Lucusta non attigerat. quem ego
Romae aggrediar et, ut arbitror, commouebo et simul M. Taurum,
quem *tibi* audio *promisisse*, qui nunc Romae erat, de aqua per
fundum eius ducenda rogabo.

5 Nicephorum, uilicum tuum, sane probaui quaesiuique ex eo *ecquid
ei de illa aedificatiuncula Lateri de qua mecum locutus es mandauisses.*
tum is mihi respondit, *se ipsum eius operis HS XVI conductorem fuisse
sed te postea multa addidisse ad opus, nihil ad pretium; itaque id se
omisisse.* mihi mehercule ualde placet, te illa ut constitueras addere;
quamquam ea uilla, quae nunc est, tamquam philosopha uidetur
esse, quae obiurget ceterarum uillarum insaniam. uerum tamen illud
additum delectabit. topiarium laudaui; ita omnia conuestit hedera,
qua basim uillae, qua intercolumnia ambulationis, ut denique illi
palliati topiariam facere uideantur et hederam uendere. iam
ἀποδυτηρίῳ nihil alsius, nihil muscosius. habes fere de rebus rusticis.

6 **urbanam expolitionem** urget ille quidem Philotimus et Cincius sed
etiam ipse crebro interuiso, quod est facile factu. quamobrem ea te
cura liberatum uolo.

7 **de Cicerone** quod me semper rogas, ignosco equidem tibi sed tu
quoque mihi uelim ignoscas. non enim concedo tibi plus ut illum
ames quam ipse amo. atque utinam his diebus in Arpinati, quod et
ipse cupierat et ego non minus, mecum fuisset. quod ad Pompo-
niam, si tibi uidetur, scribas uelim, *cum aliquo exibimus eat nobiscum
puerumque educat.* clamores efficiam si eum mecum habuero otiosus;
nam Romae respirandi non est locus. id me scis antea gratis tibi esse
pollicitum, quid nunc putas tanta mihi abs te mercede proposita?

8 uenio nunc ad **tuas litteras** quas pluribus epistulis accepi dum sum in Arpinati; nam mihi uno die **tres** sunt redditae et quidem, ut uidebatur, eodem abs te datae tempore, **una** pluribus uerbis in qua primum erat quod *antiquior dies in tuis fuisset ascripta litteris quam in Caesaris.* id facit Oppius nonnumquam necessario ut, cum tabellarios constituerit mittere litterasque a nobis acceperit, aliqua re noua impediatur et necessario serius quam constituerat mittat neque nos datis iam epistulis diem commutari curamus.

9 scribis *de Caesaris summo in nos amore.* hunc et tu fouebis et nos quibuscumque poterimus rebus augebimus.

de Pompeio et facio diligenter et faciam quod mones.

quod tibi permissio **mansionis tuae** grata est, id ego summo meo dolore et desiderio tamen ex parte gaudeo.

in Hippodamo et nonnullis aliis arcessendis quid cogites non intellego. nemo istorum est quin abs te munus fundi suburbani instar exspectet.

Trebatium uero meum quod isto admisceas nihil est. ego illum ad Caesarem misi, qui mihi iam satis fecit; si ipsi minus, praestare nihil debeo teque item ab eo uindico et libero. quod scribis *te a Caesare quotidie plus diligi,* immortaliter gaudeo.

Balbum uero, qui est *istius rei* quemadmodum scribis *adiutor,* in oculis fero.

Trebonium meum *a te amari, teque ab illo,* pergaudeo.

10 **de tribunatu** quod scribis, ego uero nominatim petiui Curtio et mihi ipse Caesar nominatim *Curtio paratum esse* rescripsit *meamque in rogando uerecundiam* obiurgauit. si cui praeterea petiero (id quod etiam Oppio dixi ut ad illum scriberet) *facile patiar mihi negari, quoniam illi qui mihi molesti sunt sibi negari a me non facile patiuntur.* ego *Curtium,* id quod ipsi dixi, *non modo rogatione sed etiam testimonio tuo diligo quod litteris tuis studium illius in salutem nostram facile perspexi.*

de Britannicis rebus, cognoui ex tuis litteris nihil esse nec quod metuamus nec quod gaudeamus.

de publicis negotiis *quae uis ad te Tironem scribere,* neglegentius ad te ante scribebam quod omnia minima maxima ad Caesarem mitti sciebam. rescripsi epistulae maximae.

11 audi nunc **de minuscula**, in qua primum est **de Clodi ad Caesarem litteris**. in quo Caesaris consilium probo, quod tibi amantissime petenti ueniam non dedit uti ullum ad illam furiam uerbum rescriberet.

alterum est **de Caluenti Mari oratione**. quod scribis, miror, *tibi placere me ad eam rescribere*, praesertim cum illam nemo lecturus sit si ego nihil rescripsero, meam in illum pueri omnes tamquam dictata perdiscant.

libros meos omnis quos exspectas incohaui sed conficere non possum his diebus. orationes efflagitatas *pro Scauro* et *pro Plancio* absolui. poema *ad Caesarem*, quod composueram, incidi. tibi quod rogas, quoniam ipsi fontes iam sitiunt, siquid habebo spati, scribam.

12 uenio **ad tertiam. Balbum** quod ais *mature Romam bene comitatum esse uenturum mecumque assidue usque ad Id. Mai. futurum*, id mihi pergratum perque iucundum. quod me in eadem epistula sicut saepe antea cohortaris *ad ambitionem et ad laborem*, faciam equidem, sed quando uiuemus?

13 *quarta* epistula mihi reddita est Id. Sept. quam a. d. IIII Id. Sext. ex Britannia dederas. in ea nihil sane erat noui praeter *Erigonam* (quam si ab Oppio accepero, scribam ad te quid sentiam, nec dubito quin mihi placitura sit) et, quod paene praeterii, de eo quem scripsisti *de Milonis plausu* scripsisse ad Caesarem. ego uero facile patior ita Caesarem existimare illum quam maximum fuisse plausum. et prorsus ita fuit. et tamen ille plausus qui illi datur quodam modo nobis uidetur dari.

14 reddita etiam mihi est **peruetus epistula**, sed sero allata, in qua **de aede Telluris et de porticu Catuli** me admones. fit utrumque diligenter. ad Telluris quidem etiam tuam statuam locaui.

item **de hortis** me quod admones, nec fui umquam ualde cupidus et nunc domus suppeditat mihi hortorum amoenitatem.

Romam cum uenissem a. d. XIII Kal. Oct., absolutum offendi in aedibus tuis tectum, quod supra conclauia non placuerat tibi esse multorum fastigiorum, id nunc honeste uergit in tectum inferioris porticus.

Cicero noster dum ego absum non cessauit apud rhetorem. de eius eruditione quod labores nihil est, quoniam ingenium eius nosti, studium ego uideo. cetera eius suscipio ut me putem praestare debere.

15 **Gabinium** tres adhuc factiones postulant, L. Lentulus, flaminis filius, qui iam de maiestate postulauit, Ti. Nero cum bonis subscriptoribus, C. Memmius tribunus pl. cum L. Capitone. ad urbem accessit a. d. XII Kal. Oct. nihil turpius nec desertius. sed his iudiciis nihil audeo confidere. quod Cato non ualebat, adhuc de pecuniis repetundis non erat postulatus.

Pompeius a me ualde contendit de reditu in gratiam sed adhuc nihil profecit nec, si ullam partem libertatis tenebo, proficiet. tuas litteras uehementer exspecto.

16 quod scribis *te audisse* **in candidatorum consularium coitione** *me interfuisse*, id falsum est. eiusmodi enim pactiones in ea coitione factae sunt, quas postea Memmius patefecit, ut nemo bonus interesse debuerit, et simul mihi committendum non fuit ut iis coitionibus interessem quibus Messalla excluderetur. cui quidem uehementer satis facio rebus omnibus, ut arbitror, etiam Memmio. Domitio ipsi multa iam feci quae uoluit quaeque a me petiuit. Scaurum beneficio defensionis ualde obligaui. adhuc erat ualde incertum et quando comitia et qui consules futuri essent.

17 cum hanc iam epistulam complicarem, **tabellarii a uobis** uenerunt a. d. XI Kal. septimo uicesimo die.

o me sollicitum. quantum ego dolui **in Caesaris** suauissimis **litteris**. sed quo erant suauiores, eo maiorem dolorem illius ille casus afferebat.

sed ad **tuas** uenio *litteras*. primum **tuam remansionem** etiam atque etiam probo, praesertim cum, ut scribis, *cum Caesare communicaris.*

18 **Oppium** miror quicquam cum Publio; mihi enim non placuerat.

quod inferiore epistula scribis, me *Id. Sept.* **Pompeio legatum** *iri,* id ego non audiui scripsique ad Caesarem *neque Vibullium Caesaris mandata de mea mansione ad Pompeium pertulisse nec Oppium.* quo consilio? quamquam Oppium ego tenui quod priores partes Vibulli erant; cum eo enim coram Caesar egerat, ad Oppium scripserat.

ego uero nullas δευτέρας φροντίδας habere possum *in Caesaris rebus.*
ille mihi secundum te et liberos nostros ita est, ut sit paene par. uideor
id iudicio facere, iam enim debeo, sed tamen amore sum incensus.

19 cum scripsissem haec infima quae sunt mea manu,
uenit ad nos **Cicero tuus** ad cenam, cum Pomponia
foris cenaret.

dedit mihi **epistulam** legendam **tuam**, quam paulo
ante acceperat, Aristophaneo modo ualde mehercule
et suauem et grauem; qua sum admodum delectatus.

dedit etiam **alteram** illam mihi, qua iubes eum
mihi esse affixum tamquam magistro. quam illum
epistulae illae delectarunt, quam me. nihil puero
illo suauius, nihil nostri amantius. hoc inter
cenam Tironi dictaui, ne mirere alia manu esse.

20 **Annali** pergratae litterae tuae fuerunt, quod *et curares de se diligenter et tamen consilio se uerissimo iuuares.*

P. **Seruilius** pater ex litteris, quas *sibi a Caesare missas esse* dicebat, significat ualde *te sibi gratum fecisse quod de sua uoluntate erga Caesarem humanissime diligentissimeque locutus esses.*

21 cum **Romam** ex Arpinati reuertissem, dictum mihi est **Hippodamum** *ad te profectum esse.* non possum scribere *me miratum esse illum tam inhumaniter fecisse ut sine meis litteris ad te proficisceretur;* illud scribo, *mihi molestum fuisse.* iam enim diu cogitaueram ex eo quod tu ad me scripseras ut, *si quid esset quod ad te diligentius perferri uellem, illi darem,* quod mehercule hisce litteris, quas uulgo ad te mitto, nihil fere scribo, quod si in alicuius manus inciderit, moleste ferendum sit. Minucio me et Saluio et Labieno reseruabam. Labeo aut tarde proficiscetur aut hic manebit. Hippodamus ne numquid uellem quidem rogauit.

22 T. **Pinarius** amabiles ad me de te litteras mittit; *se maxime litteris, sermonibus, cenis denique tuis delectari.* is homo semper me delectauit fraterque eius mecum est multum. qua re, uti instituisti, complectere adulescentem.

23 quod multos dies **epistulam in manibus** habui propter commoratio-nem tabellariorum, ideo multa coniecta sunt, aliud alio tempore uelut hoc: T. **Anicius** mihi saepe iam dixit *sese tibi* **suburbanum** *si quod inuenisset non dubitaturum esse emere.* in eius sermone ego

utrumque soleo admirari, et te de suburbano emendo cum ad illum
scribas non modo ad me non scribere sed etiam aliam in sententiam
de suburbano scribere, et cum ad illum scribas nihil te recordari de
se de epistulis illis quas in Tusculano eius tu mihi ostendisti, nihil
de praeceptis Epicharmi: Γνῶθι πῶς ἄλλῳ κέχρηται, totum denique
uultum, sermonem, animum eius, quemadmodum conicio, quasi...

24 sed haec tu uideris. **de suburbano** cura ut sciam quid uelis, et simul
ne quid ille turbet uide. quid praeterea? quid? etiam.

    Gabinius a. d. IIII Kal. Oct. noctu in urbem introierat et hodie
hora VIII, cum edicto C. Alfi de maiestate eum adesse oporteret,
concursu magno et odio uniuersi populi paene afflictus est. nihil illo
turpius. proximus est tamen Piso. itaque mirificum ἐμβόλιον cogito
in secundum librum *Meorum Temporum* includere, dicentem Apollinem in concilio deorum, *qualis reditus duorum imperatorum futurus
esset; quorum alter exercitum perdidisset, alter uendidisset.*

25 ex Britannia **Caesar** ad me Kal. Sept. dedit litteras quas ego accepi a.
d. IIII Kal. Oct., satis commodas **de Britannicis rebus**, quibus, ne
admirer quod a te nullas acceperim, scribit *se sine te fuisse cum ad
mare accesserit.* ad eas ego ei litteras nihil rescripsi, ne gratulandi
quidem causa, propter eius luctum.

        te oro etiam atque etiam, mi frater, ut ualeas.

GREETINGS TO QUIFFER FROM MARCUS

1 It's me. Away from temperatures way up high, can't recall higher,
down **at the Arpinum place**, back with best beloved river, re-fitted
myself over holiday fortnight (the folks on our register forwarded c/o
Philotimus).

    I was **at Arcanum** 10 Sept. Mescidius & Philoxenus + water they
were piping not far from house, saw it running real purty, esp. given
height of drought, & telling me they're going to pull in a fair amount
fuller yield.

    All straight **at Herus'**.

At **Manilius'**, bumped into Diphilus out-dawdling Diphilus. All the same, no jobs left to go, apart from: baths; walkway; birdhouse. House yes got my vote and how, for why because flooring brings colonnade top-notch class, as finally dawned on me, now that (i) the whole show's wide open; (ii) pillars have their finish. Whole effect's all in the—I'll take care of it—rendering, getting it harmonized. Flooring seems going fine; some ceilings I've flunked & ordered alterations.

2 The spot in colonnade they say you specify *for turning into mini-patio* gets my vote as is: (*a*) spot don't seem enough room for an m-p, (*b*) not normally done thing, except in units including jumbo patio, (*c*) couldn't have rooms off + that type of annex. Now it'll find room for, oh, genteel vault or ace suntrap. Still if you feel different write back asap. In bathhouse I brought roasterator forward into the other corner of de-togs for why because it's located such that its steamer (where the flames pop out) wd be stuck underneath bedrooms. Fair-sized bedroom + tall one for winter passed muster and how, as: (i) roomy; (ii) occupies space on one side of walkway, closest to bathhouse. Pillars weren't either in line or aligned where Diphilus had 'em rigged—course he'll be taking THEM down. One day soon he's going to learn the use of T-square and plumbline. I hope 100% D's work will be done and dusted in a month or two—Caesius is taking care strenuous as anything. (He was with me at the time.)

3 From that spot straight off we went down Veal Broadway to **Fufidius' farm**, we bought it for you at Arpinum last market day from F. @ 101K. Me, I never did see a spot shadier in summer, water welling at loadsa spots, good 'n' full, at that. No need to wonder: Caesius reckons that *you'll irrigate 1 doz. hectares easy*, and I—coming on strong on what I know better—that *you'll have stunning sweetie of a house, put in pool, fountains, work-out and greenwood*. I'm told you *now want to hang on to this Babuleian district farm:* on that you'll settle the way you see fit. Caesius, he say *subtract the water, settle its water rights, stick service easement on the farm, and we can* still *preserve cost-price should we want to sell.* Mescidius I've had with me. Claims *his bargain with you was 3/- per foot*, says *he measured it out in paces @ 3K's worth.* Seemed more to me, but I'll guarantee it,

the money couldn't be better spent anywhere. Cillo I sent for from Venafrum, but that very day 4 of his slave mates and apprentices got crushed by a Venafrum tunnel.

4 13 Sept. I was **at Laterium**. Gave road the once over. Got my vote, such that it could pass for state works, apart from 150 paces (measured 'em myself) from little bridge, the one by St Furina's, towards Satricum. At that spot surface is layer of dirt not gravel (changes will be made) + that bit of road's on slope and how; but I realized it couldn't be put through any other way, specially as you didn't want to put it through Locust's or Varro's. This Varro's built road in front of his farm good and proper, Locust hasn't touched it—I'll get after him in Rome and (I bet) I'll get his skates on, + in one go M. Taurus (he's *currently at Rome*), I'm told *he promised you*, I'll chase up on question of putting water through his farm.

5 Your estates manager Nicephorus I sure do rate, asked him *whether you gave him any orders on that little chalet at Laterium you talked about to me*, then he answered me *he had the contract for the work @ 16K but afterwards you added lots to work, zilch to price, so he's dropped it*. My vote by crikey goes like how to adding stuff as per your plan—although that house the way it is now seems sort of like a mantra there to put to scorn the mania of rest of houses. Still and all, add-on extension'll be fun. Gardener I congratulated, for carpeting the lot with ivy this way, here house plinth, there walkway gaps in-between pillars, so in fact those characters dressed in Greek look like THEY'RE doing the gardening, peddling their ivy. Next, the DE-TOGS—nothing so cool, nothing so MOSSY . . . You pretty well got it for news out of town.

6 **Finishing touches in Rome** are hustled along by him—Philotimus, + Cincius, but, again, I frequently run an eye over too, easy done, so you be carefree on that score, just for me.

7 On **Cicero**—you keep on asking, and I don't mind, but you too please don't you mind my not backing down on your loving him any more than I do myself. In fact just wish these days at the Arpinum place, as (1) he fancied and (2) I did, just as much, he'd been with me. Do please write Pomponia if you see fit, *when we go off somewhere she should come with us & fetch the boy out.* I'll cause a sensation if I have him with me when I'm on vacation—see, there's no room to

breathe in Rome—you know I promised you this before, for free, so what you reckon now you've offered me such a big pay-off?

8 Now I get to **your letters**, received them in quite a few bulletins while at the Arpinum place—you see, *3* were delivered to me on one day and actually, so it seems, your end they were sent same time—**No. 1** in quite a few words, in it point 1 being, *an older dateline was noted on your letter than on Caesar's*. This is Oppius' doing, sometimes it's necessity: when he's planned sending off couriers & got a letter from me, gets tangled up in some development and . . . *it's necessity*, sends it off later than he planned, 'n' we don't bother getting date altered once letter's handed over.

9 You write of *Caesar's* **deepest love for us**—you'll tend it and, whatever's in my power, I'll grow it.

On **Pompey**, I'm studiously doing and will do as you advise.

As for my leave for **you to stay on** being swell with you, it means my deepest pain & longing, but a *bit* of me feels joy.

In having **Hippodamus + a good no. of others** sent for, I don't get your thinking. Nary a one of that lot don't anticipate a gift from you the size of a farm outside Rome.

My **Trebatius**, now, no cause to mix him up with them. Sent him to Caesar and *he's* already done plenty by me—if not for T., I'm not obliged to deliver on anything, & as for you—I clear/free you, too. You write *you're adored more every day by Caesar*—I'm in heaven, the joy.

So **Balbus**, who is *in this*, so you write, *your lieutenant*—I only have eyes for him.

My **Trebonius** *being loved by you & you by him* means I'm overjoyed.

10 On **the tribunate**, in your write, well I did lobby for Curtius, by name, & Caesar did write back that *it was waiting for Curtius, by name +* put me to scorn for *my shamefacedness in lobbying*. If I lobby for somebody besides, as I told Oppius to write to him as well again, *I'll easy take a no* FOR *me, because the ones who are being a drag for me don't easily take a no* FROM *me*. Me and Curtius, as I told you, I adore him not just because you ask me to but again because of yr reference, as I easy spotted right through your letter his fervour for my well-being.

On **the Britain front,** I realize from yr letter there's nada, no call for fright, no call for joy.

On **the political situation,** *on which you want Tiro to write you,* I've been writing you before now a bit nonchalantly because I've known that EVERYTHING, mini through maxi, gets sent Caesar. I've answered the mega-max bulletin.

11 Listen up now on **the tiddler,** in it 1st point being on **Clodius' letter to Caesar,** and in this I approve Caesar's strategy, not giving in to you 'n' yr lobbying out of deepest love by writing back to that demon, not one single word.

No. 2 is on **Calventius Marius' speech.** You writing that *my writing back*—you amaze me—*gets your vote*—specially as nobody'll read THAT if I write no reply, whereas mine is getting swotted up by all the boys like a homework assignment.

All my books you're hanging on for, I've made a start but can't manage to knock on head these days: *For Scaurus* and *For Plancius* speeches I've wrapped up after the badgering. *To Caesar* poem I got organized, I've put on hold. *For Qfr* thing you ask for, given the actual wells are gasping right now, if I've got any legroom, I'll write it.

12 I've got up to **letter 3.** *Balbus*—you say *he'll get up to Rome good and early,* + *fine escort, & will be with me non-stop till 15 May,* which is real nice by me, real fun. You pushing me in said bulletin, like so many times before, *into hustling and grafting*—sure I'll do my bit. But when's life gonna begin?

13 **Bulletin No. 4.** Reached me 13 Sept. Mailed from Britain 10 Aug. In it no news at all, bar *Erigone*—once I get it from Oppy, I'll write you my take, no qualms 'case she won't get my vote; and—nearly skipped him—on the guy you wrote *as having written to Caesar about Milo's standing ovation.* Me, I'll easy let Caesar go think that ovation was big as it gets, and that's entirely how it was; & yet & still that ovation handed him looked at one way does seem handed *me.*

14 Again, reached me, extra, ***real ancient bulletin.*** Delivery late in day though. In it, *on* **Earth Shrine/Catulus colonnade:** your memo. Both happening full tilt. Again, fact, at Earth's I've sited the statue of you.

Likewise *on* **a place outside Rome**, your memo: well I never did fancy one tons/now The HQ supplies me with an estate's worth of pleasure.

Rome, upon getting here 18 Sept., found roof complete on yr house. Above living rooms, it didn't get your vote for being multi-gabled: now slopes classy to roof of lower colonnade.

Our **Cicero** while I was away no slacking with Rhetoric tutor. On his education, no cause for you to make heavy weather. 'Cos *you* know his ability 'n' *I* witness his agility. Rest of his stuff I'm onto, so I'll reckon making it a pledge a must for me.

15 **Gabinius.** To date 3 syndicates are after seeing him in court: L. Lentulus, the *Flamen*'s son, he's already charged him under public interest; Tib. Nero + back-up team of worthies; C. Memmius, *Tribune* + L. Capito. He marched up to Rome 19 Sept.: tarnished nadir, no-show. But THESE courts, don't dare trust 'em an inch. As Cato was unwell, to date not yet been charged on a count of extortion.

Pompey's really pushing for return to my good books, but to date not got anywhere, and if I hang on to any %age of freedom, he'll get nowhere. I'm waiting and waiting on a letter from you.

16 Your writing that *you heard I was in on* **the candidates for consul pact**: no truth in it. See, the deals done in the pact were the sort that (Memmius went public on 'em afterwards) no good guy *should* have been in on them, plus, as well, I was bound not to commit to any deal Messalla was locked out from. Yes, I really am performing to HIS heart's content, all round; methinks, to Memmius', again, too. For actual Domitius, I've now done lots he wanted/requested from me. Scaurus I've really got one owing by doing him a favour 'n' defending him in court. To date it's really not clear (i) when elections will come (ii) who'll be consuls.

17 I'm just folding this bulletin, when couriers from you lot got here, on 20th (day 27). Wow I was alarmed.

Me, the pain I felt over **Caesar's** sweet, sweet **letter**—sweeter it is, greater the pain that **calamity** of his brought along... but I get to **yr letter:**

(i) **your staying on** I approve, again and again, specially since (you write) *you've shared it with Caesar.*

18 **Oppius.** I'm amazed at any truck with Publius—did *not* get *my* vote.

Your writing, lower down bulletin, *I shall be made lieutenant to Pompey 13 Sept.*, first I've heard of it, and I've written Caesar to say (i) Vibullius brought no instructions to Pompey about my staying put, (ii) & neither did Oppius. The thinking? Though I did put Opp. on hold, as the lead role was Vib.'s (you see Caesar's dealings with him were in person—he WROTE to Oppy)...

In fact, I can have no *deuxièmes-pensées* in the Caesar dept., for me he comes close second to you and our kid*s*... nearly joint equal. In my eyes I'm doing this judiciously (time I did now, a must)—but still I AM ablaze, passionately ablaze.

19 When I'd written these bottom bits, the ones in my own hand, **your Cicero** got over to us for dinner, as Pomponia's dining out.

He gave me **your bulletin** to read, a short while after he received it, in the Aristophanes mood, real sweet 'n' serious both, by crikey, I was pretty well delighted.

Again, gave me **2nd letter** also where you tell him to staple himself to me for sort of DoS. These bulletins so delighted HIM. Me, too. Nowt sweeter than that lad. Nowt loves me more. (This dictated over dinner to Tiro, so don't puzzle over the change of hand.)

20 **Annalis** much obliged by your letter, *as (i) you're so focused looking after him, (ii) but also helping him with the sincerest advice going.*

P. Servilius Sr., on the basis of *letter sent him* he says *by Caesar,* indicates that *you really did oblige him in having spoken on his good will toward Caesar in* THE *most civilized,* THE *most focused, terms going.*

21 When I got back from the Arpinum place to **Rome** it was told me *Hippodamus'd started out bound for you.* I can't write down *I was amazed at him behaving so uncivilized: starting out for you minus letter from me.* But I AM writing this down, *it was drag for me.* See, I'd been reckoning, long since, that *arising from what you wrote me any item I might want delivered to you with extra special care, I'd give it him,*'cos crikey in these letters I send you run-of-the-mill, I write pretty well nowt, should it fall into anybody else's hands, it'd be a drag to put up with. Minucius, Salvius, Labeo—I'm

saving myself up for them. Labeo'll either start out late or else stay here. Hippodamus—didn't even ask me for any wants.

22 Titus **Pinarius** sends me lovely letter about you, *how extremely delighted he is by yr writing, conversation, and esp.* YOUR DINNERS. This hombre always has been a delight to me, his brother's with me loads. So: the way you've begun—keep the lad in your clutches.

23 Because I had **the bulletin on my hands** day after day on a/c of courier delay, that's why item after item has got bunged in together, each at a different time, e.g. this: **T. Anicius** has by now told me often *he'd not bat an eyelid about buying you a place outside Rome.* In his talk, both things I keep finding amazing, (i) you on buying a place outside Rome, while you write him, you not only don't write me but, again, even write in a different vein, (ii) while you write him you remember nowt of him, his letters you showed me at the Tusculum place, nowt on Epicharmus' commandment,

> *Reconnaissance!*
> *Regarde comment*
> *On traite les gens,*

in short, his entire face-talk-thinking, my best guess, you sorta . . .

24 —But that's yours to see to. **On the place outside Rome** take care I know your wants + meantime see he doesn't mess up at all. What . . . else? Umm.

Again—**Gabinius** on 27 Oct made his entry to the City & 2 p.m. today when he had to attend, under public interest, by order of Gaius Alfius, in massive hate demo of the united citizens of Rome he NEARLY got squashed. Nowt more tarnished, though close second is Piso. So it is I'm thinking of amazement-factor *entr'acte* to hypertext into *Cicero, In Time of Crisis,* Book II, Apollo's bubble at the gods' assembly saying *what kind of homecoming the brace of generalissimos are going to have when 1 from 2 lost, and 2 of 2 sold, his army.*

25 From Britain **Caesar** mailed me a letter on 1 Sept., received 27 Sept., plenty agreeable on the Britain front, writing in it so I don't get fazed at receiving no mail from you *he was minus you when he reached the*

sea. I've written nothing by way of letter back to him, not even by way of congratulations. Because he's in mourning.

I ask you, and ask again and again, brother mio, do see you fare well.

E. BIBLIOGRAPHICAL NOTE

On Ciceronian epistoliterarity:

GUNDERSON, E. (4thcoming, 2007) 'S.V.B.E.V.', CA 26.

On Ciceronian letters and confidentiality:

NICHOLSON, J. (1994–5) 'The delivery and confidentiality of Cicero's letters', *Classical Journal* 90: 33–63.

On M and Q Cicerones:

BANNON, C. (1997) *The Brothers of Romulus. Fraternal Pietas in Roman Law, Literature, and Society*, Princeton: 101–16, 'Cicero and Quintus: A case study'

and their separation/pooling of finances: DIXON, S. (1993) 'The meaning of gift and debt in the Roman elite', *Échos du Monde Classique* 12: 451–64; VERBOVEN, K. (2002) *The Economy of Friends. Economic Aspects of Amicitia and Patronage in the Late Republic*, Brussels: 74, 82, 84, 94, 122, 155–6.

On Q. Cicero:

McDERMOTT W. C. (1971) 'Q. Cicero', *Historia* 20: 702–17

and the consulate: WISEMAN, T. P. (1987) *Roman Studies, Literary and Historical*, Liverpool: 34–41, 'The ambitions of Quintus Cicero'

in Asia: MAMOOJEE, A.-H. (1994) 'Le Proconsulat de Q. Cicéron en Asie', *Échos du Monde Classique* 38: 23–50

and Sardinia: RUNCHINA, G. (1992) 'La Sardegna e i Tullii Cicerones', in (1992) *Sardinia Antiqua: Studi in Onore di Piero Meloni in Occasione del suo Settantesimo Compleanno*, Cagliari: 441–54

as writer: CUGUSI P. (1970) *Un Letterato della Tarda Repubblica: Q. Tullio Cicerone* (= *Annali di Facoltà di Lettere e Filologia dell'Università di Cagliari* 33: 1–29), Cagliari

property management: SHATZMAN, L. (1975) *Senatorial Wealth and Roman Politics*, Brussels: 425–7, no. 212.

On M. Cicero's property management and domestic economy:

BRUNO P. (1960) '*Cicero in re familiari versatus*', *Latinitas* 8: 123–7

FRIER B. W. (1978) 'Cicero's management of his urban properties', *Classical Journal* 74: 1–6

GARLAND A. (1992) 'Cicero's *familia urbana*', *Greece & Rome* 39: 163–72

HAVAS, L. (1992) 'Work organization in Cicero's letters', *Acta Classica Universitatis Scientiarum Debreceniensis* 28: 51–63

KUZISCIN V. I. (1960) 'Cicéron propriétaire de maisons (A propos de la concentration des biens à Rome, à la fin de la République)', *Vestnik Moskovskogo Universiteta. Seriia istoriia* 5: 69–79

RAWSON, E. (1976) 'The Ciceronian aristocracy and its properties', in M. I. Finley (ed.), *Studies in Roman Property*, Cambridge: 85–102

SHATZMAN, L. (1975) *Senatorial Wealth and Roman Politics*, Brussels: 403–25, no. 211.

On Ciceronian prestige invested in the *domus*:

HALES, S. (2000) 'At home with Cicero', *Greece & Rome* 47: 44–55

KRAUSE, C. (2001) '"*In conspectu prope totius urbis*" (Cic. dom. 100): il tempio della Libertà e il quartiere alto del Palatino', *Eutopia*: 1: 169–201

TREGGIARI, S. M. (1999) 'The upper-class house as symbol and focus of emotion in Cicero', *Journal of Roman Archaeology* 12: 33–56.

On M. Cicero's epic for Caesar:

BYRNE, S. N. (1998) 'Flattery and inspiration: Cicero's epic for Caesar', in C. DEROUX (ed.), *Studies in Latin literature and Roman history* 9 (= Collection Latomus 244), Brussels: 129–37.

On M. Cicero *De temporibus suis*:

DUGAN, J. (2005) *Making a New Man. Ciceronian Self-Fashioning in the Rhetorical Works*, Oxford: 67–9

HARRISON, S. J. (1990) 'Cicero's "De Temporibus Suis": the evidence reconsidered', *Hermes* 118: 455–63.

3

Cicero's 'Stomach': Political Indignation and the Use of Repeated Allusive Expressions in Cicero's Correspondence

Stanley E. Hoffer

The Ciceronian letter collection is a rare and precious example of an informal and almost spontaneous writing style among the Roman elite. Especially in some of Cicero's letters to Atticus we can sometimes track the writer's thoughts and manner of expression from day to day, even hour to hour. It is tempting to wonder how much this epistolary style reflects casual spoken Latin among the elite, and to what degree it is still only a formalized literary representation of actual conversation. I shall try to shed light on this question by examining a prominent feature of Cicero's letters, the use of repeated allusive expressions, paying special attention to expressions that refer to resentment and suppressed indignation (often involving the word *stomachus*). These repeated, allusive expressions have received little scholarly attention except insofar as they overlap with other familiar epistolary categories such as quotations, humour, Greek, health or greeting formulae, or echo-repetition. I shall examine such features as their tendency to cluster together, their tendency to be used at rhetorical turning-points and in connection with epistolary content and style, and, most notably, their tendency to have loaded political

I am grateful to the editors, referees, and conference participants for many helpful suggestions. Work on this article was made possible through support by Tel Aviv University.

significance in expressing resentment at the despotism of Julius Caesar and other dynasts; hence my choice of the *stomachus*-expression as the example *par excellence* of such expressions. I hope to show how one can simultaneously analyse Cicero's intimate letters both as rare windows into casual Latin conversation and as masterpieces of literary construction in the epistolary genre.

I shall begin by examining Cicero's epistolary use of the term *stomachus* ('indigestion'), along with some related terms that describe indignation through the metaphor of physical disease and discomfort. It is not surprising that this term is especially frequent in the letters, since it belongs simultaneously to many categories of colloquial and epistolary language: technical or medical language, references to health, jokes, 'low' bodily metaphors, repeated expressions, and even Greek.[1] On the one hand, the word *stomachus* encapsulates the dominant mode of the letters, a sense of indignation at political events combined with impotence and suppression, both external political suppression and the ensuing internal emotional suppression, the frustration that comes from no longer being able to express one's views and shape one's plans freely. The characteristic metaphor for this mood, indigestion, is an ailment of frustrated aggression redirected against the self. Accordingly, the expression appears mostly in negative contexts: Cicero proclaims that he must stop 'retching', or that his *stomachus* either no longer exists or has been hardened over. On the other hand, this metaphor is a representative example of Cicero's use of repeated marked expressions in the letters, and accordingly it shares their characteristically epistolary rhetorical functions. For example, in the epistolary list-style, it tends to be used either as an introductory device or as a concluding or dismissive device. This epistolary rhetorical *structure* of the dismissive device functions collaboratively with the epistolary *mode* of indignation, since the rhetorical need for foreclosing a topic derives from, and expresses, the political and emotional need for suppression.

---

[1] Once the term appears with full code-switching, εὐστομάχως 'with good digestion' (*Att.* 9.5.2). On these epistolary categories, see e.g. Cugusi (1983) 83–98, Iulius Victor, *Ars Rhetorica* 27, 448 Halm. These categories of epistolary style frequently overlap. For example, literary quotations in the letters are frequently proverbial or Greek or both, Greek is frequently technical or humorous, etc.; see e.g. Dunkel (2000) 127, Adams (2003) 323, 335, 340, Albrecht (2003) 52–5, 64–5.

Thus, the use of the 'stomach' metaphor illustrates why such repeated expressions are so prevalent in the letters. The contrast between Cicero's letters and later collections both in the use of such repeated expressions and in the use of bodily images can also serve as a diagnostic for the striking transformation in elite epistolary practice under the empire.[2] In short, examining the 'stomach' metaphor, along with other repeated expression in the letters, allows us to get beyond the simple and compartmentalized listing of elements of epistolary style (e.g. colloquialisms, proverbs, Greek), structure (e.g. greetings, echo, list), and contents (e.g. health, news, requests), and to understand their interrelationship, as well as giving us fresh insight into the special nature of the Ciceronian collection, a remarkable representation of intimate conversations at a time of political crisis.

The physical connection between bile and anger has extremely ancient origins, pre-dating developed humoral theory of Greek medicine and attested in such Homeric words as χόλος, 'anger' (connected with χολή, 'bile') or καταπέπτει, 'digest bile', 'suppress anger'.[3] (Of course, χολή or *bilis* is not only the digestive fluid secreted by the gall bladder, but also digestive juice and reflux, or even the semi-mythical cardinal bodily fluid of humoral theory.)[4] Seneca lists some Latin subcategories of *ira* at the start of his *De Ira*; although he does not define them, we can distinguish the screaming fury of the *clamosus* and the insane rage of the *rabiosus* from the dyspeptic indignant or suppressed anger of the *stomachosus*.[5] Although the word *stomachari* is not common in Cicero's speeches and treatises, the variety of

---

[2] See n. 40 on the absence of repeated allusive expressions from later collections such as Pliny's and Fronto's, and the different use that Augustus makes of them. See also Freisenbruch in this volume on the use of bodily images in the correspondence of Fronto.

[3] *Il.* 1.81, 4.513, 9.565.

[4] The familiar symptom of indigestion from anger or grief makes this one of the most ancient, long-lasting, and widespread elements of the humoral theory. It is more alive in modern languages than most linguistic relics of humoral theory, and is probably connected with the well-nigh universal association between bitterness and grief. English examples are 'I can't stomach it', 'it's galling', 'it turns my stomach', 'it makes me retch', or to 'swallow an insult' or 'vent one's spleen'. On humoral survivals in modern languages, see Geeraerts and Grondelaers (1995).

[5] *Amarum ... acerbumque ... stomachosum rabiosum clamosum difficilem asperum*, 1.4.2.

contexts in which it appears illustrates its comic flavour, which is probably due to the combined colloquial and technical tone, the low bodily image joined to a mock-technical medical reference. Often the indigestion of indignation is connected either with telling aggressive jokes or with being the victim of such a joke. For example, people joked that *ius Uerrinum,* Verrine justice or pork gravy, was bad, and others told worse jokes when they were 'dyspeptic' (*stomachabantur*) from the injustice (*Verr.* 2.1.121). In the *Pro Cluentio* (59), a defence advocate, Caespasius, was 'dyspeptic' when his peroration was ruined; he started to say *respicite C. Fabrici senectutem* 'have regard for the old age of Fabricius', but the defendant had already slinked away. Cicero himself is 'dyspeptic' in the *Pro Plancio* when bad jokes are falsely attributed to him, or when he returns from his glorious quaestorship at Lilybaeum and no one noticed that he had been gone except for the know-it-all who said 'What? Don't you know he's been quaestor at *Syracuse*?' (35, 65); similarly the rich knight C. Canius who was duped into overpaying for a coastal estate when the owner got all the local fisherman to go fishing in front of it (*Off.* 3.60). Thus, although indignation is a basic mode of oratory (*Inv. Rhet.* 1.100–5), the word *stomachari* is too colloquial to be used very often in it. Besides, one arouses indignation not by mentioning it, but by describing injustice; even the word *indignari* is used only once outside the *De Inventione* (at *QRosc.* 5).

In the letters, the term *stomachus* is a central item in a range of metaphors of physical illness for frustrated anger, including indigestion (*bilis, concoquere, deuorare*), scabs and festering (*occallesco, obduresco, ὕπουλος*) and even bursting (*dirumpi*).[6] The thirty-odd instances of the term in the letters can be divided into several categories, by positive or negative formulation (someone either does or does not have indigestion), by first-, second-, or third-person reference, or by topic—political, 'epistolary', or other topics.[7] The

---

[6] I have not found the verb *obduresco* used literally for 'scabbing', but the collocation *obduruerat et percalluerat...patientia* (Cic. *Mil.* 76) suggests that the medical sense was present in the metaphorical use 'to become hardened, insensitive'.

[7] *Att.* *2.6.2, *4.18.2, 4.18.4, 5.1.4, 5.11.2, 6.3.7, *7.18.2, *9.5.2, *9.19.2, 10.5.3, 12.37.2, *14.21.3, (*)15.15.2 s.v.l., *16.1.1, 16.2.3, 16.3.1, 16.16f.1; *Fam.* *1.9.10 Dec. 54, 7.1.2 Sept. 55, 3.11.5 June 50 quoting Appius?, 8.13.2 June 50 by Caelius, (*)2.16.2 May 49, 2.16.7, *9.2.3 Apr. 46, 15.16.3 Jan. 45, 10.26.1 June 43; *QFr.* 3.5.2 Oct.–Nov.

largest sub-group of the instances (marked with an asterisk) are those with the negative, first-person, political uses as described above: Cicero declares that he does not, will not, or cannot react with 'indigestion' to the political situation under the dynasts Caesar (and/or Pompey), and later, Antony. (The only negative instance aside from these instances is at *Att.* 6.3.7, which resembles them.) As we might expect, these passages of (negative) political indigestion occur in the parts of the corpus dominated by the mood of suppressed political indignation, approximately books 2, 4, 7–10, and 13–16 to Atticus and the portions of the other collections from the same periods. This epistolary rhetoric of political indignation is relatively absent both from periods of intense activity—the return from exile (57), the pro-consulship (51–50), and the struggle against Antony (43)—and from periods of depression or paralysis—Cicero's exile (58–57), his wait at Brundisium (47), and his mourning over Tullia (45).[8]

The positive uses, on the other hand, illustrate a different function of the term *stomachus*: a reference to any kind of anger, a sensitive and taboo epistolary topic, can be softened by the jocular tone and admitted into a letter when necessary.[9] Accordingly, they cluster around epistolary topics such as possible ill-feelings that can be aroused by the wrong kind of letter, or social resentments that are to be appeased or prevented through letters. The softening expression is one of the defence mechanisms to protect against a cardinal problem of letter-writing, that the imperfect written communication as opposed to personal conversation can lead to

---

54, 3.6.1 Nov. 54, *3.7.2 Dec. 54; *Brut.* 1.13.2 July 43 by Brutus, 1.17.6 ?June 43 by Brutus?; *Cic. ad Caerelliam apud Quint. *Inst.* 6.3.112 ?45–44. Some examples of related expressions are: *Att.* 2.7.2 *bilem id commouet*, 4.5.1 *deuorandum est*, QFr. 3.7.5 *non sorbeam solum sed etiam concoquam*. Literal meaning: *Fam.* 14.7.1, χολὴν ἄκρατον, *Fam.* 16.4.1 κακοστόμαχος. At *Att.* 16.3.1 Cicero seems to play on the literal meaning: if Atticus has entertained (fed) his guests before reading them *De Gloria,* they will not have 'indigestion' against Cicero.

[8] We can compare the relative absence of such epistolary features as the use of Greek, quotations, and humour from the latter group; see Dunkel (2000) 128, Swain (2002) 157, Adams (2003) 343–4, Albrecht (2003) 119.

[9] This taboo is mentioned in epistolary theory: 'It is never proper to quarrel, least of all for a letter' (Iulius Victor, *Ars Rhetorica* 27, 448 Halm *iurgari numquam oportet, sed epistolae minime*). See e.g. Trapp (2003) 40–1.

misunderstanding and unnecessary bad feelings.[10] Thus Cicero tells
Appius, 'I don't understand what you mean by "my rather dyspeptic letter"' (*stomachosiores meas litteras quas dicas esse non intellego,*
Fam. 3.11.5); the epistolary colloquialism is reinforced by an epistolary modest comparative.[11] The epistolary anger was resolved
when Appius returned to Rome and was able to learn in person
what Cicero had done for him. Several other positive expressions of
stomachus involve epistolary anger. For example, after Cicero had
written to Vettienus 'rather dyspeptically' over the latter's unsatisfactory financial arrangements and curt letter, Cicero wrote to him
again to say that Atticus' conversation with Vettienus in person had
clarified the matter (*Att.* 10.5.3). Cicero softens a follow-up request
for political assistance on behalf of Atticus by saying that he does
not doubt that Capito will be amazed and even dyspeptic at the
repeated request (*Att.* 16.16f.1). He wonders whether Cassius will
be dyspeptic over his mocking epistolary use of Epicurean εἴδολα,
as if the addressee's 'image' is present in the writer's mind while
writing a letter (*Fam.* 15.16.3). And in a negative epistolary use, he
says that Brutus' letters, which always contain something arrogant
and 'unsociable' (ἀκοινονόητον), generally arouse his laughter more
than his indigestion (*Att.* 6.3.7).[12]

   Among the passages referring to political resentment, two fixed
types stand out, a longer, metaphorical expression, the claim that his

---

[10] By contrast, see Hodkinson in this volume on advantages of letters.

[11] Similar softening or distancing formulae (Greek, absolute comparatives, and
diminutive prefixes or suffixes) are used to describe angry epistolary exchange at
Att. 6.1.2 (*Appius... bis terue* ὑπομεμψιμοίρους *litteras miserat,* 'Appius sent me
somewhat critical letters two or three times), 10.5.3 (*rescripsi ei stomachosius,* "I
wrote back to him rather dyspeptically"), 10.11.5 θυμικώτερον *eram iocatus,* "I
joked **rather** angrily"), *Fam.* 3.9.1 (*rescripsi tibi subiratus,* "I wrote back to you
somewhat angrily"), and *QFr.* 1.2.12 (*iracundius scripseram,* "I wrote **rather** angrily"); compare the softening diminutive at Plin. *Ep.* 6.17.1 *indignatiuncula,* "a bit
of indignation". It is hard to know whether the urbane expression *stomachosiores* is
Appius' own, or Cicero's softening (compare the joking mis-quotation at *Fam.*
2.10.2 *quod esset ad laureolam satis* ∼ Caelius 8.5.1 *quantum gloriae triumphoque
opus esset*). On Greek for a softening effect see e.g. Hutchinson (1998) 15, Adams
(2003) 330–5.

[12] *Ille mihi risum magis quam stomachum mouere solet.* The verb renders the
standard medical expression χολὴν κινεῖν, already in Ar. *Vesp.* 403; cf. Plaut. *Bacch.*
537, Cic. *Mur.* 28, *Att.* 2.7.2.

stomachus is missing or hardened, and a short phrase, *sed stomachari desinamus*, 'but let's stop retching'.[13] These two types demonstrate the basic rhetorical and political functions of the term. The short phrase is used for dismissing a topic; after describing a political situation indignantly he cuts off the discussion with self-irony ('but enough of this belly-aching'). The longer form serves to explain how he can endure the political humiliation of capitulating to the dynasts: Cicero no longer has a bodily organ to produce the bile necessary for angry resentment. In normal circumstances this resentment would drive him to fight back, but in his current impotence it would only lead to self-destructive indigestion, so its absence or hardening is a form of self-defence. This is an exaggeration of an ordinary characteristic that any public figure needs. For example, Marcus Pupius Piso 'could not put up with the absurd and stupid behaviour of others *which we orators have to swallow*, and he would *spit it up* rather angrily, whether from peevishness, as people thought, or from a squeamishness suitable to a free-born person' (*hominum ineptias ac stultitias, quae deuorandae nobis sunt, non ferebat iracundiusque respuebat siue morose, ut putabatur, siue ingenuo liberoque fastidio, Brut.* 236).[14] But since the appropriate degree of 'swallowing' one's pride is a matter of judgement, the absence of 'stomach' can be either a trait one willingly confesses in oneself, or an accusation of not having enough moral backbone, as Cicero to Caelius in 49: 'you know the squeamishness not only of my stomach—*you once had a similar one*—but even of my eyes over the outrageous behaviour of arrogant people (*nosti enim non modo stomachi mei, cuius tu similem quondam habebas, sed etiam oculorum in hominum insolentium indignitate fastidium, Fam.* 2.16.2).

The shorter phrase *sed stomachari desinamus* occurs twice in the space of two months (*Att.* 7.18.2, 9.19.2) and nowhere else in Latin literature; it is an example of the sort of recurring, marked epistolary expressions which I shall discuss below. In the first example, Cicero denounces Caesar for actively prosecuting the war, seizing and fortifying positions, while negotiating for peace with Pompey:

[13] The longer form: *Att.* 4.18.2, *Fam.* 1.9.10, *Fam.* 9.2.3; cf. *Fam.* 2.16.2. The short form: *Att.* 7.18.2, 9.19.2; cf. 14.21.3, 16.1.1.
[14] See Kaster (2001) 150 on *fastidium*.

O perditum latronem! ⟨o⟩ uix ullo otio compensandam hanc rei publicae turpitudinem! sed stomachari desinamus, tempori pareamus, cum
Pompeio in Hispaniam eamus. haec optima in malis...sed haec
hactenus. (*Att.* 7.18.2)

What a shameless thug! What a disgrace is this to the Republic, which
scarcely any peace can make up for! But let's stop retching, let's submit to
circumstances, and go to Spain with Pompey. That's the best of a bad
situation...but so much for this.

Cicero's impotence forces him to swallow his anger and his pride, and
acquiesce in the humiliating peace settlement that he expects. The
dismissive function is also clear in the second passage, where it is
used in aposiopesis, cutting off the indignant irony against Servius in
mid-sentence (with Shackleton Bailey's punctuation):

sed erit immitissimus Seruius, qui filium misit ad effligendum Cn. Pompeium aut certe capiendum cum Pontio Titiniano. etsi hic quidem timoris
causa, ille uero—sed stomachari desinamus et aliquando sentiamus nihil
nobis nisi, id quod minime uellem, spiritum reliquum esse...sed haec satis
deplorata sunt. (*Att.* 9.19.2)

But no doubt Servius will be very savage [in opposing Caesar's wishes in the
Senate]—Servius, who sent his son with Titinianus to destroy or at least
capture Pompey! Titinianus, at least, acted out of fear, but Servius—but let's
stop retching, and let's understand at last that nothing of ours is left but our
breath—though I wish it weren't...but I have lamented enough about these
matters.

Although rhetorical self-interruption (aposiopesis) can be used to
amplify the impression of anger (Quint. *Inst.* 9.2.54), Cicero's self-
reflective tone is aimed more at allaying his own feeling of anger.

These passages also illustrate the clustering tendency of dismissive
formulae. The passages end with common epistolary dismissive formulae (*hactenus/satis*), but in order to dismiss a topic that is so loaded
with indignation and humiliation, Cicero uses several preliminary
dismissive formulae to lower the emotional tone, or to process the
indigestible emotional residue, so to speak. In the first example he first
goes through several formulae of dismissal and self-therapy (*sed
stomachari desinamus, tempori pareamus,...haec opt ima in malis*)
before the actual closing formula (*sed haec hactenus*); alongside
the stomach-formula he includes two formulae of proverbial,

philosophical wisdom for dealing with a bad situation.[15] The bitter residue of anger and humiliation is not acceptable for ending a letter, and the clustering of dismissive formulae allows him to reach the generic requirement of a quiet or even-tempered ending, in these instances business requests (7.18) and an epistolary request to write back (9.19).[16] In May 44 Cicero dismisses his indignation (over the ineffectual way in which the 'tyrannicides' carried out their plan) with a similar sequence of dismissive tags. 'I need to read my *De Senectute* more often, old age is making me more bitter—I am dyspeptic over everything. But I have lived my life, let the young men see to things' (*legendus mihi saepius est 'Cato maior' ad te missus. amariorem enim me senectus facit. stomachor omnia. sed mihi quidem βεβίωται; uiderint iuuenes, Att.* 14.21.3). The positive formulation is virtually negative, since he blames his indignation not so much on the outrageous circumstances as on his old age, which makes him both more crotchety and less able to affect things; he needs another dose of philosophy to acquire serenity. The philosophical formula βεβίωται rephrases the suicide wish of 9.19.2 in a more cheerful mode, and the setting brings out the humorous and softening potential of the 'indigestion' motif. Someone who says 'let's stop this belly-aching' has already switched from fury to sullen or witty resignation, so the idea of ceasing to be angry is instantiated by the very word *stomachari*, especially in light-hearted passages such as *Att.* 14.21.3 or 16.1.1, where the literal escape to Greece serves as a safety-valve for his indignation.[17]

The repeated joke that the organ of indigestion no longer exists can be thought of as a variant of this dismissive figure, although in the form of *paraleipsis* (*praeteritio*) rather than aposiopesis or dismissal:

---

[15] In his philosophical writings Cicero advocates the elimination of anger through reason (e.g. *Tusc.* 4.52–5). In particular, the idea of 'obeying circumstances' was considered part of the wisdom of the Seven Sages (*Fin.* 3.73). The idea 'best among evils' also occurs at *Att.* 7.7.7 (*quid sit optimum male contractis rebus*); the similar proverb 'least among evils' appears at Sen. *Tranq.* 7.4, Quint. *Inst.* 7.1.37.

[16] Some letters, to be sure, express such extreme despair that they explicitly flout this generic requirement. For example, the close of *Att.* 9.12 reverses the conventional request to write back, saying that it would be useless, and instead he only wants to die; cf. *Att.* 3.2, 8.8.

[17] At *Att.* 12.2.2 Cicero sarcastically says that Balbus can forget about the political and military horrors and enjoy life with the Epicurean thought βεβίωται, 'I have had a life of adequate pleasure and therefore have a clear "conscience" for the future' (Shackleton Bailey (1965–70) 5.299 ad loc.).

instead of interrupting an outburst of dyspeptic description of injustice, he cuts it off in advance by saying that he no longer gets indignant about such incurable matters. This form of the *stomachus* motif occurs from the years 54 (*Att.* 4.18.2, *Fam.* 1.9.10) to 46 (*Fam.* 9.2.3), and even merited citation by Quintilian, from a lost letter to Caerellia, as an example of urbanity, a sort of grim humour, 'expressions which are of the same category as funny expressions but are nevertheless not funny': '"these circumstances must be borne either with Cato's spirit or with Cicero's stomach"—this "*stomachus*" has something similar to a joke in it' (Quint. *Inst.* 6.3.112 *haec aut animo Catonis ferenda sunt aut Ciceronis stomacho—stomachus enim ille habet aliquid ioco simile*).[18] In its first appearance (*Att.* 4.18.2) it is used in a fixed nexus of topics that recurs in a letter to his brother later in the same year (*QFr.* 3.7.1–2): Gabinius' acquittal, the sorry condition of the Republic, Cicero's equanimity and lack of *stomachus*, and his non-political consolations (literature, villas, friends and family). I shall investigate this use of marked expressions to encapsulate a larger group of ideas below.

We might also ask how this epistolary-political use of a medical expression for dyspeptic anger fits in with two related motifs, first, the frequent use of health as an epistolary topic, especially for opening and closing letters, and second, the conventional metaphor of political trouble as a disease of the body politic. On the surface it would appear that the 'indigestion' image is unrelated to epistolary greetings and health; Cicero usually uses it as a local rhetorical commentary on political matters, not as a report on his general physical and mental state in the opening or closing of a letter. Even the use of the image in the context of 'epistolary anger' discussed above seems remote from discussions of health. The one use of the term *stomachus* in a purely medical sense shows how far the epistolary-medical use is from the metaphorical use: in a letter entirely devoted to Tiro's health Cicero complains that the doctor should not have given Tiro soup when he was 'dyspeptic' (*ius enim dandum tibi non fuit cum* κακοστόμαχος *esses*, *Fam.* 16.4.1). On the other hand, almost the same Greek medical term reappears in a purely political context: 'come, imagine my bearing it with ever so

---

[18] See Corbeill (1996) 209.

good a digestion [to sit in Caesar's Senate and listen to the insolent speeches]' (*age, finge me quamuis εὐστομάχως haec ferentem, Att.* 9.5.2).[19] Epistolary discussions of health do not always distinguish sharply between bodily and mental health; the shared terminology (such as κακο-/εὐστόμαχος) reflects a shared conceptual basis, the humoral theory. An example of the term *stomachus* in a passage parallel to an epistolary health report is in Brutus' letter pleading on behalf of Lepidus' children. 'I neither can nor should write to you at length on account of my anxious and embittered feelings' (*scribere multa ad te neque possum prae sollicitudine ac stomacho neque debeo, Ad Brut.* 1.13.2). Brutus seems to use the term in a slightly different sense than does Cicero, emphasizing more the eating away at oneself than the flare-up of resentment; this sense is better suited to descriptions of epistolary physical and mental health.

If we extend our purview to terms synonymous with *stomachus* we can find parallel examples in Cicero's letters as well. Cicero's reply in May 49 to Caelius' plea on behalf of Caesar opens with a variant of the 'hardened *stomachus*' theme, used as an epistolary opening description of mental health and pain: 'Your letter would have caused me great pain if Reason itself had not already driven away all griefs, and long despair at political affairs had not already hardened over my mind against new pain' (*magno dolore me adfecissent tuae litterae nisi iam et ratio ipsa depulisset omnis molestias et diuturna desperatione rerum obduruisset animus ad dolorem nouum, Fam.* 2.16.1). And an even more striking overlap between epistolary health and political indigestion can be found in the letter to Terentia a month later, during his departure for Greece and for Pompey's camp. 'All the griefs and anxieties with which I made you so miserable... I have laid aside and thrown off. The day after I left you I understood what had been the cause. I threw up pure bile at night. I was immediately so recovered that I think it was some god that healed me' (*omnis molestias et sollicitudines quibus et te miserrimam habui...deposui et eieci. quid causae autem fuerit postridie intellexi quam a uobis discessi. χολὴν ἄκρατον noctu eieci. statim ita sum leuatus ut mihi*

---

[19] Greek adjectives such as these or στομαχικός ('with upset digestion') appear to have influenced the semantic shift of στόμαχος from 'throat, opening of the stomach' to 'stomach' in later Greek and in Latin.

deus aliquis medicinam fecisse uideatur, Fam. 14.7.1).[20] Cicero explicitly intermingles the physical and mental illnesses, lest the reader should imagine a purely physical cause of the seasickness.[21] The overlap is underlined by the verbal parallel between 'throwing off' anxieties and 'throwing up' digestive fluid (*eieci*). The impotent and dyspeptic anger has come to an end with his escape out from under Caesar's control and his decisive action (though no doubt it returned when he saw the situation in Pompey's camp, e.g. Plut. *Cic.* 38.2 δυσχεραίνων ὑπούλως, 'with festering annoyance'). The emotional significance of vomiting forth months of repressed indignation is so striking that we might almost wonder if Cicero is speaking symbolically and did not actually vomit; but the term *statim* ('immediately') and the ensuing request for Terentia to offer satisfaction to the god supports the literal meaning.[22] On the contrary, this moment of purgation shows that the numerous political uses of 'indigestion' should be understood as more than mere metaphor. Cicero finally understood the reason for his bad mental state, with which he had plagued his family: he had been literally dyspeptic through resentment and repression.

The medical metaphor for the political 'health' of the body politic is widespread.[23] Furthermore, ever since 63 it had been a staple of Ciceronian praise that the fortunes of the Republic were intimately connected with the fortunes of Cicero.[24] We might therefore wonder whether Cicero ever explicitly connects his own oppression-induced ailment with that of the State. To be sure, he repeatedly connects his non-existent *stomachus* with the ruin of the Republic, as in the letters of 54 discussed above. But in addition,

[20] The distancing function of the Greek here, the only Greek to Terentia, has been widely noted; compare Adams (2003) 416 on the humoral theory.

[21] Contrast nausea, *Att.* 5.13.1, 5.21.3, *Fam.* 16.11.1.

[22] The intimate connection between physical and mental health recurs in the letters, e.g. *Att.* 11.4a, 11.5.3.

[23] e.g. *Att.* 2.9.1 *remedia rei publicae* ('remedies for the Republic'), 2.20.3 *morbo... moritur... cum omnes... doleant... medicina nulla* ('it is dying by a disease... although it... pains everyone... there is no remedy'), 2.21.1 *uenenis* ('poisons'), *Cat.* 1.31 *in uenis atque in uisceribus rei publicae* ('in the veins and internal organs of the Republic'). I am obliged to David Langslow for suggesting this comparison.

[24] e.g. *Cat.* 1.11, *Fam.* 1.9.12–13, 12.13.1.

he twice mentions his *stomachus* alongside a specific reference to the *diseased* State. At *Att.* 9.5.2, after imagining himself enduring insolence in the Senate without indigestion (εὐστομάχως), he calls the cause of the Republic lost not only on account of its wounds but especially on account of the medicines that are in preparation (*cum uulneribus... tum medicamentis*). Perhaps the impossible idea of his own forced show of a healthy digestion of outrageous sights finds resonance with the impossible idea of the Senate under Caesar's domination bringing the State to health. More revealing is the connection between his health and the State's at *Att.* 4.18.2: 'We have lost not only all the vital fluid and blood of the State, but even its former complexion and appearance... that place in our mental anatomy where the stomach was once situated has long since calloused over' (*amisimus... omnem non modo sucum ac sanguinem sed etiam colorem et speciem pristinam ciuitatis... locus ille animi nostri stomachus ubi habitabat olim concalluit*). The 'drying up' of the State has necessitated a corresponding hardening in Cicero's political sensitivities.[25]

REPEATED MARKED EXPRESSIONS IN THE INTIMATE LETTERS

I should now like to consider the kind of repeated shorthand or coded expressions of which the *stomachus* expression is one example among many, either single words such as νέκυια for Caesar's 'conjuring up' followers out of the 'underworld', or allusive quotations such as αἰδέομαι Τρῶας ('I am in fearful awe of the Trojans') for Cicero's sensitivity to optimate opinion, or other coded expressions such as *Dic, M. Tulli* ('Speak, Cicero') for being put on the spot in the Senate to declare his position.[26] As we saw in the case of the *stomachus*-motif, so too repeated expressions in general have a special connection with letters, especially intimate letters, in many ways: in style, in structure,

---

[25] Compare the physical-mental medical term *doleant* above, n. 23 (2.20.3).

[26] Respectively at *Att.* 9.10.7, 9.11.2, 9.18.2; at 2.5.1, 7.1.4, 7.12.3, 8.16.2, 13.13.2, 13.24.1; and at 7.1.4, 7.3.5, 7.7.7, 9.5.2.

and in content. First, many of the linguistic types associated with these expressions belong to informal or intimate style, whereas their use in formal prose is more restricted; these types include the use of Greek, literary quotations, proverbs, colloquial features such as diminutives, and secret or coded language. Second, they often have a cardinal role in epistolary structure, appearing at the start or end of letters or topics, recalling a prior letter in echo style, or dismissing a topic which has transgressed the acceptable epistolary limits of length or emotion. Third, they are associated with epistolary topics, such as descriptions of separation, travel and meeting, or references to prior letters. Their association with both epistolary structure and content is also demonstrated by two other features, their mutuality (the reuse of the same expression by both correspondents) and their gregariousness (the use of several expressions in a cluster). In short, the remarkable interconnection which we found among the *stomachus* motif, the epistolary categories of style, structure, and content, and the conditions of political and emotional expression dominating the collection, is merely one example of a similar connection which is more or less detectable for repeated marked expressions in general.

This category of expression is striking and obvious, but hard to define, since it represents a spectrum of possibilities rather than a precise category. The clearest examples, such as those given above, satisfy three criteria: they are repeated, marked, and allusive. First, they are used repeatedly by one or both correspondents. Second, they have some marked use of language, such as the use of literary or other quotations, Greek, striking metaphors, or a divergent linguistic register such as colloquial or technical language, often with what appears to be a jocular tone; sometimes several of these linguistic markers are present at the same time. And third, they are allusive or riddling, sometimes even secretive, hinting at their meaning by metonymic reference. Many intermediate examples lie somewhere on a continuum, or rather on three continua, with one or more of these three criteria partially or wholly absent: some repeated marked expressions lack coded allusiveness, and some marked allusive expressions appear only once (although they may have been repeated in lost letters, or in conversation). The choice of an appropriate name for these expressions is also not obvious. We might call them a form of private slang, emphasizing the private and marked (especially colloquial) aspects. I shall also call them epistolary 'leitmotifs' after the Wagnerian opera term, emphasizing their repeated and allusive nature, although to be sure these are casual and often improvisatory usages rather than explicit techniques in 'high' art, and they are verbal rather than musical symbols; nevertheless, I consider these differences less important than the similarities.

As marked expressions, epistolary leitmotifs are almost by definition connected with the familiar categories of epistolary style mentioned above (literary quotations or allusions, proverbs, Greek, colloquial language, humour, etc.); they are instances of these categories which occur repeatedly, often with a consistent allusive or epistolary function. One obvious category of repeated or allusive use is the nickname or epithet, often colloquial or Greek, and generally for invective; for example Βοῶπις for Clodia 'the sister and wife' of Clodius (*Att.* 2.9.1 etc.), Pulchellus for Clodius (1.16.10 etc.), or Sampsiceramus (2.14.1 etc.) for Pompey the 'eastern grandee'. This category is not exclusively epistolary, but is also found in political invective in oratory (e.g. *Phil.* 13.26 *Philadelphus Annius*), epigram (e.g. Catull. 94 *Mentula*), and other genres.[27] This type of kenning is also used for groups, such as Atticus' term νέκυια for Caesar's followers, *barbatuli* for former Catilinarian sympathizers (*Att.* 1.14.5, 1.16.11), *piscinarii* for selfish optimates (1.19.6 etc., apparently also used by Atticus, 2.9.1), *barones* for Epicureans (5.11.6), or *Pelopides* in the recurring quotation expressing indignation against Caesar and the Caesarians (14.12.2 etc.). The recurring Iliadic line αἰδέομαι Τρῶας (*Il.* 22.105), on the other hand, is sometimes used as an honorific kenning; the neighbouring line 22.100 on Poulydamas is glossed once as Cato (*Att.* 2.5.1) and once as Atticus (7.1.4). The function of this category as an outlet for political resentment is clear, and we sometimes find further, specifically epistolary functions, such as introducing a topic or letter (e.g. 2.14.1) or secrecy (e.g. *Att.* 6.9.2 τοῦ φυρατοῦ, and perhaps some of the epithets for Pompey and Clodius in book 2). A parallel type of allusive expression, however, the metonymic use

---

[27] It even gave rise to cognomina; see Corbeill (1996) 57–98.

of a date ('the Ides of March', used to mean 'the killing of Caesar'),
is not found in Cicero's oratory.[28]

Other specifically epistolary features of style include literary quotations and proverbs (which are themselves often cited as poetic
quotations, although of course many were pre-existing proverbs that
were used by poets).[29] Some examples are 'fully repaired' *sartum et
tectum* (*Fam.* 13.50, Plaut. *Trinumm.* 317), 'I have lost oil and effort' *et
oleum et operam perdidi* (*Att.* 2.17.1, 13.38.1, *Fam.* 7.1.3, Plaut. *Poen.*
332), 'what's done is done' *actum ne agas* (*Att.* 9.18.3, Ter. *Phorm.* 418;
cf. *Att.* 9.6.7 *sed acta ne agamus*, *Att.* 15.20.3 *sed acta missa*), 'on his own
head!' *suo capiti* (*Att.* 8.5.1, *Phil.* 11.12, Ter. *Phorm.* 491; cf. *Fam.* 8.1.4
Caelius), 'let each do [the craft he knows]' ἔρδοι τις *Att.* 5.10.3, Ar. *Vesp.*
1431), or 'when two go together [one sees first]' σύν τε δύ᾽ ἐρχομένω
(*Att.* 9.6.6, *Fam.* 9.7.1, *Il.* 10.224). Here the allusive aspect tends to be
weak; the meaning is given either explicitly or through a frozen metaphor. Sometimes, however, quotations are used allusively, even serving
as code-words to keep politically dangerous thoughts or plans secret.
Thus, Cicero's projected voyage to Pompey is designated by the 'twit-
tering' of the swallow that signals 'seasonable weather' (Leonidas *Anth.
Pal.* 10.1 ὁ πλόος ὡραῖος *Att.* 9.7.5, originally by Atticus; λαλαγεῦσαν
Att. 9.18.3, *Att.* 10.2.1).

Among colloquial or conversational types, along with the diminutive epithet *barbatuli*, we can add the diminutive *raudusculum* ('scrap
[of money]'), perhaps a joke invented by Atticus and then passed back
and forth.[30] The urbane scorn of money seems characteristic of
Atticus, but we might venture to call it an 'epistolary' attitude, to
the degree that mental and philosophical balance is a central social
ideal that the letters maintain and reinforce.[31] Its structural use is

[28] It is used as a dismissive-consolatory formula for closing off political anger and
disgust (e.g. *Att.* 14.4.2, 14.13.3, 14.14.3), apparently also by Atticus (14.14.3), but is
not used allusively in the *Philippics*. Perhaps the impression of jaded neutrality that
we have of Atticus is partly due to the overrepresentation of such dismissive formulae
in Cicero's quotations.

[29] The epistolary theorists mention proverbs (Demetrius, *De Elocutione* 232) and
quotations (Iulius Victor, *Ars Rhetorica* 27, 448 Halm).

[30] *Att.* 4.8.1 *de raudusculo quod scribis*; 6.8.5, 7.2.7, 14.14.5.

[31] Among the few known leitmotifs in Augustus' letters is an imperial transformation of this urbane scorn of money, this time presumably connected with the
imperial finances: 'they will pay on the Greek Kalends' (Suet. *Aug.* 87.1).

characteristically epistolary, varying between echo-opening (4.8.1), announcement of a new topic in a list structure (6.8.5, 7.2.7), and closing a topic with a dismissive gesture (14.14.5). The associated Greek joke, *tyrotarichus* ('cheese and salt-fish', a meagre dish), is used in epistolary ring structure to open and close the topic of dinner at Paetus'.[32] Colloquial slang references to the body include such epistolary topics as a plea to write back 'whatever comes into your chops' (e.g. *Att.* 1.12.4 *quod in buccam uenerit*), and an invitation to 'sniff out' coded language (6.4.3) or someone's intentions through conversation (*Att.* 4.8a.4, 12.22.3). Greek is of course a widely studied conversational element; among its numerous uses is the structural function of introducing new topics (see below) or closing them with dismissive tags (e.g. *Att.* 2.1.8, 15.3.2 ἅλις, both echoing Atticus).[33] And finally, in view of the conversational nature of letters it should not be surprising that the vast majority of literary quotations, including the Homeric quotations, are originally from dialogue and not narrative passages; we would have to compare quotations in other genres to see how much of this is because of the epistolary genre and how much simply because most famous Homeric passages are in dialogue.

The use of leitmotifs with epistolary structure is perhaps more significant than their use with epistolary style or content, since for the latter two it is hard to avoid circular reasoning: I am selecting them on the basis of marked (and therefore epistolary) style, and almost all the content of the intimate letters is epistolary—topics such as greetings and health, news and favours, letters and travel, affection and consultation—so it is no surprise that most marked expressions are associated with epistolary content. One clear structural location that attracts the use of repeated marked expressions is the introduction of new topics. When this is in reply to a topic of the prior letter, it has been called the 'echo' style, since the 'echo' headline is often a brief phrase or word from the prior letter, and it is sometimes marked in some way—humorous, allusive, secretive, etc. We have already seen the scornful diminutive joke for introducing a financial topic, *de raudusculo* (*Att.* 6.8.5, 7.2.7). This position can have a proverb (8.15.2 *Ioui ipsi iniquum*),

[32] *Fam.* 9.16.7, 9; also *Att.* 4.8.1, 14.16.1.
[33] Shackleton-Bailey interprets ἅλις σπουδῆς as Atticus' conversational tag (1965–70: 1.57); I should think that his letters are a likelier source (but see below).

a metaphoric allusion (7.3.8 *de serpirastris* '[moral] splints'), a coded secret (10.15.2 *Caelianum illud*, 5.21.14 *de* ἐνδομύχῳ), a learned allusion (5.20.6 *Ligurino Μώμῳ*), or some other Greek expression (6.1.20 τί λοιπόν; *QFr.* 2.5.1 ἀμφιλαφίαν).[34]

Aside from the echo function, leitmotifs often begin or end a letter or section.[35] Letters that begin with such marked phrases, especially quotations, tend to have a light-hearted or effusive mood.[36] Sometimes one senses an artificial light-heartedness covering over resentments or anxieties.[37] By contrast, at *Att.* 13.11.1 Cicero's grim mood upon returning to the scene of Tullia's death is expressed, or mitigated, by the distancing of literary quotation (οὐ ταὐτὸν εἶδος 'a different view' = Eur. *Ion* 585). The ending of a letter or section is a typical place for simple epistolary closing or dismissive formulae (e.g. *sed haec hactenus* 'but enough of this', *sed haec coram* 'but about this in person', *sed tu uidebis* 'but you will see to this', *sed de ioco satis est* 'but enough joking'), but more marked or allusive expressions also cluster here. For example, the Homeric tag 'gold for bronze' summarizes Cicero's reply to a letter (*Att.* 6.1.22), whereas the tag 'one omen is best, to fight for one's country' is used to conclude a political discussion with a proclamation of bravery, and is immediately followed by an epistolary dismissive formula, 'let's save this for our holiday strolls' (*Att.* 2.3.4). As we have seen, the stomach motif is used gregariously with other repeated leitmotifs for winding down from a peak of indignation at the close of a letter or section (*Att.* 7.18.2, 9.19.2). Other such expressions are proverbs such as *acta ne agamus* (9.6.7), or philosophical declarations that the end of life is near.[38]

The related function of the start and end of a section is sometimes demonstrated by the use of similar or identical leitmotifs in both

[34] It is therefore not accurate to say that Greek is not used to change topics, Dunkel (2000) 127.

[35] Wenskus (2001) 220 comments that markers of group membership and personal relationship, including Greek, cluster at the end of letters.

[36] e.g. *Att.* 12.5, 12.6a, 13.42, *Fam.* 7.16, 7.15.

[37] e.g. *Fam.* 15.6.1 to Cato, 'I am happy to be praised by a praised man', *laetus sum laudari me . . . a laudato uiro* = Naevius trag. fr. 15; *Fam.* 12.4.1 'I wish you had invited me to dinner on March 15', *uellem Idibus Martiis me ad cenam inuitasses* ∼ *Fam.* 10.28.1.

[38] *Att.* 14.21.3 *sed mihi quidem* βεβίωται; *uiderint iuuenes*; *Ad Brut.* 1.2a = Plaut. *Trinumm.* 219 *sed de hoc tu uideris . . . 'mihi quidem aetas acta ferme est . . .'*.

positions. Some expressions are first used as introductory motifs and later appear as closing formulae. The formula of 'Parthian stroke of luck' first appears as the apotropaic opening of Cicero's first extensive civil-war consultation (*Att.* 7.1.2), and is used thereafter to prevent closing on an impossibly grim note.[39] We might compare the verse 'unsettled for favourable times, good for bad times', which is used to summarize the long first letter after exile (4.1.8), and then reused in echo fashion to open the second letter the next month, explicitly quoting the first letter (4.2.2). Frequently a major section such as a political discussion has both beginning and ending leitmotif-formulae, as if to signal or excuse a change of register and then to return to the ordinary lighter epistolary tone. For example, at *Att.* 14.13.1–3, after some opening travel pleasantries (in echo style) Cicero shifts to the ominous political situation with one marked expression (a quotation of a similar transitional device from the *Iliad*, 9.228–30) and then winds down from the political topic with a series of marked dismissive expressions, first an Iliadic dismissal passage (5.428–9), then the 'let him/them see to it' formula (*sed haec fors uiderit*), then philosophical proverbs and commonplaces on bravely enduring human fortune as mere humans, and finally the allusive consolatory reference to the Ides of March. A discussion of a political favour at *QFr.* 2.8.1–2 opens with an admonitory allusion to Jupiter's speech in Cicero's *De Temporibus* advising against politics (echoing Quintus), and closes with a consolatory-dismissive allusion to the same passage.

We have already seen some of the many topics of epistolary content associated with leitmotifs: epistolary pleasure or anger over letters or conversations (e.g. *Att.* 6.3.7, *Fam.* 15.6.1), invitations (*Fam.* 9.16.7, 9), travel and travel plans (*Fam.* 9.18.3), and of course political resentment (which both epitomizes and transgresses the generic mode). Instead of providing more examples, which could be multiplied at will, I should like to point out some similarities and differences between epistolary and conversational topics. I would suggest that the reason for the surprising prevalence of these repeated, marked expressions in Cicero's letters, and almost nowhere else in classical Latin prose, is that through these letters we get closer to ordinary conversation, or rather to elite conversation at a time of

---

[39] *Att.* 7.2.8, 7.26.3 echoing Atticus; cf. 8.11.7.

crisis, than through any other texts: people wrote this way because
they spoke this way, and this feature is not much found in other texts
because of a conventional taboo against repetition, comparable to the
conventional taboo against Greek, colloquialisms, or quotations.[40]
Letters are of course not real conversation but a literary artefact
representing conversation, but of course real conversation is itself a
literary artefact embracing many of the features of style and structure
found in the intimate letters. The ancients not only advised that
letters should resemble conversation, but even used letters as evidence for conversational style (e.g. Suet. *Aug.* 87), and in several of
the examples cited above Cicero seems to say that these are conversational expressions (*Att.* 9.18.2 *ut tu soles dicere*; cf. 6.3.7, *QFr.* 2.5.1).

It is therefore interesting that although many of the epistolary
topics and structures for which leitmotifs are especially used are
conversational as well as epistolary, some are not. Cicero and Atticus
surely talked about health, social favours and disagreements, and
political resentments, and no doubt they used many of the well-
known features of epistolary style, even literary quotations as a
coded shorthand (*Att.* 6.3.7). But surely quotations would be limited
to a few words; the longer quotations are an epistolary artefact. Also,
traces of the epistolary structures of echoes, list-headings, and dismissive irony might have been used in conversation, but probably
not the more formal epistolary ring composition. Similarly, formulae
of secrecy, of longing and absence (e.g. *Att.* 9.6.6), and perhaps even
of uncertainty (e.g. *Att.* 6.6.3, 6.9.3 ἐπέχειν) would be less applicable.
In short, this is not simply a conversational style, but a conversational
style adapted to intimate epistolary use.

---

[40] Except for Augustus' letters (Suet. *Aug.* 87), the repeated leitmotivic style is rare
in the surviving classical Latin letters, being absent not only from Pliny's official
letters and his edited private letters (except for 'Diana and Minerva', *Ep.* 9.10.1 ∼
1.6.3) but even from the Frontonian collection, perhaps being unsuited to the
dynamics of imperial power. By contrast, in Augustus' letters, the Ciceronian tone
of ironic or detached resentment has turned into the characteristically Augustan
modesty of imperial power.

4

Didacticism and Epistolarity in Horace's *Epistles* 1

A. D. Morrison

LETTERS AND TEACHING

Horace is the first poet to compose or construct a book of verse-letters, a dedicated poetry-book in epistolary form, *Epistles* book 1 (in 20/19 BC). This in itself makes him and his first book of *Epistles* a fitting subject for a paper in a volume on ancient letters.[1] *Epistles* 1 also plays an important role in the development of ancient philosophical epistolography. It adapts, in part, the letters of Epicurus, and itself forms a model (along with those same letters of Epicurus) for Seneca's letters to Lucilius,[2] but it also engages with Lucretius' philosophical didactic poem, the *De Rerum Natura*, as well as the figure and methods of the archetypal ancient philosopher, Socrates.

In *Epistles* 1 Horace explicitly employs what can be usefully described as the 'didactic mode':[3] the collection of letters contains very many imperatives, and other 'imperatival expressions',[4] directing, instructing,

---

[1] I concentrate on the first book of *Epistles*—I make no reference to *Epistles* 'book 2', the so-called literary epistles and the *Ars Poetica*. When I talk about 'the *Epistles*' I mean *Epistles* 1. Translations are my own unless otherwise indicated.

[2] See Inwood in this volume.

[3] See Volk (2002) 42–3.

[4] Imperatival expressions are 'expressions which communicate an instruction, implicitly or explicitly' (Gibson (1997) 67). E.g., in addition to ordinary imperatives, we find in Latin imperatives in -*to*, jussive subjunctives, etc.

and exhorting its internal addressees in various ways. In various parts of the different epistles, then, 'Horace', the narrator (as I'm going to call him), seems to be teaching or advising his addressees. This invites comparison with the genre of didactic poetry, and more particularly the *De Rerum Natura* of Lucretius.[5] We are also pointed to poems like the *De Rerum Natura* by the clear philosophical material in *Epistles* 1,[6] which can even be said to play a part in the architecture or structure of the book.[7] The aim of this paper, then, is simple—to investigate how the 'epistolarity', the 'letteriness' of the *Epistles* relates to and complements the didactic, instructive element of the book and vice versa. Appropriately enough for a paper where Epicureanism will feature heavily, I use 'epistolarity' in a non-technical sense—anything which reminds us that the *Epistles* are indeed letters.[8]

EPISTOLARY MARKERS

The epistolary markers in *Epistles* 1 are well understood,[9] but it would be useful to summarize them here. The first epistolary signal we get from *Epistles* 1 is, of course, the title.[10] But was this the ancient or original title? There is nothing as convenient as the internal reference in the *Ars Amatoria* (*si quis ... artem ... non novit amandi*, 'if anyone doesn't know the art of love', 1.1),[11] and there have been sceptics,[12] but there seems little good reason to doubt it—it's alluded to in Statius' *Silvae* (1.3.102–4) and already the title for Porphyrio,

---

[5] A common metre too points us to didactic poetry, although the hexameter *Epistles* obviously develop Horace's own hexameter satire (see Mayer (1994) 13–15 for a comparison of Horace's metrical practice in the *Satires* and *Epistles*). Nevertheless, hexameter poetry with a prominent didactic element reminds us of Didactic.

[6] See e.g. McGann (1969), Moles (1985), Harrison (1995).

[7] See Moles (2002).

[8] For a more theoretical discussion of 'epistolarity' in *Epistles* 1 and the models of the collection see de Pretis (2002) 4–32, and also more generally Trapp (2003) 1–46.

[9] See in particular Trapp (2003) 23–4 and de Pretis (2002) 21–3, whose summaries I depend on here.

[10] See Trapp (2003) 23.

[11] See Hollis (1977) 31.   [12] e.g. Horsfall (1979).

Horace's third-century commentator (*nam hos priores duos libros Sermonum, posteriores Epistularum inscripsit,* 'He titled the first two books *Conversations* and the latter two *Letters*', ad *Sat.* 1.1.1).[13]

There are also some clear epistolary openings, for example in imitation of standard Greek and Latin letter-beginnings:[14]

Celso gaudere et bene rem gerere Albinouano

[Say] to Celsus Albinovanus to be happy and to prosper   (*Epist.* 1.8.1)

Urbis amatorem Fuscum saluere iubemus
ruris amatores

To Fuscus the lover of the city we bid well-being
as lovers of the country   (*Epist.* 1.10.1–2)

Some ends echo standard epistolary closing formulas: *uiue, uale,* 'good-bye and farewell' (*Epist.* 1.6.67), *uade, uale,* 'go, farewell' (*Epist.* 1.13.19), while we find an epistolary imperfect in *Epist.* 1.10—*haec tibi dictabam,* 'I was writing this' (*Epist.* 1.10.49),[15] and examples of common epistolary types, such as letters of recommendation (of a sort) in *Epistles* 1.9 and 1.12.[16] There are of course other signs—notably the separation of narrator and addressee (e.g. in *Epist.* 1.2: *dum tu declamas Romae, Praeneste relegi,* 'while you're practising speeches in Rome, at Praeneste I've reread...', v. 2), which gets the whole epistolary situation going, and the length of the epistles.[17] Thirteen of the twenty epistles are less than sixty lines long, and nine of these are less than forty lines in length. Eight of these thirteen shorter epistles are clustered together in *Epistles* 1.8–15, in the 'heart' of the collection. It's worth recalling in this connection Demetrius' instruction, τὸ δὲ μέγεθος συνεστάλθω τῆς ἐπιστολῆς, 'the length of a letter should be restricted' (*Eloc.* 228),[18] and the brevity of many 'real' ancient letters, for instance, those preserved on papyrus.[19] Long letters risk, as Demetrius

[13] See Rudd (1979) 147, de Pretis (2002) 20–1.
[14] On standard epistolary openings, closings, and other formal characteristics see Trapp (2003) 34–8.
[15] De Pretis (2002) 22 notes that this epistolary signal comes half-way through the book, reasserting its epistolary character. Note also the requests to 'write back' at *Epist.* 1.3.30 and 1.5.30, and the similar invitation to write at 1.15.25.
[16] On letters of recommendation in Latin see Rees in this volume.
[17] For (restricted) length as an epistolary characteristic see Trapp (2003) 1, 23.
[18] All translations from Demetrius are taken or adapted from Trapp (2003).
[19] See Hutchinson in this volume.

comments, not seeming true letters, but treatises with χαίρειν ('greetings') attached (*Eloc.* 228).

But it is true to say that some of the epistles in *Epistles* 1 are low
on or simply lacking these markers—as a whole the collection gives
what Trapp calls 'discontinuous patches of epistolary colouring'—
occasional allusion to epistolary markers, not consistent use.[20] But,
as we will see, there are more important ways in which the *Epistles*
exploit the letter-form.

THE 'DIDACTIC' MODE

An admittedly crude, but also effective, way of measuring the degree
to which *Epistles* 1 tells its addressees to do things, the degree to which
it instructs, exhorts, and advises is to look at the use of imperatival
expressions in the collection. Space precludes a full list of all the
imperatival expressions in *Epistles* 1, so I list below the examples in
the first two poems of *Epistles* 1 of a representative selection of
imperatival expressions:[21] ordinary imperatives, so-called 'future'
imperatives in *-to*, jussive subjunctives, and constructions with
debeo ('I should'), whether spoken directly by 'Horace' or a character
he quotes (such quotations are indicated by quotation marks):

1.1: solue senescentem mature sanus equum (be reasonable and free the
ageing horse in time, 8), hic murus aeneus esto, | nil conscire sibi, nulla
pallescere culpa (make this your bronze wall: don't have anything on your
conscience, and have no blame to make you go pale, 60–1), dic sodes (tell
me, if you please, 62), uerum | esto aliis alios rebus studiisque teneri (but
grant that different people are captivated by different things, 80–1), ride
(laugh, 91).

1.2: audi (listen, 5), sapere aude: | incipe (dare to be wise, begin, 40–1),
sperne uoluptates (reject pleasure, 55), certum uoto pete finem (seek a fixed
limit to your desire, 56), animum rege (restrain your temper, 62), hunc

[20] Trapp (2003) 23.
[21] For a full list of the types of imperatival expression in Latin didactic literature,
see Gibson (1997) 70–3. My list is not meant as exhaustive, only as an indication of
the amount of direction and exhortation in *Epistles* 1. I attempt no statistical analysis
on the basis of my list.

frenis, hunc tu compesce catena (check it with a bridle, check it with chains, 63), nunc adbibe puro | pectore uerba puer, nunc te melioribus offer (now drink my words into a pure heart while you're young, and give yourself to your betters, 67–8).

This list is not unrepresentative of the book as a whole.[22] Even such a list as this, however, omits much of the considerable engagement with the addressee through the regular use of the second person,[23] questions and so forth,[24] and makes no allowance for ironic or conditional direction or suggestion, but it does make the point that there is a lot of telling the addressees to do things in *Epistles* 1. But this shouldn't surprise us—these are letters, and letters are an obvious way of disseminating advice between friends, and even philosophical knowledge, as in the *Letters* of Epicurus, for example, to Herodotus (physics) or Menoeceus (ethics).[25]

More importantly still, as Rolando Ferri has explored, *Epistles* 1 is in many ways a response to one particular didactic poem, the *De Rerum Natura*, and we should see the didactic manner and matter in *Epistles* 1 in this light.[26] Recalling the genre of didactic poetry and its basic teacher-student set-up inevitably recalls the *De Rerum Natura*, which quickly became a text fundamental, in different ways, to all Latin didactic poems (most obviously the *Georgics*), and the language and manner they use.[27] That the subject-matter of the *De Rerum Natura* is philosophical and Epicurean means that any reader of the hexameter *Epistles*, which boast of a narrator who is *Epicuri de grege porcum* ('a pig from the herd of Epicurus', 1.4.16), and an author

[22] Even in the short *Epist.* 1.3–5 we find the following examples: 1.3: *hoc opus, hoc studium parui properemus et ampli* (let's get going on this task, this pursuit, whether small or great, 28), *debes hoc etiam rescribere* (you should also write this back, 30); 1.4: *omnem crede diem tibi diluxisse supremum* (believe every day has dawned on you as your last, 13); 1.5: *arcesse uel imperium fer* (fetch it or submit to my authority, 6), *mitte leuis spes* (drop your trifling hopes, 8), *tu quotus esse uelis rescribe* (write back how many you'd like, 30), *atria seruantem postico falle clientem* (trick the client waiting in the hall by the back door, 31).

[23] e.g. *Epist.* 1.1.42–8, 95–105, 1.2.32–40.

[24] e.g. *Epist.* 1.1.48: *discere et audire et meliori credere non uis?* ('don't you want to learn and listen and trust in a better?'), 1.2.37–9, 1.3.1–21, 1.4.1–5.

[25] See in this volume Inwood on Epicurean letters, and also Langslow on the communication of medical knowledge by letter.

[26] See Ferri (1993).

[27] See on the influence of Lucretius on the *Georgics* Farrell (1991) and Gale (2000).

with strong Epicurean associations is led to Lucretius.[28] Armstrong
has recently re-emphasized the close connections of Horace to Epicureanism, particularly as it is formulated and adapted in the works
of Philodemus.[29] He cites, for example, the affinities between *Epist.*
1.2 and Philodemus' *On the Good King According to Homer*,[30] the
clear preference for the Epicurean secret life in *Epist.* 1.17 and 1.18,
which oppose the *secretum iter et fallentis semita uitae* ('secret way
and the path of an unnoticed life', 1.18.103) to *honos an dulce
lucellum* ('public office or a nice little earner', 1.18.102),[31] and the
relevance of Philodemus' *On Frank Speaking* for a full understanding
of the tone of the advice 'Horace' gives in *Epist.* 1.7, 1.17, and 1.18.[32]
It may well be, as Armstrong suggests,[33] that Philodemus' modifications of Epicurus' teaching and an eclecticism which permitted
adapting elements of the teaching of rival philosophical schools,[34]
may have attracted Horace in contrast to Lucretius' Epicurean 'fun-
damentalism', which as David Sedley has proposed, very much
looked to Epicurus himself, rather than the modifications of later
Epicureans.[35] In any case Horace's choice of form and style in the
Epistles prompts contrast and comparison with Lucretius' very different approach. This does not mean, I should emphasize, that I think
we should see Horace simply as an Epicurean—we need to take
seriously his warning that he is *nullius addictus iurare in uerba
magistri* ('bound to swear to the words of no master', 1.1.14), and
the importance of the ideas of philosophical schools other than
Epicurus' to the structure and argument of the *Epistles.*[36] The
importance of Panaetian *decorum* is clear from the announcement
in *Epist.* 1.1.11 of a concentration on what is *decens* ('appropriate'),

[28] On Horace's Epicurean connections see Armstrong (1993) 195–9.
[29] See Armstrong (2004), esp. 277–93.
[30] Both texts subject Homer to a moralistic rereading, and cite similar positive and
negative *exempla* from among the characters in the *Iliad* and *Odyssey.* See Gigante
(1995) 75–8, Armstrong (2004) 277–81.
[31] Compare also *nec uixit male qui natus moriensque fefellit* ('he has not lived badly
who from birth to death goes unnoticed', 1.17.10). See Armstrong (2004) 286–7.
[32] See Armstrong (2004) 287–8.
[33] See Armstrong (2004) 272–3.
[34] On Philodemus' eclecticism see Gigante (1999) 19.
[35] See Sedley (1998) 62–93.
[36] See Moles (2002) 141–3, 149–56.

and amply explored by McGann,[37] while even the central halting progress of the narrator, 'Horace', in the collection reflects the Panaetian Stoic *proficiens*.[38] Nevertheless, one important text with which we are directed to compare the *Epistles* is the Epicurean didactic poem of Lucretius.

THE *EPISTLES* AND THE *DE RERUM NATURA*

Epistles 1 plays off the *De Rerum Natura* in a number of ways, and the relationship can be traced out, as it is by Ferri, through the many intertexts between the poems (e.g. Lucr. 1.410 ∼ *Epist.* 1.2.70; Lucr. 1.936–41 ∼ *Epist.* 1.2.67–8). In particular, as I shall show here, it is in the relationship between the two texts where the interaction between didacticism and epistolarity in *Epistles* 1 becomes clear. The letter-form is in fact vital to the differences between *Epistles* 1 and the *De Rerum Natura*, and the differences which Horace wants to emphasize. The *Epistles*, I think, set themselves up in some ways as a correction of the *De Rerum Natura*, as overcoming, or trying to overcome, some of the deficiencies of Lucretius' poem. Ferri, it should be said, also argues along these lines to some extent, and he thinks that in choosing the letter-form Horace is 'going back to Epicurus',[39] pointedly not taking up the form of the *De Rerum Natura*.[40] He constructs a model of Epicurean epistolography with an attention to the specific addressee (contrast the 'revelatory' Lucretian manner), which he thinks Horace might be trying to recreate. Ferri bases this not on those letters of Epicurus which survive complete, but largely on the Senecan letters to Lucilius, which seem clearly to develop Epicurus' wider epistolography.[41] This Epicurean epistolography would have been directed at the maintenance of an Epicurean community spread across the Greek

---

[37] See McGann (1969), esp. 10–15.

[38] See McGann (1969) 10–11, who cites as an example the end of *Epist.* 1.2, where 'Horace' says he will progress at his own pace (vv. 70–1).

[39] The importance of Epicurus' letters for Horace was already suggested by Heinze (1919) 305–7.

[40] Ferri (1993) 85–94.

[41] See Inwood in this volume on the importance of Epicurean epistolography to Seneca's letters.

world,[42] and this sense of a scattered community of friends united by letters is also shared by *Epistles* 1, where several of the letters are to addressees across the Roman world.[43] As Inwood's survey of the fragmentary letters of Epicurus shows,[44] they seem to have had a wide range of addressees, and ethics and advice were prominent (though not the only topics treated), while the style of many seems to have been clearly more informal and epistolary than the wholly extant letters preserved in Diogenes Laertius. Epicurus' own experience seems to have been drawn on several times, another reminder of Horace's *Epistles*.[45]

It is also possible to see, I think, signs of a difference in Epicurean letter-styles in the letters of Epicurus in Diogenes Laertius. The letter to Menoeceus (on ethics), though it still expounds Epicurean doctrine, is written in a much more lively style than the longer letter to Herodotus (on physics),[46] and makes a much greater attempt to engage the addressee with second-person and first-person plural pronouns and verbs, and also imperatives and questions.[47] It is also much more obviously epistolary in character, which is partly connected to its comparative brevity.[48] It may also be that the subject-matter of the letter to Menoeceus is closer to the material in Epicurus' more individualized letters, as it is to prominent themes in *Epistles* 1. Horace's choice of the letter-form probably owes much, then, to this

---

[42] See Ferri (1993) 87.

[43] e.g. *Epist.* 1.3 (in the East), 1.4 (near Praeneste), 1.8 (in the East), 1.11 (Bullatius has been travelling in the East), 1.12 (Sicily), 1.14 (Horace's Sabine farm), 1.15 (southern Italy). See Armstrong (2004) 269–71.

[44] See Inwood in this volume.

[45] A good example of all of these characteristics is fr. 52 Arrighetti from the *Letter to Idomeneus*, where Epicurus complains of great pain in his bladder and stomach, against which he sets the pleasure in his soul at the memory of philosophical discussion with Idomeneus, and then asks him to look after Metrodorus' children.

[46] e.g. in the section explaining the meaning of Epicurean pleasure (Diog. Laert. 10.131–2), where Epicurus points out that this does *not* mean 'continuous drinking and *komoi*, enjoying boys and women, fish and other things provided by a lavish table…'.

[47] e.g. the imperatives πρᾶττε ('do'), μελέτα ('practise'), πρόσαπτε ('[do not] attach'), δόξαζε ('believe', Diog. Laert. 10.123), several first-person plural pronouns (124–5), first-person plural verbs (127), and the question to the addressee, 'who do you judge better than that man who holds a holy belief about the gods and doesn't fear death?' (133). The letter to Herodotus has much less direct engagement with the addressee, and relies more on impersonal verbal adjectives such as νομιστέον ('it must be believed', e.g. Diog. Laert. 10.53, 54).

[48] Though its formal epistolary close is missing—see Inwood in this volume on the signs this and the other Epicurean letters show of modification to fit their context in Diogenes Laertius.

(largely lost) type of Epicurean epistolography. But there are other important philosophical models and methods with which Horace is playing, which deserve examination.

What, then, do the *Epistles* 'teach'? If you believe Roland Mayer, they tell the young Roman aristocrat on the make 'how to get on'.[49] These men are only interested in philosophy as part of what it is to be a gentleman:[50]

Horace's object is, after all, the young man of general culture in good society: his addressees write poetry and serve the state abroad, they play games, administer the property of others and interest themselves in the mysteries of natural science. Horace assumes that, in addition to all this, they want to understand how to live.

But this, it seems to me, neglects and marginalizes the great (indeed, central) prominence given in *Epistles* 1 to ethics:

nunc itaque et uersus et cetera ludicra pono;
quid uerum atque decens, curo et rogo et omnis in hoc sum.

So now I put aside both verses and the rest of my trifles;
what's right and appropriate, that's what I consider and ask, and I am
entirely devoted to this.   (*Epist.* 1.1.10–11)

qui quid sit pulchrum, quid turpe, quid utile, quid non,
planius ac melius Chrysippo et Crantore dicit.

he tells us what is noble, what is shameful, what is useful, what is not,
better and more clearly than Chrysippus and Crantor.   (*Epist.* 1.2.3–4)

More particularly, Mayer's formulation leaves out the urgency (the *need* 'to understand how to live' rather than simply to 'want') in *Epistles* 1 of considering what is *uerum* ('true') and what is *decens* ('appropriate'), a phrase, of course, which recalls the Panaetian (ethical) τὸ πρέπον ('the appropriate'):

ut iugulent hominem surgunt de nocte latrones:
ut te ipsum serues non expergisceris?

thieves get up while it's still night to cut a man's throat,
will you not wake up to save yourself?   (*Epist.* 1.2.32–3)

---

[49] Mayer (1995) 282.   [50] Mayer (1994) 42.

> nam cur
> quae laedunt oculos festinas demere, si quid
> est animum, differs curandi tempus in annum?
>
> Why
> do you rush to get rid of things which hurt your eyes,
> but if something is eating your soul, you put off the time to
> take care of it for a year?   (*Epist.* 1.2.37–9)

The main concern of the *Epistles* is with ethics, with *recte uiuere*, 'how to live correctly': *qui* recte uiuendi *prorogat horam...* ('the man who delays the time of living correctly...', *Epist.* 1.2.41), *uis* recte uiuere: *quis non?* ('you want to live correctly—who doesn't?', *Epist.* 1.6.29), uiuere nec recte *nec suauiter* ('living neither correctly nor gently', *Epist.* 1.8.4), *tu* recte uiuis, *si curas esse quod audis* ('you're living correctly, if you take care to be what you're said to be', *Epist.* 1.16.17). This stress on the importance of ethics, on how to act correctly or morally, is central to understanding the relationship of the *Epistles* to the *De Rerum Natura*. The *Epistles*, I think, sets up 'Horace'/itself as Socrates to Lucretius' (pre-Socratic) Empedocles, urging a greater attention to ethics as opposed to the physics which concerns the *De Rerum Natura*.

As John Moles has recently emphasized,[51] Socrates features prominently in the characterization of 'Horace' in the *Epistles*, starting with the *daimonion*-like voice 'Horace' hears in the first epistle:

est mihi purgatam crebro qui personet aurem...

I have a voice which rings repeatedly in my cleaned ear...   (*Epist.* 1.1.7)

The Socratic *daimonion*, a 'divine' voice which warns Socrates against particular actions, is familiar from both Plato and Xenophon.[52] Particularly relevant is a passage from the *Phaedrus*, where Socrates tells Phaedrus that his *daimonion* has come and from it he has heard a voice (φωνή, 242c) which prompts him to correct his wrong against Eros, saying later that he wants to 'rinse out my salt-blocked ear with clear speech' (ποτίμῳ λόγῳ οἷον ἀλμυρὰν ἀκοὴν ἀποκλύσασθαι, 243d).[53]

'Horace' also meets the Roman people in public (*Epist.* 1.1.70–5), which reminds us of Socrates in the Athenian *agora*,[54] while his professed

[51] Moles (2002) 141–3, 146–9. See also Macleod (1979) 21, Johnson (1993) 88–9.
[52] e.g. Pl. *Ap.* 31c–d, Xen. *Ap.* 4.
[53] I am indebted to an anonymous reader for the Press for pointing out the importance of this parallel.
[54] See Moles (2002) 146–7.

independence from any one philosophical school can also be connected with Socrates, given Socrates' popularity as a model for more than one Hellenistic philosophical school.[55] Fraenkel, of course, pointed out the similarities of the openings of several of the satires of Horace's second book of *Satires* to Plato's dialogues,[56] and Anderson called the Horace of the *Satires* the 'Roman Socrates'.[57] But the 'Horace' of the *Epistles* is more Socratic still, and there are some important Socratic intertexts at the end of the collection, such as the reference to Plato's *Gorgias* in the use of Zethus and Amphion from Euripides' (now fragmentary) *Antiope* at *Epist.* 1.18.41–5.[58] 'Horace' cites the example of Amphion's yielding to his brother as a model for Lollius' own attitude to his powerful friend. The use of this parallel, however, brings complications. Zethus and Amphion are representative of the practical and the contemplative life respectively, and there is a striking difference between the Euripidean resolution of their conflict in the *Antiope* (via a *deus ex machina*), and its employment in the *Gorgias*, where Socrates represents himself as an Amphion who will not yield to Callicles' Zethus,[59] which hints strongly at the trial and execution this will lead to.[60] But later in *Epist.* 1.18 'Horace' himself sets up a choice between the active and philosophical lives, but one which strongly favours the latter (vv. 96–103). The use of Zethus and Amphion in *Epist.* 1.18, who were employed by Plato to emphasize the necessity of choosing philosophy (even if this leads to one's death), makes the implication that Lollius should choose the contemplative life even more uncompromising.

Empedocles' own didactic poem *On Nature* is of course the model for the form of the *De Rerum Natura*,[61] and Empedocles receives great praise from Lucretius:[62]

carmina quin etiam diuini pectoris eius
uociferantur et exponunt praeclara reperta,
ut uix humana uideatur stirpe creatus.

---

[55] See Mayer (1986) 58 n. 13, Long (1988).
[56] See Fraenkel (1957) 136–7.   [57] See Anderson (1963) 28–49.
[58] I examine these intertexts at greater length in a recent article (Morrison 2006).
[59] *Gorg.* 506b. Callicles earlier (*Gorg.* 485e–486a) represents himself as Zethus, urging Socrates to abandon philosophy for oratory.
[60] See Rutherford (1995) 166–7.
[61] See e.g. Gale (1994) 59–75, Sedley (1998) esp. 16–34. For Empedocles as a philosophical model also see Furley (1970).
[62] All translations of Lucretius are taken or adapted from Rouse–Smith (1992).

> Moreover, the songs of his divine heart
> utter a loud voice and declare illustrious discoveries
> so he seems hardly to be born of human stock.   (Lucr. 1.731–3)

Again, the main concern is with physics. But the *Epistles* urges its addressees, and us, to concentrate on how we act or behave. A (Socratic) desire to shift from a Lucretian concern for physics towards ethics is clearest in *Epistles* 1.12 and 1.6:

> miramur, si Democriti pecus edit agellos
> cultaque, dum peregre est animus sine corpore uelox,
> cum tu inter scabiem tantam et contagia lucri
> nil paruum sapias et adhuc sublimia cures;
> quae mare compescant causae, quid temperet annum,
> stellae sponte sua iussaene uagentur et errent,
> quid premat obscurum lunae, quid proferat orbem,
> quid uelit et possit rerum concordia discors,
> Empedocles an Stertinium deliret acumen.

> we wonder that Democritus' herd ate his fields
> and crops, while his swift mind was abroad without his body,
> whereas you, among such a contagious itch for wealth,
> have no trivial knowledge and still attend to matters on high—
> what causes check the sea, what controls the year,
> do the stars wander of their own accord or are they controlled,
> what obscures and what reveals the disc of the moon,
> what is the significance of the discordant harmony of the universe,
> is Empedocles or clever Stertinius mad?   (*Epist.* 1.12.12–20)

The description of Democritus here in vv. 12–13, whose crops suffer because of the philosophical wandering of his mind recalls one description of Epicurus himself in the *De Rerum Natura*:[63]

> ergo uiuida uis animi peruicit, et extra
> processit longe flammantia moenia mundi
> atque omne immensum peragrauit mente animoque...

> And so the lively power of his mind prevailed,
> and forth he marched far beyond the flaming walls of the world,
> and travelled through all immensity in mind and spirit...
>
>   (Lucr. 1.72–4)

---

[63] See Ferri (1993) 120–1.

The subject-matter and language of the passage from *Epist.* 1.12, the movement and causes of celestial phenomena also recall the *De Rerum Natura*, especially 5.509–770. On the surface, of course, the comparison with Democritus praises Iccius, the addressee of 1.12: he, unlike the philosopher, successfully combines estate-keeping with an interest in physics. But there are also strong hints that Iccius ought to have different concerns—note the description of a point at issue between Empedocles (again, the poetic model for the *De Rerum Natura*) and one Stertinius in terms of which one 'is mad'. Iccius is unhappy with his lot, the management of Agrippa's estates on Sicily, and he's told:

> tolle querelas:
> pauper enim non est cui rerum suppetit usus.
> si uentri bene, si lateri est pedibusque tuis, nil
> diuitiae poterunt regales addere maius.

> stop complaining:
> the man who can use resources when he needs them is not poor.
> If your stomach, chest and feet are well, royal
> riches can add nothing greater. (*Epist.* 1.12.3–6)

This is put in Epicurean terms—the notion that luxury cannot increase one's pleasure when one's basic needs like health and food have been satisfied recalls the Epicurean idea that pleasure is the absence of pain, and, once achieved, luxury can only vary the pleasure, not increase it.[64] But more importantly *Epist.* 1.12 shows us that philosophical consideration of the causes of celestial phenomena, in a manner which recalls the *De Rerum Natura* is not enough to bring spiritual peace to Iccius. He is still complaining, still dissatisfied. But it is a state of mental peace which Epicurean physics is supposed to bring about:

εἰ μηθὲν ἡμᾶς αἱ τῶν μετεώρων ὑποψίαι ἠνώχλουν καὶ αἱ περὶ θανάτου, μή ποτε πρὸς ἡμᾶς ᾖ τι, ἔτι τε τὸ μὴ κατανοεῖν τοὺς ὅρους τῶν ἀλγηδόνων καὶ τῶν ἐπιθυμιῶν, οὐκ ἂν προσεδεόμεθα φυσιολογίας.

If we had never been molested by alarms at celestial and atmospheric phenomena, nor by the misgiving that death somehow affects us, nor by the neglect of the proper limits of pains and desires, we should have had no need to study natural science. (Epicurus, *RS* 11)[65]

---

[64] See Trapp (2003) 246, Long (1986) 63–7.
[65] Translation from Hicks (1931).

> hunc igitur terrorem animi tenebrasque necessest
> non radii solis neque lucida tela diei
> discutiant, sed naturae species ratioque....
>
> quippe ita formido mortalis continet omnis,
> quod multa in terris fieri caeloque tuentur
> quorum operum causas nulla ratione uidere
> possunt...
>
> This mental terror therefore and this gloom must be
> scattered not by the sun's rays or the shining shafts of day
> but by the aspect and law of nature....
>
> Certainly a dread holds all mortals in this way,
> because they see many things happening in heaven and earth
> whose causes they can by no means see...
>
> (Lucr. 1.146–8, 151–4)

But though the *De Rerum Natura* certainly *implies* changes in ethical behaviour and attitudes, such as the behaviour caused by an irrational fear of death, or mistaken beliefs about the nature of the gods, the attention of the poem is on explaining Epicurean physics. There is little in the way of direct ethical instruction.[66] We need to make the leap from readers enlightened in Epicurean physics to the state of mental peace such knowledge should bring about.

The *Epistles*, in contrast, focuses firmly on the ethical dimension, suggesting that the concentration on physics in the *De Rerum Natura* doesn't quite do the trick:

> hunc solem et stellas et decedentia certis
> tempora momentis sunt qui formidine nulla
> imbuti spectent
>
> there are those who can gaze on the sun there, and the stars,
> and the seasons passing by fixed degrees tainted
> by no fear... (*Epist.* 1.6.3–5)

This again refers to the state of fearlessness and equanimity Lucretius aims to bring about in the *De Rerum Natura*, and the principle of *nil admirari*, 'idolize nothing' (*Epist.* 1.6.1) with which the letter begins

---

[66] See Gibson (1997) 91–2 on the imperatival expressions in the *De Rerum Natura*. He concludes there is less instruction than in comparable didactic texts—Lucretius is engaged on exposition, and the reader is asked simply to accept the truth of what Lucretius expounds.

is Epicurean (though not exclusively so).[67] But again *Epist.* 1.6 contains a long parade of false ethical principles by which to live one's life—the acquisition of wealth, eating to excess, sex. The suggestion again seems to be that equanimity about celestial phenomena is at least not *automatically* productive of ethical behaviour. There is still a potential gap between learning about Epicurean physics and doing what is right. The regular stress throughout the *Epistles* on *asking* 'what should I/you do?', 'what is right?', etc. is a corrective to the concentration in the *De Rerum Natura* on physics, and itself is reminiscent of Socrates' constant ethical questioning. Horace is shifting the focus from physics onto one of the other three parts of philosophy,[68] ethics.

Such a move from physics to ethics cannot fail to remind us of Socrates—this move on Socrates' part 'is the most fundamental characteristic of Socrates in the doxographical tradition',[69] and that this 'ethical turn' was originated by Socrates is clear for Cicero (*Tusc.* 5.4.10). We also find such a characterization in Timon of Phlius (Timon fr. 799 *Suppl. Hell.*), in Aristotle (*Metaph. A.6*, 987^{b}1–2), and of course in Plato (e.g. *Ap.* 19b–d, 26b–d).[70] Xenophon's version seems to have been the most influential on the later tradition about Socrates,[71] and is worth quoting at length here. Xenophon begins by rejecting any interest on Socrates' part in physics:

οὐδὲ γὰρ περὶ τῆς τῶν πάντων φύσεως, ᾗπερ τῶν ἄλλων οἱ πλεῖστοι, διελέγετο σκοπῶν ὅπως ὁ καλούμενος ὑπὸ τῶν σοφιστῶν κόσμος ἔχει καὶ τίσιν ἀνάγκαις ἕκαστα γίγνεται τῶν οὐρανίων . . .

He did not discourse about the nature of the physical universe, as most other philosophers did, inquiring into the constitution of the cosmos (as the sages call it) and the causes of the various celestial phenomena . . .   (Xen. *Mem.* 1.1.11)[72]

---

[67] See Armstrong (2004) 284–5. It could also be associated with others, notably Democritus (see McGann (1969) 46–7), an atomist like Lucretius and Epicurus, and praised in the *De Rerum Natura*: *Democriti quod sancta uiri sententia ponit* ('which the holy judgement of the great man Democritus laid down', Lucr. 3.371, 5.622).

[68] For the threefold division of philosophy, specifically Epicurean philosophy, see (e.g.) Diog. Laert. 10.29–30.

[69] Long (1988) 151.

[70] See in general on Socrates as rejecting physics in favour of ethics Long (1988) 150–4.

[71] So Long (1988) 151.

[72] Translations of Xenophon are taken from Waterfield–Tredennick (1990).

Xenophon goes on to report that Socrates compared the disagreements of natural philosophers to those between lunatics, who can disagree radically with each other and with normal standards of behaviour. Although the direct comparison is between the large degree of disagreement within both groups, the description of the lunatics as not behaving correctly or rationally suggests that correct or rational behaviour may not be a characteristic of natural philosophers either (*Mem.* 1.1.14). Xenophon then depicts Socrates as asking about the effects these natural philosophers and their students seek—what do they want to gain from their studies? The contrast with ethics is clear—this has consequences for how you live, what you do. But physics?

ἐσκόπει δὲ περὶ αὐτῶν καὶ τάδε, ἆρ', ὥσπερ οἱ τἀνθρώπεια μανθάνοντες ἡγοῦνται τοῦθ' ὅ τι ἂν μάθωσιν ἑαυτοῖς τε καὶ τῶν ἄλλων ὅτῳ ἂν βούλωνται ποιήσειν, οὕτω καὶ οἱ τὰ θεῖα ζητοῦντες νομίζουσιν, ἐπειδὰν γνῶσιν αἷς ἀνάγκαις ἕκαστα γίγνεται, ποιήσειν, ὅταν βούλωνται, καὶ ἀνέμους καὶ ὕδατα καὶ ὥρας καὶ ὅτου ἂν ἄλλου δέωνται τῶν τοιούτων, ἢ τοιοῦτον μὲν οὐδὲν οὐδ' ἐλπίζουσιν, ἀρκεῖ δ' αὐτοῖς γνῶναι μόνον ᾗ τῶν τοιούτων ἕκαστα γίγνεται.

He also raised this further question about them: whether, just as those who study human nature expect to achieve some result from their studies for the benefit of themselves or of some other selected person, so these students of divine matters expect that, when they have discovered the laws that govern the various phenomena, they will produce at will winds and rain and changes of season and any other such required effect; or whether they have no such expectation, but are content with the mere knowledge of how these various phenomena occur.   (Xen. *Mem.* 1.1.15)

Either such studies are irrelevant or they are pursued for ridiculous ends, such as control of the weather and the seasons. This latter possibility reminds us of Empedocles, who claims he is able to impart just these abilities.[73] Hence the model for Horace in *Epistles* 1 is clear—just as Socrates rejected the study of physics, with its questionable effects on natural philosophers, 'Horace' turns to ethics, to the part of philosophy whose effects are clear and whose relevance for life is unambiguous. This part of philosophy, of course, involves

[73] Fr. B111 D.–K. See Waterfield–Tredennick (1990) 71 n. 2 for this Empedoclean parallel for the description in Xenophon.

questioning and the investigation of moral concepts, another aspect of Socrates' endeavours emphasized by Xenophon:

αὐτὸς δὲ περὶ τῶν ἀνθρωπείων ἀεὶ διελέγετο σκοπῶν τί εὐσεβές, τί ἀσεβές, τί καλόν, τί αἰσχρόν, τί δίκαιον, τί ἄδικον, τί σωφροσύνη, τί μανία, τί ἀνδρεία, τί δειλία, τί πόλις, τί πολιτικός, τί ἀρχὴ ἀνθρώπων, τί ἀρχικὸς ἀνθρώπων . . .

He himself always discussed human matters, trying to find out the nature of piety and impiety, honour and dishonour, right and wrong, sanity and lunacy, courage and cowardice, State and statesman, government and the capacity for government. . .   (Xen. *Mem*.1.1.16)

DIDACTIC 'PLOT' AND DIDACTIC ADDRESSEE

Don Fowler suggested there were various implied 'plots' or impressions of plots running through didactic poems like the *De Rerum Natura*, which help the reader make sense of the instruction being given in the poem.[74] Prominent among these in the *De Rerum Natura* is the progress of the addressee, Memmius, down a path or journey from ignorance to knowledge already followed by the teacher:

> haec sic pernosces parua perductus opella;
> namque alid ex alio clarescet, nec tibi caeca
> nox iter eripiet quin ultima naturai
> peruideas: ita res accendent lumina rebus.

> So you will gain a thorough understanding
> of these matters, led on with very little effort;
> for one thing will become clear by another, and
> blind night will not steal away your path and prevent
> you seeing nature's deepest recesses—
> so will truths light the way for truths.
>
> (Lucr. 1.1114–17)

Along this path or progress in the *De Rerum Natura* there is some encouragement for the addressee:[75]

> uerum animo satis haec uestigia parua sagaci
> sunt per quae possis cognoscere cetera tute.
> namque canes ut montiuagae persaepe ferarum

---

[74] See Fowler (2000).   [75] See also Lucr. 1.140–5.

> naribus inveniunt intectas fronde quietes,
> cum semel institerunt uestigia certa uiai,
> sic alid ex alio per te tute ipse uidere
> talibus in rebus poteris caecasque latebras
> insinuare omnis et uerum protrahere inde.

> But for a keen-scented mind, these little tracks
> are enough to enable you to recognize others for yourself.
> For as mountain-ranging dogs very often find
> by their scent the leaf-hidden resting-places of beasts,
> once they have hit on certain traces of its path,
> so you will be able for yourself to see one thing after
> another in such matters as these, and to penetrate
> all unseen hiding-places, and draw forth the truth from them.
>   (Lucr. 1.402–9)

But in general the *De Rerum Natura* is very 'teachery', and the situation developed in the poem is clearly one of enlightened instructor and struggling, ignorant addressee. Another crude index—Lucretius regularly describes himself as 'teaching' using *doceo/docui* ('I teach', 'I taught'): *magnis doceo de rebus*, 'I teach about great matters' (Lucr. 1.931).[76]

The teacher has to battle lack of trust and forestall objections by Memmius and his going astray or 'backsliding' in his progress:[77]

> nequa forte tamen coeptes diffidere dictis,
> quod nequeunt oculis rerum primordia cerni...

> lest you may by any chance begin nevertheless to distrust
> my words, because the first-beginnings of things
> cannot be seen with one's eyes...   (Lucr. 1.267–8)

> illud in his rebus ne te deducere uero
> possit, quod quidam fingunt, praecurrere cogor.

> And here in this matter I am driven to forestall
> what some imagine, lest it should lead you away from the truth.
>   (Lucr. 1.370–1)

For Philip Mitsis this adds up to an 'aggressive, condescending tone of paternalism',[78] and it seems that Memmius doesn't get very far along the path to knowledge. He is a difficult pupil and does not

---

[76] See also Lucr. 1.265, 1.499–50, 1.531, 1.539, 1.951, 4.6, 5.55–6, 6.1094, etc.
[77] See also Lucr. 1.332–3, 1.398–9.   [78] Mitsis (1993) 112.

progress much, which Mitsis identifies as a strategy for getting readers to identify with and accept the doctrines being propounded by Lucretius. But this is only another example of the 'didactic *nepios*', the presentation of the addressee of some didactic poems as a 'fool' in great need of the teaching provided by the narrator of a didactic poem—similar situations are to be found in Hesiod's *Works and Days* with Perses, and also Pausanias in Empedocles' *On Nature*.[79]

EPISTOLARY NARRATIVE AND EPISTOLARY ADDRESSEES

Horace tries something different in the *Epistles*. There we get an epistolary version of the implied narrative or plot of a path or progress in the *De Rerum Natura*.[80] This time, however, this is focused on the narrator, on 'Horace'. De Pretis has suggested that the order of the epistles leads us to assume a narrative of sorts, they create 'an illusion of temporal sequence':[81] in 1.1 we get an announcement of a turn from poetry to ethics, in 1.2 we seem to get an example of this—'Horace' writing about ethics to a friend.[82] When we get to 1.7, where 'Horace' apologizes to Maecenas for having been away from Rome for longer than he said (vv. 1–2), the impression is created that this absence is a result of the decision announced in 1.1, and perhaps has prompted 'pressure' from Maecenas. We also, perhaps, assume *Epist.* 1.2–6 have been written in the absence from Rome (though 1.5 is a problem for this impression of narrative). But there are other ways of reading the 'progress' of the *Epistles*—'Horace' announces a turn away from poetry in 1.1 (*uersus et cetera ludicra pono*, 'I put aside both verses and the rest of my trifles', v. 10), but in 1.2 is rereading Homer (*Troiani belli scriptorem*, 'the writer of the Trojan war', v. 1)—a kind of 'backsliding'?

[79] See Mitsis (1993) 124, Clay (1993) 24.

[80] See Beard (2002) on the kind of implied or quasi-narrative which can be created by a letter-collection.

[81] See de Pretis (2002) 141–4.

[82] On the turn from poetry to philosophy by 'Horace' see Harrison (1995) 49–50 and Moles (2002) 143–8. As Harrison notes, it is not simply that 'Horace' puts aside lyric poetry, but that he is announcing a turn away from poetry altogether, though this is deconstructed by the paradox that the *Epistles* are in verse.

We get more of this kind of backsliding in the confession of spiritual malaise in 1.8:

> nil audire uelim, nil discere, quod leuet aegrum;
> fidis offendar medicis, irascar amicis,
> cur me funesto properent arcere ueterno;
> quae nocuere sequar, fugiam quae profore credam;
> Romae Tibur amem uentosus, Tibure Romam.

> I want to hear nothing, to learn nothing which might alleviate
> my sickness. I am rude to my loyal doctors, angry at my friends,
> because they fuss to keep me safe from deadly depression.
> I chase what harms me, I shun what I think would benefit me.
> Fickle, at Rome I love Tibur, at Tibur, Rome.   (*Epist.* 1.8.8–12)

This is not only in marked contrast to the moral soundness 'Horace' has just displayed in 1.7, as McGann suggests,[83] but it even sounds as if the (philosophical) *uerba et uoces, libellus* and *piacula* of 1.1, which marked out the whole project of philosophical self-examination of *Epistles* 1 itself,[84] which was meant to bring spiritual peace, no longer work:

> sunt certa piacula quae te
> ter pure lecto poterunt recreare libello.

> there are surefire rituals which
> can revive you, when the booklet is read three times with a pure heart.
> (*Epist.* 1.1.36–7)

Note also the confession to a satisfaction with simplicity (remember the Epicurean disregard for luxury) which turns out to be superficial in 1.15:

> nam tuta et paruula laudo
> cum res deficiunt, satis inter uilia fortis;
> uerum ubi quid melius contingit et unctius, idem
> uos sapere et solos aio bene uiuere, quorum
> conspicitur nitidis fundata pecunia uillis.

> I praise safe and small things
> when resources are lacking, strong enough amid cheap stuff;
> but when something better and more delectable comes my way,

---

[83] McGann (1969) 56.

[84] These sound (partly) Epicurean, as Armstrong (2004) 275–6 suggests, reminiscent of Epicurean memorizing of phrases and books, but also epistolary, as the tags, proverbs, and one-liners are at home in letters (see Harrison (1995) 51–3 and also below).

all the same I say only your sort are wise, whose money
can be seen to be poured into shining villas.

(*Epist.* 1.15.42–6)

This kind of 'backsliding', now by the narrator/teacher rather than the addressee itself plays the same kind of role as the encouragement of the addressee in the *De Rerum Natura*—'Horace' himself struggles with the ethical problems they have to face.[85] Sometimes it's 'Horace' himself who needs the lesson, or the advice—he is not the lofty teacher of the *De Rerum Natura*, dispensing the truths of Epicurean physics from a position of certainty.[86] The reader of the *Epistles* also gets 'breaks' like 1.5, the invitation to Torquatus to a boozy (but simple) party, which relieve one from the moralizing of *Epist.* 1.1, 1.2, and 1.6, or *Epist.* 1.13, the instructions to one Vinnius on how to take 'Horace's' *carmina* ('poems') to Augustus, in a tone which seems a displaced version of the irritation a didactic narrator could show with his didactic *nepios* (particularly in the first line, where *docui... saepe* ('I have instructed several times') parallels the *doceo/docui* language of the *De Rerum Natura*), but which again forms a 'break' from discussion of ethics:

> Ut proficiscentem docui te saepe diuque,
> Augusto reddes signata uolumina, Uinni,
> si ualidus, si laetus erit, si denique poscet;
> ne studio nostri pecces odiumque libellis
> sedulus importes opera uehemente minister.

> As I said several times and at length to you as you were off,
> make sure you deliver Augustus the rolls still sealed, Vinnius,
> if he's well, in a good mood and only if he asks for them,
> so you don't stumble in your zeal for me and inflict distaste on
> my little books by doing your duty over-keenly.

(*Epist.* 1.13.1–5)

If the didactic *nepios* strategy is one way of getting the wider audience of a didactic poem on the side of the teacher, of making the instruction being offered more appealing to a general readership,[87] then this is achieved in the *Epistles* by the very variety of

---

[85] See Harrison (1995) 50–1. There is similar epistolary encouragement for the addressee in Seneca, who also confesses his own struggles: see (e.g.) *Ep.* 68 and Inwood in this volume, who suggests that Seneca's writing of his own personal experience probably resembled Epicurus' in his wider epistolography.

[86] See Ferri (1993) 86, 94.   [87] See Mitsis (1993) 124–7.

addressees of the different epistles (all different save Maecenas in 1.1, 1.7, and 1.19, Lollius in 1.2 and 1.18, and the book itself in 1.20). This in itself opens out the advice being given—though the content and manner of each epistle is carefully modified with each addressee (e.g. 1.7 to Maecenas, or 1.12 to Iccius, with his interest in natural philosophy), the fact that there are so many internal addressees suggests the wider applicability of the ethical lessons being urged:

> qui semel aspexit quantum dimissa petitis
> praestent, mature redeat repetatque relicta.
> metiri se quemque suo modulo ac pede uerum est.

> A man who sees by how much his old life is better than
> the one he sought, should quickly return to and seek out what
> he left. It's right for each man to measure himself by his own footrule.
>   (*Epist.* 1.7.96–8)

The form too of the ethical advice being urged aids this suggestion of wider applicability—proverbs and memorable tags:[88]

> uirtus est uitium fugere, et sapientia prima
> stultitia caruisse.

> Virtue is to avoid vice, and the first wisdom to
> have got rid of stupidity.   (*Epist.* 1.1.41–2)

>   hic murus aeneus esto,
> nil conscire sibi, nulla pallescere culpa
>   Make this your bronze wall:
> don't have anything on your conscience, and have no blame
> to make you go pale.   (*Epist.* 1.1.60–1)

> caelum non animum mutant qui trans mare currunt.

> those who run across the sea change their sky, not their soul.
>   (*Epist.* 1.11.27)

Proverbs, of course, are an appropriate epistolary means of including philosophy in letters:

> κάλλος μέντοι αὐτῆς αἵ τε φιλικαὶ φιλοφρονήσεις καὶ πυκναὶ παροιμίαι
> ἐνοῦσαι· καὶ τοῦτο γὰρ μόνον ἐνέστω αὐτῇ σοφόν . . .

> The beauty of a letter lies in the feelings of warm friendship it conveys and the numerous proverbs it contains; this should be the only element of philosophy in it . . .   (Demetr. *Eloc.* 232)

---

[88] See Harrison (1995) 51–3.

But the most important 'lesson' of the *Epistles* is the urgent need to *ask*, 'how should I act?', 'what should I do?':

quid uerum atque decens, curo et rogo

what's right and appropriate, that's what I consider and ask   (*Epist.* 1.1.11)

quid minuat curas, quid te tibi reddat amicum;
quid pure tranquillet, honos an dulce lucellum,
an secretum iter et fallentis semita uitae.

what reduces your cares, what makes you a friend to yourself,
what brings absolute calm, public office or a nice little earner,
or the secret way and the path of an unnoticed life?
                                        (*Epist.* 1.18.101–3)

Hence the great many questions in the *Epistles* (another reminder of Socrates). And this interrogative aspect is, I think, another important aspect of the choice of the letter-form in the *Epistles*, in contrast to the didactic poem of Lucretius. Socrates asks his interlocutors in discussion to consider the motivations for their actions and their ideas of various moral concepts—his philosophy, which concentrates on ethics to the exclusion of physics, is one which takes place in conversation.[89] Questions to one's addressee, particularly about what he/she is doing, or what he/she should do, or what one should do, are a natural aspect of epistolary communication. Both the subject of ethics and the mode of questioning are at home in letters. It is of course an often quoted maxim from ancient epistolary theory that a letter is one half of a dialogue.[90] But although this is not without its problems as a definition, it reminds us that letters do have the potential to be answered by other letters, and the recommendations, doubts, backsliding, and progress of 'Horace' in *Epistles* 1 also have such potential replies from 'Horace's' addressees. This marks *Epistles* 1 out as very different from the *De Rerum Natura*, and as much more 'Socratic'. The letter-form may be Horace's solution to the problem of representing Socratic dialectic in writing (a paradox flagged in Plato's *Phaedrus*),[91] to which Plato's answer was the dialogue.[92]

---

[89] Indeed, as an anonymous reader for the Press points out, one distinctive characteristic of Socrates was thought to be his use of a wide variety of everyday situations and meetings to pass on ethical advice—see Plut. *Mor.* 796c–797a.

[90] See Demetr. *Eloc.* 223.   [91] See Pl. *Phdr.* 275d–e.

[92] See also Inwood in this volume who draws attention to the dialogic, conversational character of Seneca's letters to Lucilius.

RESOLUTION, OPENNESS, AND
THE DIDACTIC PLOT

And this urging of the need to ask 'what is right?' in the *Epistles*, and the figure of 'Horace', the backsliding narrator whose own progress is halting and problematic, brings us to another (final) difference from the *De Rerum Natura*. Don Fowler saw a tension between the nature of didactic poems like the *De Rerum Natura*, which teach a body of knowledge which the pupil/reader learns, thus removing the need for the poem, and the fact that such works are poems, and ought to be reread, reused, often taken as a mark of the 'literary'. But the *Epistles* presents us with an ethical project which can't finish—asking yourself how to live right, *recte uiuere*. The fact that 'Horace', at the end of the collection, hasn't reached a state of spiritual peace, or indeed abandoned poetry for philosophy, as *Epistle* 1.19 on models and innovation in poetry, and 1.20, addressed to the book itself show, points us to this 'openness'. 'Horace' won't even be living in secret like a good Epicurean (see the 'secret path' of 18)—the book of *Epistles* itself is going to tell the world all about him:

> me libertino natum patre et in tenui re
> maiores pennas nido extendisse loqueris,
> ut quantum generi demas uirtutibus addas;
> me primis Urbis belli placuisse domique;
> corporis exigui, praecanum, solibus aptum,
> irasci celerem, tamen ut placabilis essem.
> forte meum si quis te percontabitur aeuum,
> me quater undenos sciat impleuisse Decembris
> collegam Lepidum quo dixit Lollius anno.

> you'll say that my father was a freedman, and that in modest
> circumstances I stretched my wings which were too big for the nest.
> Hence what you subtract from my birth you'll add to my good points.
> You'll say I pleased the city's leaders in war and at home in peace,
> that I was small, grey before my time, suited to the sun,
> quick to get angry, though I am also easy to appease.
> If by chance someone asks you for my age, tell him
> I completed forty-four Decembers in the year Lepidus
> was Lollius' new colleague.

(Epist. 1.20.20–8)

Philosophy, which in the *Epistles* as for Socrates means ethics, is too important to be left for us to deduce from an exposition of physics like the *De Rerum Natura*, or to be put aside like a completed correspondence course at the end of reading such a poem. It is too urgent, and it needs to be 'done' every day—another reason for the everyday form Horace chooses, the letter.

5

The Importance of Form in Seneca's Philosophical Letters

Brad Inwood

Seneca's letters are clearly his most influential work—whether rightly or not is neither determinable nor to the point. Students of Stoicism might wish that his other prose works, such as the massive *Natural Questions* and *On Favours* or the more compact but still treatise-like *On Anger* or even the shorter addresses and consolations grouped as the *dialogi*,[1] matched the letters for impact on the later tradition. But they do not. The striking literary power and influence of the letters has shaped our understanding of Seneca's legacy, and through the intense interest in these letters of Michel Foucault and Pierre Hadot it has recently affected the common understanding of Imperial Stoicism more generally. So for me, as a student of Stoicism and also as a keen admirer of Seneca, it matters rather a lot to get a reasonable understanding of what makes the letters work the way they do for their readers and some grasp of why they were written the way they were. In this discussion I would like to suggest that some of the striking features of his letters owe more than has yet been appreciated to the influence of the models Seneca had in view when he composed the collection and the formal constraints imposed by the epistolary genre.[2]

---

[1] For a sensible account of the Senecan *dialogus*, see Griffin (1992) appendix B 2.

[2] For a compelling account of why the letters should be read as being fundamentally epistolary see Wilson (2001). I only became aware of Wilson's essay when my fundamental approach to the letters was well worked out and the first version of this paper had been written. It should never have been necessary to argue for something so obvious as the epistolary quality of Seneca's letters, but Wilson both gives an

Let me start with a few basics.[3] The entire collection of letters that we have was almost certainly written late in Seneca's life (after the year AD 62 and before his death in 65). Our collection is incomplete; we know that originally there were more than the twenty books which now survive, thanks to a lengthy quotation by Aulus Gellius (*Noctes Atticae* 12.2) from book 22. The collection seems to have circulated in at least two volumes in late antiquity (letters 1–88 and 89–124). Hence Reynolds[4] has suggested that the incompleteness at the end of our collection was the result of an early loss of one entire volume of letters, possibly not a very long one. It is also possible that small groups of letters have been lost within the span of our transmitted collection, and the volume join between 88 and 89 would be a particularly likely location for such a loss.[5] The maimed state of our collection is probably not a result of its being left incomplete by Seneca's death; and whatever we think about the integrity of our collection, it clearly suffered less from the indignities of transmission than the *Natural Questions*, for example, did.[6]

It was established over 25 years ago, by Miriam Griffin, that the correspondence with Lucilius is essentially fictitious;[7] it is unnecessary to repeat the arguments for that now.[8] There has always been a

excellent brief account of how the generic character of the letters came to be misperceived in our scholarly tradition and of why it is fundamentally misguided to treat the letters as 'essays'.

[3] See Cancik (1967); also Cancik-Lindemaier (1998) 102–9. In addition to other works cited below, see also Mazzoli (1989) for a broad overview of important issues in recent scholarship dealing with the letters; also Cugusi (1983) 195–206. A bibliographical survey covering the years 1945–85 was prepared by F.-R. Chaumartin and published in *ANRW* 2.36.3: 1585–96.

[4] Reynolds (1965) 17.

[5] See Cancik (1967) 8–12 for sensible discussion of the internal completeness of our collection. In n. 18, p. 8, she notes that Reynolds fails to consider the possibility that letters may have been lost at the join between the two volumes of letters that came down separately through the medieval manuscript tradition.

[6] In addition to the loss of two half-books, the order of the books in our *QNat.* seems to have become seriously confused in the course of transmission. It is likely that the original order was 3, 4a, 4b, 5, 6, 7, 8, 1, 2 and quite possible that the work was left incomplete on Seneca's death. For further discussion and references, see Inwood (2002).

[7] Griffin (1992) appendix B 4. For a generous survey of earlier views see Mazzoli (1989) 1846–50.

[8] See also the admirably crisp argument to this effect by Leeman (1951) 175–81, a perceptive study of one letter which discusses Seneca's references to alleged previous

considerable interest in the internal articulation of the letters—how they were meant to be grouped for reading or publication—and the hermeneutical issues attendant on this issue are certainly complex, probably insoluble. This is partly because we cannot any longer look at the whole collection of letters as Seneca meant it to be read and partly because it has proved difficult to separate philosophical interpretation from questions of structure and literary form.[9] If one's ultimate goal is a philosophical interpretation of the letters, it won't help much to seek guidance from a view about their literary form which is itself partly shaped by an incipient philosophical interpretation.

Still, even with these challenges to the reader, the *Letters to Lucilius* remain Seneca's masterpiece. Yet it is his only work in this genre and it is not at all clear how to regard it when assessing its philosophical significance. Here, then, is my question. Why did he write in epistolary form? Why, at the end of a long life, a long and tumultuous political career, and (perhaps most relevant) at the end of a brilliant literary career of unmatched versatility, write letters?

Any answer is bound to be speculative and so to require constraints to guide the guesswork. My first assumption is about Seneca's character and motivation. I think—and I argued for this some years ago,[10] though it is scarcely an original view—that the best general description of Seneca is as a 'man of letters', someone whose central point of pride and ambition would have been his career as a writer. A poet, a dramatist, a public speaker (and tutor to Nero in the same),

letters by Lucilius and himself (as well as the difficult question of Seneca's attitude to dialectic); this is further developed in Leeman (1953) 307–13. Note also Abel (1981) and the sensible comments of Cancik (1967) 53–4. Margaret Graver reviews the issue more recently in her unpublished dissertation (Graver 1996), ch. 1.

[9] See Maurach (1970). Also: Schönegg (1999), Hachmann (1995); Cancik (1967), who commits herself to the view that the organizational principle of the collection is pedagogical rather than doctrinal, is unusually sensitive to the methodological problems involved in discussing the plan and organization of the collection and emphasizes the complexity of the techniques used by Seneca (in her view) to give unity and texture to the work. I restrict myself here to citing a few detailed discussions of letter grouping and articulation, but it should be noted that virtually everyone who writes on Seneca's philosophical letters has taken an at least implicit position on their pedagogical or literary structure and a review of the issue would be both lengthy and inconclusive.

[10] Inwood (1995), now reprinted as ch. 1 of Inwood (2005).

and an essayist in a wide variety of genres—who else in his generation spanned such a wide range of literary forms? And who else did so well in them all? If this is the right picture of Seneca, then when we consider his motivations in approaching the *Letters* it will be reasonable, perhaps even compelling, to consider the influence of the obvious target for literary emulation, Cicero's correspondence, alongside that of the more obvious models, collections of philosophical correspondence.[11]

But first let me say a bit about the tradition of philosophical letter writing into which Seneca inserted himself with his choice to write in this genre.[12] There are, of course, many corpora of philosophical letters, beginning perhaps with Plato's letters, whose authenticity remains highly controversial. But in addition to this most famous set of letters, we also find letters of Aristotle, pseudo-Pythagorean letters from the Hellenistic era,[13] Cynic epistles,[14] and a very important body of philosophical letters by Epicurus—and this list is certainly not complete. Epicurus' letters were of particular importance for Seneca, as is suggested by Seneca's frequent use of them.[15]

The collections of philosophical letters which may have shaped Seneca's practice were certainly varied. Some were genuine, some pseudepigraphic; some highly doctrinal and technical, some quite informal; some real correspondence and some artificial. Seneca's own letters, then, need to be seen against the background of the genre in which he chose to write near the end of his life. And of course, we

---

[11] This view is essentially that of Griffin (1992) 418–19, whom I also follow in most matters of the chronology of Seneca's works. For background see Maurach (1970) ii.181 ff. The major limitation of his assessment of generic influence on Seneca's letters is his nearly exclusive concentration on literary form and his emphasis on Seneca's situation within his Latin literary tradition. Hence (pp. 197–8) he downplays the importance of Epicurus' letters and focuses more on Horace and Lucilius. Similarly, his grudging concession of possible Ciceronian influence on the project of the letters (p. 197) seems to underestimate the motivational power of authorial *aemulatio.*

[12] See also Hodkinson in this volume.

[13] These can be found in Thesleff (1965). Three Pythagorean women are represented in this collection (Melissa, pp. 115–16, Muia, pp. 123–4, and Theano, pp. 194–200), as well as letters attributed to Pythagoras himself (pp. 185–6) and to Telauges (p. 189).

[14] See Malherbe (1977).

[15] See especially Maurach (1970) 186–8.

must also bear in mind that when he chose to write in this way it was a significant decision, for at the same time he seems to have been engaged in at least the groundwork for a large theoretical treatise (the *Moralis Philosophia*, of which only a few fragments survive)[16] and the strikingly different *Natural Questions*. We should not be thinking of the letters of Seneca as a product of the weary personalism of an ageing and disillusioned man, as a choice he could not help but make. He was, at the same period of his life, keen to sort out the varieties of hail and the causes of earthquakes. So the not infrequent notion that the Seneca we know from the letters is the man himself should not be accepted uncritically.[17]

Self-consciously, then, Seneca writes his letters.[18] Beyond an admiration for Epicurus and a keen desire to rival Cicero (whose letters he quotes just often enough to signal awareness) and the influence of Horace's epistles (again, signalled by occasional quotations),[19] what expectations was Seneca willingly bringing on to himself when he chose to cast a major intellectual labour in this form?

[16] See Leeman (1953) for a discussion of how the plan to write such a work may have related to the letters. The fragments preserved in Lactantius (see frr. 119–24 Haase) do not cohere very well with the description of the treatise given by Seneca in letters 106, 108, and 109. Although Lactantius may not be the most reliable source for the content of the lost treatise, it is worth noting that the fragments are devoid of the dialectical and metaphysical technicality which Seneca's account of his own work would lead us to expect. It is worth asking whether Seneca's invocation of the *Moralis Philosophia* functioned in part to motivate the introduction of technical material into the letters.

[17] Compare Freisenbruch's chapter in this volume, section III, on epistolary role-playing in the correspondence of Fronto and Marcus.

[18] Cf. Graver (1996) 30–5.

[19] See the chapter by Morrison in this volume, who also emphasizes the relationship between Horace and Lucretius (another author of great importance to Seneca). See in particular *Ep.* 118 for Cicero and *Epp.* 119 and 120 for Horace. Cancik (1967) 54–8 summarizes literature on Horace's epistles and concludes that two of the features which stand out in Seneca's letters (deliberate self-presentation and moral exhortation) are shared with Horace's letters and that these are to be seen as artefacts of the genre of literary epistle. I think this is very likely to be right and highly significant, but some caution is indicated by the need to take account of two important generic differences: Horace wrote in verse and was surely affected by traditions of hexameter satire; and Seneca wrote explicitly philosophical letters against the background of an established genre of such letters.

Let's look for a moment at what one Greek authority, pseudo-Demetrius *On Style*, has to say.[20] In sections 223–35 the author deals with the 'epistolary style', a type of the plain style. He cites the opinion of Artemon, the editor of Aristotle's letters (most of which are now thought to be inauthentic), on the question of the general character of letters. One should, he says, 'write both dialogue and letters in the same manner (*tropos*)' on the grounds that 'the letter is, as it were, one of the two sides of a dialogue'.[21] Pseudo-Demetrius himself wants to modify this perhaps excessive claim. A letter should be, he thinks, a little more carefully worked up than a dialogue just because the latter is a representation of someone who is improvising while a letter 'is written out and then sent, in a way, as a gift' to the recipient. Examples of things which are inappropriate in conversational dialogues but acceptable in letters and vice versa follow. Tragic diction might work in some letters, but would fail in dialogues. Sudden elliptical omissions are acceptable in conversation, but merely cause unclarity in letters. A vivid representation of two-sided conversation is not as suitable in written letters as it is in Platonic dialogues (the example used in 226 comes from the *Euthydemus*).

Positive recommendations for letters sometimes emphasize similarities to the dialogue—for example, letters reveal a person's character (*ēthos* or *psuchē*) quite clearly. Pseudo-Demetrius also recommends length limits on letters so as to avoid the appearance that a letter is nothing more than a treatise with a salutation at the beginning (some Platonic letters are indicated as failing on this criterion).[22] A fluid rather than a highly periodic structure is best, and so is the frankness characteristic of daily life. Some themes are picked out as being inappropriate to the genre of the letter while others are a particularly

---

[20] Rhys Roberts (1902). Ps.-Demetrius is not the only ancient authority on the epistolary genre, but due to his date and interests he is more revealing in the present context than (for example) ps.-Libanius, *On Letter Form*. On epistolary theory in antiquity generally, see the succinct account of Trapp (2003) 42–6.

[21] Seneca's remarks about the *sermo* over the *disputatio* at *Ep.* 38 do not, *pace* Griffin (1992) 419, quite constitute a norm for writing letters; but the spirit of the remark is nevertheless quite close to the recommendation of ps.-Demetrius.

[22] Compare the recommendation of C. Iulius Victor, *Ars Rhetorica* 27, pp. 447–8 Halm: a more learned letter should be kept brief in order to conform to the *modus epistulae*; personal letters in particular should be short and obscurity should be especially avoided. Iulius Victor's model for epistolary practice is clearly Cicero. On Victor see also Trapp (2003) 44.

good fit. Logical puzzles (*sophismata*)[23] and natural philosophy (*phusiologia*) are unsuitable to letters—so much the worse for Epicurus' letter to Herodotus, we might say. Simplicity, expressions of personal sentiment, and proverbs or maxims (*paroimiai*) are *in*, while highly wrought *gnōmologiai* and protreptic exhortations are *out*. Our author, using Aristotle's letters as a benchmark for the genre, concedes that it is occasionally acceptable to raise the stylistic level (if one is addressing a king or potentate, for instance) or to throw in a bit of logical proof if the underlying theme of the letter is appropriate. But even so, this authority takes a firm stand on the appropriate epistolary style: letters should be written in a blend of the plain and the graceful style (235), balanced—precariously, we might think—between the simplicity and vigour of the dialogue and the complexity and rhetorical ambitions of treatises and speeches.

If one were to judge Seneca's letters against the expectations generated by pseudo-Demetrius' discussion, one's reaction might well be mixed. Certainly many letters (such as 94 and 95) cross dangerously over the line towards being treatises with a salutation—overly long, excessively complex, too full of sententious bits and protreptic flights of enthusiasm. But in other respects it will help us to understand some features of Seneca's letters which might otherwise get in the way of our philosophical understanding of his letters. For example, two philosophical topics are thought of as being particularly unsuitable for letters, natural philosophy and logical puzzles and subtleties. Seneca's tastes and predilections in philosophy are often gauged by his letters, and on the basis of this a great deal is made of his dismissive attitude to logic and to physics—hence the widespread but misleading impression that later Stoicism is concerned excessively with ethics, that somehow the school which started out preaching the equal importance of all three branches of philosophy and the need for a mixed manner of teaching and writing about them (the *miktē paradosis* mentioned at Diogenes Laertius 7.40) went intellectually soft in the Imperial period.

---

[23] Ps.-Libanius 41 (pp. 20–1 Weichert) has a more relaxed attitude to length than ps.-Demetrius or Iulius Victor (see above) but insists that if philosophical material is to be introduced into the letter it must not be presented in a 'dialectical manner'.

This view has always been strange, in my opinion. Seneca wrote his *Natural Questions* and for all its ethical import it is still a work on natural philosophy. Cornutus' work on theology falls under physics and so does everything written by Cleomedes. Epictetus may deprecate logic, but he knows it well and insists that his students learn it. Jonathan Barnes, in *Logic and the Imperial Stoa*,[24] argues forcefully that the frequent complaints made by Seneca and others about the over-valuation of logic demonstrate how much attention was actually being paid to logic in the early empire, not how little. So how do we explain the widespread conviction that Stoicism as practised in the early empire took such a purely ethical turn?

Part of the answer, surely, is that Seneca's letters have become paradigmatic for us as modern intepreters of Stoicism. Since the seventeenth century if not before, to think of Stoicism is to think of the *Epistulae Morales*. And this isn't surprising, from a literary point of view. Aside from bits of Cleanthes and Aratus, Seneca's works are the earliest non-fragmentary texts of Stoicism that we have. And for centuries they were enjoyed by a much larger audience than other works—which is one great advantage of being written in Latin. And they are, from a literary point of view, *really* good: engaging, personal, seductive even, rather like the best Platonic dialogues—and our notion of a Platonic dialogue is shaped fundamentally by the vivid 'Socratic' dialogues rather than by the *Timaeus* or the *Laws*, or even the *Sophist* and *Statesman*. So the letters of Seneca have had a disproportionate impact on our conception of Stoicism. The two branches of Stoicism that get slighted (physics and logic) are the very ones which Seneca either omits or ridicules in the letters. He tells us often that logical subtleties are a waste of time, that details of Stoic ontology represent a finicky branch of philosophy and are beneath his dignity. Letters 113 and 117 leap to mind. Letter 45 is brutal on the topic of dialectical argumentation; letter 82 ridicules Zeno for it.[25] Letters 102, 108, and 111 present the reader with a relentless attack on this sort of philosophical activity.[26]

---

[24] Barnes (1997).   [25] See the apt comment by Wilson (1987) 114–15.

[26] On the question of Seneca's attitude to dialectic, see also Leeman (1951) esp. 177 and 179; Leeman is quite right to point out that despite his disparaging remarks Seneca *chose* to include the dialectical themes for his own purposes; he was under no obligation to do so.

No doubt Seneca is more interested in ethical argumentation than in physics (though I dare anyone to argue that he disliked physics after a second consecutive reading of the *Natural Questions*—remembering that you are only reading it and he had to write it!). But it is certainly worth considering the possibility that a major motivation for Seneca's attitude is his awareness of and interest in the genre he is working in. If the rules of the letter-writing game indicate that in general (though not absolutely, as the example of the letters of Epicurus shows) logic and physics should be absent from letters, Seneca (not out of character) goes one step further. He not only omits them, he attacks them; he flaunts before the reader his awareness of generic constraints—and plays with the reader as well, for there really is a great deal of physics in the letters, not just in 113 and 117, where the topic is dismissed only to be raised, in the manner of a clever *recusatio*, but also in more straightforward treatments such as letter 121 on *oikeiōsis*.[27]

If these are some of the generic constraints on philosophical letters which Seneca faced, then it is, I hope, clear that being aware of them will make a difference to our interpretation not just of Seneca's own authorial strategy but also to our understanding of the nature of ancient Stoicism. I want to turn now to a brief consideration of the importance of a more specific model, Epicurus, as an example of how reading Seneca against the background of his literary models can help with philosophical interpretation. In so doing I do not wish to neglect Cicero's influence. If it is right to see Seneca's desire to make his mark on Latin literature as part of his authorial strategy, then of course Cicero must have played a central role for Seneca. Cicero was, after all, his main predecessor in the project of writing philosophy in Latin prose and in several letters we can detect the importance of the themes of his *De Finibus* as part of the intellectual background;[28] the *Letters to Atticus* are noted as a source of literary fame for their recipient in *Ep.* 21 (where Epicurus' letters to Idomeneus are compared to them)[29] and in *Ep.* 118 Seneca unmistakably targets these

---

[27] Similarly, Jula Wildberger's recent Habilitationsschrift, *Seneca und die Stoa, Teil I: Der Platz des Menschen in der Welt* (2003), makes extensive use of the *Epistulae Morales*, confirming how thoroughly the themes of physics run through a major work on ethics.

[28] Letters 66, 71, 76 are three examples.

[29] Cf. Cancik (1967) 79, Graver (1996) 26–8.

letters with an eye to philosophical and moral one-upmanship. In *Ep.* 58 Cicero is cited as a precedent for philosophical terminology in Latin and any survey of Cicero's role in the letters will leave the inescapable impression that he more than any other Latin author sets the benchmark for Seneca's ambitions. It is quite likely that Seneca's decision to compose a collection of letters addressed to a single correspondent, and a close friend at that, was determined by the model of Cicero's *Letters to Atticus.* If so, then we would be well advised to take this into consideration when thinking about the relationship (literary or real) between Lucilius and Seneca.[30]

But even so, there can be no doubt that it was the letters of Epicurus which constituted the most important point of reference for Seneca and so it is to them that I now turn. To modern readers, Epicurus' letters seem to fall into two categories. First, there are the long doctrinal summaries which we know through their inclusion in book 10 of Diogenes Laertius—not particularly 'epistolary' in their character, perhaps, but letters nonetheless in many of their features. And second, there are many short quotations from and allusions to other letters in a wide variety of ancient authors. And if these fragments are at all indicative of their original content, then many of these other letters were in fact much more obviously epistolary in character. Although direct evidence is lacking, there seems to be no reason to doubt that the letters we know about formed a single collection in antiquity, and I think the general consensus now is that many of these letters had orginally been written to cement the structure of the far-flung Epicurean intellectual community around the Aegean basin as well as to propagate doctrine. Seneca clearly knew many of these letters and, to judge from his citations from them in his own collection of letters, admired them.

Without launching into a major study of them—a separate job in itself and one eminently worth undertaking—one can still learn a great deal of importance from a survey of our surviving evidence in the standard collection of Epicurus' literary remains, Graziano Arrighetti's *Epicuro: Opere.*[31] From this we learn that, in addition

[30] See Wilson (2001) 186–7. See also the perceptive remarks of Graver (1996) 20–30. Robert Coleman (1974) esp. 287–8 comments briefly on the contrast between Seneca's and Cicero's corresondence.
[31] Arrighetti (1973).

to three lengthy letters preserved in book 10 of Diogenes Laertius' *Lives and Opinions of the Philosophers*, there was available to readers in antiquity a large and varied collection of correspondence. The letters preserved by Diogenes Laertius include a massive summary of Epicurus' natural philosophy, set out in a letter addressed to the Epicurean Herodotus. In the standard modern edition it runs to 22 pages of dense and difficult prose, a summary of many of the central themes of Epicurus' massive treatise *On Nature* and our best surviving source for most of this material. The letter to Pythocles is shorter (15 pages) and deals exclusively with 'meteorology', detailed questions about natural phenomena that had been subject to explanatory analysis by philosophers since the days of the Presocratics; this letter also gives us the best account of Epicurus' scientific method, with its notorious tolerance of 'multiple explanations'. Seneca's *Natural Questions* flirts with this un-Stoic approach as it surveys a similar range of phenomena in a highly literary style. Finally, the letter to Menoeceus puts the key points of Epicurean ethical doctrine into a sharply formulated five-page summary having a markedly protreptic and practical character.

Both Herodotus and Pythocles are known to have been recipients of other letters (49, 88–91 A, respectively) and it is therefore very possible that Menoeceus was too, although no direct evidence of this survives. Although the preserved letters have naturally been decisive in shaping our image of the Epicurean epistolary corpus, it is worth noting that they show some signs of having been normalized for inclusion in the work of Diogenes Laertius. First, they begin with the standard salutation of most Greek letters in antiquity, *chairein*, although Lucian tells us (40 A)[32] that Epicurus (like some other philosophers) favoured the salutation *hugiainein* ('be healthy', an allusion no doubt to moral health and well-being) in both the small number of 'more serious' letters (*spoudaioterai*) and in the ones addressed to his friends. And second, they lack the archon-dating formula which fixes the year of composition for so many of the fragmentary letters (50, 60, 62, 63, 67, 68, 74–7, 79, 80, 83, 84, 93, 94, 96, 105–13 A) that we can only conclude that it was a standard

---

[32] Lucian, *Pro Lapsu inter Salutandum* 6. On epistolary formulae see Trapp (2003) 34–5.

feature of the collection. Epicurean authors citing the letters (often preserved in Herculaneum papyri) preserve this information more often than other sources, but lest we conclude that this was a feature of some documentary archive accessible only to school insiders and absent from the published collection, it must be noted that Seneca (*Ep.* 18.9, fr. 83 A) cites in the same form: Epicurus 'certainly says this in those letters which he wrote to Polyaenus in the archonship of Charinus'.[33] In fact, it wouldn't be unreasonable to suspect that the collection of Epicurus letters was organized by recipient and date (though this can hardly be proved and we have no basis for guessing whether recipient or date was the primary organizational category).[34]

Other named recipients of the letters include quite a few lesser known characters[35] and several major Epicurean philosophers such as Hermarchus, Metrodorus, Polyaenus, Idomeneus, Timocrates, and Kolotes, his mother (though Pamela Gordon has convincingly argued that this letter was inauthentic),[36] and philosophical groups in Lampsacus, Mytilene, and elsewhere in Asia. The identity of the 'great men' to whom several letters were apparently written (100 A) can only be guessed at.

As to the themes of the letters, beyond the doctrinal summaries preserved by Diogenes Laertius, there is a great variety.[37] Many are certainly personal in focus; many deal with ethics and practical advice for living a good life, but in a less technical and formal tone than the letter to Menoeceus; others look like mini-treatises on moral

[33] Setaioli (1988) 176 concluded that the collection of letters consulted by Seneca was probably quite similar to the collections used within the Epicurean school itself. Setaioli argues convincingly that Seneca was not reliant on the bits of letters which may have been preserved in anthologies of Epicurean sayings. His general discussion runs from p. 171 to p. 248. See also Mutschmann (1915) esp. 324–7, 355 and Gigante (2000) esp. 32.

[34] Cf. Mutschmann (1915) 330.

[35] Athenaeus, Anaxarchus, Apelles, Aristoboulus, Dositheus, Purson (or Phurson), Eurylochus, Themista (possibly as part of a group), Leontion the courtesan, Leonteus, Mithres.

[36] Gordon (1996), ch. 3. The inauthenticity of the letter matters little for the question of how it was used and understood by readers of the collection. It is, at all events, quite likely that the letter was written and included in the collection before Seneca's time. It is also clear that inauthentic letters intended to reflect badly on Epicurus' morals circulated; see Gordon (1996) 81–2.

[37] Griffin (1992) 418 understates the variety in the collection, no doubt due to focusing only on the preserved letters.

themes with the author's own personal example often adduced for purposes of illustration or inspiration; quite a few deal with the organization and regulation of financial and other contributions to the upkeep of the school in Athens; quite a few mention other schools in a polemical spirit; his own imminent death (and his attitude to it) was the subject of several letters that became famous; theology and religious practice were also topics, as was physics. The range and variety of Epicurus' epistolary activity was sneered at by Plutarch (98 A). We hear of others' letters to Epicurus (71 A). Epicurus evidently boasted that his letters would suffice to make his recipient famous (Seneca, *Ep.* 21.3, 55 A), a common literary trope, and Seneca's wording in his description of a letter to Idomeneus (*Ep.* 22.5, 56 A) suggests that *Letter to Idomeneus* was a title or heading of some separately published letter, which must, then, have been of considerable length and ambition.

The picture which emerges helps us, I think, to understand some of the characteristics of Seneca's letters. He had available a large collection of formally published letters, some very personal and others highly technical. They were, for the most part, genuine letters, though the epistolary character of some mini-treatises in letter form was no doubt tenuous. The author talked about himself and his own experience a good deal, and frequently wove together that experience and detailed moral and ethical guidance. One important series of letters dwelt at length on the author's imminent death and its moral significance. Although the moral philosophy no doubt dominated, other themes were included. Polemic against other schools was a feature of the collection, though probably not a dominant feature.

All in all, with the exception of the actual historicity of the letters and the number of recipients, the letters of Epicurus must have been a very close model indeed for the collection of Seneca's letters as we now have it. It is particularly important to note that the blend of personal experience and moral advice (so often thought to be a distinctive characteristic of Seneca's letters), the combination of technical and non-technical letters, and especially the inclusion of mini-treatises alongside more plausibly epistolary compositions were all features of Seneca's most important generic model. And if the range of themes and compositional texture of Seneca's letters seem so similar to what we can reconstruct for his model, then we need,

I suggest, to begin from that fact in our interpretation of the literary and philosophical significance of the letters.

Philosophical readers of Seneca, then, have a lot to learn from an awareness of where they are situated in the genre, though I cannot undertake here the thorough study this issue obviously deserves. It might, however, be worth asking, just briefly, if one motivation for Seneca's apparent Epicurean 'sympathies' in the letters might not be generic rivalry rather than uncomplicated philosophical sympathy. Commentators have often worried, needlessly in my view, about the oddity of Seneca's openness to Epicurean influence. How could a Stoic welcome the enemy into his own camp? Is it perhaps because Lucilius needs to be 'converted'? Anything is possible, of course, but it is to my mind more likely that the entire theme of Epicureanism in the early letters is a tribute to a generic model and a deliberate indication of the target of Seneca's literary rivalry. Its philosophical significance may be much less than has been routinely assumed in the past.

There is one final issue I wish to raise, though briefly, in connection with the impact of form and generic models on our interpretation of Seneca's letters. As Griffin once said, perhaps a bit dismissively, Seneca's letters can sometimes seem to be 'dialogues with an epistolary veneer'.[38] This is not an unusual observation; I limit myself to citing Maurach on the point.[39] It is worth emphasizing that there is nothing in what we know of Epicurus' letters which suggests that this dialogical nature was among the traits Seneca took from his Epicurean model.[40] In fact, since the shared stylistic traits go beyond those which characterize the simple personal style of genuine letters and also include flamboyant rhetorical tropes, it is more plausible to see here the impact of Seneca's own dramatic and rhetorical experience.

To illustrate this point, let me draw attention briefly to one of Seneca's actual dialogues, the *De Tranquillitate Animi.* As is well

[38] Griffin (1992) 419. Note the corrective views of Wilson (1987) 109–10 and (2001). See too the brief remarks of Lana (1991) 271–4.

[39] Maurach (1970) 198–9.

[40] The closest thing to a model for this feature of Seneca's epistolary philosophy is perhaps the Socratic dialogue. There are particularly acute remarks about the similarities in Teichert (1990) 71–2.

known, Michel Foucault once described the opening of this address to Serenus as a 'letter'[41] rather than as a dialogue. Foucault, of course, often reacts somewhat impressionistically to his texts so this perception of the style and voice is ambivalent. On the one hand, he exhibits a freshness of perception often lost to those burdened with professional philological obligations. But on the other hand he runs the risk of projecting his personal enthusiasms into the texts he reads. But in this case Foucault's sensitivity as a reader has the upper hand, for the scrupulous Gregor Maurach comes to the same conclusion as a result of careful analysis. In *Seneca: Leben und Werk*,[42] he says:

Seneca stellt einen Brief des Adressaten Serenus voran und antwortet dann auf dessen Frage. Man kann diese Form als Vorform der späteren 'Epistulae Morales' betrachten...jedenfalls wird auf diese Weise das Epistular-Dialogische an Senecas Traktaten hier so deutlich betont wie sonst nirgends.

Seneca sets out first a letter of his addressee Serenus, and then answers his questions. One can regard this structure as an antecedent of the later 'Epistulae Morales'...in any case in this manner the epistolary-dialogic character of Seneca's treatises is emphasized nowhere else so clearly.

If critics as different in method and temperament as Maurach and Foucault detect the same stylistic trait, surely this should command our attention and our credence.

I do not think that this intensely dialogical style is typical of any of Seneca's literary models for writing epistolary philosophy.[43] It seems not to be a feature of Epicurus' letters; it is not typical of Platonic letters nor even really of the non-philosophical letters of Cicero.[44] No, this is almost certainly a personally distinctive feature of Seneca's own writing style.[45] Seneca comments in *Ep.* 38 that *sermo* is a particularly effective way to communicate philosophically—a truth

---

[41] See Foucault (2001*a*) 151; see the more cautious remarks at Foucault (2001*b*) 86.

[42] Maurach (1991) 123–4.

[43] Attention to the uniquely dialogical quality of the letters does not, of course, derogate from their epistolary character. The *dialogi* which most share this quality with the letters are precisely the ones least similar to the 'essay' genre to which the letters used to be assimilated. See Wilson (2001).

[44] See, however, Morrison in this volume on the 'Socratic' nature of Horace's *Epistles*.

[45] I speculate briefly about the impact of this on our interpretation of Seneca's philosophical work in ch. 12 of Inwood (2005) 346–9. See too the brief remarks of Schönegg (1999) 94.

made canonical by the success of Platonic dialogues. Seneca is not, I think, claiming here that the *sermo* style is a norm for letter-writing; rather, it is a feature of discourse which letter-writing makes more difficult because of the remoteness in time and space that it presupposes. Nevertheless, for his own reasons Seneca is unconsciously echoing what pseudo-Demetrius (*On Style* 223) reports from the editor of the corpus of Aristotelian letters, that a letter should be one half of a dialogue. It is a curious feature of Seneca's relationship to his tradition and to his models that he should conform so closely to their norms in a manner that is uniquely his own.

6

Letters of Recommendation and the Rhetoric of Praise

Roger Rees

1. THE CRITICAL 'I'

In an envelope addressed to the Governors of Cowbridge Grammar School, in Glamorgan, South Wales:

From M. P. Charlesworth, Esq., *President, Director of Classical Studies, St. John's College, Cambridge: Laurence Reader of Ancient History in the University of Cambridge.*

St. John's College,
Cambridge 25ᵀᴴ May 1938

Mr. J. Idwal Rees has informed me that he is applying for the post of Headmaster at Cowbridge Grammar School, and I am glad indeed to write on his behalf, because I believe him to be deserving of very serious consideration as a candidate. To his career at Swansea others can testify, and I would only speak here of the man as I have known him at this College and afterwards. During the two years that he was here (1931–33), he did a good deal of work for me and I saw him frequently. His essays always reached a good standard, showing thoughtfulness and care, and that gained him a Second Class in Part II of the Classical Tripos in 1933. In addition to his Classics, I would mention that he got his Blue for Rugby Football and for two years was a member of the Cambridge team. But in recommending a man for a high post, one must take account not only of his standing in work or games, but also of his character, and it is that which I should like to stress. During his time here he made a definite mark: he was modest and unassuming, but he was perfectly firm and definite, and he won the respect and admiration of his contemporaries in a way that was very striking. I believe that as a Headmaster he would not only be a sympathetic and helpful teacher, but that his strength of character and level-headedness would make people combine willingly under him and work well together, and so obtain the best possible for the School. I recommend him very strongly.

M. P. CHARLESWORTH

The opening salutation: 'This is me'; 'this is a letter'.
The background formula: 'I know him'; 'I like him'.
The petition: 'Consider appointing him—he will be good for you'.
The closing salutation: 'This is me'; 'this is a letter'.

Characteristic features of this letter of reference from nearly 70 years ago remain familiar: the structure is ancient;[1] the clichés of their time. The style confirms its vintage, with the formal pairing of substantives and adjectives, the fondness for abstractions and the contrastive 'but' and certain details of phrasing, such as 'I am glad indeed' or 'standing in work or games'. It is easy to identify both continuities and changes.

Few nowadays would share the ethical dissatisfaction with the letter of recommendation as a form of representation on behalf of another which troubled Epictetus. The philosopher tells of how he was asked for a letter of reference by a man who wanted an introduction to high society in Rome; but that Epictetus wrote ταπεινῶς (perhaps here, 'with humility') and the man rejected it (*Discourses* 1.9.27–34). Epictetus goes on to vaunt the merits of self-sufficiency over reliance on others, but the anecdote reveals the advantages of inflated and astute rhetoric, and at the same time, the discomfort it might inspire. But in our own very different situation, we might experience vaguely similar feelings. References take precious time to write and read, and they can be dull and untrustworthy. When Referee A writes to head of Appointment Committee B in support of Candidate C, today they may claim to write 'without reservation' but they certainly compose within distinctive and restrictive parameters which give the form a notoriously monotonous character. This can be further accentuated when A is urged to follow notes of guidance, which request comment on particular areas, or limit word count or even stipulate font size. The genre's notoriety affects A and B

---

[1] For structural formulae, Kim (1972) 7.

to different ends: A might strive to rise above the conventions of expression and argument to make their reference eye-catching; B meanwhile, oppressed by the genre's tendency to inflate and oversell, might interpret A's bland expression as tantamount to disapproval of C, or read any fulsome commendation as exaggerated and incredible, or suspect that brevity masks a lukewarm sentiment. C remains the candidate, but as B tries to read between the lines, on the line, at least in part, is the integrity of A. Precisely because letters of reference are intended to have practical effects—such as the appointment of C to the vacant position—and yet the implied strategies of writing and reading may be so at odds, the letters can have a mercurial quality.

Ancient letters of reference—*litterae commendaticiae* in Latin, συστατικὴ ἐπιστολή in Greek—survive in considerable number, from sources of two types, the documentary and, in particular, the literary. Documentary letters of reference survive in Greek and Latin, predominantly papyri.[2] More prolific are the literary letters of reference preserved and published in the collections of Cicero, Pliny, and Fronto.[3] All but one of the seventy-nine letters in Cicero's *Ad Familiares* 13 are *litterae commendaticiae*, dating mainly to 46–45 BC;[4] a few others appear elsewhere in the *Ad Familiares*.[5] In Pliny's letters there are over twenty *litterae commendaticiae*, including several addressed to Trajan himself.[6] A further sixteen survive from Fronto, to private individuals and to emperors.[7] This survival record provides a promising set for consideration of formulae and variations.[8]

Charlesworth's reference survived amongst the various papers discovered on Rees's death in 1991. That the letter was preserved in this private context seems entirely in line with regular modern practice, informed by sensibilities about modesty and confidentiality. No such inhibitions seem to have applied in antiquity, and in the case

---

[2] Kim (1972) and Cotton (1981); Cugusi (1983) 111–13; White (1986) 193–4.

[3] For a selection of texts with commentary, see Trapp (2003) 86–95, 236–45. From late antiquity letters of reference appear in the collections of Symmachus and Paulinus.

[4] The odd one out is 13.68. On problems of dating, Shackleton Bailey (1977) 22–4.

[5] Cotton (1985) 328.

[6] Sherwin White (1966) 44–5; Bérenger-Badel (2000) 165–71.

[7] Van den Hout (1999) 399; Bérenger-Badel (2000) 165–71.

[8] Cugusi (1983) 111–15.

of the literary collections lead to questions concerning publication and distribution. Genre and authorship clearly provide book 13 of Cicero's *Ad Familiares* with its coherence and integrity, and have led to the now orthodox conclusion that the book was prepared and published during Cicero's lifetime, perhaps even by Cicero himself.[9] The collation and publication of so many letters of recommendation from a two-year period is curious—especially as a few letters of recommendation from both before and after 46–45 BC survive else-where in the 16 books of the *Ad Familiares*. In 46–45 BC Cicero enjoyed celebrity but no power, and the collection and publication of his *litterae commendaticiae* from the time would serve to heighten appreciation of the influence he was still able to wield through social contacts and networks. No individual letter of reference could convey this impression, so perhaps the monotony of book 13 was a price worth paying in the service of the promotion—or commemoration, if publication was in fact posthumous—of Cicero as a widely-connected and respected patron.

Pliny provides an interesting contrast to Cicero. Rather than concentrating and publishing his references together in a single book, Pliny distributed them across several books, especially 1–4, 7, and 10.[10] This schema has a more measured effect, and with its regular and consistent reminders of Pliny's influence as a patron across a broad chronological stretch, is less suggestive of the crucial ambition we can detect in the concentrated collection of *Ad Famil-iares* 13. Our ignorance of the date and circumstances of publication of Fronto's letters leave us less well placed to calibrate the effect of their collectivity, but what remains clear is that compilation and publication of letters of reference could be instrumental to plays for power in a society structured around patronage.[11] Across *Ad Famil-iares* 13 many different individuals and even a few communities are promoted; but, of course, a constant—and indeed the *raison d'être* for the collection—is Cicero himself. The collection becomes a showcase to present Cicero as the master-patron, the influential agent whose judgement, esteem, and contacts make him the ideal man to court. The heightened sense of the author we get from a

[9] Cotton (1985) 328 n. 3.   [10] Sherwin White (1966) 46–50.
[11] Cugusi (1983) 257–8; Pavis d'Escurac (1992); Pani (1992) 149.

collection of letters of recommendation is reflected in paler form in details within certain examples. The following letter, obscure in details of date and context, is typical of Cicero:[12]

Cicero Curio Pro Cos.
Q. Pompeius, Sexti filius, multis et ueteribus causis necessitudinis mihi coniunctus est. is, cum antea meis commendationibus et rem et gratiam et auctoritatem suam tueri consuerit, nunc profecto, te prouinciam obtinente, meis litteris assequi debet, ut nemini se intellegat commendatiorem umquam fuisse. quamobrem a te maiorem in modum peto ut, cum omnes meos aeque ac tuos obseruare, pro nostra necessitudine, debeas hunc in primis ita in tuam fidem recipias, ut ipse intellegat, nullam rem sibi maiori usui aut ornamento quam meam commendationem esse potuisse. uale.   (*Fam.* 13.49)

Cicero to the proconsul Curius
Quintus Pompeius, the son of Sextus, has been attached to me for many long-standing reasons of *necessitudo*. As in the past it is in my recommendations that he has been used to finding support for his fortunes, reputation and influence, now indeed, when you are in charge of the province, he ought to benefit from my letter so far as to understand he has never been more highly recommended to anyone. For this reason I make request of you to an unusual degree, since because of our *necessitudo* you ought to treat my friends equally as yours, that you so receive him especially in your care, that he understands that nothing could have been of more use or distinction to him than my recommendation. Farewell.

The opening salutation: 'This is me'; 'this is a letter'.
The background formula: 'He is bound to me by *necessitudo*'.
The petition: 'Consider receiving him—you are bound to me by *necessitudo*'.
The closing salutation: 'This is me'; 'this is a letter'.

Clearly, the circumstances are not very like those which Charlesworth faced in 1938; for a start, in 1938 there was a vacancy and applications, complete with letters of reference, had been invited, a procedure with little in the way of an ancient equivalent. In this case rather, Cicero appears to have been prompted to write on behalf of Pompeius because Curius was now governor of the province—that is, not only was there not a vacancy for a position, but the original

---

[12] Shackleton Bailey (1977) 456.

motivation for the letter was the recipient, not the ultimate subject of
the petition. Accordingly, the argument is different; where Charlesworth's petition is based upon his evaluation of the candidate's
capacity to fill the vacancy, Cicero hardly discusses Pompeius at all.
Pompeius is identified clearly (as his father's son), but he is barely
characterized and the letter gets its force from the relationship
between Cicero and Curius. By the tie of *necessitudo* between them,
Cicero and Curius have obligations and responsibilities to each other
which this letter is designed to invoke. That invocation is made more
urgent by the insistence that Cicero himself respects the protocols of
necessitudo—a point brought home by the occurrence of the word in
respect of Cicero's relationship with Pompeius. Typical of Cicero too
is this letter's closing request that Pompeius be made aware of the
good effects of Cicero's petition—a common conceit which reveals
Cicero's concern to be seen to be influential.[13]

The paramount importance of the identity and influence of the
writer to the letter's leverage can be seen in many of the shorter
surviving examples. Cicero wrote the following letter for the sculptor
Avianus Evander sometime before 46:[14]

Cicero Memmio suo
C. Auiano Euandro, qui habitat in tuo sacrario, et ipso multum utor, et
patrono eius M. Aemilio familiarissime. peto igitur a te in maiorem modum,
quod sine tua molestia fiat, ut ei de habitatione accommmodes. nam propter
opera instituta multa multorum subitum est ei remigrare Kal. Quint. impe-
dior uerecundia ne te pluribus uerbis rogem; neque tamen dubito, quin, si
tua nihil aut non multum intersit, eo sis animo quo ego essem, si quid tu me
rogares. mihi certe gratissimum feceris.   (*Fam.* 13.2)

Cicero to his friend Memmius.
I am rather close to C. Avianus Evander, who is living in your family shrine,
and am very close to his patron M. Aemilius. Therefore, with unusual force,
I ask of you that without it being a nuisance to you, you sort him out
regarding his residence. For, he has so many works commissioned for
numerous people, it would be a scramble for him to return home on July
1st. Shyness prevents me from making this request of you at greater length,
yet I have no doubt that if it is all the same to you, you will be of the same

13 Cf. *Fam.* 13.20, 25–6, 34–6, 38–9, 45–6, 58–9, 71.
14 Shackleton Bailey (1977) 456.

mind as I would be if you were making some request of me. Certainly you will have done me a very great favour.

The opening salutation: 'This is me'; 'this is a letter'.
The background formula: 'He is bound to me by *familiaritas*'.
The petition: 'Help him—I would do the same for you. I will be grateful'.

The letter's simple request is hardly onerous, but in his argument Cicero relies on himself and his own relationship with Memmius rather than on Avianus. This is a clear example of the subordinate position characterization of the subject of a letter of recommendation would hold in the attempt to persuade the recipient. In this case, the inflected echoes of *te rogem* in *tu me rogares* highlight the parallel obligations Cicero and Memmius share and which exert their own persuasive force over Memmius. Whether this letter is structured to imply that Avianus *must* be a worthy character to be recommended by Cicero, or simply that his worth is not significant in the negotiation that is being pressed, it is Cicero who is most prominent. This strategy underpins a great number of surviving letters, from documentary and literary sources, where the subject is sometimes not characterized beyond a brief mention of their name and their relationship to the writer, and instead the petition made on the subject's behalf gets its persuasive force from the relationship between the author and the recipient.[15]

A curious, perhaps extreme, variant of this technique seems to have occurred in a letter to Pompeius Falco from Pliny, now lost, but mentioned in a sequel which does survive.[16]

C. Plinius Falconi suo s.
minus miraberis me tam instanter petisse, ut in amicum meum conferres tribunatum, cum scieris quis ille qualisque. possum autem iam tibi et nomen indicare et describere ipsum postquam polliceris. est Cornelius Minicianus ...   (*Letters* 7.22.1)

C. Pliny to his friend Falco, greetings.
You will be less surprised that I asked you so relentlessly to grant the tribunate on my friend when you learn who he is and what he is like. Now you have promised, I can give you his name and describe him to you. He is Cornelius Minicianus ...

---

[15] Kim (1972) 49–53.
[16] I am assuming here that 7.22 follows up an earlier letter, but it is possible that the request to Falco was made by word of mouth.

It is difficult to determine Pliny's purpose in the original letter, but
it might be that he deliberately withheld Cornelius' name as a test of
Falco's faith in him; and now that Falco had passed that test by
granting the tribunate, Cornelius' identity could be revealed in this
subsequent letter.[17] What is decisively illustrated by this example is
the minor role the identity and qualities of the subject could have in
an ancient letter of recommendation, subordinate to the force the
author could exert through their own influence. Nowadays length
might vaguely be thought an indicator of the seriousness and sincerity of a reference, but the marked brevity of many ancient letters
which attempt no characterization of their subject certainly did not
disqualify them from inclusion in the published collection—in fact, a
number of such short letters better serves to signify the extent and
variety of the author's influence. When the collectivity of surviving
literary letters of recommendation serves to promote the author and
when, in many individual examples, the author promotes the subject
by giving greater prominence to himself, the irony emerges that the
letter of recommendation—a form we might expect to serve the
ambitions of others—was at least as much about the promotion of
the author as it was about the subject. The author is critical.[18]

2. THE *AMICITIA* TRIANGLE

More persuasive as an argument than the bald assertion of the
relationship between the author and the subject, or between the
author and the recipient, was the integration of all three parties.[19]
In the following example, Cicero offers to Caesius some details of the
character of his subject Messenius, but the letter gets its essential
purchase by linking the three of them:

M. Cicero P. Caesio S. D.
P. Messienum, equitem Romanum omnibus rebus ornatum meumque
perfamiliarem, tibi commendo ea commendatione, quae potest esse

[17] Sherwin White (1966) 429–30 for Cornelius' career.
[18] See Fitzgerald in this volume for discussion of the manipulation of relationships
in Pliny's letters.
[19] See Fitzgerald in this volume for three-way relationships.

diligentissima: peto a te et pro nostra et pro paterna amicitia, ut eum in
tuam fidem recipias eiusque rem famamque tueare: uirum bonum tuaque
amicitia dignum tibi adiunxeris mihique gratissimum feceris. (*Fami.*
13.51)

Cicero greets Caesius
I recommend to you Publius Messenius, a Roman knight with all the
accomplishments and my close friend; I do so with as pressing a commendation as can be. I ask this of you for our own friendship and our fathers',
that you may welcome him into your trust and look out for his affairs and
reputation: you will join to yourself a good man and one deserving of your
friendship; and you will be doing me a great favour.

The opening salutation: 'This is me'; 'this is a letter'.
The background formula: 'He is a good man and is bound to me by
familiaritas'.
The petition: 'Consider receiving him—you are bound to me by
amicitia; he will become your *amicus*'.

In letters of recommendation, Cicero most frequently specifies the
relationships of *amicitia, hospitium, familiaritas,* and *necessitudo*.[20] In
this example Cicero employs his typical strategy of invoking the relationships to triangulate the inherent obligations. Messenius is clearly
deemed by Cicero to have merits, although they are barely touched
upon; instead the attempt at triangulation makes it difficult for Caesius
to resist, for to do so would be to reject Cicero's *amicitia* and to deny
himself the possibility of a new friendship. Social triangulation is made
to look logical and cogent by repeated patterns of the vocabulary of
personal relationships. Particularly common too is the coercive assertion
that the subject, by definition a friend of the author, will prove to be
deserving of the friendship of the recipient, expressed in the phrase
amicitia dignus (and variants).[21] This formula completes the triangle
of *amicitia*, a contract of reciprocal obligations; insidiously too, *dignus*
implies an element of meritocratic discretion in the commendation of
the subject (Rees was said by Charlesworth to be 'deserving of very
serious consideration as a candidate'). Thus while the letter extends
and consolidates the relationships which define the specific and broader
interests of author, addressee, and subject it affects an ethical integrity
which it fails to substantiate.[22]

[20] Kim (1972) 50.   [21] See (e.g.) *Fam.* 13.3, 6a.4, 13, 17.3, 67.2, 78.2.
[22] For the strategy, see Hoffer (1999) 181–2, 193.

Pliny too uses *amicitia* triangulation as a means to persuade, but the unusual efficacy of this strategy is best illustrated in two letters from Fronto.[23] In the prefatory sentences to his letter recommending Sulpicius Cornelianus to Claudius Severus, Fronto identifies the origins of recommendation in the introduction of one friend to another—*commendandi mos initio dicitur benivolentia ortus cum suum quisque amicum ali amico suo demonstratum conciliatumque vellet* ('the custom of recommendation is said to have first arisen from goodwill, when everybody wanted his friend to be introduced to and united with another friend', *Ad Amicos* 1.1).[24] This principle can even be seen to underlie the ambition of a letter of recommendation from Fronto to a man with whom he seems to have had no direct contact before:

Fronto Passieno Rufo salutem.
Aemilius Pius cum studiorum elegantia tum morum eximia probitate mihi carus est. commendo eum tibi, frater. nec ignoro nullum adusque inter nos mutuo scriptitantium usum fuisse, quamquam ego te optimum uirum bonarumque artium sectatorem communium amicorum fama cognossem, et tu fortasse aliquid de me secundi rumoris acceperis. sed nullum pulchrius uinculum amicitiae copulandae reperire potui quam adulescentis optimi conciliandi tibi occasionem. ama eum, oro te, cum ipsius causa hoc peto tum mea quoque, nam me etiam magis amabis, si cum Pio familiarius egeris. nouit enim Pius nostra omnia et in primis quam cupidissimus sim amicitiarum quom eiusmodi uiris, qualis tu es, copulandarum. (*Ad Amicos* 1.8; 2.190 Haines)

Fronto greets Passienus Rufus
Aemilius Pius is dear to me for his refined tastes and his outstanding integrity. I commend him to you, brother. I am not unaware that we have not been correspondents until now, although I have known from the opinions of mutual friends that you are an excellent man and a follower of the noble arts—perhaps you have heard some favourable report about me. But I could discover no finer bond to cement a friendship than the chance to introduce to you an excellent young man. Love him, I beg you. I ask this for his sake and for mine too—for you will love me if you become closer to Pius. Pius knows my every wish and especially how much I wish to join in friendship with men such as yourself.

[23] For sterling examples in Pliny, see *Letters* 2.13.10, 3.2.4, 4.15.2, 7.22, 7.31; in Fronto, see *Ad Amicos* 1.3, 1.9, 2.6.
[24] Cugusi (1983) 247.

Characteristically, to configure mutual obligations, the letter urges its petition through echoes of key terminology and associated cognates: Pius and Passienus are *optimus*; the *studia* of one mirror the *artes* of the other; the *fama* about Passienus might match the *rumor* about Fronto; and Fronto and Pius are united by the lexis of *amicitia* (*ama eum, me amabis*). That this elaborate series coordinates all three to triangulate *amicitia* is extraordinary because at the time of writing neither Fronto nor Aemilius knew Passienus; the letter's ambition is clearly to introduce both the author and the subject to the recipient, and the fact that it seeks to do so by triangulating *amicitia* indicates the efficacy of the strategy.

3. THE RHETORIC OF PRAISE

Alignment of interests and obligations through triangulation can be seen throughout surviving letters of recommendation and identify them as our best textual evidence for the processes of Roman patronage in action. As a social system, patronage extended throughout private and public areas of human activity, and in the vast majority of cases in our sources was concerned with men rather than women.[25] The following letter from Pliny demonstrates the monopoly of male power in the organization of marriage. Triangulation is Pliny's strategy for recommendation, but the letter is quoted in full to give the sense of the expansive description of the subject.

C. Plinius Iunio Maurico suo s.
(1) petis ut fratris tui filiae prospiciam maritum; quod merito mihi potissimum iniungis. scis enim quanto opere summum illum uirum suspexerim dilexerimque, quibus ille adulescentiam meam exhortationibus fouerit, quibus etiam laudibus ut laudandus uiderer effecerit. (2) nihil est quod a te mandari mihi aut maius aut gratius, nihil quod honestius a me suscipi possit, quam ut eligam iuuenem, ex quo nasci nepotes Aruleno Rustico deceat. (3) qui quidem diu quaerendus fuisset, nisi paratus et quasi prouisus esset Minicius Acilianus, qui me ut iuuenis iuvenem—est enim minor pauculis annis—familiarissime diligit, reueretur ut senem. (4) nam ita formari a me et institui cupit, ut ego a uobis solebam. patria est ei Brixia, ex illa nostra Italia

[25] Hoffer (1999) 132–3.

quae multum adhuc uerecundiae frugalitatis, atque etiam rusticitatis anti-
quae, retinet ac seruat. (5) pater Minicius Macrinus, equestris ordinis
princeps, quia nihil altius uoluit; allectus enim a Diuo Vespasiano inter
praetorios honestam quietem huic nostrae—ambitioni dicam an digni-
tati?—constantissime praetulit. (6) habet auiam maternam Serranam Procu-
lam e municipio Patauio. nosti loci mores: Serrana tamen Patauinis quoque
seueritatis exemplum est. contigit et auunculus ei P. Acilius grauitate prudentia fide prope singulari. in summa nihil erit in domo tota, quod non tibi
tamquam in tua placeat. (7) Aciliano uero ipsi plurimum uigoris industriae,
quamquam in maxima uerecundia. quaesturam tribunatum praeturam hon-
estissime percucurrit, ac iam pro se tibi necessitatem ambiendi remisit. (8) est
illi facies liberalis, multo sanguine multo rubore suffusa, est ingenua totius
corporis pulchritudo et quidam senatorius decor. quae ego nequaquam arbitror neglegenda; debet enim hoc castitati puellarum quasi praemium dari. (9)
nescio an adiciam esse patri eius amplas facultates. nam cum imaginor uos
quibus quaerimus generum, silendum de facultatibus puto; cum publicos
mores atque etiam leges civitatis intueor, quae uel in primis census hominum
spectandos arbitrantur, ne id quidem praetereundum uidetur. et sane de
posteris et his pluribus cogitanti, hic quoque in condicionibus deligendis
ponendus est calculus. (10) tu fortasse me putes indulsisse amori meo,
supraque ista quam res patitur sustulisse. at ego fide mea spondeo futurum
ut omnia longe ampliora quam a me praedicantur inuenias. diligo quidem
adulescentem ardentissime sicut meretur; sed hoc ipsum amantis est, non
onerare eum laudibus. uale.   (*Letters* 1.14)

C. Pliny greets his friend Iunius Mauricus

You ask me to look out for a husband for your brother's daughter, a duty you
very rightly impose on me, for you know how much I have respected and
admired him, the encouragement with which he supported me when I was a
young man, and the praise with which he made me aspire to be praised. No
order from you could be greater or more pleasing for me, no undertaking
more honourable, than to choose a young man to be worthy father to the
grandchildren of Arulenus Rusticus. Indeed, the search for the man would
have been very long had not Minicius Acilianus been at hand and, you might
even say, expected. As one young man does another (he is younger by a few
years) he loves me most warmly, and respects me as an elder. For he wishes
to be shaped and taught by me, as I was by you and your brother. His home
is Brescia from our part of Italy which still retains and preserves much
modesty, frugality and ancient rusticity. His father Minicius Macrinus was
the leading knight, because he aspired no higher; when chosen for the
Praetorians by the deified Vespasian, he determinedly preferred his honest
and quiet lifestyle to our ambitions—or should I say to our rank. His

maternal grandmother is Serrana Procula from the town of Patavium—you know the customs of the place, but Serrana is a model of austerity even to the Patavians. His uncle, Publius Acilius is of almost unique dignity, wisdom and integrity. In sum there is nothing in his whole household which you would not be pleased to find in your own.

In Acilianus himself there is a great deal of energy and industry, although with greatest modesty. With the greatest honesty he held the quaestorship, the tribunate and the praetorship, thus removing the need for you to canvas for him. His appearance is handsome, flushed with plenty of high colour; his overall good looks are natural, with a certain senatorial grace. (I think these points should not be neglected, as if a due reward for a girl's innocence.) I don't know whether I should add his father's considerable means, for when I picture you and your brother, for whom we are looking for a son-in-law, I think I should be silent about finances; but when I see public conventions and even the country's laws which consider a man's wealth to be of first importance, it seems not even that should be passed over. For sure, when considering the many future generations, finances must be counted amongst the selection criteria.

Perhaps you think I have indulged my love for him and gone further than the facts permit; but I promise on my honour that you will find the reality better by far than my words. Indeed I love the young man most warmly, as he deserves; but it is a mark of love not to overload him with praise. Goodbye.

The letter has a very studied air. Pliny is careful to delineate the various relationships he discusses with precise phrasing and repeated vocabulary: he is to Acilianus what the brothers were to him, an idea expressed in the poised *nam ita...a uobis solebam* (1.14.4) and the echoes of the letter's opening themes of adolescence, love, merit, and praise (*merito, dilexerim, adulescentiam, laudibus, laudandus,* 1) at its close (*diligo, adulescentem, meretur, laudibus,* 10). Structured in this way, the recommendation is difficult for Junius Mauricus to resist; to reject Acilianus is to reject Pliny, and to reject Pliny is to abandon the principles the brothers have kept at the centre of their own lives. The letter is then not only a commendation of Acilianus but also a conspicuous affirmation of the aristocratic value-system to which all the parties subscribe.[26]

These sentences which align the personalities by echoing key vocabulary surround a section in which the subject, Acilianus, is

[26] Hoffer (1999) 177–93.

characterized in unusual detail. Characterization of the subject is a
central feature of modern recommendations—in 1938, for example,
Charlesworth devoted a considerable section of his recommendation
of Rees to ethical description. But whereas we have noted above that
the character of the subject of a typical Ciceronian or documentary
litterae commendaticiae is relatively unimportant in the petition, distinctly subordinate to that of the author in the construction of the
argument, in Pliny's recommendation of Acilianus, the elaborate dis-
closure of details of Acilianus' native town, his father, grandmother
and uncle, his qualities, career to date, appearance and income go far
beyond the regularly bald statement of the subject's relationship to the
author.[27] Pliny's characterization of Acilianus corresponds to the
schema which appears in essentially consistent form in treatises on
epideictic oratory from the late Republic and Empire. The anonymous
Ad Herennium says that praise in epideictic can be of external affairs
(such as descent, education, wealth, power, titles, citizenship, and
friendships), physique (such as agility, strength, and beauty) and
character (specifying wisdom, justice, courage, and modesty) (*Ad
Her.* 3.10–14). In the *De Oratore*, Cicero lists family, money, intimates,
friends, wealth, health, appearance, strength, intellect, and other features, of body or otherwise (2.46) and modifies this later with a
distinction between the benefits bestowed by nature and fortune and
the genuinely praiseworthy exercise of virtues such as clemency, justice, kindness, honesty, and bravery (2.342–3). The mind, the body, and
external affairs (including family, money, and homeland) are the three
areas for praise in the *De Inventione* (2.177). A similar tripartite
division of subjects for praise also features in his *Partitiones Oratoriae*
(74). While recommending all three subjects, Quintilian urges the
distinction between praise of the subject's mind and the categories of
body or external matters; he also suggests a broadly chronological
arrangement, dealing first with subject matter antedating the subject,
such as their homeland and parentage (*Instit. Orat.* 3.7.10).[28]

Pliny's recommendation of Acilianus follows the contours of this
panegyrical schema in spirit and in detail. And although we might

---

[27] Pani (1992) 146–8; Bérenger-Badel (2000) 172–9.
[28] This schema is also proposed by Greek writers, including the late antique
Menander Rhetor, *Basilikos Logos* 369–70; Theon 2.110–11.

expect this letter of recommendation above all others to include a character sketch of its subject because it proposes a man as a candidate for marriage, it is not unique for its use of epideictic conventions. In the letter quoted in part above to Pompeius Falco, after Pliny disclosed the name of the subject of his earlier, anonymous, recommendation, he launched into a characterization of Cornelius Minicianus as follows:

... est Cornelius Minicianus, ornamentum regionis meae seu dignitate seu moribus. natus splendide abundat facultatibus, amat studia ut solent pauperes. idem rectissimus iudex, fortissimus aduocatus, amicus fidelissimus. accepisse te beneficium credes, cum propius inspexeris hominem omnibus honoribus, omnibus titulis—nihil uolo elatius de modestissimo uiro dicere—parem. uale. (*Letters* 7.22.2–3)

... he is Cornelius Minicianus, by rank and habits the pride of my region. Of illustrious birth, he has abundant means, [but] loves to apply himself as poor people do. Likewise, he is the most proper judge, the bravest advocate, the most loyal friend. You will think you have received a benefit when at closer quarters you have seen the man equal to all his honours, all his titles—I want to say nothing more exalting about a most modest man. Goodbye.

As he touches briefly on his subject's birthplace, wealth, and interests before the elaborate tricolon with superlatives to quantify his justice, bravery, and loyalty, Pliny here rehearses the main subjects of panegyrical oratory, as recommended in contemporary treatises. Less pronounced but comparably epideictic in its inspiration is the characterization of Sextus Erucius in *Letters* 2.9.3–4, where Pliny catalogues his subject's moral qualities in the superlative before detailing those of his father and uncle. Characterization of Voconius Romanus (2.13.4–10) begins with his father and mother, touches on his appearance and devotes a series of adjectives to his intellectual qualities. The short recommendation of Maturus Arrianus begins with his birthplace, mentions his means in decorous *praeteritio*, and then catalogues his virtues—*castitas, iustitia, grauitas, prudentia, fides, ueritas*, and *intellegentia* (3.2). Pliny's letters of recommendation to Trajan in book 10 tend to be direct and clipped in comparison to these more elaborate appeals.[29] Much of Fronto's most expansive

---

[29] 10.10, 11, 12, 26, 85, 86a, 86b, 87, 94, 104, 106.

letter of recommendation to an emperor is taken up with an apologetic explanation of the tight financial circumstances of the subject, Gavius Clarus, but a typically panegyrical section details his various virtues (*Ad Verum Imp.* 2.7.6).

What can be seen, then, in the letters of recommendation of Pliny and Fronto is considerable continuity in the form from Cicero's *Ad Familiares*, but also a tendency towards amplification of the character of the subject.[30] Epideictic rhetoric provided the methods for such amplification, and although there persisted in Roman society some resistance to epideictic—or display oratory—as a Greek cultural phenomenon rarely suited to the *Realien* of Roman life, the letter of recommendation seems to have constituted something of an exception.[31] The letter of recommendation aimed to fulfil a particular function in the smooth operation of the networks of patronage in Roman society, and so the importation of panegyrical method, specifically developed to articulate and urge favourable disposition, could have very useful application. Pliny and Fronto, both orators, of course, and both authors of imperial panegyric, were ideally placed to use the rhetoric of praise in their letters of recommendation.

4. ANXIETY AS A RHETORICAL POSE

When he says, 'in recommending a man for a high post . . .' Charlesworth signals the direction of his argument and reveals his sharp awareness of the discourse in which he is involved. Self-consciousness seems something of a burden to Cicero, Pliny, and Fronto in their letters of recommendation. In his letter to Acilius Glabrio recommending Archagathus and Philo, Cicero dwells introspectively for a minute, *sed uereor, ne, quia complures tibi praecipue commendo, exaequare uidear ambitione quadam commendationes meas* ('But I fear that because I recommend many people to you in special terms, I may seem to be putting all my recommendations on a level by some

---

[30] The breakdown of several letters of recommendation from Cicero, Pliny, and Fronto by Plantera (1977–8) 10–15 illustrates how the latter two authors amplify passages on their subject's character.

[31] Cic. *De Or.* 2.341, Quint. *Inst.* 3.7.1–2.

ambition of mine', *Fam.* 13.32.1).[32] When Cicero returns to his current petition and remarks that it is *in maiorem modum* ('with unusual urgency', 13.32.2) it becomes apparent that the opening apologetic is in fact a protestation intended to disarm any diffidence or indifference from Acilius. Cicero was aware of the formulaic nature of letters of recommendation (an impression that is heightened by the collectivity of book 13 of *Ad Familiares*);[33] and by admitting that formulaic nature and representing it as a cause of anxiety, he could insist with greater conviction on the sincerity of his own letters. Thus the anxious note of awareness of form serves a useful rhetorical purpose.

Awareness of rhetorical reputation and commonplaces features prominently in the letters of recommendation of Pliny and Fronto too, and in their different ways, it was transformed into a rhetorical stance in the service of their argument. Later in the letter in which he identified the practice of the introduction of friends as the origin of the custom of recommendation, Fronto observes that recommendations in the form of character witnesses had become established features of court hearings. Fronto notes in conclusion *item istae commendantium litterae laudationis munere fungi uisae sunt* ('likewise, these letters of recommendation seem to fulfil the task of a panegyric', *Ad Amicos* 1.1.1). Pliny has no such explicit comment about the relationship between letters of recommendation and panegyric, but in the closing sentence of *Letters* 1.14, quoted above, his concern not to overload Acilianus with praise (*onerare laudibus*) reveals his awareness of the panegyrical nature of the preceding characterization.[34] Fronto's preface contributes to the economy of the letter's rhetoric as it explains and therefore normalizes panegyrical elements in recommendation; thus when Fronto moves onto the character of Sulpicius Cornelianus, he has cleared the way to treat him in a panegyrical manner without need for apology or further justification. Fronto squarely confronts the transition from

---

[32] Shackleton Bailey (1977) 452.

[33] e.g. *Fam.* 13.15.3; 27.1; 35.2; Keyes (1935) 42–4; Plantera (1977–8) 8; Cotton (1985); for some recurrent phrases in Cicero's recommendations, Cugusi (1983) 99–100.

[34] Cf. 2.9.3, where Pliny combines the concepts of praise and merit *omni denique laude dignissimum* ('in sum, most worthy of all praise').

his preface to the characterization *sed ut dixi ueteris instituti exemplo
necessarium meum laudare apud te ausus sum* ('but as I said, following the example of traditional practice, I have dared to praise my
close friend before you', *Ad Amicos* 1.1.2). This justification suggests a
degree of disquiet in Fronto, situated between his wish to employ
panegyrical method to best represent his subject and his realization
that any such practice requires some explanation. In response to the
problems raised by this culture of praise within recommendation
Pliny takes a more unembarrassed stand. It is not clear if his letter to
Septicius refers to recommendations in letter form rather than in
conversation, but the sentiment remains unaffected:

C. Plinius Septicio suo s.
(1) ais quosdam apud te reprehendisse, tamquam amicos meos ex omni
occasione ultra modum laudem. (2) agnosco crimen, amplector etiam. quid
enim honestius culpa benignitatis? qui sunt tamen isti, qui amicos meos
melius norint? sed, ut norint, quid inuident mihi felicissimo errore? ut enim
non sint tales quales a me praedicantur, ego tamen beatus quod mihi
uidentur. (3) igitur ad alios hanc sinistram diligentiam conferant; nec sunt
parum multi, qui carpere amicos suos iudicium uocant. mihi numquam
persuadebunt ut meos amari a me nimium putem. uale.   (*Letters* 7.28)

C. Pliny to his friend Septicius
You say certain people reprimand me in your presence as if I praise my
friends beyond measure at every opportunity. I acknowledge the charge, I
welcome it even, for what is more honourable than the blame for being
kind? But who are these people who know my friends better than I? And, just
as they know, why do they grudge me my most delightful delusion? For if my
friends are not as I declare them, still I am lucky that they seem so to me. So
let these people direct their misplaced good-intentions to others; there are
plenty of people who call it discretion to criticize their friends. They will
never persuade me that I love my friends too much. Goodbye.

The letter strikes a piously self-regarding note even in isolation; in
the published context where it features in a collection which includes
several letters of recommendation which adopt panegyrical rhetoric
as a means to promote the subject, the letter constitutes a guide on
how to read Pliny's recommendations. By the reign of Trajan, it
seems, panegyrical discourse commanded little trust of its audience;
when Pliny himself labours to insist on the sincerity of his speech of
praise to Trajan, the audience might realize that inflated statements

of flattery actually signal heartfelt and diametrically opposed senti-ment.[35] The orator or (in the case of letters of recommendation) the author is in a bind when the genre is discredited. One way to assert the sincerity of claims which others might assume are inflated is to admit to the general problem of inflation in the genre only then to deny it in one's own case (as Pliny does in his *Panegyricus*); or to admit to it in an endearing display of sincerely held passion (as Pliny does in *Letters* 7.28).[36] Either way, if the anxiety is acknowledged, it can be confronted and transformed to a weapon in the author's armoury.

5. CONCLUSION

The inclusion in the *Τύποι 'Επιστολικοί* of pseudo-Demetrius of the letter of reference or recommendation suggests it was a well-known form in antiquity.[37] The function of the letter is said to be to introduce the subject and recipient to each other whilst weaving in praise (ἔπαινον συγκαταπλέκοντες) and to make them better acquainted; pseudo-Demetrius then gives a brief example, in which the subject is said to be judged, trusted, and loved by the writer and worthy of due reception by the recipient; the recipient will not regret this and will indeed praise the subject to others in future, such are the services they will provide. The date of pseudo-Demetrius and his intended reader-ship are notorious problems, but the text highlights some of the issues which informed the collected letters of recommendation from Cicero to Fronto:[38] networks of personal relationships provide the frame-work, and indeed will be extended, to the benefit of all parties, if the letter is successful; the author is to emphasize their own discretion in

---

[35] e.g. Pliny, *Pan.* 3.4; Bartsch (1994) 148–66.

[36] See Morello in this volume for discussion of the instruction in social-literary inclusiveness that this letter about praise urges. Pliny's attitude to *inuidia*, and the marked difference in this respect from Cicero that Morello highlights might be closely related to an increase in, and increased awareness of, praise discourse in Roman (literary) culture.

[37] Text in Weichert (1910) 3–4; discussions in Keyes (1935), Kim (1972), Plantera (1977–8) 6–7, Trapp (2003) 45.

[38] Weichert (1910) xviii–xx.

offering their evaluation of the subject; and their statements about the subject's merit can be interwoven with praise. All these feature in the letters of our authors, where they are complicated by the factors of literary awareness and of collectivity itself. The naivety we might identify in pseudo-Demetrius' template is hardly apparent in Cicero, Pliny, and Fronto, each of whom in different ways considers the problematic reputation and reliability of the genre. For Cicero the formulaic nature of the letter might be held to compromise its sincerity; and for Pliny and Fronto, the increased influence of epideictic method in the letters of recommendation increased anxiety by the attendant issue of the trustworthiness of praise-discourse. That their solutions to these problems were to address them directly as a disarming strategy of denial, and then to preserve the letters for later readers, reveals their ambition to present themselves as powerful literary and social patrons.

The culture of confidentiality which prevailed when Charlesworth wrote his letter of recommendation for Idwal Rees, and the ideology of meritocratic promotion on which Charlesworth insists together signal profound differences between ancient and modern society; at the same time, the rhetoric of his letter has many continuities with the past. Patronage, it seems, was alive and well. My grandfather got the job.[39]

[39] For their suggestions and improvements, my thanks to audiences at Manchester and Edinburgh, the anonymous readers, and the editors.

7

Confidence, *Inuidia*, and Pliny's Epistolary Curriculum

Ruth Morello

Stanley Hoffer's book on Pliny the Younger, the first major study in English for some years, set the agenda for those interested in how letters work by examining the 'anxieties' of Pliny and the ways in which his letters reveal or attempt to conceal them. As Hoffer says, 'the leading trait in Pliny's epistolary self-portrait is his confidence', but that confidence masks anxieties about his status, reputation, career, and longed-for literary immortality.[1] Since then, Greg Woolf has re-examined the anxieties of Roman *readers*; in the light of the now familiar assertion that 'a common literary culture had the potential to bind together as an elite group those who were confident readers of this esoteric discourse', he notes the sense of cultural distance and exclusion which Latin literature might generate in the less confident reader.[2] He argues, however, that Pliny, unlike, say, Statius, deliberately minimizes the elements which trigger that anxiety of exclusion:

Reading Latin literary texts was clearly hard work, and meant to be. Even when an author deliberately adopted a more inclusive style, as the Younger Pliny did in his letters, that effect is achieved partly by ostentatious abstention from the devices of routine exclusion, in order to signal a (temporary and voluntary) departure from the norm.

---

[1] Hoffer (1999) 1.   [2] Woolf (2003) 211–12.

This suggestion—which itself invokes a scholarly insider's easy familiarity with 'the devices of routine exclusion'—depends partly on the relative rarity in Pliny of the challenging literary/mytho-logical/historical allusions which are the pheromones, as it were, whereby one educated polymath might catch the interest of another but repel those unlike himself. Woolf's observation that Pliny has an unusually inclusive style is amply borne out by the experiences of anyone who has taught the letters of both Pliny and his model Cicero to undergraduates: even the numerous students who dislike Pliny himself still find his letters more 'accessible' than those of his model. Woolf's approach, however, is not unproblematic, since letters are not expected to exclude as much as other literary production might; as a more informal genre, they demand a simpler register than the Silver epic which Woolf rather unfairly sets up in contrast to them. The accessibility or inclusiveness of Pliny's letters (if that is under-stood to mean a restraint in allusion) is also partly illusory, and there is still plenty in Pliny's letters that an 'undereducated' or anxious reader might miss; as Quintilian's student he does, after all, expect familiarity at least with the republican orators (including one of his own favourite models, Catullus' friend Calvus), as well as with the great epics and with Demosthenes. His slightly bizarre choice of Catullus as a model not only for his own poetry but also for the *nugae* among his letters is another example (see below)—and one which does not automatically suggest an inclusive agenda. Neverthe-less, even if we compare them with an epistolary model alone, Pliny's letters do lack the dazzling pyrotechnic range of Cicero's packed, gossipy, bitchy, allusive, jumbled, Greek-sprinkled, commentary-hungry correspondence.

This paper looks in more detail at Pliny's 'inclusive' persona, and particularly at the ways in which his correspondence fosters a com-munity of addressees and develops a didactic project in literary friendship and literary criticism.[3] It argues that Pliny's 'inclusive' strategy in dealing with his readership is more extensive and even

[3] For more on letters being used to create, teach, maintain, or assert membership of, a community of like-minded people, see also Morrison, Rees, and Fear in this volume. For the Frontonian strategy of using letters to set writer and addressee outside and above the wider community of letter writers, see Freisenbruch in this volume.

more explicitly outlined than Woolf suggests: Pliny proceeds not by exclusion of the unworthy masses (and the concomitant creation of a select 'in crowd') but by ostentatious inclusion and encouragement of as wide a range of people as possible, even of those who seem, on the face of it, unlikely citizens of the world of littérateurs. Think, for example, of his reaction to Terentius Iunior, an irreproachably worthy landowner, but one from whom Pliny expects little in the way of intellectual fireworks over dinner. Terentius, however, refuses to allow Pliny to restrict the conversation to matters of common interest to farmers and landowners, and reveals himself to be a conversationalist of sophistication and learning, who nevertheless chooses rural retirement over the bustle of urban soirées. After their evening together, Pliny articulates the danger of making judgements on the basis of *fama* alone:

Auxit sollicitudinem meam effecitque ut illis quos doctissimos noui, non minus hos seductos et quasi rusticos uerear. Idem suadeo tibi: sunt enim ut in castris sic etiam in litteris nostris, plures cultu pagano quos cinctos et armatos, et quidem ardentissimo ingenio, diligenter scrutatus inuenies.

He has increased my nervousness and made me respect these retired somewhat countrified people as much as the persons I know to be learned scholars. I suggest you do the same, for in the field of letters, as of battle, there are men who may be rustic in appearance, but are found on closer inspection to be well armed and equipped and full of the most spirited intelligence.   (7.25.5–6)[4]

Hasty exclusion based on appearances or reputation is risky—hence the metaphor of military danger at the didactic climax of the letter (*idem suadeo tibi: sunt enim* ...).[5] Terentius might, as it turns out, be an alarming presence in the front row at a recitation, and vigilance is essential, since well-armed adversaries or sophisticated associates (depending on your perspective) could be anywhere. That Pliny expresses his discovery as a matter for anxiety (*auxit sollicitudinem*

---

[4] All translations of Pliny are taken or adapted from Radice (1963). Those of Seneca are taken from Gummere (1917).

[5] The metaphor is not especially appropriate to the addressee, if Sherwin-White is right to identify him as one of Pliny's two *literary* correspondents named Rufus (Sherwin-White (1966) 434). Given that Pliny is elsewhere rather fond of elegantly appropriate allusions to an addressee's military environment (e.g. 4.26.2; 9.25.3), this Rufus might be better identified as a soldier.

meam) rather than for surprised delight is revealing, but entirely in keeping with other aspects of his epistolary persona. In the *literary* sphere, at least, he makes much of his anxieties, deliberately revealing a lack of self-confidence which drives him to teach and practise inclusiveness.

It is remarkable, indeed, how often Pliny parades such self-doubt, together with a carefully edited selection of moral shortcomings, all of which demand—or so it seems—compensatory practices in his literary work. He claims to be a lazy man, for example, especially by comparison with such powerhouses of *industria* as his uncle,[6] who wrote vast amounts on every conceivable subject in the interstices of a busy public career, and who rebuked his nephew for wasting valuable study time by walking through Rome instead of taking a sedan-chair. *Industria* is always to be commended in others,[7] but (again, in his *literary* life only) laziness is one of the first faults this feckless nephew 'confesses'.[8] In 1.2.6, for example, he says one should publish *something*—and as a lazy man he looks for something ready to hand (*desidiae uotum*, 'a wish born of laziness').[9] At 1.8.2 Pompeius Saturninus has asked to read some of Pliny's work but *desidia* dictates that the work he receives is one which he has already seen and commented upon: *non est tamen quod ab homine desidioso aliquid noui operis exspectes* ('there is no reason for you to expect some new work from a lazy man'). Pliny is (he would have us believe) a naturally lazy man hampered in his literary practice by his own failings as much as by the demands of a busy career.

The one respect, however, in which he does not fail or succumb to laziness is in encouraging his friends' literary activities, and in this area he develops a distinctive didactic agenda. In 1.13 he

[6] 3.5.19 *si comparer illi sum desidiosissimus*, 'compared with him I am the idlest of men'.

[7] The prospective husband, for example, for Iunius Mauricus' niece is a model of *industria* (1.14.7).

[8] This laziness is not part of his dourly self-disciplined public persona in his professional career (see e.g. 3.21).

[9] This works as a rationale for the publication of his letters too, none of which, he says, will be kept back (*si quas addidero non supprimam*, 'I shall not suppress any which I may write in future', 1.1.2). We should not take his claim to laziness too seriously: the rest of 1.2 is all about how carefully he crafted the book that he is sending Arrianus, and this is a minor example of what Hoffer calls Pliny's bad faith (Hoffer (1999) 227).

complains to Sosius Senecio about the restless inattentiveness of a typical contemporary audience, many of whom carefully time their arrival at a recitation to avoid having to sit through the whole of the work they have been invited to hear—and even then rarely stay long.[10] An imperial *exemplum* should shame them: supposedly the emperor Claudius, attracted by the hubbub, came voluntarily and unexpectedly to listen to one of Nonianus' recitations (*subitum recitanti inopinatumque uenisse*). Today, however, even invited guests complain about time wasted at such an event:

Nunc otiosissimus quisque multo ante rogatus et identidem admonitus aut non uenit aut, si uenit, queritur se diem (quia non perdidit) perdidisse. Sed tanto magis laudandi probandique sunt, quos a scribendi recitandique studio haec auditorum uel desidia uel superbia non retardat. Equidem prope nemini defui.

Today even the most leisured of men, after an early invitation and frequent reminders, either never comes at all, or, if he does, complains that he has wasted a day—just because he has not wasted it. The more praise and honour then is due to those whose interest in writing and reading aloud is not damped by the idleness and arrogance of their listeners. Personally I have let almost no-one down.   (1.13.4–5)

These reluctant auditors cannot use their *otium* well, and their hardworking literary hosts are all the more praiseworthy for persisting in their efforts despite the *desidia* and *superbia* of such audiences. Pliny, however, punctiliously sacrifices his own literary *otium* (*his ex causis longius quam destinaueram tempus in urbe consumpsi*, 'that is why I have spent more time in the city than I had planned', 1.13.6), even without specific expectations of reciprocity (*ne uidear... non auditor fuisse sed creditor*, 'lest I should seem not to have listened to them but to have made them indebted to me'). Pliny's laziness, then, hinders his literary productivity, but does not inhibit his performance of 'socio-literary' duty.

This begins a didactic project in living well in literary society which 'teaches' correct behaviour to auditors and critics. As 'teacher', though, he generally presents himself not as an expert or *exemplum*, nor even (like Seneca) as the man just slightly further ahead of his

---

[10] For another epistolary treatment of this problem, see Seneca's anecdote about Iulius Montanus (*Ep.* 122.11–13).

addressee on the road to wisdom, but as merely the first grateful beneficiary of his re-educated circle's generosity.

Such pedagogical strategies may be seen in letters which respond to surprise or criticism. His addressees and their friends seem quite reasonably to think, for example, that this often infuriatingly priggish man is a most unlikely author of risqué verse. Pliny handles this issue in three letters in particular, gradually developing (as the books proceed) a stance of exaggerated openness in response to such criticism as he reveals to us. His main focus, though, is not on how or what to write, but on how to be a friendly critic.

In 4.14, a 'cover letter' for the collection of Pliny's poetry which Decimus Paternus has received instead of the speech he asked for, Pliny pre-empts disapproval with a show of hesitancy. Having explicitly advertised his model as Catullus, he admits that some of the work may be indelicate but reassures his addressee that really indecent language is not his style—not because he is the kind of *homo seuerior* Catullus attacked, nor because he cannot be the chaste poet of unchaste verse, but because he is just too timid to write immodestly:

> Ex quibus tamen si non nulla tibi petulantiora paulo uidebuntur, erit eruditionis tuae cogitare summos illos et grauissimos uiros qui talia scripserunt non modo lasciuia rerum, sed ne uerbis quidem nudis abstinuisse; quae nos refugimus, non quia seueriores (unde enim?), sed quia timidiores sumus. Scimus alioqui huius opusculi illam esse uerissimam legem, quam Catullus expressit: 'Nam castum esse decet pium poetam / ipsum, uersiculos nihil necesse est.'

> But if some of the passages strike you as rather indelicate, your reading ought to tell you how many distinguished and serious writers in dealing with such themes neither avoided lascivious subjects nor refrained from expressing them in plain language. If I have shrunk from this, it is not because my principles are stricter than theirs (why should they be?) but because I am less courageous; and yet I know that the best rule for this kind of thing is the one in Catullus, when he says that 'the true poet should be chaste himself, though his poetry need not be.' (4.14.4)

He is demurely unspecific about what he means by *non nulla petu-lantiora* or *uerba nuda*.[11] Instead, he slides away from that issue to give a most polite lesson in a reader's obligations: to understand how

---

[11] Contrast Cicero's long and detailed letter about indecent language (*Fam.* 9.22), in which he discusses specific words and the problems their indecent meanings create for the writer. Timid Pliny is no Catullus—but he cannot even bring himself to be Cicero.

to approach a collection of small works and how to respond in friendship.[12] He has sent the whole work to Paternus so that he may judge it properly (*malui* omnia *a te pensitari quam electa laudari*, 'I preferred you to consider all of it than to praise selections') and respond honestly:

A simplicitate tua peto, quod de libello meo dicturus es alii, mihi dicas; neque est difficile quod postulo. Nam si hoc opusculum nostrum aut potissimum esset aut solum, fortasse posset durum uideri dicere: 'Quaere quod agas'; molle et humanum est: 'Habes quod agas.'

I want a man of your straightforwardness to say to me now what you are likely to say about my book to someone else. It is not much to ask, for if this little work were my chief or sole effort it might perhaps seem harsh to tell me to 'find something else to do'; but it is gentle and polite to say 'You *have* something else to do'. (4.14.10)

Pliny gives his addressee a safely courteous escape route: a letter about poetry which began by establishing Paternus as a fan of Pliny's *oratory* can end by allowing him to tell Pliny to stick to the day job. On this basis Pliny asks for the frank opinion Paternus might express to a third party, and this emphasis on amicable frankness becomes an important part of his strategy.[13]

---

[12] *Praeterea sapiens subtilisque lector debet non diuersis conferre diuersa, sed singula expendere, nec deterius alio putare quod est in suo genere perfectum*, 'Besides, an intelligent and sensitive reader should not compare totally different passages, but should evaluate each passage individually, nor think one inferior to another if each is perfect of its kind' (4.14.7). For the importance of reading a whole work, cf. Seneca's emphasis in *Ep*. 33.5 on leaving behind the habit of learning maxims and instead studying complete masterpieces.

[13] Cf. 7.20 for Pliny's joy at the open exchanges of literary criticism between himself and Tacitus. For *simplicitas* in friendship, cf. 1.15.4 (*potes adparatius cenare apud multos, nusquam hilarius simplicius incautius*, 'you can eat more sumptuously at many houses, but nowhere with more merriment, honesty or lack of constraint'). For the importance of presenting *whole* works to friends, see 8.21 on a two-day recitation of a complete collection of Pliny's poetry. His thoroughness is depicted as a mark of openness and of true friendship (*lego enim omnia ut omnia emendem, quod contingere non potest electa recitantibus. At illud modestius et fortasse reuerentius; sed hoc simplicius et amantius*, 'I read every word so as to correct every word, a thing which is impossible for readers of selected passages. It may be said that theirs is the more restrained and possibly more considerate practice, but mine is more honest and affectionate'). Restraint, self-editing, and withholding of literary work even in its early stages or in its less respectable forms mark the man who, though laudably modest, still lacks the crucial clubbableness of the Plinian littérateur.

In 5.3, Pliny is ready to field a third party's disapproval after it has actually been expressed. Aristo has sent him a commendably frank report of discussions of Pliny's poetry among his friends:

Cum plurima officia tua mihi grata et iucunda sunt, tum uel maxime quod me celandum non putasti, fuisse apud te de uersiculis meis multum copio- sumque sermonem, eumque diuersitate iudiciorum longius processisse, exstitisse etiam quosdam, qui scripta quidem ipsa non improbarent, me tamen amice simpliciterque reprehenderunt, quod haec scriberem recitar- emque.

I have many welcome acts of kindness to thank you for, but you do me a real service by thinking that you ought not to hide from me that my verses have been the subject of long and full discussion at your house, a discussion which was prolonged because of a divergence of opinions. There were some people, you say, who found no fault with the actual poems, but thought I deserved censure—in a frank and friendly way—for composing them and for reciting them in public.   (5.3.1)

The quality of the work is not in doubt, it seems, but there are divergent views (expressed *amice simpliciterque*) about his decision to produce and then to publicize it. Such undisguised criticism from cordial friends causes no offence (they do like the poems, after all, and their frankness is laudable) but it elicits an apologia for the practice of recitation: ostensibly—as in 4.14—Pliny lacks confidence in his own judgements and can only produce literary work with the support or example of others. *This* is the difference between himself and his great models from the Republic: they could write poetry without need of recitation:

Recito tamen, quod illi an fecerint nescio. Etiam: sed illi iudicio suo poterant esse contenti, mihi modestior constantia est quam ut satis absolutum putem, quod a me probetur.

However, it can be said that I give readings of my work without knowing if these authors did. So I do; but they could be content with their own judgement, whereas I am too diffident to feel confident that I have done everything I can to what has only my own approval.   (5.3.7)

Pliny's own *iudicium* is insufficient: he needs to see, hear, and act on the responses of his friends, and the recitation is part of the process of literary production:

Multa etiam multis admonetur, et si non admoneatur, quid quisque sentiat perspicit ex uultu oculis nutu manu murmure silentio; quae satis apertis notis iudicium ab humanitate discernunt.

He receives many suggestions from different members of the audience, and, failing this, he can see what everyone thinks from expressions, glances, nods, applause, murmurs and silence, signs which make clear the distinction between their critical judgement and politeness.   (5.3.9)

That Pliny *writes* poetry is not the issue in 5.3, despite the disapproval of Aristo's friends, since he has established respectable precedent in 4.14. The question is why he *recites* it, and his defence is that recitation is not an act of self-display (*quasi populum in auditorium ... aduocarim*), but an occasion for the simultaneous performance of friendship and good literary criticism on the part of his friends. That he has successfully shifted the agenda is shown by the letter's 'relocation' from Aristo's house and his guests' literary reproaches at the beginning to Pliny's *cubiculum* packed with his own friends at the end:[14]

Atque haec ita disputo quasi populum in auditorium, non in cubiculum amicos aduocarim, quos plures habere multis gloriosum, reprehensioni nemini fuit.

But now I am arguing this point as if I invited the general public to a lecture hall instead of a group of friends to my own room—and having many friends has been a source of pride to many and a reproach to none.   (5.3.11)

This letter is another lesson in how to operate in literary society, taught by a man who seems unsure of himself in literary production, but confident that he does at least know how the social sides of literary activity should function. This letter serves, in a sense, as a response to Seneca's epistolary disapproval both of recitation and of the wish for a large social circle on the grounds that only a few people here and there will really understand what is being said—and even they will need some further intellectual moulding:

Non est quod te gloria publicandi ingenii producat in medium, ut recitare istis uelis aut disputare... nemo est, qui intellegere te possit. Aliquis fortasse, unus aut alter incidet, et hic ipse formandus tibi erit instituendusque ad intellectum tui.

---

[14] Even critics of Pliny's verse could hardly criticize Pliny for having lots of poetry-loving friends (*reprehenderunt* ~ *reprehensioni nemini*).

There is no reason why pride in advertising your abilities should lure you into publicity, so that you should desire to recite or harangue before the general public... there is not a man of them who can understand you. One or two individuals will perhaps come in your way, but even these will have to be moulded and trained by you so that they will understand you.   (Seneca, *Ep.* 7.9)

The small audience (ideally consisting only of one like-minded individual) is the model in Seneca's teaching on shared intellectual life. He quotes Epicurus as saying, for example, to one of his intellectual companions: *satis enim magnum alter alteri theatrum sumus*, 'each of us is a sufficient audience for the other' (*Ep.* 7.11). Pliny is also teaching on the same subject, but for him the right audience (unlike Aristo's guests, well-disposed though they were), will assist his literary work and help him to the fame he desires, and his credibility as a teacher of literary life is attested precisely by the *large* friendly audience he can attract. Friendship, social gatherings, and literary production are intimately connected for Pliny: drafts may be written or polished in the *secessus* of a country villa, but much real work is done in recitations to friends[15] or in epistolary sociability, and the letters enact his growing confidence as the books progress.[16]

By 7.4, Pliny can be even more bullish. He answers Pontius' question about how a *seuerus homo* like himself ever came to write hendecasyllables not with a defence but with even more to be startled by: his early poetic works include a tragedy (written when he was 14), elegies inspired by an Aegean journey, and an attempt at epic. Next came a first attempt at hendecasyllables (inspired by an erotic poem by Cicero), then more elegy, and only at last the verse which Pontius has just read. Here, instead of citing august precedent, or acknowledging indebtedness to the kindness and tolerance of his friends, Pliny piles up a literary career filled with *nugae*[17]—more, in other

---

[15] In 7.4.8, for example, Pliny's first elegies, written *in Laurentino*, were read to friends as soon as he returned to the city (*deinde in urbem reuersus sodalibus legi; probauerunt*).

[16] On the development in Pliny's confidence during the collection, see Morello (2003) 208.

[17] Listed with little discernible progression; contrast his account of Pliny the Elder's carefully graduated literary production, which develops from youthful specialism to grand comprehensiveness (3.5; see Henderson (2002) 69–102).

words, of precisely the kind of thing which prompted Pontius' surprise.

Affable candour (in both writers and readers) becomes a criterion of friendship in his epistolary world. In 8.4, for example, Pliny implores Caninius Rufus to send him even the unpolished drafts of his poem on the Dacian wars:

> Patere hoc me super cetera habere amoris tui pignus, ut ea quoque norim quae nosse neminem uelles. In summa potero fortasse scripta tua magis probare laudare, quanto illa tardius cautiusque, sed ipsum te magis amabo magisque laudabo, quanto celerius et incautius miseris.

> Allow me this further pledge of your affection—let me into the secrets you would prefer no one to know. The bottom line is that I may perhaps be better able to commend and praise your writings if you are rather slow and cautious in sending them, but I shall love and praise you yourself all the more if you send them more swiftly and with less hesitation.   (8.4.7–8)

No one is ever attacked in Pliny's world (except his one egregious enemy, Regulus) and few fail or even risk failure except Pliny himself. There are no bores in Pliny (not from his point of view, anyway) and no incompetent littérateurs. Pliny's 'teaching' may be staged in the exclusive environment of the Esquiline, but within its limits the programme is unusually inclusive.

When friends fail in their duty to encourage and to provide frank substantive criticism, disapproval can degenerate into *inuidia*, a vice to which he refers explicitly 25 times in 23 letters across all the books of the collection save for book 10, and it is to the examination of *inuidia* in Pliny's 'episto-literary' project that the remainder of this paper is devoted.[18] *Inuidia*, the resentment (potentially resulting in malicious action) of another's success or material benefit, or the generalized ill-feeling incurred by inappropriate behaviour, is a prominent motif in Cicero's letters; indeed the negotiation of *inuidia* was one of the principal challenges of Cicero's public life as we see it represented in his letters (and even in his philosophical and oratorical works). Examples are too numerous for a comprehensive list, but

---

[18] Hoffer (1999) 137 n. 40: 'the opposite of the epistolary ideal of mutually beneficial exchange (e.g. 1.4.3) is to begrudge *both* oneself *and* other people some pleasure or benefit'. As Hoffer says, *inuidia* is one of the 'canonical' vices of Pliny's collection. For a careful treatment of *inuidia*, see Kaster (2003).

the *inuidia* stirred up against Cicero by Clodius, or the ill-will of those he calls *piscinarii nostri*, 'our fish-fancying friends' (*Att.* 1.20), or of the *inuidi* at the time of his exile (Att. 3.7.2) are familiar enough, as is the generalised *inuidia* attached to his name, which he fears will afflict his son (*Att.* 3.23.5). Of 78 instances in Cicero's letters, though, only four locate *inuidia* in the literary sphere,[19] and only three others are specifically about the relationship between praise (or fame) and *inuidia*.[20]

Three features of Pliny's handling of *inuidia* are particularly striking to the reader of Cicero. The first is that Pliny's 'taxonomy' of *inuidia* looks much more varied than that of Cicero, for whom *inuidia* means primarily either political *inuidia* or the ill-will which may be stirred up or allayed in court.[21] Pliny, however, depicts the action of *inuidia* not only in political or legal contexts (although in a remarkably restricted fashion in those contexts) but also in precisely the literary environment in which he has been trying to inculcate a positive and productive economy of literary interaction. The second is that Pliny himself is only very rarely the victim of *inuidia*, and his own envious emotions are carefully minimized.[22] The third is that whereas Cicero takes *inuidia* as an inevitable (if deplorable) part of public life, and makes no visible effort to combat it,[23] Pliny attempts to educate his circle to abandon *inuidia* in social literary life, and instead promotes its antitheses, *miratio* or *favor*.

In 6.17, a case study in invidious misbehaviour, he writes that he has returned from a recitation faintly annoyed (*indignatiunculam*)— not by the work recited, which was most polished, but by the conduct of some fellow-listeners, who sat like deaf mutes throughout, showing no sign of appreciation or engagement. Pliny's letters on his own recitations[24] show how important an audience's gestures and body language were for an apparently unconfident literary host, offering, as they did, another medium for receiving the honest criticism he desires. Here, though, a few limp sophisticates have begrudged the

---

[19] *Att.* 1.20; 2.4.2; *Fam.* 5.12; 7.33.   [20] *Fam.* 7.2; 12.5; Q fr. 1.15.44.

[21] There is one rare and interesting exception in *Fam.* 16.18, where Cicero writes to Tiro about the possible *inuidia* of a letter greeting.

[22] See Hoffer (1999) 116–17 on *others'* responsibility for uncharitable attacks of which Pliny is only ever the reluctant hearer.

[23] See e.g. *De Oratore* 2.52.210.   [24] e.g. 5.3 and 5.12.

speaker that natural benefit which is the only appropriate return for his friendly hospitality, and in their graceless condescension they destroy the *amicitia* which brought them there:

Quae tanta grauitas? quae tanta sapientia? Quae immo pigritia adrogantia sinisteritas ac potius amentia, in hoc totum diem impendere ut offendas, ut inimicum relinquas ad quem tamquam amicissimum ueneris?

What is the point of all this dignity and learning, or rather this laziness and conceit, this want of tact and good sense, which makes you spend a whole day giving offence and leaving an enemy in the man you came to hear as your dearest friend? (6.17.3)

The rule to apply in life is addressed to everyone:

Disertior ipse es? Tanto magis ne inuideris; nam qui inuidet minor est. Denique siue plus siue minus siue idem praestas, lauda uel inferiorem uel superiorem uel parem: superiorem quia nisi laudandus ille non potes ipse laudari, inferiorem aut parem quia pertinet ad tuam gloriam quam maximum uideri, quem praecedis uel exaequas.

Are you cleverer than he is? All the more reason not to begrudge him his success, for jealousy is a sign of inferiority. In fact, whether your own performance is better or worse or on a par with his, you should show your appreciation; for if your superior does not meet with applause neither will you, and it is in your own interests that anyone you equal or surpass should be well received. (6.17.4)

This is common courtesy, we might say, but for Pliny it is motivated also by pragmatism.[25] Cicero acknowledged (*De Oratore* 2.52.209–10) that *inuidia* thrives in social hierarchies: equals or inferiors incur *inuidia* if they seem successful beyond their due, especially if they have overtaken the *inuidus* in the social league tables, while even superiors may suffer it in punishment for anti-social self-aggrandizement.[26] Pliny is well aware of social and intellectual league tables, but in his conception of them, any individual's *relative* position is likely to be permanently fixed; the only person who loses standing, for himself and others, is the practitioner of *inuidia*

---

[25] Though it is elsewhere very much a moral issue (e.g. 7.26.2, on the spiritual benefits of illness; cf. Cic. *Timaeus* 3: *probus inuidet nemini*).

[26] For persistent *inuidia* as a feature of social hierarchies, cf. also Seneca, *Ep.* 14.10; 84.11; 104.9.

himself. Praise of all, one's inferiors and equals as well as one's superiors, is the only safe course of action.

By contrast, Pliny's enthusiasm for *all* literary efforts leaves no room for invidious thoughts.[27] He advocates hierarchy without exclusion—or more precisely, perhaps, a peculiar kind of competitive inclusiveness, whereby all involved are safely on the receiving end of praise; his approach makes that ultimate invidious situation—in which an inferior surpasses his superior—substantially less likely. This creates a group in which literary friendship is safe, and seeming to praise one's friends too much is merely a laudable enactment of principle, as 7.28 demonstrates. Instead of simply observing the phenomenon of *inuidia* within the social hierarchy, as Cicero did in the *De Oratore*, Pliny seeks to establish standards of generous behaviour which will guarantee the status and success of everyone in the league table: nobody will win praise if his superior is begrudged it, while praise for an outstanding equal or inferior can only boost one's own image. Therefore, everyone at every level benefits from the inclusiveness of this system of praise, while *inuidia* damages the whole literary 'economy'. Pliny is, then, taking on the job of re-engineering (at least in the epistolary micro-world which he creates for himself and his friends) the behaviour of his circle, to common and reciprocal benefit.

The other occurrences of *inuidia* in Pliny's world are all remarkably safe, in that *inuidia* is either in the past or at least comfortably distant from Pliny himself. An atmosphere of generalized political *inuidia* is strongly associated in Pliny's letters, for example, with the reigns of earlier, tyrannical, emperors (especially Domitian, but also Nero)—and in no case is that *inuidia* directed against Pliny himself. In 3.9.31, the egregious Norbanus fails to save himself partly because of the backwash of Domitianic *inuidia* (*tanta conflagrauit inuidia homo alioqui flagitiosus et Domitiani temporibus usus ut multi,* 'he was consumed in the general indignation, a man disgraceful also in other respects, who had profited, like many, from the reign of Domitian') whereas in 4.11.5, Domitian himself is beset by *inuidia* (*ingenti inuidia*).[28] In 3.7, Silius' life *sine potentia, sine inuidia* is a welcome atonement in *otium* for his early career as a Neronian stooge. One of

---

[27] Compare his uncle's dictum at 3.5.10.   [28] Cf. Pliny, *Pan.* 14.

Pliny's most important sets of speeches, *De Helvidi Ultione*, was delayed after Domitian's death precisely in order to avoid the period of post-mortem *inuidia*.[29] In this instance, not only was he unwilling to exploit the witch-hunting rage of the post-Domitianic senate, but he demonstrated that even at the most crucial time for self-positioning, personal *inuidia* was alien to him, since he tells us at 9.13.5 that he offered to share the glory of the project with Helvidius' widow (*sed non ita gloriae meae fauerim, ut uobis societate eius inuideam*, 'I am not so devoted to my own glory as to begrudge you a share in it'). He wants this seen as an inclusive project—though one which will produce one of his finest literary achievements.

In the forensic environment, Pliny even capitalizes on the risks of *inuidia* and parades his own success in avoiding or outwitting it. In 7.33, he even tries to get Tacitus to include in the *Histories* the story of his courage in sharing with Herennius Senecio the risk of *inuidia* after the case against Baebius Massa. In this letter, the virtuous association with Senecio automatically outweighs (though perhaps only with epistolary hindsight) any *inuidia* Pliny might actually have risked incurring, but the story as he tells it turns the whole situation stunningly to his advantage—so much so that he is able to report a letter of congratulation from Nerva for his handling of the affair.[30] On other occasions, though, Pliny shows himself simply avoiding *inuidia* altogether. In 3.4, for example, he manages to pre-empt *inuidia*, since his senatorial opponent, Caecilius Classicus, is conveniently dead. Another (less serious) kind of *inuidia* which might be incurred in a legal action—that aroused by speaking too long—is jokily evaded by Pliny in 6.2.3, where Regulus, his co-advocate, is responsible for requesting the extra time.[31] Finally, even when speculating about the motives of others, Pliny seems to prefer to discount the possibility of *inuidia* if an alternative is available. In 2.11 Pliny considers Tuccius Cerialis' three possible motives for requiring

[29] *Ego et modestius et constantius arbitratus immanissimum reum non communi temporum inuidia, sed proprio crimine urgere*, 'I believed that the more moderate and more steadfast course was to deal with this atrocious criminal not through the universal hatred of Domitian's time, but by bringing a specific charge against him' (9.13.4).

[30] For further discussion of this letter, see Fitzgerald in this volume.

[31] Regulus invokes *inuidia* in a different context in 2.20.8, where he shamefully accuses a dying testator's doctors of begrudging their patient a quick and easy death.

Priscus' presence at Marcianus' hearing: to excite pity, to stir up *inuidia*, or because of natural justice (if a charge is made against two people, both should be present to defend themselves). It is the final, safely procedural, explanation, which naturally attracts Pliny. We never, though, see Pliny explicitly attempt to instruct an addressee in how to negotiate *inuidia* in the legal or political world. Pliny's confidence in his professional sphere means that he need not try to adjust the realities of *inuidia*, since he can successfully avoid or pre-empt it in his *negotia* (or so he would have us believe).[32] It is only in the context of *literary* activity in *otium* that he consciously designs a code of conduct for his circle.

Just occasionally, however, polite *inuidia*, elegantly expressed, has a special epistolary function, since it can bring writer and addressee together in shared leisure interests and can allow Pliny to break out of his own exclusion from envied pleasures. In 4.3, a literary fan letter to Arrius Antoninus, Pliny confines *aemulatio*, together with the most innocuously courteous *inuidia* (*inuideo Graecis quod illorum lingua scribere maluisti*, 'I envy the Greeks because you preferred to write in their language') to the verses, rather than to the public career (*ego tamen te uel magis in remissionibus miror*, 'yet for your recreations I personally admire you even more'). So also, in the apparently trifling 2.8, in which Pliny asks his countryman Caninius whether he is using his enviable *otium* for hunting, fishing, or *studia*, Pliny demonstrates that he is no stranger to these activities at Comum, by using the very vocabulary of such pursuits—in a letter showcasing his skill and experience in *studia*—to articulate his temporary exclusion from them: *numquamne hos artissimos laqueos, si soluere negatur, abrumpam... tot nexibus, tot quasi catenis maius in dies occupationum agmen extenditur* ('I wonder if I shall ever be able to shake off these constricting fetters if I am not allowed to undo them... as more and more links are added to the chain, I see my work stretching out

---

[32] The only letter in which *inuidia* seems to have caused serious discomfort is 8.22. This is one of Pliny's many evasive letters, but it is clear that he has encountered some unpleasant behaviour which now prompts general reflections. His unspecified critics/ enemies have said something harsh, in terms which suggest a quasi-*inuidia* (*sic aliorum uitiis irascuntur quasi inuideant*, 'they are enraged at the faults of others, as if they feel jealous resentment'). Pliny ends by demonstrating his own *humanitas* in refraining from further comment and withholding the offender's name.

farther and farther every day').[33] Pliny who envies the hunter in the
country is himself the prey in the city.[34]

Similarly, in 1.10—a letter generously eschewing *inuidia* against a
friend who is enjoying the company of the philosopher Euphrates—
Pliny reveals that he has already made all his complaints to Euphrates
himself and been reassured that the unremitting public duties which
might cause him to feel envy towards his less busy friend may in fact
be the best kind of philosophy:

Soleo non numquam (nam id ipsum quando contigit!) de his occupationi-
bus apud Euphraten queri. Ille me consolatur, adfirmat etiam esse hanc
philosophiae et quidem pulcherrimam partem, agere negotium publicum,
cognoscere, iudicare, promere et exercere iustitiam, quaeque ipsi doceant in
usu habere.

Whenever I have the chance I complain about these duties to Euphrates,
who consoles me by saying that anyone who holds public office, presides at
trials and passes judgement, expounds and administers justice, and thereby
puts into practice what the philosopher only teaches, has a part in the
philosophic life and indeed the noblest part of all.   (1.10.10)

Pliny does talk to Euphrates; what he lacks is the opportunity to
listen to Euphrates *all day,* and it is that only which he finally and
ostentatiously—as a matter of principle—does not begrudge to
Attius Clemens:

Neque enim ego ut multi inuideo aliis bono quo ipse careo, sed contra:
sensum quendam uoluptatemque percipio, si ea quae mihi denegantur
amicis uideo superesse.

For unlike many people, I don't grudge others the advantages which I cannot
have myself: on the contrary, I feel a real sense of pleasure if I see my friends
enjoying the plenty which is denied to me.   (1.10.12)

---

[33] For a letter as itself an enactment (and performance) of pursuits from which the
writer claims to feel barred by external circumstances, see also Fitzgerald in this
volume.

[34] Cf. 4.18 and 5.15. Other activities (especially acts of public munificence) at
Comum, however, could fall prone to *inuidia.* As a cautionary tale in 6.31.3, Claudius
Ariston of Ephesus, who fell victim to an informer at the instigation of enemies who
lacked his popularity and good character, is vindicated only by acquittal before the
emperor (*princeps Ephesiorum, homo munificus et innoxie popularis; inde inuidia et a
dissimillimis delator immissus, itaque absolutus uindicatusque est,* 6.31.3). Pliny has
similar worries about his own munificence, though they are re-focused in 1.8, for
example, on the awkwardness of self-praise.

So Pliny has taken a painful emotion and made it pleasurable.[35] He has also trumped his friend's good fortune (since he has the *pulcherrima pars* of philosophy) and demonstrated that he is only formally (though not in spirit) excluded from the pleasures enjoyed by his friends. This sort of *inuidia* does no one any harm, and contributes to the picture of the world of shared interests and abundant praise supported by the didactic project discussed in the first part of this paper.[36]

However, that this project could itself incur criticism is clear in 7.28, a programmatic letter addressed to Septicius Clarus, the addressee of 1.1 (and so of the whole collection), where he resists malicious criticism that he routinely *over-praises* his friends. This important addressee brings me finally to a slightly unusual occurrence of *inuidia* and a suggestion for its interpretation. 1.15 shows us a different type of failure in literary social life from that witnessed in 6.17 (with which this discussion of *inuidia* began). Septicius Clarus agreed to come to dinner, but then ate elsewhere instead:

Heus tu! Promittis ad cenam, nec uenis? Dicitur ius: ad assem impendium reddes, nec id modicum. Paratae erant lactucae singulae, cochleae ternae, oua bina, halica cum mulso et niue—nam hanc quoque computabis, immo hanc in primis quae perit in ferculo—, oliuae betacei cucurbitae bulbi, alia mille non minus lauta. Audisses comoedos uel lectorem uel lyristen uel— quae mea liberalitas—omnes. At tu apud nescio quem ostrea uuluas echinos Gaditanas maluisti. Dabis poenas, non dico quas. Dure fecisti: inuidisti, nescio an tibi, certe mihi, sed tamen et tibi. Quantum nos *lusissemus* risissemus studuissemus! Potes apparatius cenare apud multos, nusquam hilarius simplicius incautius. In summa experire, et nisi postea te aliis potius excusaueris, mihi semper excusa.

Who are you, to accept my invitation to dinner and never come? I have a good case and you shall pay my costs in full, no small sum either. It was all laid out, one lettuce each, three snails, two eggs, barley-cake, and wine with honey chilled with snow (you will reckon this too, please, and as an expensive item,

---

[35] On *inuidia* as *aegritudo*, see Cicero, *Tusc. Disp.* 4.7.16; 3.9.21.

[36] All this is, of course, so much dry ice on Pliny's part. It obscures the existence of real *inuidia* in Pliny's world, or of secrets that might endanger him or his friends. We are seduced into believing that (unlike Cicero) Pliny has no dangerous secrets. Such things belong in the past, and they were always somebody else's secrets anyway (so at 1.12.7 Pliny was privy to Corellius' innermost thoughts, which he had kept hidden even from his entirely admirable and trustworthy wife).

seeing that it disappears in the dish), besides olives, beetroots, gherkins, onions and any number of similar delicacies. You would have heard a comic play, a reader or singer, or all three if I felt generous. Instead you chose to go where you could have oysters, sow's innards, sea-urchins, and Spanish dancing-girls. You will suffer for this—I won't say how. It was a cruel trick done to spite one of us—yourself or most likely me, and possibly both of us, if you think what a feast of fun, laughter and learning we were going to have. You can eat richer food at many houses, but nowhere with such free and easy enjoyment. All I can say is, try me; and then, if you don't prefer to decline invitations elsewhere, you can always make excuses to me.

The literary genealogy of this letter is familiar, but quite complex; the branches of the family tree are not only poetic but also prosaic and (specifically) epistolary. The letter has obvious affinities with the tradition of invitation poems (e.g. the detailed menu and entertainments list).[37] It also recalls, however, a tradition of post-party 'letters' in both prose and verse: these include Cicero's letter to the jurist, Trebatius, in which he follows up a stimulating conversation on a legal topic of shared interest.[38] A sexier, poetic, specimen of the genre is Catullus 50 (*hesterno, Licini, die otiosi | multum* lusimus *in meis tabellis*). Catullus and his friend Calvus—both important models for Pliny—have spent a stimulating day together playing in verse. Catullus goes home too excited to eat or sleep, so he writes to Calvus of his longing to see him again. Finally he threatens Calvus with the penalties of Nemesis if he rejects Catullus' advances.

Pliny's letter 1.15 is a hybrid: a detailed invitation has been issued, and this is a post-party letter but it is one with an air of satirical reproach. Septicius had a better offer from an unnamed host for a more vulgarly expensive (and exclusive) party—he chose oysters, caviar, and lapdancers at another house instead of a simple cold platter and shared literary fun at Pliny's.[39] Pliny crucially characterizes Septicius' choice as an example of *inuidia*—Septicius begrudged them both a lovely evening. This may be just a version of the courteous epistolary *inuidia* discussed above. However, I would like to suggest that *inuidisti* here—not a natural or normal verb in this context—helps to indicate that the addressee has done more than

---

[37] Edmunds (1982) 184–5. For another 'epistolary' version, see Horace, *Epist.* 1.5.
[38] *Fam.* 7.22 illuseras *heri inter scyphos*...
[39] On this letter, see especially Gunderson (1997) 216–21; Gowers (1993) 267–79.

disappoint Pliny's hopes of an entertaining dinner. What Pliny loses by Septicius' choice is the chance to show that he belongs in the illustrious company of Cicero and Trebatius (lawyers and orators like himself, one of them his principal model) or Catullus and Calvus (both poets, one also an orator, both models for Pliny). Pliny *tried* to create a party like the day shared by Catullus and Calvus (*multum lusimus* ∼ *quantum nos lusissemus*) or by the two boozy lawyers of *Fam.* 7.22, but was foiled in his attempt to build the right sort of literary social life because *his* guest, the dedicatee and instigator of the whole Ciceronian/Catullan/Calvian letter collection, failed to turn up to a Catullan/Ciceronian/Calvian dinner. In such circumstances, how can he, as emulator of Catullus and Cicero, write a version of Catullus 50 or *Fam.* 7.22?[40] Although he 'salvages' and develops the legal joke at the end of Catullus 50, in other respects his only recourse is reproach—not a suitable mode for letters, according to ancient theorists, and certainly not Pliny's normal mode. *Inuidia,* even of the most apparently innocuous kind, can derail not only a social occasion between friends, but a literary project as well—Septicius has not fostered Pliny's literary activity as he should have done (in Pliny's co-operative programme). Once again, Pliny demonstrates his adherence to the right values but shows himself frustrated in his desire to live them out.

To summarize: Pliny 'teaches' the rules of social conduct within a literary world, and demonstrates his own adherence to those rules, together with the benefits that accrue. The rules are based on reciprocity, generosity in praise, and most of all on inclusiveness. There *is* an 'in-crowd' in Pliny's world, as there was in those of Cicero and Catullus, of well-educated men who attend each other's recitations and exchange drafts of literary work. However, where Cicero or Catullus might have participated in the practices which form what Gunderson and others call 'a zone of constitutive exclusion', in which insiders understand and follow rules of conduct which are often only explicitly defined when they are breached (when someone has been a bore, for example, or behaved inappropriately), Pliny, by contrast,

---

[40] As Gunderson (1997) 221 says, 'Clarus purloined from Pliny the letter and the spirit of the evening.'

adopts a self-depreciating and confiding tone, which suggests that in fact, although morally and intellectually the right sort of person, he still regularly almost fails to make it in this world himself. Rather than showing off to the world his right to define the 'in-crowd' by excluding those who can't keep up, he ensures that everyone is included (apparently because of his own anxiety), and that the rules against *inuidia* are clearly articulated in a didactic programme for improvement addressed to those from whom he can derive most benefit himself. In choosing to implement this programme in an epistolary collection, which includes letters to many different people (as well as letters to mutual acquaintances *about* some of his address-ees), he can show himself both convening and shaping a large literary group of friends; in so doing, he protects himself from failure by proposing the epistolary curriculum for the literary critics he has gathered together in his recital room and in the pages of his collected *Epistulae.*

8

The Letter's the Thing (in Pliny, Book 7)

William Fitzgerald

There is something paradoxical about being famous for one's letters.[1] Letters usually become interesting because their writers are famous, which is certainly true for the Ciceronian corpus.[2] One wonders what Pliny would have made of the fact that he is famous, two thousand years later, for his *Letters*—not for the oratory we find him so busily polishing, nor because he plays a distinguished role in Roman history or even Tacitus' *Histories*, and certainly not (and here we must be grateful) for his *nugae*.[3] Would he have thought that we had got things back to front, that the *Letters* were just commentary on the true achievements, prefaces to the oratory, background to the great man's *vita*? Or would he simply have been interested to see which of his several bids for survival had paid off, knowing that he had hedged his bets heavily enough to guarantee that *something* would come through (so, it was the *Letters!*). Perhaps Pliny the all-rounder would have been happy to survive through his letters, the most appropriate medium for a man of parts.[4]

Pliny was obsessed with his survival into posterity and the *gloria* that would ensure it, but he was not entirely decided as to how to achieve it.[5] In 5.8 he tells Titinius Capito that he has seriously

---

[1] On Pliny's Letters and the problem of fame, see Ludolph (1997) 60–88.

[2] If you were to read all of Cicero's letters to Atticus you wouldn't feel the lack of a continuous history of the period, comments Nepos (*Att.* 16.3).

[3] The possibility that Pliny's *nugae* might survive is raised at 7.4.10 and 7.9.10.

[4] 9.29.1 Pliny will do many things *mediocriter* because feels unable to do *unum aliquid insigniter*.

[5] On *gloria*, see Guillemin (1929) 13–22; Mayer (2003) 227–9. In Book 7, my focus in this chapter, see 7.17.5; 9.14 is perhaps the most poignant expression of Pliny's aspirations.

considered the urging of Titinius and others to write a history. He is driven above all by the ambition to survive, to 'raise himself from the earth' and 'fly victorious through the mouths of men' (5.8.3). History is more likely to find favour with posterity than are oratory and poetry, but he has decided against this path to immortality, or at least put it on one side, because of the need to polish and publish his speeches. His successful career at the bar can only be parlayed into lasting fame by publication, without which his career might as well never have been (*quidquid non est peractum pro non incohato est,* 5.8.7). Thrift dictates that he gamble on his speeches.

The speeches are a major topic of the *Letters,* and Mayer (2003) makes a powerful argument that the *Letters* were intended to com- plement the speeches, whether as prefaces, advertisements, substi- tutes, records of their reception, or simply as catalogue. So, are the *Letters* a kind of insurance policy for the survival of the speeches?[6] If so, it is strange that, as Morello points out, a full 57 per cent of the cover letters do not identify the speech in question.[7] Perhaps this very silence works to enhance the literary production that it fails to identify by virtue of its vagueness: 'It is the rich hinterland of literary activity just at the periphery of the reader's sight which is the most important creation of the vaguer letters' (Morello (2003) 207).

Nowhere does Pliny directly express hopes for the *Letters* as a path to posterity, but there are indications that they too might have a role to play in the pursuit of lasting *gloria.* Writing to Tacitus, the addressee who receives the most letters in the collection (11), Pliny exclaims that 'everywhere the story of our unanimity, straight- forwardness and mutual trust will be told' (*usquequaque narrabitur, qua concordia simplicitate fide uiximus,* 7.20.2). By Book 9, it appears that the *Letters* may have a future: Geminus asks Pliny to address something to him which could be included in his books (9.11.1 *aliquod ad te scribi uolebas, quod libris inseri posset*) and informs Pliny that they are selling well in Lyon. So it seems that while Pliny was clear about where he would make his main push to posterity, other fronts might be opened too.

---

[6] Janson (1964) 106–7 (apud Morello (2003) 201) compares Pliny's cover letters to Statius' prefaces. 6.33.7 is a good example.

[7] Morello (2003) 199.

The question of the status of Pliny's *Letters* in his project of self-immortalization is not unrelated to the status of the Letter itself, which always raises, in some form or other, the question of whether it is the thing itself or an adjunct, substitute, or signpost. On one account, the letter is a *pis aller*, the substitute for a conversation, a dinner, or some other kind of social intercourse that is prevented by the separation of the participants; it may refer back to some social event, or even anticipate it, but it is not the thing itself.[8] Alternatively, the letter is the distillation of the self in the presence of the other, its words and gestures unaffected by chance, distraction, misunderstanding and all the mishaps that interfere with communication, causing intentions to go astray and meanings to be imperfectly conveyed.[9] It is the thing itself and not a substitute.[10] A cliché of blurbs and reviews of letter collections has it that they conjure up the life and times of the correspondents in all their immediacy: letters help us to imagine the life to which they defer. 'I felt... that I'd lived for years in that set', as Lytton Strachey put it.[11] But, for the writers themselves it might be equally accurate to say that life aspires to the condition of the letter: the titbit of gossip, the anecdote, the pithy character study, the put-down—to share these is what constitutes living 'in that set'. The letter, on this account, is the genre whose content is what is worth communicating and, as a corollary, what is worth communicating must become suitable material for a letter.

Pliny dramatizes vividly the ambiguous status of the letter in the last letter of Book 7, where he recounts an anecdote about himself and offers it to Tacitus for inclusion in his *Histories*. His letter provides raw material for a genre where this anecdote will find a more appropriate and glorious home, and it would seem to defer to the superior genre. But, as we shall see, it's not quite as simple as that, and this same letter then proceeds to reclaim the anecdote for the genre of the letter and for the *Letters* of Pliny. The final letter of

---

[8] Trapp (2003) 38–9.

[9] Compare Hodkinson's 'advantages of the letter' in this volume.

[10] This tension is related to that between the letter as bridge and as barrier in Altman's account of epistolarity (Altman (1982) 186). A good example is provided by Pliny's letter to his wife, 6.7.

[11] Quoted by Peter Parker, reviewing *The Letters of Lytton Strachey* in the *TLS* 29 Apr. 2005. I owe this reference to Roy Gibson.

Book 7 relates to the first in a number of ways, with the result that the
status of the Letter is marked as a significant theme for this book,
which will be the main text for my discussion. I will return to the
relation between the first and last letter of the book later, but I want
to start by looking at some of the ways in which Pliny plays with the
possibility that the letter is the thing itself right from the start of the
book.

The first letter of Book 7 begins with a formulaic reaction to the
news of Geminus' illness: 'Your very persistent ill-health frightens
me' (*Terret me haec tua tam pertinax ualetudo*).[12] It turns out that
Pliny's concern is not purely for Geminus' physical well-being, for he
is more worried about the danger to his friend's moral health.[13]
Illness can impair a man's self-control, and Pliny trusts that it will
find no purchase with his steadfast friend. As usual, it does not take
him long to switch the focus to himself: to assure Geminus that the
self-control he is urging is not beyond human capacity (*admittit
humana natura quod suadeo*, 7.1.3), he instances his own behaviour
in similar circumstances. Pliny's slaves, he reports, are under standing orders to restrain him forcibly from doing anything unworthy
should he fall ill, and they have been warned that if they allow him
anything against doctor's orders they will be punished as severely as
anyone else would punish his slaves for refusing. So much for *self-
control*! But, so far, the slaves have not been tested; indeed, once
when he was suffering from a raging fever Pliny refused the bath that
had been prepared for him because the doctors, while not forbidding
it, had mixed feelings as to whether it was advisable (4–6). This story,
he tells Geminus, is intended both to provide an *exemplum* for his
addressee and to compel the writer himself to live up to the self-
control he has displayed in the past, now that he has bound himself
with the pledge of this letter (*cum me hac epistula quasi pignore
obligauissem*, 7.1.7).[14] The spectre of humiliating compulsion by
slaves is exorcized here by a form of self-determination as the letter
itself takes over the role of the restraining slaves. What Pliny tells

---

[12] See Sherwin-White (1966) 6–9 for a classification of opening gestures.

[13] The issue of how we behave when ill returns in 7.21 and 7.26.

[14] For the letter's double role (for addressee and for writer), see 7.24.8: *haec quia
soles siquid incidit noui non inuitus audire, deinde quia iucundum est mihi quod
ceperam gaudium scribendo retractare.*

Geminus has the same *effect* as what he tells his slaves. As *pignus*, the letter acquires a materiality that takes it one step beyond the speech act it performs (*monerem*, 7.1.7). The letter's the thing.[15]

In 7.13, the status of the letter is the subject of a riddle.

Eadem epistula et non studere te et studere significat. Aenigmata loquor? Ita plane, donec distinctius quod sentio enuntiem. Negat enim te studere, sed est tam polita quam nisi a studente non potest scribi; aut es tu super omnes beatus, si talia per desidiam et otium perficis. Uale.

The same letter conveys to me that you are not engaged in your literary pursuits and that you are. Am I speaking in riddles? Obviously I am, until I make my meaning clearer. It says that you are not, but it is so polished that it could only have been written if you are; or else you are luckier than all the rest in being able to reach such perfection in idleness and leisure. Farewell.

Pliny's riddle depends on the mild zeugma of *significat*. The letter 'conveys' something in two different senses. It conveys what it reports and it conveys (for instance) the culture of the writer. Ferox has made the common complaint that he has no time for his *studia*. But that cannot be, for his letter is the work of a man who is reading the right books or (more mischievously) who is *working* at it. As the product of *studium*, Ferox's letter is the thing itself, and cancels its own statement. Unless Ferox is uniquely lucky to be able to toss this sort of thing off, an alternative that provides a perfect flourish with which to end the letter, rescuing it from the laboured symmetry of riddle and solution with a spontaneous afterthought. Pliny may be telling Ferox that his letter is both a report and the thing itself, but his own letter is an example of the same phenomenon: while encouraging us to imagine the letter that elicited his praise, Pliny pre-empts Ferox with this consummate performance of the very *sprezzatura* to which he alludes in his final flourish.

Pliny's collection gives us only one side of a correspondence, and many of the letters begin with some reference to what the addressee has written, but, like the unnamed and non-extant speeches accompanied by the cover letters, that is something we have to imagine. The reply points to the word of someone else and to a continuing

---

[15] For self-praise as a morally salutary act, see 1.8.8, on the advantage of writing in praise of his own gift: Pliny is bringing himself to the proper attitude to giving, and he is forestalling the regret that sometimes ensues on a generous gift.

correspondence of which this letter is but an excerpt, and yet the
reply also stands on its own, duplicating what it attributes to its
addressee's letter. But it would be churlish to claim that Pliny has
simply covered the letter he is praising with his own, for Ferox's letter
has elicited this from Pliny as a counterperformance.[16] The society
that Pliny imagines in the *Letters* is one in which the correspondents
are constantly encouraging each other to go out and do likewise.[17]
Without the 'challenge' of Ferox's letter there would be no Plinian
response, and the letter maintains a delicate balance between inviting
us to imagine its inspiration and insisting on its own performance.

Pliny's *aenigma* of 7.13 is anticipated in the opening words of 7.2
(*Quemadmodum congruit...?*), where he asks how Justus can both
complain that he is encumbered by business and still request Pliny's
writings of him. The letter closes by assimilating itself to the works that
Justus has solicited. Pliny will wait until winter, when Justus will at least
have his evenings to himself before he sends the requested writings.
'Meanwhile, it is enough if *letters* aren't a nuisance; but they are and so
they will be shorter' (*Interim abunde est si epistulae non sunt molestae;
sunt autem et ideo breuiores erunt. Uale*). The same point is made in 7.9,
where Pliny concludes a letter of advice about how to pursue one's
studies with an apology for having written such a long letter that he has
eaten into Fuscus' study time (*et alioqui tam immodice epistulam
extendi ut dum tibi quemadmodum studere debeas suadeo, studendi
tempus abstulerim*, 7.9.16). The effect is to remind us that these letters,
too, are *scripta*. Ironically, it is the letters that have survived to reach an
audience far beyond the addressee, whereas even the identity of the
anonymous 'writing' that Pliny is sending is lost to posterity.

From the above, it will be clear that one of the most significant topics
of the *Letters* is the pursuit of *studia*, through which Pliny and many of
his correspondents aspire to achieve a lasting fame.[18] 7.13 is a good
example of the role that this common pursuit plays in epistolary

[16] See Wray (2001) 96–109 on epistolary exchanges in Catullus.
[17] Hoffer (1999) 11, citing as examples 3.7.15, 7.20.3.
[18] The most direct statement of this is 3.7.14: *sed tanto magis hoc, quidquid est
temporis futilis et caduci, si non datur factis (nam horum materia in aliena manu), certe
studiis proferamus*. In the cases with which I am concerned, *studium* is used in the
sense 'intellectual activity, esp. of a literary kind' (*OLD* 7a). Pliny's *Letters* feature
studeo 25 times, *studia* 113 times, and *studiosus* 13 times (Jacques and Ooteghem
(1967) ad locc.).

communication. Ferox has evidently complained, perhaps in answer to a query from Pliny, that he is not finding time for his *studia* and Pliny reassures him that his letter is the thing itself. Encouragement, commiseration, confession, and advice about finding time for one's *studia* are significant topics for Pliny's 'set'. But the status of *studia* is complex, for though they are central to the project of survival they can never be the main substance of a worthy life. They are and they aren't the thing itself, as the opening of 7.15 indicates:

Requiris quid agam. Quae nosti: distringor officio, amicis deseruio, studeo interdum, quod non interdum sed solum semperque facere, non audeo dicere rectius, certe beatius erat.

You ask what I am doing. You know the story: I am pulled this way and that by commitments; I slave away for my friends; from time to time I write. Writing full-time instead of from time to time would perhaps not be the better thing, but it would certainly make for a happier existence.

We are given conflicting accounts of the relative value of *studia* and *officia* right from the beginning of Pliny's epistolary oeuvre. In 1.9 Pliny reflects on the dissipating effect of the city's various claims on him and contrasts the distracted life of the city with the undisturbed concentration afforded by his Laurentian villa, where he speaks with nobody but himself and his books (1.9.5). He ends the letter by inviting Minicius to leave the bustle of the city and consign himself to *studia* or to leisure (*strepitum istum inanemque discursum et multum ineptos labores... relinque teque studiis uel otio trade*, 1.9.7). In the following letter he laments to Clemens that he has not had the time he would have liked to devote to the philosopher Euphrates, being preoccupied with duties (*nam distringor officio*, 1.10.9). But then he consoles himself with the thought that when he made the same lament to Euphrates, the philosopher reassured him that it is the better part of philosophy to engage in public life and to put into practice what the philosophers teach. To Caninius Rufus, at the beginning of Book 1, he exclaims 'When will you hand over your lowly and squalid business to others and claim yourself for your writing in that deep and rich retirement of yours. It's high time.'[19]

---

[19] *Quin te (tempus enim) humiles et sordidas curas aliis mandas, et ipse te in alto isto pinguique secessu studiis adseris?* 1.3.3. Contrast 9.3, where the same phrase recurs, but in a negative sense: *ac mihi nisi praemium aeternitatis ante oculos*, pingue illud

In Book 7, he asks Praesens 'When will you finally return to the city, the place of honours and offices, of influential friends and clients. How long will you play the king?' (*quin ergo aliquando in urbem redis? ubi dignitas honor amicitiae tam superiores quam minores. quousque regnabis?* 7.3.2). Here Pliny urges on the absent Praesens (!) the intermittence that he elsewhere deplores (*otium . . . quod ego non abrumpi sed intermitti uolo*, 7.3.4). Throughout the *Letters* Pliny maintains a constant tension between these two positions.[20]

The fact that, though *studia* are the best hope for lasting fame and the happiest choice of activity, they cannot form the substance of a worthy life, gives a particular rhythm to the existence reflected in the *Letters*. *Studia* are, and must be, pursued intermittently in time snatched from *officia*; *otium* and *negotium* must be rotated.[21] Even *studia* themselves must be varied, for the mind, like a field, needs rotation and must apply itself to a variety of genres (7.9.7 ff.). Alternation, intermittency, postponement, and provisionality are the characteristics of elite life as reflected in the *Letters*, and they constitute a recurrent theme of Book 7, marked repeatedly by compounds of *inter-* and *re-*.[22] It is appropriate, then, for this life to be reflected in a collection of letters, a genre which drops and resumes relationships and themes, updates news (7.6 and 10; compare 6.16 and 20), and interrupts the very *studia* whose pursuit it urges (7.9.16; cf.7.2.3). The connection between the intermittence of *studia* and that of an epistolary correspondence is brought to the fore by a striking sequence. Pliny ends 7.9 with the words 'why don't you resume the writing that my letter interrupted?' He then begins the following letter by prefacing its update of the news related in 7.6 with the words 'When I have heard the beginning of a story I want to hear the rest, as though it had been wrenched away from me'.

altumque *otium placeat* (on which, see Hoffer (1999) 39–40 n. 28). Leach (2003) discusses the difference between productive and unproductive *otium*.

[20] Compare 8.9, where Pliny complains that for a long time he has not taken up a pen, for the n*egotia amicorum* have allowed him neither to retire (*secedere*) nor *studere*. But he concludes: *nulla enim studia tanti sunt, ut amicitiae officium deseratur, quod religiosissime custodiendum studia ipsa praecipiunt.*

[21] Pliny's workaholic uncle is the prime example of *studia* pursued in rescued time (3.5.7–10, on which see Henderson (2002) 69–102). Rotation of *otium* and *negotium*: 7.3.4 and 7.7.2.

[22] For instance, 7.6.14; 7.9.5–8; 7.31.4.

If the welcome seclusion of *studia* alternates with the distractions of *officia* in the life of Pliny and his peers, these two poles produce distinctive epistolary positions. To return to 1.9, when Pliny reports that in his villa he speaks only with himself (*mecum tantum et cum libellis loquor*, 1.9.5), he is in fact speaking with (only) one other.[23] The retirement of the villa and the virtual conversation with the self are given body by the ideal of virtual conversation with the addressee in the focus of letter. Pliny invites Minicius to 'join' him in a distinctly epistolary place ('I wish you were "here"...'). In the following letter, after lamenting that he has no time to devote himself to philosophy, he recommends Euphrates to his addressee Clemens, who will be able to take advantage of him as the distracted Pliny cannot. This letter is in some respects a recommendation, and Pliny delegates to Clemens the pursuits in which he cannot indulge ('I wish I were there...'; cf. 2.8). Instead of creating a shared virtual space, as in 1.9, the letter here becomes a means of delegation through which the intermittency that dissipates and distracts the individual becomes a principle of community. We can see these two epistolary positions combined in 7.15, a short letter to Saturninus which confirms that mutual commiseration on the difficulty of finding time for *studia* is a sufficient motivation for an exchange of letters. The opening, quoted above, contains Pliny's account of himself, summed up in the characteristic phrase *distringor officio*.[24] As a consequence of this distraction, Pliny can only pursue his *studia* intermittently (*studeo interdum*). Evidently, Saturninus had made the same complaint in his letter to Pliny, who then reassures him, as Euphrates did Pliny in 1.10, that mediating between friends is thoroughly deserving of praise. It is no accident that when Pliny comes to reassure Saturninus, urging that arbitration among friends is thoroughly deserving of praise, the characteristic pairing of *dis-* and *inter-* recurs, but now in positive senses: dis*ceptare* inter *amicos laude dignissimum est* (7.15.2). The prefix and the preposition now convey connection rather than

---

[23] The conversation with the self is related to the conversation with another at 9.3.3: *haec ego tecum quae cotidie mecum, ut desinam mecum, si dissenties tu.*

[24] Morello (2003) 188 on *distringor*. Compare 1.10.9 and 3.5.19. The phrase *amicis deseruio* is striking, since the same verb has been used in the previous letter to Saturninus, but there with *studia* as its object (*te negotiis distineri ob hoc moleste fero, quod deseruire studiis non potes*, 7.7.2).

dispersal or interruption. Pliny then proceeds to practise what he preaches, speaking of their mutual friend Priscus, whose relationship with Saturninus Pliny had fostered in 7.7 (to Saturninus) and 7.8 (to Priscus). The *dis-* that scatters the individual between a variety of *officia* and the *inter-* that consigns true value to the interstices of the business of life become the *dis-* and the *inter-* that make, mend, and sustain friendships. Pliny's collection of letters is both a fractured series of shared moments snatched from the hurly-burly and a network of relations maintained, connected, and mediated by Pliny himself.[25] If the Letter is in general the locus of absent presences or present absences, in the case of Pliny and his correspondents this is given a particular inflection by the role that *studia* and *otium* play in elite life.[26]

In the finale of Book 7, the adequacy of the Letter to represent what is of value to Pliny comes into question, and this brings us back to the issue of whether the letter can be the thing itself rather than, for instance, the raw material for a history. An important prong of Pliny's pursuit of *gloria* is his claim to have been associated with the heroic opposition under Domitian.[27] Like the speeches that are to be his main path to immortality, the record of his career under Domitian must undergo careful revision. In the final letter of Book 7, Pliny consigns an anecdote about himself to Tacitus' safe keeping (cf. 9.11). When Pliny ends his book by offering Tacitus an anecdote about himself to be grafted onto (*inseri*) the latter's sure-to-be-immortal *Histories*, he would appear to defer to the superior genre. Tacitus will make more of this story in every way (*notiora clariora maiora*, 7.33.10). And yet the final word of the letter is *sufficit*: history must not exceed the bounds of truth, and the truth is enough for what has been well done (*et honeste factis ueritas sufficit*, 7.33.10). This final word has much the same effect as the concluding *perficis* of 7.13.2 (*aut es tu super omnes beatus, si talia per desidiam et otium perficis*), which by virtue of its closural position points to the elegant perfection of the present letter itself. For Pliny's anecdote, the plain

---

[25] This dialectic is given a different colour by Leach (2003) 158–9, who describes how *otium* becomes a medium of exchange, a social reciprocity 'that pre-empts the *otium* of some men in order to display the *otium* of others'.

[26] On 'epistolary presence', see Hardie (2002) 106–9; 283–5.

[27] Ludolph (1997) 44–8; Shelton (1987).

speaking of a letter is adequate after all.[28] Furthermore, Tacitus could hardly enhance an *exemplum* which, as Pliny goes on to relate, prompted Nerva himself to write and congratulate not only Pliny but the age itself for having produced such *exempla*.[29] In the end, this letter defers not to another genre but to another letter. Nerva's letter of congratulation brings full circle the book that had begun with Pliny providing an *exemplum* for Geminus; now he provides another, worthy of the ancients themselves (*ut te non sine exemplo monerem*, 7.1.7; *exemplum... simile antiquis*, 7.33.9). One might almost say that Pliny makes good on the *pignus* of the opening letter, in which he obligated himself to come through in difficult times, with this anecdote of grace under pressure. Admittedly, he makes good on his pledge with an anecdote about the *past*, but, as he points out elsewhere, he is not writing a history.[30] So Pliny retains this anecdote for his letter, the (genre of the) Letter and (Book 7 of) the *Letters*.

The anecdote entrusted to Tacitus is of a distinctively Plinian kind. It features Pliny the orator and advocate and it displays an exercise of eloquence, but not in the same way that the speeches would have done. Pliny's triumphant anecdote concerns his participation in the prosecution of Baebius Massa for extortion while governor of Baetica. After the successful prosecution his co-prosecutor, Senecio, wanted to secure the property of Massa in custody. Pliny opined that their involvement in the case was at an end, but that he would nevertheless support Senecio, who had a personal interest in the province. When the matter went before the consuls, Massa protested that Senecio was acting out of personal animosity, at which Pliny declared 'I fear... most illustrious consuls that by his silence Massa has accused me of complicity in that he has not made this accusation of me as well' (*uereor... clarissimi consules, ne mihi Massa silentio suo praeuaricationem obiecerit, quod non et me reum postulauit*, 7.33.8).

---

[28] For a similar, but more explicit, ending, see 7.26.4: *possum ergo quod plurimis uerbis, plurimis etiam uoluminibus philosophi docere conantur ipse breuiter tibi mihique praecipere, ut tales esse sani perseueremus, quales nos futuros profitemur infirmi. Uale.* (!)

[29] *Diuus quidem Nerua... missis ad me grauissimis litteris non mihi solum sed etiam saeculo est gratulatus, cui exemplum (sic enim scripsit) simile antiquis contigisset* (7.33.9).

[30] *Neque enim historiam componebam*, 1.1; compare 6.16.22, *aliud est enim pistulam, aliud historiam, aliud amico, aliud omnibus scribere.*

The anecdote, in which Massa's silence is replaced by Pliny's *vox*, nicely displaces Pliny's anxiety at the prospect of a Tacitean history of the Flavian period silent (*tacitus!*) about Pliny; as we shall see, the theme of silence is prominent in this book. Furthermore, his retort to Massa perfectly represents the non-oratory of the Letter. It may not impress by weight and *copia*, like a speech, but it achieves the same effect of tying the speaker's voice to authority. Its very brevity projects a confidence that need not display authority because it assumes it. In this moment of truth, Pliny comes through with a display of verbal finesse that is peculiarly the province of his letters, for Massa is outmanoeuvred with the same grace that Ferox is both complimented and trumped in 7.13.

From other letters it is clear that Pliny would have us believe that the ability and nerve to say the right thing under pressure is the form that heroism takes in the dangerous world of Domitianic (and post-Domitianic) Rome.[31] In this book, we might compare the defiantly laconic answers of Fannia to Mettius' questioning in 7.19: Fannia utters 'no word that is influenced by danger'.[32] Pliny's response to Massa is more elegant and less defiant; it can be compared to the witty put-down with which he declines to respond to Africanus in 7.6.12. After repeating that *mot*, Pliny comments 'I can't easily remember receiving such applause for giving a speech as I did then for not making one' (*non facile me repeto tantum adsensum agendo consecutum, quantum tunc non agendo*, 7.6.13). Certainly Massa's silence in the final letter is as pointed as Pliny's refusal to respond to Africanus, and in the anecdote entrusted to Tacitus we see Pliny himself threatened by the very principle which introduces his response to Africanus: 'sometimes it's no less the job of an orator to hold one's peace than to speak' (*non minus interdum oratorium esse tacere quam dicere*). Is Pliny as unworthy an adversary as he made Africanus in 7.6? Massa's silence dismisses Pliny as his own did Africanus. Earlier in 7.6 Pliny tells us that he had decided to hold his peace, because to speak on his client's behalf would have been to

---

[31] For example, the letters on the courage of Mauricus (4.22) and on Pliny's run-in with Regulus (1.5, especially 5–8).

[32] *Quaerente minaciter Mettio Caro, an rogasset respondit: 'Rogaui'; an commentarios scripturo dedisset: 'Dedi'; an sciente matre: 'Nesciente'; postremo nullam uocem cedentem periculo emisit*, 7.19.5.

admit that he needed defending.[33] But Massa's silence manages to make Pliny look guilty, not innocent. The treacherous times require mastery of an eloquent non-oratory that may take the form of a speaking silence. But silence is not the exclusive prerogative of advocates and prosecutors; audiences, too may wield it. 7.25 is another letter that concerns silence and judgement, but this time in the context of recitations. 'How many scholars are hidden and lost to fame by their own modesty or a retiring life! But we who are about to read or to speak fear only those who parade their learning, while those who do not speak are far superior in that they respect a great work by their silence' (7.25.1).[34] Silence, then, is respect. Or is it? The letter is a puff for Terentius Iunior, whom Pliny has just visited in rural retirement. Imagining Terentius to be something of a rustic, Pliny keeps off the intellectual talk until he finds that his interlocutor is leading him back to scholarly topics and proves to be a fount of learning. The result? 'It increased my worry and ensured that I fear those retired "rustics" no less than those whom I know as extremely learned.'[35] The letter takes us from respect (*reuerentia*) to fear (*uer-ear*), from the audience's respect for the reciter to the reciter's fear of his audience. Silence is unstable, and in this book it raises issues of guilt, innocence, complicity, and judgement; its ambiguity renders the oratorical situation treacherous. In the final letter, Pliny proves that he can turn silence to account. His retort to Massa is both a protest against a silence that would leave him out of account and an exercise of the non-oratory (*non agendo*, 7.6.13) that masters a situation by sheer finesse. Whether or not his friend Silent sees fit to graft this anecdote onto his *Histories*, it belongs firmly to the agenda of this book and, more broadly, of the *Letters*.[36]

---

[33] *Adsistebam Uareno iam tantum ut amicus et tacere decreueram. Nihil enim tam contrarium quam si aduocatus a senatu datus defenderem ut reum, cui opus esset ne reus uideretur, 7.6.3.*

[34] *O quantum eruditorum aut modestia ipsorum aut quies operit ac subtrahit famae! At nos eos tantum dicturi aliquid aut lecturi timemus, qui studia sua proferunt, cum illi qui tacent hoc amplius praestent, quod maximum opus silentio reuerentur.*

[35] *Auxit sollicitudinem meam effecitque ut illis quos doctissimos noui, non minus hos seductos et quasi rusticos uerear, 7.25.5.*

[36] See Hoffer (1999) 90–1 on the role of 'doing nothing' in Pliny's concept of prudence under the emperors.

I have been pursuing some epistolary tensions that cluster around the issue of 'the thing itself' and I will end, appropriately, with pretexts. Those who would downplay the epistolary element in Pliny's *Letters* describe them as essays for which the epistolary form provides merely an excuse.[37] Compared to Cicero's letters, they do indeed tend to focus on a single topic, and the pretext for enlarging on some aspect of the author's experience or achievement often seems quite flimsy. But we should not simply discount the epistolary 'pretext' as a sham, for the play with pretext and purpose is itself an aspect of epistolarity. The 'response' to another's letter becomes an opportunity to tell one's own story in an epistolary equivalent of the conversational 'That reminds me of…'. The skill and even, as I will now suggest, the clumsiness with which Pliny moves onto his own ground, may be a significant factor in the letter's effect.

Pliny's epistolary openings have been usefully categorized by Sherwin-White, who includes in his list of opening gambits the expression of concern, sorrow, or pain in response to some piece of news, often conveyed in the addressee's letter (*angit, terret…me*, etc.).[38] The opening of 7.30 belongs to this class: 'I am tormented that you have lost a highly promising pupil, as you tell me' (*Torqueor quod discipulum, ut scribis, optimae spei amisisti*).[39] Genitor's secretary has died, but the transition from you to I is particularly swift and brutal. First, the slave's death is taken as an interruption of Genitor's *studia*, and this establishes us on the familiar Plinian ground of mutual commiseration about interrupted *studia*. Pliny, too, has been distracted from his *studia* by city business, even on his country estate.[40] From there, Pliny doubles back to Genitor's letter and its flattering comparison of Pliny's speech *De Ultione Helvidii* with Demosthenes' *Against Meidias*. Pliny did indeed have the Demosthenes in his hand while composing his speech, not out of a spirit of

---

[37] Most recently, Fantham (1996) 200–1. On the history of the dispute about whether Pliny wrote 'genuine' letters or not, see Gamberini (1983) 122–36.

[38] Sherwin-White (1966) 6–9.

[39] This letter can be paired with the next but one (7.32), which opens with a contrasting *delector* and concerns the manumission of slaves rather than the death of a secretary.

[40] *Cuius et ualetudine et morte impedita studia tua quidni sciam?… me huc quoque urbana negotia persequuntur… quibus ex causis precario studeo*, 7.30.1–4.

rivalry (how could that be?) but in order to imitate Demosthenes' speech, as much as the difference between their talents and their respective cases would allow. The focus has now shifted from the part of Genitor's letter which concerns his own news to the part which concerns Pliny. But the arbitrariness of the letter's transitions leaves a mark in the final words of the letter with their reference to the difference of the cases (*aut causae dissimilitudo pateretur*, 7.30.5). Demosthenes' *Against Meidias* was a speech against a personal enemy in a matter that engaged Demosthenes directly and immediately, whereas Pliny's *De Ultione Helvidii* was an attempt to associate himself retrospectively and from a (relatively) safe distance with the opposition to the previous dynasty by accusing Helvidius' accuser Certus.[41] Similarly, Pliny's *reasons* for interrupting his *studia* are less immediate and less tragic than Genitor's (*quibus ex* causis, *precario studeo* 7.30.4; compare causae *dissimilitudo*, 7.30.5). The final reference to different causes transmutes the connection between writer and addressee made in the opening of the letter into something grander. The letter is upgraded, but the fact that the death of Genitor's secretary becomes a pretext for a transition to Pliny's *studia* is intrinsic to the letter's effect. We are invited to compare the intense personal involvement of Demosthenes' *Against Meidias* to Genitor's loss of his slave, and to contrast these with Pliny's once-removed defence of Helvidius and his lesser reasons to be distracted from his work. The abrupt transition from Genitor's loss to Pliny's problems with his *studia* is, as it were, a pre-echo of the anxiety that attends Pliny's tardy enrolment in the opposition to the late emperor. Pliny's 'me too' is not entirely convincing in either case, but this epistolary gesture becomes the filter through which we read Pliny's political claims.

7.30 is fairly transparent in its agenda, but I turn now to one of Pliny's most oblique, and famous, letters. 7.27 is celebrated for its ghost story, but the story of the philosopher Athenodorus and the haunted house is one of three tales of the supernatural told in this letter.[42]

---

[41] Shelton (1987) 129–33 discusses this speech. Pliny's own account of the circumstances is in 9.13.

[42] No doubt the three stories conform to the *lex scholastica*, cited by Pliny at 2.20.9, which demands three illustrations of a thesis.

Idle curiosity provides the ostensible motive, as Pliny asks his addressee to put him out of his indecision: do ghosts exist, or are they projections of our own fears (*Et mihi discendi et tibi docendi facultatem* otium *praebet*, 7.27.1)? Naturally, Pliny himself has something to say about the subject, and he launches on the first story, which inclines him to believe in ghosts. The disinterested question, born of *otium*, that is posed in the opening words is repeated at the end of the letter with an urgency that would seem facetious did we not feel that the stakes had shifted in the meantime.[43] For with the last story Pliny finally comes round to himself and recounts a tale that has serious implications for his claim to have been a member of the opposition under Domitian. The letter finally reveals its agenda! And yet, though the third of Pliny's anecdotes clearly has a significance for him for which the other two have not prepared us, it is the second which is the longest and the most elaborate. This ghost story is set in Athens and far removed from the world of Roman politics, which is the context of the other two. If the final story turns the whole letter into an elaborate pretext for Pliny's political claim, the second makes broader connections with the themes of the book and serves as the neutral ground on which they can meet. This letter plays, perhaps coyly, with the structure of pretext that we come to expect from Pliny's letters. But it stretches the play of pretext and agenda to its limit, so that the imbalance produces a complex interplay of elements that works both within the letter and across the book.

In Pliny's first story, Curtius Rufus, on a tour of duty with the governor of Africa, encounters a woman of superhuman size and beauty who identifies herself as the spirit of Africa.[44] She tells him that he will return to Africa as governor, covered in glory, but that he will also die there. When one half of the prophecy comes true, Rufus despairs of his life and dies. The second story, introduced simply as 'more frightening and no less remarkable' (*magis terribile et non minus mirum*, 4) is the longest and most vivid. Once upon a time,

---

[43] *Proinde rogo, eruditionem tuam intendas. Digna res est . . . cui copiam scientiae tuae facias*, 7.27.15.

[44] The story is also recounted by Tacitus (*Annals* 11.21).

there was a haunted house in Athens whose inhabitants, terrorized at night and terrified by day, had fled, advertising the house in the hope that some ignorant soul might buy or rent it. Along comes the philosopher Athenodorus, looking for somewhere to rent, and finds this house available for a suspiciously low price. On making enquiries, he learns the history of the house. Not only is he undeterred by this, but he positively welcomes the opportunity to prove his mettle, and on the first evening of his possession he sets up his materials for work, determined not to let an idle mind conjure up fearful visions of the house ghost. The ghost duly appears, rattling his chains and beckoning to Athenodorus, who continues writing while the ghost stands over him. Eventually the distraction proves too much, even for him, and he follows the ghost to a courtyard, where it promptly disappears. The next day, with the permission of the magistrates, he has the place dug up and finds human bones still loaded with chains. Once these have been duly collected and buried, the ghost ceases to haunt the house. Athenodorus the Greek philosopher inhabits a world quite different from that of the other two stories, both concerned with Roman politics, and the sensational nature of the events is congruent with their exotic setting in the removed world of Greek philosophy. And yet, this story of *studia* interrupted and then (presumably) continued has obvious resonances with other letters in the book and in the Plinian corpus as a whole. The very location of the story, sandwiched between two that concern Roman political careers, echoes the location of *studia* in elite life, at the centre of value and yet snatched from the distractions of *officia*.

For his third story, Pliny moves closer to home and a phenomenon he can vouch for from his own experience. A slave and a freedman of his household both had the same dream that someone came to cut their hair; lo and behold! in the morning their heads were shorn and the cuttings lay on the floor. Pliny, quite perversely, understands this as a dream about *himself*, and one that portends a non-event. Since defendants on trial let their hair grow long, this haircutting, he declares, indicates that he will *not* be a defendant, and indeed he wasn't. But why should he have been? Here Pliny delivers his *coup de foudre*. On Domitian's death a denunciation (*libellus*) of Pliny by Carus was found in the emperor's desk. Had Domitian lived longer, Pliny might have been a martyr of the opposition. The dreams were a sign of danger avoided.

When Pliny ends his letter by repeating his request that Sura put him out of his indecision about the status of ghosts, we know that this is no longer a matter of idle curiosity: the status of Pliny's claim to be associated with the opposition is at stake (3.11.2–3 and 4.24.4–5; also 9.13). Does this claim require as hefty a suspension of disbelief as the story of Athenodorus' ghost? Anxiety about Pliny's political plausibility is cleverly interwoven with questions about the reality of ghosts. Perhaps the story of the denunciation found in Domitian's desk is a less fantastic version of a skeleton exhumed than Athenodorus' ghost story, which this anecdote brings down to earth and closer to home. Applying Athenodorus' story metaphorically to Pliny's anecdote, we might see his career under Domitian as a haunting source of unease that needs to be dug up and reburied once and for all. So the Athenodorus story lends Pliny's a sense of completeness: now we can put the past behind us and get on with living. In return, Pliny's story 'solves' the mystery of the chains on Athenodorus' ghost, which are never explained. Those chains might belong to a man (not) on trial. The two stories from utterly different worlds complement each other.

We could be excused for thinking that the whole of 7.27 is a pretext for introducing the denunciation in Domitian's desk, a silent witness to Pliny's political credibility, which he forces to speak as advantageously as he will Massa's dismissive silence in the book's final letter. The letter feints. But, once again, we cannot simply discount the pretext, which not only takes up the major part of the letter but provides the context for reading the last anecdote.

The story of Athenodorus and the ghost, obliquely related to Pliny's prime agenda in this letter, acquires, by its very uniqueness, a prominence which allows it to serve as a focal point for other themes in this book. I have already suggested that it relates to the theme of *studia* interrupted and resumed, a theme which is recurrent in the *Letters* as a whole. But Book 7 features another ghost, and it appears in a quite different context. It is the ghost of Pliny's absent wife, which appears in a short love letter telling his wife how much he misses her (7.5). He is living in a house that is haunted by her, for a great part of the night is spent in wakeful visualization of her image (*magnam noctium partem in imagine tua uigil exigo*, 1; *imago* of the ghost, 7.27.6) while during the day his feet carry him to her empty room, from which he returns like an *exclusus amator*.[45] The only respite from these torments is the time he spends in court (*unum tempus his tormentis caret, quo in foro et amicorum litibus conteror*). The letter concludes with an epigrammatic paradox which plays cleverly with the *Letters'* running theme of distracting *officia*: 'imagine what a life is mine, for whom rest is found in work and solace in trouble and anxiety'. We might almost see the story of Athenodorus' ghost as a parody of this letter, with its ghost (*imago*) from whose haunting Pliny finds relief only in the distraction of *officia*; Athenodorus, by contrast, had sought to avert his thoughts from the ghost by applying himself to his writing.[46]

I want to suggest another, slightly less obvious, parallel to the Athenodorus ghost story. It is the obituary letter for Ummidia Quadratilla (7.24), the object of one of the most attractive character studies in Pliny's letters. Pliny describes how this fun-loving (decadent?) lady lived in the same house as her upstanding grandson, but did not live the same life. Unlike Athenodorus, the young Quadratus is not distracted from his *studia* by his housemate (7.24.5) and that largely because Ummidia is careful to protect him from her own influence. This odd couple manages a mutually respectful cohabitation until Ummidia dies and Quadratus emerges as the proper heir to continue the glorious tradition of the house (*uixit in contubernio auiae delicatae seuerissime, et tamen obsequentissime*, 3). The Quadratus house is everything Athenodorus' rented lodgings are not. Not just a place to live, nor even a household, it is an aristocratic 'house': a link in the continuity of Roman history, a source of honour (or disgrace), a tradition. But the parallels allow the lone Greek scholar to locate the more connected Romans by contrast: what the ghost is to Athenodorus, his grandmother is to

---

[45] *Inde quod interdiu . . . ad diaetam tuam ipsi me, ut uerissime dicitur, pedes ducunt; quod denique aeger et maestus ac* similis excluso *a uacuo limine recedo*, 7.5.1.

[46] Notice also that the preceding letter, about Pliny's *nugae*, contains his homosexual erotic poem in imitation of Cicero on Tiro (7.4.5). Pliny now writes a letter which recasts heterosexual erotic *topoi* (most strikingly, the *exclusus amator*) and reclaims this material for the Letter. On Pliny's letters to his wife (6.4, 6.7, 7.5), see de Pretis (2003) and Shelton (1990).

Quadratus and his absent wife is to Pliny.[47] The philosopher finally lays to rest the ghost which caused the house in question to be abandoned and, similarly, Quadratus restores the standing of his house after the not-entirely-respectable goings-on under Ummidia. Pliny's love letter has no such denouement, for it is not a story. The letter itself is testimony that the right state of affairs pertains *chez* Pliny.

Ghostly presences and imperfectly shared cohabitation seem appropriate figures for the Letter. But if the narrative forms of this motif have to be 'resolved', the epistolary form does not. The letter's the thing.

[47] 7.24 makes a pair with the letter on the utterly different Fannia (7.19). There Pliny worries that the family will never produce a comparable scion: *ac mihi domus ipsa nutare, conuulsaque sedibus suis ruitura supra uidetur* (7.19.8). In the present letter, Quadratus will restore the house to its proper glory, obscured under the genial regime of Ummidia (*laetor etiam quod domus aliquando C.Cassi... seruiet domino non minori* (7.24.8).

9

The *Epistula* in Ancient Scientific and Technical Literature, with Special Reference to Medicine

D. R. Langslow

In two recent volumes of collected essays on, respectively, the dissemination and transmission of knowledge in Greek culture,[1] and genres of ancient technical literature,[2] the letter, or epistle,[3] is notable by its absence.[4] This absence, whether accidental or not, is in spite of the fact that letters constitute a small but not insignificant portion of surviving Greek and Latin technical literature on a wide range of

I should like to thank the editors for inviting me to contribute to this volume, so inspiring me to begin a new line of inquiry, and for their patience and encouragement. Successive draft versions of this paper were delivered at the universities of La Coruña, in October 2005, Glasgow, in January 2006, and Newcastle, in February 2006. I am indebted to all participants in the discussion on all three occasions for their insightful comments and pause-giving questions. For comments and information I am especially grateful to Jim Adams, Mary Beagon, Philip van der Eijk, Heinrich von Staden, and Klaus-Dietrich Fischer (to the last-named also for letting me see the text of Mavroudis and Fischer (2005) and Fischer (forthcoming *a* and *b*) before publication).

[1] Kullmann and Althoff (1993).

[2] Kullmann, Althoff, and Asper (1998).

[3] The special use of 'epistle' to refer to a letter intended from the first for publication, and lacking the particular private motivation of the 'letter' proper, goes back to Deissmann (1923) 194–6. I shall not employ it here.

[4] Letters on technical subjects are ignored also by Fögen (2002) 34–7, and they receive only cursory notice in Castillo (1974) 437. The forms of technical literature are not a concern of De Meo (1986), nor, it seems, of Meißner (1999).

disciplines, and were evidently both heterogeneous and popular from early in our record to the end of antiquity and throughout the Middle Ages.[5]

The absence of the letter from the wide-ranging volumes just referred to may be symptomatic of a wider neglect, for anything approaching a systematic study of ancient scientific and technical letters has yet to be undertaken.[6] Ideally, such a study will one day form part of a comprehensive account of ancient literary letters of all types, to the mutual benefit of the loftiest literary and the lowliest 'technical' examples of the form, since the boundaries between, say, a letter of Horace and one of 'Hippocrates' addressed to Maecenas may ultimately be regarded as matters of degree rather than of kind, and the study of each stands to gain from at least an awareness of the other.[7] While literary form is quite a different matter from language, there is still force in the caveat that I have urged elsewhere,[8] that we risk 'impoverishing our appreciation of literature by relegating technical works too fiercely below canonical *belles lettres*, or to put this positively, there is a real general value for our appreciation of ancient and medieval canons in the best possible understanding of the... diversity within which the canonical texts stand and with which they inevitably interact'.

This essay has two aims: namely, to offer a critical survey of some of those ancient letters which form part of scientific and technical literature, and, at the same time, to consider, in outline at least, certain more particular questions under the following four, inter-related, headings, the first at much greater length than the other three:

1. the content of the letter, with regard to its ostensible purpose, and its subject-matter, length, and degree of technicality;

[5] The popularity and heterogeneity of surviving letters of this sort are inadequately illustrated even by the *TLL*, s.v. 'epistula', v, 683, 23 ff., although it bears to be remembered that this article was published in 1935.

[6] Note, however, that Aimilios Mavroudis has recently announced a project to assemble a corpus of all Greek and Latin medical letters, from the earliest examples to the Middle Ages (in Greek, from the 4th cent. BC to the 14th cent. AD; in Latin from the 1st to the 12th cent. AD): see Mavroudis and Fischer (2005).

[7] Any such comprehensive account, identified as a desideratum by Wilamowitz in 1881 (see Sykutris (1931) 188), remains to be attempted.

[8] Langslow (2005) 302.

2. the identity and standing of the letter's professed author and recipient;
3. the function of the letter-form; and
4. the style of the letter.

I consider both Greek and Latin letters, and take account of testimonia as well as surviving examples. The emphasis throughout is on letters relating in some way to (human) medicine or medical texts, but comparisons and contrasts are drawn with letters transmitted in the context of other technical disciplines and with letters of other types altogether.

The wider literary setting is important for several reasons, which offer themselves as helpful if obvious axiomatic preliminaries. In the first place, the juxtaposing of better-known, classical examples may help to situate the less familiar, later letters with which we are here mainly concerned. In the face of so much uncertainty, and in advance of a comprehensive study, it makes little sense to treat in isolation letters from a single period or of one particular type[9]—and, in fact, each of the four main categories of letter (private, official, literary, pseudepigraphic)[10] is relevant to our survey of medical letters. I do not mean that any such situating should be taken to imply genetic or generic dependence. While the possibility of inspiration and influence in either direction between private and public letters, and between Greek and Latin epistolography, is in principle, let us suppose, available at any time, we should not exclude the possibility of polygenesis. So, for example, if the letters of the Roman jurists to their pupils under Nerva, Trajan, and Pius are said[11] to be reminiscent of those of Epicurus to his, this need be no more than a typological parallel (rather than a statement of dependence). Moreover, it is in general terms risky, and potentially seriously misleading, to identify a single point of departure for a manifold literary phenomenon.[12]

---

[9] Zelzer (1997) quite rightly includes classical antecedents in her review of late-antique letters.

[10] This is essentially the typology of Schneider (1954), which is followed by Wiedemann (1976). Other important partitions include those of Sykutris (1931) and Schmidt (1997).

[11] Peter (1901) 220.

[12] For example, by naming only the *ethopoiia*-exercises of the rhetorical schools among the origins of the fictional letter (cf. Zelzer (1997) 336), while ignoring

Then there are the perils of transmission. These also urge the broad view, for, just as (in principle) any sort of text[13] can be turned into a letter by additions made,[14] if not by the author, by later copyists or editors, so a letter can become anything by trimming in the process of transmission. This has off-putting implications for one setting out to collect a corpus of letters on a given subject, in virtue of its important implications for the definition of a letter. In other words, any formal definition of 'letter' is in danger of catching the spurious and missing the genuine, and it is mainly for this reason that I cast my net wide in what follows, although definitional criteria recur in the discussion.[15]

various forms of poetry, including drama, and (e.g.) the exchange between Pausanias and Xerxes in Thucydides, 1.128–9. On the Greek 'letter novel', see Holzberg (1994) and his introduction to the volume.

[13] Esp. perhaps those with 2nd-person verb-forms, but clearly not only those (cf. the examples towards the end of (1) below). There is also the draft letter, not yet a letter because lacking the epistolary salutations, which survives e.g. in the extensive correspondence of Cerialis at Vindolanda (*Tab. Vindol.* ii, 225). I am grateful to Jim Adams for reminding me of this phenomenon.

[14] Cf. the preface to bk. 2 of Martial's epigrams, cast in the form of a prefatory letter replying to his friend Decianus, who has objected to Martial prefacing his epigrams with a letter, on the grounds that, while ' "tragedy or comedy get a letter [i.e. a prologue], not being able to speak for themselves, . . . they [epigrams] make a letter on any page they think proper" ' (tr. Shackleton Bailey); for excellent discussion and further references, see Trapp (2003) 291–3. Seneca is famously castigated by Peter (1901) 232–3, 248, for making his 'letters' by topping and tailing tracts, in contrast with the more personal approach of Epicurus (Peter (1901) 229); cf. Inwood in this volume. Similarly, if from a quite different context, Fink (1971) 348, generalizing from military reports, aptly observes that '[a] very large part of the public as well as the private business of the Roman world was conducted in the formal guise of letters'; Fink is quoted by Tomlin (1998) 55 n. 83 commenting on a military letter from Carlisle, 'which is really a report'. I owe these references to Jim Adams.

[15] Wiedemann, who gives in the introduction to his dissertation (Wiedemann (1976) 5–81) one of the best available historical overviews of the phenomenon, both Greek and Latin, seems, to judge from the texts that he reviews, to understand 'Lehrbrief' to include (in addition to the more obvious, as well as much less promising texts called 'epistula', on which more below) any short tract on a single theme that creates the impression through 2nd-person pronouns and verb-forms, and dialogue-orientated discourse-particles, even in the absence of straight vocative forms, that it is addressed to a particular reader (or readers).

1. CONTENT

I begin by considering the ostensible purpose of the letter as a whole. If the letter constitutes the vehicle—the illocutionary force, as it were—what is the meaning, or perlocutionary force, of (that portion of) the work conveyed within the letter? What job is the body of the letter doing?

The polar distinction here is between letters serving as dedications, or prefaces, separate from the principal work that follows,[16] and those standing as treatises in their own right. A few important examples seem to serve both functions, providing, in the manner of a substantial introduction, information on a theme related to that of the main work and/or indicating the arrangement of the main work, so serving as an articulate index or table of contents.[17]

There is a clear—and originally perhaps important—formal distinction between, on the one hand, the dedicatory letter proper, with its opening and closing formula of greeting, and its consistent 2nd-person address from sender to recipient, and, on the other, the sparer dedication achieved by means of a simple 'to X' in the title and/or one or more vocative forms, especially in the opening and closing sections.[18] While it is important to stress the apparent fluidity of the boundaries between the various types, it may be helpful to take this simple typology (schematically represented in Table 1) as a set of

[16] Many Latin examples are usefully introduced and discussed in the three volumes on prefaces to Latin works on technical-scientific subjects, Santini and Scivoletto (1990–2) and Santini, Scivoletto, and Zurli (1998).

[17] With or without the conventional rhetorical commonplaces of the ancient preface. On the relation between dedication and index, see Peter (1901) 242–3; on some famous classical examples, including Varro to Cicero in the preface to *Ling.* bk. 5 and Pliny's 'rather free letter' to the emperor in *HN* bk. 1, see Peter (1901) 244–9.

[18] If the vocative of the personal name of the addressee was avoided in certain sets of prose letters (and this is clearly not true of all, e.g. of Seneca's), its presence may be an indication that the text was not originally a letter as such, even if an epistolary salutation is also present. Alternatively, we must reckon with the existence of a mixed type, as e.g. in A. Hirtius' dedication of *B Gall.* 8, which, although it begins without epistolary greeting and with the bare vocative 'Balbe', ends, at least in part of the tradition, with 'Vale' ('Fare well!') and without a reprise of the vocative—or with authorial or editorial incompetence.

TABLE 1. *The ancient 'Lehrbrief': formal types and textual domains*

THE LETTER'S TEXTUAL DOMAIN → THE LETTER'S FORMAL MARKERS ↓	1. Preface only	2. Preface and introduction	3. Main work
Type A. Opening and/ or closing salutation			
Type B. 'To X' in the title and/or vocative(s) in the opening (and concluding) section(s)			

cardinal reference points within the formal variation encountered among surviving ancient letters.[19]

In prose at least, on some definitions,[20] a text of type B (in Table 1) would not count as a letter, although Greek ἐπιστολή and Latin *epistula* sometimes refer clearly to such forms, at any rate in verse,[21] and it is perhaps for this reason that the two types are commonly conflated in modern critical literature.[22] Obviously, if we include type B as letters, we increase very significantly the size of our corpus, and we considerably stretch the chronology. This is not only because of the large number of surviving examples, but also because we can then include systematically numerous lost works, both from pre-classical Rome and from archaic, classical, and even Hellenistic Greece, which may be the early forebears of later scientific

[19] One might complete the typology with a Type C in which the whole discourse is in the 3rd person: apart from some of the examples mentioned towards the end of (1) below, there is the interesting case of Galen's preface to what emerges is the second, improved edition of his *Anatomical Procedures* (2. 215–18 Kühn), dedicated to the late Flavius Boëthus, who inspired the first edition (all copies of which were consumed in a fire), and entirely in the 3rd person, except for the final clause, 'But now attend as I begin my account.'

[20] On the formal definition of a letter, and epistolary formulae, see the concise but rich and useful discussion in Trapp (2003) 1–3, 34–8.

[21] So e.g. pseudo-Archimedes' *Cattle Problem* (in 44 epic hexameters; II, 528–32 Heiberg–Stamatis) is characterized in its heading as a letter (ἐπιστολή) to Eratosthenes of Cyrene, although its only epistolary features are the repeated vocative 'stranger' (ξεῖνε) and 2nd-person verb-forms.

[22] They are not clearly distinguished even by Peter (1901) 242–9, and type B is often referred to as 'epistolary' by more recent scholars, e.g. by Flammini (1990) 70 on Firmicus Maternus, which raises the serious issue of whether, and if so how, to distinguish the letter from any work beginning with, or containing, a vocative form.

letters, but on whose form we can only speculate on the strength of titles, testimonia, or fragments. I have in mind works such as that *On Nature, to Brotinus, Leo and Bathyllus* by Alcmaeon of Croton (6th/ 5th cent. BC); Empedocles' *On Nature, to Pausanias* (5th cent.); the *Matters of Health, to Plistarchus* by the fourth-century doctor Diocles of Carystus.[23] While these works and others like them may have been prefaced by a dedicatory letter of type A, a safer comparison is likely to be with later surviving works such as that bible of pharmacy the *On the Raw Material of Medicine* (Περὶ ὕλης ἰατρικῆς) of Dioscorides (1st cent. AD),[24] and the three principal surviving works of the fourth-century medical compiler Oribasius,[25] all with prefaces of type B, or with works of which the dedication is confined to the opening vocative address, or to the title alone, such as Galen's *On prognosis, to Epigenes* (14. 599–673 Kühn) or his *On Whether Health is a Matter of Medicine or Exercise, to Thrasybulus* (5. 806–98 K.), respectively.[26]

In early Latin we have less to go on. This type may or may not be represented already by the Elder Cato's 'books' addressed to his son Marcus.[27] The first secure instance is literary, namely the dedication by the historian L. Coelius Antipater (late 2nd cent. BC) of his seven books on the Punic Wars to his friend L. Aelius Stilo,[28] and dedications of type B are certainly common in later works on technical subjects, as, for example, in the work of the land-surveyor Balbus (time of Domitian or Trajan),[29] or the astrological treatise of Firmicus Maternus (AD 334–7).[30]

---

[23] See Wiedemann (1976) 25–6, and van der Eijk (2000) xxxiv for a list of the testimonia.

[24] Dedicated to Areius of Tarsus, one of his teachers. See Wiedemann (1976) 26.

[25] That is, the *Medical Collection* (Συναγωγαί), dedicated to the Emperor Julian, the *Summary* (Σύνοψις) to his son Eustathius, and the *Ready Remedies* (Εὐπόριστα) to Eunapius.

[26] Cf. also Galen's *On the Medical Profession, to Patrophilos* (1. 224–304 Kühn), and *On the Order of his Own Books, to Eugenianus* (19. 49–61 Kühn). On those works of Galen which are in one way or another, however slightly, epistolary in character, see Wiedemann (1976) 26–31.

[27] On these see Schmidt (1972), LeMoine (1991) 344–7, Suerbaum (2002a) 409–13.

[28] Cf. Peter (1901) 243, with references to other early Latin examples. The vocative ('Luci...Aeli') in the quotation used at *Rhet. Her.* 4. 12. 18 to illustrate a feature of word-order, would suggest that this was a preface of type B.

[29] See Santini (1990) 137–42.

[30] Peter (1901) 248 n.

Letters of type A functioning as prefaces or dedications are common and various in Greek and Latin prose, and scientific and technical works on a wide range of subjects including medicine were apt to be prefaced by a letter. Famous examples include several mathematical works by Archimedes (*c.*287–212 or 211 BC) and Apollonius of Perge (late 3rd cent. BC),[31] and in Latin the astronomical work by Hyginus (?2nd cent. AD).[32] Medical examples of prefatory letters of type A seem to be commoner in Latin than in Greek.[33] Latin examples range in date from that of Scribonius Largus (time of Claudius) dedicating his pharmaceutical *Compositiones* to the imperial freedman C. Iulius Callistus,[34] to that of Anthimus (*c.* AD 500) addressing advice on diet to Theoderic, King of the Franks.[35] Scribonius' letter is included (although here falsely attributed to Celsus) as the fifth of the seven medical letters collected by the nobleman and imperial minister Marcellus among the prefatory material to his vast collection of medical recipes (under Theodosius, *c.* AD 410), material which begins with an index of chapters plus information on weights and measures copied from three separate sources, and which is headed by Marcellus' own prefatory letter to his sons.[36] Of the seven letters copied from his sources, the first (that of Largius Designatianus to his sons) and the sixth (that of Celsus to Pullius Natalis) are also purely prefatory, both purporting to

[31] For example, both books of Archimedes' *On the Sphere and the Cylinder*, prefaced with a letter to Dositheus; the first two books of Apollonius' *Conics*, to Eudemus, or the fourth, following the death of Eudemus, to Attalus. It is noteworthy that Eutocius of Ascalon, the 6th-cent. AD commentator on these great mathematicians, observes (p. 314 Heiberg) that Apollonius' third book lacks a prefatory letter. Eutocius himself uses only vocative forms to address each of his four books of commentary on Apollonius to the great architect and engineer Anthemius, and the first of the two books on Archimedes to 'Ammonius, best of the philosophers'.

[32] Peter (1901) 247; Santini (1990).

[33] Indeed, as far as I can see, none of the Galenic and pseudo-Galenic works of epistolary character listed by Wiedemann (1976) 26–33 is of type A.

[34] On Scribonius, see Römer (1987) and (1990).

[35] The latter is sometimes misleadingly referred to as a letter as a whole: there is a clear change of tone and form, and virtually an end of 1st- and 2nd-person forms— albeit without a closing salutation—at p. 4, 7, the end of the prefatory letter to the King.

[36] On Marcellus' own letter, see Segoloni (1990); in general on Marcellus, Kind (1930), Sabbah, Corsetti, and Fischer (1987) 111–13, Fischer (2000) 36–7, and esp. Fischer (forthcoming *a*).

introduce translations of Greek works.[37] A surprising omission from
Marcellus' collection is the letter of 'Apuleius Platonicus' to his fellow
citizens, the preface to the famous *Herbarius*,[38] which Marcellus uses,
and indeed refers to in his own prefatory letter (*Prol.* 2, p. 2, 13):
possibly, it has been suggested,[39] his copy of 'Apuleius' was acephal-
ous. Conversely, the fourth of Marcellus' letters—the *Letter of Plinius
Secundus to his Friends concerning Medicine*[40]—is of interest in being
a reworking as a letter of an older, extant prologue, and so an early
illustration of the strong appeal especially in Latin-speaking circles of
the medical prefatory letter.[41] A further general phenomenon that
finds illustration in Marcellus' collection is the detaching of a prefatory letter from the work which it introduces.[42] This has early,
literary antecedents, a famous surviving example being Cicero's
dedication to Varro of the revised version of the *Academica Posteriora*
(published separately as *Fam.* 9. 8). The pharmaceutical collection
prefaced by Marcellus' sixth letter (that of Celsus to Pullius Natalis) is
lost, as are the works purportedly introduced by the seventh (that of
Vindicianus to the Emperor Valentinian) and, possibly, by the third

---

[37] The Designatianus letter introduces a Latin translation (allegedly made from
memory!) of a letter from Hippocrates to King Antiochus, the second item in
Marcellus' collection. The Celsus letter, earlier attributed to Scribonius Largus (see
Wiedemann (1976) 45), purports to introduce another translation (not extant), in
which Greek 2nd-person verb-forms are systematically rendered impersonal. If the
ascription to Celsus is false, it may imply a fine observation of the consistently—and
unusually—impersonal language of Celsus' prescriptions (on which, see Pinkster
(1995) 562–3, with further references). This is, it is true, a feature also of Scribonius'
style, albeit not to the same degree as in Celsus. On the authorship of this letter, see
now the careful survey of Schulze (2005), who concludes tentatively in favour of the
earlier attribution to Scribonius.
[38] Ed. Howald and Sigerist (1927), together with other 'letters' mentioned below,
notably that attributed to Antonius Musa on the herb betony, and the anonymous
letter on the medicinal uses of the badger.
[39] Maggiulli (1997).
[40] Buffa Giolito (2000) presents a detailed comparison of this with Marcellus' own
preface and the preface to the pseudo-Apuleian *Herbarius*.
[41] This 'letter of Pliny' is a careless précis of the prologue to the *Medicina Plinii*, the
3rd- or 4th-cent. AD compilation of ready remedies, nearly all from Pliny, *HN* 20–32.
See Boscherini (2000) 7, and, for lit. on the *Med. Plin.*, Langslow (2000*a*) 64.
[42] Both this and the last point—the Latin taste for the letter form—are seen together
in the separate transmission in early MSS in letter form of Latin translations of the
prefaces of Galen, *To Glaucon, on the Method of Healing*, and of Oribasius, *Summary*
and *Ready Remedies*; see Wiedemann (1976) 47, 49, and Boscherini (2000) 8.

(that of Hippocrates to Maecenas). The last two belong to a sub-type of prefatory letter that is perhaps especially prone to separate transmission in that it combines the functions of preface and treatise in containing at least a substantive introduction to the subject announced (cf. my type A2 in Table 1), and thus has greater intrinsic value:[43] Vindician recounts two cases which demonstrate the superiority of his therapeutic approach, while 'Hippocrates'[44] teaches 'Maecenas' on the basis of an elementary Hippocratic physiology how to diagnose ailments at an early stage and prevent them from developing.

The technical letter as treatise (my type 3) is first securely attested in Greek in those of Plato and Epicurus. In Latin, it may be represented first in the shadowy pieces on political behaviour, which may have been used as political pamphlets, addressed to their respective sons by the Elder Cato and by Cornelia, the mother of the Gracchi.[45] Political precepts are taught also in Cicero's first letter to his brother Quintus and in Q. Cicero's own *Commentariolum Petitionis*. The latter treatise and much longer works of M. Cicero, including the *Orator*, the *Topica*, and the *De Officiis*,[46] are cast in the form of letters, although their length—and even that of the *Comment. Pet.*—strains the credibility of this conceit.

Medical tracts in letter form are well attested in both Greek and Latin, especially in the later Imperial period, although a few— surprisingly few—of the letters transmitted with the Hippocratic corpus belong here (at most, 19–24),[47] and some survive among Galen's works (to the best of my knowledge, all of my type B), including one giving advice to the father of an epileptic boy (11.357–78 K.), one on the pulse to Theutras (8.453–92 K.), another on the veins and arteries to Antisthenes (2.779–830 K.). Probably the

[43] The type intermediate between letter as preface and letter as treatise is well highlighted and illustrated for Latin medicine by Boscherini (2000) esp. 2–4.

[44] Given its references to 'Caesar', this letter was probably originally a pseudepigraph of Antonius Musa (see Fischer (forthcoming *b*)).

[45] See Suerbaum (2002*b*).

[46] On these works as letters intended from the first for a wider audience, see Schmidt (1974) 166–7. The letter of C. Cassius Parmensis to M. Antonius referred to by Pliny (*HN* 31.11) as containing a treatment for gout is likely to have been more political than medical in intent!

[47] On these letters (which are transmitted also independently of the Hippocratic corpus), see Pigeaud (1981), Smith (1990), Holzberg (1994).

best-known of all ancient medical letters is pseudonymous and survives in both Greek and (several) Latin versions. The Greek original
is the so-called letter of Diocles to King Antigonus, included in the
seventh-century *Medical excerpts* of Paul of Aegina (1.100.1–6).[48] In
Latin, this is most familiar as the letter of Hippocrates to King
Antiochus, the second item in Marcellus' prefatory corpus (above),
but it is transmitted in other traditions as well, and indeed Marcellus'
third letter—that of Hippocrates to Maecenas—is in part another
version of it. These two letters offering general advice on dietetics and
prophylaxis for the layman are the two most frequently copied
medical letters in the early Middle Ages.[49] They are closely followed
by the letter of the doctor Vindicianus (4th cent., Africa) to his
nephew Pentadius introducing Hippocratic humoral theory and
physiology, a pseudo-Hippocratic letter on blood-letting,[50] and
pseudo-Antonius Musa to M. Agrippa on the healing virtues of the
plant betony.

In the preface to the *De Herba Vettonica* we have a good example
of the minimal, token use of the letter form for what is essentially
a 3rd-person treatise. After the barest opening greeting, we plunge
straight into the doctrine and Agrippa is forgotten.[51] This is no less
true of the several versions, Greek and Latin, of the *Epistula de
Vulture*.[52] Indeed, one of the Latin versions is entitled simply *De
Medicamine Vulturis*, with the letter heading abolished; another calls
itself *Liber Vulturis*,[53] although it retains a garbled epistolary greeting
('Provinciae Babyloniae Alexandri regis Romanorum salutem').[54]
The Latin *Epistula de Taxone*,[55] purporting to be from a king of

---

[48] Most recently edited and commented on by van der Eijk (2000–1) fr. 183a.
Notice still Heinimann (1955).

[49] On these two letters, see Opsomer and Halleux (1985), Boscherini (2000) 3–4,
with further bibliography, Fischer (forthcoming *b*). On the former, see Nelson
(1932), Momigliano (1933).

[50] On these four letters, see Wiedemann (1976) 50–5.

[51] See Boscherini (2000) 2.

[52] See Mackinney (1943), Boscherini (2000) 5–7.

[53] Note that Vindicianus refers (p. 486, 2 Rose) to his letter to his nephew
Pentadius as a 'liber'.

[54] On this greeting, see Momigliano (1933). All the Greek versions purport to be
from one Bothros, variously a wise man or a king, addressing (usually) a/the king.
Momigliano suggests that Bothros is 'translated' as Alexander, Babylon as Rome.

[55] See Boscherini (2000) 7.

Egypt (Idpartus) to one Octavius (or Octavius Augustus), is again nothing more than a short compilation introduced by an obviously spurious letter formula (variously, 'Idpartus king of the Egyptians to his dear Octavius greetings', or 'Partus king of the Egyptians to Octavius Augustus greetings').

If these short compilations are letters solely in virtue of the greeting that they bear, other medical texts seem to have even less claim to 'letter status': two of the four pieces edited by Wiedemann (1976), and several others among the 33 items in the so-called *Book of Letters* (*Liber Epistularum*) of the ninth-century Brussels manuscript that forms the focus of his study (KBR 3701–15; made in western France) have no epistolary features whatever, not even 2nd-person forms.[56] This extreme point and the mention of a 'book of letters' lead us to our last category, letter-collections.

While most surviving scientific letters are transmitted as single, independent pieces, there is good, early evidence, albeit mainly testimonial, for the publication and copying of collections of scholarly letters.[57] The publication of such collections is first attested for Aristotle among Greek writers, and for Varro in Latin. If Cicero's letters to Atticus contain some items of scientific interest, these are scattered and isolated.[58] Varro's *Quaestiones Epistolicae* is the first well-documented collection of letters on scholarly topics, organized by subject and published as a collective work.[59] This collection is frequently cited by later authors, especially by Aulus Gellius, an important source of information on lost collections in general, and on Varro's in particular. The letters cited bear mostly on legal, antiquarian, and grammatical questions; none concerns medicine, although it is probable that Varro included medicine in his lost encyclopaedic work, *Disciplinae*.[60] Collections of jurists' letters are mentioned, the earliest being that of the great M. Antistius Labeo

[56] See now Fischer (2005) for an edition of two extremely non-epistolary 'letters' from the Brussels manuscript (originating in Isidore, *Origines*).

[57] Real examples of retained correspondence ('libri epistularum', letters received and copies of letters sent) are known from military contexts. Jim Adams draws my attention to Cugusi (1992) nos. 156–7, and one might note also Fink (1971) 355–6, 411, 417.

[58] Peter (1901) 216.

[59] See Peter (1901) 216–17; and cf. Morrison and Inwood in this volume.

[60] See Langslow (2000*a*) 36, 45 n. 128.

(d. AD 10/11; *Dig.* 41. 3. 30. 1), and another important early collection (*On Matters Investigated by Letter*) seems to have been published
in more than one book by the poet C. Valgius Rufus (cos. 12 BC).[61]
He, like Varro, is said to have written on medicine (Plin. *HN* 25. 4),
but the letters of his that are quoted are again on grammatical
questions, none relates to medicine.

Several (presumably published) collections of Greek medical letters are cited by the fifth-century African medical writer Caelius
Aurelianus.[62] Caelius had at his disposal at least nine books of *Epistulae*
to various named individuals by Themison of Laodicea (1st cent.
BC),[63] at least two books by Magnus of Ephesus (1st cent. AD),[64] at
least three by Antipater (?the 2nd-cent. AD Methodist);[65] Caelius also
refers (*Chron.* 2. 60) to his own book of letters, in Greek, addressed to a
certain Praetextatus. Given the abundance of testimonies to such
medical collections, it is striking that the only surviving examples of
this sort of publication should be not on human but on veterinary
medicine, in the treatises of Apsyrtus (in Greek: ?2nd/3rd cent. AD)
and Pelagonius (in Latin; ?late 4th cent. AD), both consisting of letters
to individual friends ordered by their subject-matter. These letters tend
to be very short, often stripped down to a heading (always placed at
the start of a chapter) of the form, for example, 'Pelagonius says to his
dear Falerius' or even just 'Pelagonius to Arzygius', although a few are
more developed. Adams has shown that they are stylistically uniform,
but he leaves open the question whether they are based on real letters
written by Pelagonius to his horse-owning friends and acquaintances
or rather fictional headings modelled on those of Apsyrtus—or indeed
whether the latter also are fictitious,[66] which would imply that the
form held vitality and appeal in imperial Greek as well as Roman elite
circles.

---

[61] Gell. *NA* 12.3.1. Peter (1901) 219.

[62] On these, see Boscherini (2000) 8.

[63] Cael. Aur. *Acut.* 3.186 'in a letter to Asilius'; *Chron.* 1.54; 3.80; 4.4 'in a letter to
Dimas', 4.108.

[64] Cael. Aur. *Acut.* 3.114 'in the second book'.

[65] Cael. Aur. *Chron.* 2.157, 187 'in a letter to Gallus', 'in the third book'.

[66] See Adams (1995) 9–12, on the epistolary form, 151 n. 5, for a list of the
epistolary passages, and 150–62, on the stylistic unity of the epistles. The remains
of Apsyrtus' work are published in Oder and Hoppe (1924–7). On the relation
between Pelagonius and Apsyrtus, see also Fischer (1989) 81.

Finally, mention should be made of the few corpora of letters (*libri epistularum*) surviving in early medieval manuscripts. These differ—so, at least, one presumes—from the thematically ordered collections just described in being miscellanies, but the prominent medical examples are extensive—Wiedemann's 'Lettercorpus I' comprises more than thirty items—and they were evidently popular. It is important to distinguish corpora *of* letters from corpora *including* letters (in which the letters stand as treatises, or prefaces, alongside texts cast in other forms).[67] The phenomenon of a corpus of medical texts is attested already by Cassiodorus (*Inst.* 1. 31. 2; mid-6th cent.); that the manuscript evidence for corpora of medical letters begins early, even apart from the Marcellus collection, suggests that they reflect an ancient reality.[68]

In the foregoing survey of the types of ancient scientific and technical texts presented in epistolary form, we have touched in passing on numerous examples of the subjects covered, in terms both of the technical field and of the degree of technicality of its treatment. Certain subject areas emerge as particularly inclined towards letters. Within these fields all manner of topics are treated.[69] For all the overlaps between Greek and Latin letters, notably in the areas of philosophy and medicine, some of the differences may reflect not merely accidents of survival but genuine differences in the intellectual pursuits of the respective elite (and sub-elite) groups in various periods. For example,

[67] An example of the latter type is the transmission of the letter of Hippocrates to Maecenas together with the ancient corpus of herbals which includes most famously Pseudo-Apuleius and Sextus Placitus (edited by Howald and Sigerist (1927) as vol. 4 of the *Corpus Medicorum Latinorum*).

[68] The independent tradition of 'Hippocrates' to 'Maecenas', for example, begins remarkably early, with Munich, BSB, clm 29688 [formerly 29134] (early 7th cent.; *CLA* 1312). For details of the individual letters, and of the manuscript evidence for each, see especially Wiedemann (1976) 47–81. Both of the 'letter corpora' on which he focuses (on his 'Lettercorpus II', see esp. Scherer (1976)) are transmitted, in whole or in part, in numerous pre-Salernitan manuscripts (for description and discussion of which, see above all Beccaria (1956)).

[69] As for medicine, the first five subjects in Mavroudis and Fischer (2005), ranked by number of manuscript copies, are: dietetics and prophylaxis; bloodletting; visiting the sick; history and ethics of medicine; and anatomy-physiology, including elementary humoral theory. Other subjects treated include aspects of phyto- and zoo-therapy and various individual diseases. These topics, then, appear to lie at the heart of what Heinrich von Staden helpfully suggests might be called 'epistolary medicine' (as distinct from medical epistolography).

the Hellenistic scientific culture mirrored in letters on mathematics and physics was without a counterpart in Rome, where it is not surprising that intellectual epistolography until the time of Hadrian should be dominated by political, antiquarian, grammatical, and legal interests.[70]

On the whole, however, if one excepts the Hellenistic scientists, Dziatzko's old generalization holds for both Greek and Latin letters, namely that they treat only 'rarely a technical theme... since, if it is for the sake of its lighter form that the author opts to write a letter instead of a treatise, its object must analogously be calculated to appeal to a wider audience'.[71] This accessibility is reflected also in the other aspects of the letter to which I now turn for briefer consideration, namely, the relation, real or supposed, between sender and recipient, the purpose of the letter-form, and the style of the letter.

2. SENDER AND RECIPIENT

What is the standing of the professed author and of the supposed recipient of the letter, and what is the relationship between the two? I have already touched (in (1) above) on the first point that I wish to highlight here, namely that the appropriateness of the match between a letter's theme and its recipient can range from superficial tokenism to real, personal relevance. At the one extreme, there is the accidental reusing of a 'stock' dedicatory letter already sent to someone else (to which Cicero confesses at *Att.* 16. 6. 4); at the other, is the deliberate relating of the themes of the missive to the link between author and addressee (as we see in Cicero's addressing his *Cato* and *Laelius* to Atticus, or the *De Oratore* to his brother Quintus).[72]

As for the relationship between sender and recipient of technical letters, it is only to be expected that the sender is either the recipient's superior in his control of the subject or his intellectual equal. The epistolary relationship between intellectual equals is attested in

[70] See Peter (1901) 216–20.   [71] Dziatzko (1897) 842.

[72] The classical examples are well discussed by Peter (1901) 244–9, who castigates Seneca (n. 14 above), but praises Velleius Paterculus for working quite elaborately into his *Historia Romana* its dedicatee M. Vinicius.

both Greek, from the Hellenistic period (e.g., again, in the work of Archimedes and Apollonius of Perge), and Latin, beginning with the reciprocal dedications of, respectively, the revised *Academica* and the *De Lingua Latina* by Cicero and Varro.[73] The sender is never the less knowledgeable party, although inferior competence is often conventionally feigned through the rhetorical playing down of the author's learning and/or the playing up of that of the recipient, to the extent of pretending that the work is being sent to the dedicatee for his correction.[74] Much more frequently, however, the scientific or technical letter is addressed by a senior to his junior, whether by parent to child, or by expert to non-expert.[75] As far as I can see, this holds without exception in epistolary medicine, where there are no surviving examples of the former relationship, of letters sent between intellectual equals, only of fathers writing to their sons, of the doctor writing to patients, friends, patrons, all less expert than he, often in immediate need of help and advice. We have already alluded to medical father–son letters in reviewing the letters included by Marcellus in his preface, together with his own dedication of his entire work to his own sons.[76] In the letters of Apsyrtus and Pelagonius on the care of horses, we have clear instances of the expert writing to his amateur friends. The exchange between Hippocrates and Democritus in the climactic sequence of the Hippocratic letters (18, 20–1) offers perhaps a plausible exception, although these pieces are as much about philosophy as medicine and, whether or not by this point in the sequence of letters they are still part of an epistolary novel, closer to the diatribe than the treatise.[77]

[73] See esp. *Att.* bks. 13 and 14, and, on these and other examples, Peter (1901) 244.

[74] For examples, including Hyginus, Censorinus, Justin, Solinus, and Ausonius, see Peter (1901) 247–8.

[75] Examples of fathers writing to their sons include (pseudo-)Hippocrates (letter 22) and the Elder Cato, directly, and the Elder Seneca and Quintilian, indirectly. For the 'expert to non-expert' type, note the 'introductory handbook' which Varro composed for the politically inexperienced consul designate Pompeius (Gell. *NA* 14. 7). Cf. Peter (1901) 247, and Norden (1905) 524–7, for these and other examples.

[76] That of Vindicianus to his nephew Pentadius is a close variant. If the sender (Arsenius) and recipient (Nepotianus) of the (?4th-cent. AD) letter on the correct nature of the medical profession, which begins with 'to my dearest son greetings', are correctly identified, then we have here a special, epistolary use of the word *filius* 'son'; see Boscherini (2000) 4 and n. 12. On father–son letters, cf. Ebbeler in this volume.

[77] I am grateful to Thomas Rütten for discussion of this point.

An interesting species of the 'expert to non-expert' type is of letters from the expert to the Powerful Man. This is known in other disciplines,[78] and also as a form of literary entertainment. It is prominent in surviving pseudepigraphic letters and letter collections, such as those of Plato to Dionysius II (?3rd cent. BC), those of Euripides to Archelaus, those of Aeschines to the Council and People of Athens (both ?1st/2nd cent. AD),[79] although it is important to stress that none of these are really technical or scientific letters, not even those of Hippocrates to Hystanes, Artaxerxes' 'governor of the Hellespont', early in the story told in the Hippocratic letters (nos. 4–5).[80]

Some isolated later medical examples were seen in passing in (1) above. Some of these are patently pseudepigraphic, such as those of Diocles to Antigonus (= Hippocrates to Antiochus), of Herophilus to Antiochus (in Latin),[81] and of Galen to Alexander the Great (in Greek).[82] Others, however, such as Vindicianus' to Valentinian, or Anthimus' to Theoderic, may reasonably be taken at face value, and so seen as precious proof of the plausibility of the genre, in addition to its evident vitality and appeal. Superior as he is in power, the Machthaber addressed in letters of this sort is the doctor's inferior in knowledge, and stands in need of the advice and explanations conveyed by the letter.

As it is such an eminently falsifiable hypothesis, it deserves to be stressed again that apparently the addressee of every surviving letter on a medical subject is the author's inferior in terms of expertise, being either altogether 'fachextern',[83] that is, outside the profession of medicine, or at most a student. It may be that we have simply lost the technical correspondence between Hellenistic or imperial doctors in the age of Herophilus or that of Galen. If so, the pattern of survival is

[78] So, for example, Archimedes addresses his *Sand-reckoner* (II, 216–58 Heiberg–Stamatis) to Gelon, son of Hieron II of Syracuse.

[79] For discussion of this type, see Holzberg (1994).

[80] The feeble medical compilation constituting letter 24 (to King Demetrius) would, however, count here.

[81] Ed., trans., and comm. by Fischer and von Staden (1996); and see the valuable remarks on the whole sub-genre of medical 'epistolographic pseudepigrapha' in von Staden (1989) 579–81.

[82] London, BL, Sloane 1610 (14th cent.), fo. 42ᵛ. See Mavroudis and Fischer (2005).

[83] I take the expression from Gläser (1990); cf. Roelcke (1999) 46.

telling of the tastes and interests of consumers of epistolary medicine. If the prefixing of famous names might help to advertise and sell some texts (cf. (3) below), the continued popularity of such letters must have been due in large part to their genuine utility. Only this can explain the copying of a letter on gout, written about AD 1400 to a visitor to Byzantium, composed by an assistant of the doctor Iohannes Kaloeidas, in a sense as a second go, at the request of the patient, who had been unable to understand the doctor's first attempt to explain by letter the cause, course, and dietetic treatment of the disease![84]

3. FUNCTION

Why does a technical writer—or the redactor of a technical piece—choose to present his work in the form of a letter? Or, conversely, why is this form so popular? It is presumably the popularity of the form that accounts for the curious extension of the word 'epistula' to refer to texts with few, if any, true epistolary features (cf. (1) above). Wiedemann defers an eventual answer to the time when a broader history of the 'genre' is available,[85] but this is too cautious, as some aspects of the manner of employment of the form suggest reasons for its selection.

The conclusion of section (2) above is consistent—albeit with (at least) one important qualification—with Boscherini's summary answer to this, our third question: 'in sum, the epistolary form becomes a regular means of scientific communication, especially when the intention is to teach with brevity and efficiency rules and principles regarded as fundamental'.[86] We need, however, to replace 'scientific communication' with 'instruction at a low level of technicality'; and we should add also that this can apply as well to fictitious as to genuine letters.

In the first instance, to be sure, the author writes in this form because he is writing to a real individual known to himself, whether or not he

---

[84] This 'doctor's letter' (ἐπιστολὴ ἰατροῦ) is reported and published by Schmalzbauer (1974) from a Vienna manuscript (med. graec. 47) of the late 15th cent.
[85] Wiedemann (1976) 50.   [86] Boscherini (2000) 8.

intends the contents of the letter to be made available to a wider audience. Early on, we have the vivid testimony of Archimedes and Apollonius that their main purpose in dispatching their works by letter is to ensure speedy publication among interested colleagues in other parts of the Greek world. In their cases, as we have seen, the main body of the works so transmitted is not in letter form, so that to claim that they are supplementing the earlier dialogue between fellow citizens, in the wake of the geographical expansion of the intellectual world following the conquests of Alexander, is perhaps to stretch a point.[87]

A quite different factor favouring the choice of the letter form is, however, surely related to publication, if in the slightly different sense of selling copies of the text rather than propagating the ideas within it. While in some didactic letters the *mise en scène* reflects more or less the historical reality, the use of false names is surely an element of 'sales technique'. The pretence of offering the work of an eminent physician addressed to a patient or patron of high standing will have been to reassure the prospective purchaser of the high quality and credibility of the content. This factor is attested in some earlier, historically real examples, including the oldest surviving Latin medical dedication, that of Scribonius Largus, who thanks C. Iulius Callistus for bringing his work to the attention of the emperor, Claudius.[88] This desire to associate technical writings with a famous dedicatee is reminiscent of the naming of medicaments after inventors or consumers of high standing, which is also well documented from the beginning of our Latin medical record.[89] It also explains why names are 'updated' in some of the pseudepigraphic medical letters, why, for example, Diocles and Antonius Musa give way to the universal renown of Hippocrates, and why Antoninus and Titus appear as more familiar imperial dedicatees beside, respectively, Antiochus and Theoderic.[90]

[87] Wiedemann (1976) 19.

[88] Cf. Scrib. Larg. *Epist. dedic.* 13 'sub tanti nominis editione'.

[89] See Langslow (2000a) 134–7. On 'such famous names', see also Peter (1901) 227, 245, and Paolucci (2000) 243.

[90] Boscherini (2000) 8–9. The late Latin *Letter concerning Virgins* (a two-page, 3rd-person tract on female fertility, entirely without epistolary features) is variously attributed to Hippocrates, Emogrates (?=Democritus), and 'Iustus and Erasistratus', the last combining a great physician of the past with one much closer in time to the date of manufacture of the 'letter'; on this text, see Fischer (2002).

It is well known that a letter of any sort may be, and often is, presented as a gift (δῶρον, *munus*), either in and of itself or, if it is a prefatory letter, for the more substantial work that it introduces or dedicates (cf. (1) above). This is a well-worn topos by the time of Cicero, who makes a pun on the word *munus* in a dedication to Varro (*Fam.* 9. 8; cf. (1) above), but this function is as well suited to elementary and self-help medicine as it is to the present of a letter or other work on a scholarly or a philosophical theme, and the same word is still used by pseudo-Celsus of the translation that he is sending to Pullius Natalis (p. 44, 12 Niedermann–Liechtenhan). That the gift may be the more abstract one of offering inspiration to learning is nicely illustrated in the reason that Marcellus (*Prol.* 6, p. 4, 13–16 Niedermann–Liechtenhan) gives to his sons for including in his preface the prefatory letters of his sources: 'I have included their letters, too, since their perusal will be able to inspire you to acquire the relevant knowledge as well as to instruct you in matters of health'.

4. STYLE

In ancient rhetorical theory, it is interesting that a similar set of stylistic qualities—including especially brevity, clarity, simplicity, and plainness—is enjoined by theorists and practitioners alike both for a letter and for a technical treatise.[91] This would lead us to expect that the style of the letter as preface or dedication would compare closely with that of the accompanying treatise, and that the letter as treatise should be closely comparable stylistically with treatises in non-epistolary form on the same or similar topics. There is a tension here, however, as the style of letters on technical subjects is often more elevated—less plain—than the treatises themselves.[92]

---

[91] On the recommended style of letters, see Sykutris (1931) 193–5; on that of technical literature, see most recently Fögen (2002) 38–42.

[92] Examples among those authors mentioned earlier include Archimedes and Apollonius of Perge in Greek, Scribonius Largus and Anthimus in Latin. On this tension, see already Peter (1901) 249.

Nor is this the only respect in which some surviving ancient medical letters appear to break the rules, as it were. Indeed, if we apply to the technical letters that we have reviewed here the oldest extant set of rhetorical prescriptions concerning 'the style of letters', in pseudo-Demetrius, *De Elocutione* (223–35; ? 1st cent. BC),[93] we find that they are on several counts excluded as letters by definition. Most blatantly, many of the items that we have considered are ruled out of court on grounds of their subject-matter by the injunction (*Eloc.* 230) 'It is not only a certain style but certain topics which suit letters. . . . If anyone writes on logic or science in a letter, he is writing something but certainly not a letter'![94] If some medical letters be spared here, as being on topics which do not count as science, they may yet fail if they are (228) 'too long and, furthermore, rather pompous in language', as such pieces 'can assuredly never become letters but are monographs with the conventional opening of a letter, as in the case of many of Plato's letters and that one of Thucydides'. We have certainly seen some medical examples which fall foul of the latter precept, if not in point of length.

On the other hand, many ancient medical letters follow the precept that letters should be close in style to dialogue: Demetrius recommends that a letter should be (224) 'slightly more elaborately written than a dialogue, because the latter aims at an effect of improvisation but the former [that is, the letter] is of its nature written and is sent as a sort of gift'. This is the effect created by a dominance of, and lively interchange between, 1st- and 2nd-person verb-forms, and by the use of conversational particles, such as Latin *enim*,[95] as for example in this extract from the *Letter on Features of the Pulse and the Urine in Diagnosis* (*Epistula de Pulsis et Urinis*, attributed to and in part transmitted with Alexander of Tralles):[96]

ut ex pulsu et consideratione urinae genus febris praevidere possis . . . indicant enim tibi et quasi tacite loquuntur aegrotantis color, oculi, . . . ne forte

---

[93] On this and other ancient theorizing on letters, see Sykutris (1931) 189–95.

[94] I am quoting Doreen Innes's translation (Russell and Winterbottom (1972) 211–12).

[95] In general on the illusion of dialogue in letters, see Peter (1901) 16. On conversational particles in Latin, see Kroon (1995), summarized by Langslow (2000*b*) 537–42; on the disproportionately high frequency of *enim* in (e.g.) Scribonius' dedicatory epistle, Langslow (2000*b*) 540–1.

[96] Excerpted from the edition by Stoffregen (1977) 74–8.

haec ignorantes aegros laedamus et nosmet [et]⁹⁷ ipsos deludamus... cum
enim haec omnia considerata ratione bene et uere esse cognoueris, optime
facies...

so that you can predict the type of fever from the pulse and from consideration of the urine... you see, you receive indications and tacit messages, as
it were, from the patient's colour, his eyes... to prevent us from, in ignorance of these things, doing harm to the sick and deceiving ourselves as well
as them... for when you are sure that all these things have been considered
systematically, well and truly, you will be of the greatest benefit...

The same effect, of a quasi-dialogue, can also be created by imagined
suggestions, even in the third person, as in the epistolary opening to
Anthimus' treatise on diet,⁹⁸ where 'If someone were to say...,' is
answered by, 'My suggestion is...' (*Praef.* p. 2, 16–17), and a question introduced by, 'But perhaps someone says to me...,' receives the
response, 'Still this is the account I offer' (*Praef.* p. 3, 4–8). Arguably,
a little earlier Anthimus emulates, if not dialogue, at least a sympathetic engagement with the addressee through the simile, or analogy
('exemplum') that he offers between the careful combination of food
and drink in one's diet and the proper mixing of water and lime, to
achieve a mixture strong enough for the wall of a house (*Praef.* p. 2,
9–15). For Demetrius mentions proverbs as a mark of the charm that
should, together with plainness, characterize the form of expression
of a letter (*Eloc.* 230, 235).⁹⁹

Another set of medical letters which might fit the Demetrian
mould comprises those addressed to the Powerful Man.¹⁰⁰ Of these
Demetrius writes (234), 'We sometimes write to cities and kings: give
letters of this kind a slightly more elevated style, since we must also
adapt ourselves to the character of the recipient, but not so elevated
that the letter turns into a monograph'. It is a hypothesis worth
further investigation that Vindicianus uses more elevated language
in writing to the Emperor (including e.g. *morbus, uitium, languor* for
'disease'; *medela, cura, remedium porrigere* of treatment) than he does

⁹⁷ [et] *secl.* Fischer.   ⁹⁸ Cf. n. 35 above.
⁹⁹ On some of the much wider issues raised by the question of the appropriate
rhetorical form, or 'grammar', to be used in interactive discourse on technical
subjects, see (e.g.) Lengen (2002) on Aristotle (brought to my attention by Philip
van der Eijk).
¹⁰⁰ Cf., for an interesting slant on this relationship, Freisenbruch in this volume.

in his letter to his nephew Pentadius (where he uses the more down-to-earth synonyms *aegritudo, causa* for 'disease', *occurrere* and *remedium adhibere* of treatment).

CONCLUSION

If I have been able to offer at best a superficial survey of a small part of a vast and diverse corpus, a survey based necessarily on known and edited examples, I hope that on the strength of the features considered the burden of proof leans towards those who would deny that this has anything to do with the letters of Cicero, Horace, Pliny, Statius, Fronto, Ausonius, and the rest, or who would defend the omission of the letter from the collective volumes mentioned at the outset.[101] The generalizations and working hypotheses that have been thrown up along the way—for example, that scientific, especially medical, letters, in general, or prefatory letters of type A (above), in particular, are scarcer in Greek than in Latin; or that medical letters are always from the relatively expert to the relatively inexpert—may be rendered partial or falsified in an instant by the noticing or discovering of further instances or counter-examples: these are indirect calls for further research. Other, more focused questions offer more immediate prospects for progress. Three in particular deserve to be repeated. First, are there in fact more examples of technical correspondence between academic equals, or are the *artes* in letter form—and epistolary medicine in particular—essentially elementary didactic literature for the layman? Secondly, are there observable patterns of diachronic change in the stylistic distance between the technical letter and other forms of technical literature, in Greek and Latin—especially, say, when one has to reckon in principle with ever-increasing interference from the colloquial language— and, if so, how might these patterns inform our view of the history of the literary standing of the letter form? And, thirdly, what of the use of the words ἐπιστολή and *epistula*? This simple but central question I have so far raised only obliquely, although it might

[101] Cf. nn. 1–2 above.

stand to throw important new light on the perceived essence of epistolarity, and hence perhaps on the reason for the apparent popularity of the *epistula* in the late antique and medieval West, where, as we have seen, non-epistolary prologues are given the trappings of letters, and all sorts of texts, even without the trappings, are called *epistulae*, so that one is tempted even to apply the remark made by Martial's friend Decianus on the flexibility of epigrams[102] to the predisposition of compilers and redactors of short medical tracts:

quacumque in pagina uisum est, epistolam faciunt!

---

[102] Cf. n. 14 above.

10

Back to Fronto: Doctor and Patient in his Correspondence with an Emperor

Annelise Freisenbruch

Educating oneself and taking care of oneself are interconnected activities.[1]

I

The history of scholarship on Fronto's correspondence has not strayed far from Willis's description of it fifty years ago as 'little more than a record of the crimes, the follies, and the misfortunes of his editors'.[2] It is time for a re-evaluation of Fronto's letters within the traditions of epistolary scholarship and against the backdrop of a surge of interest in the epistolarity of the letter collections of antiquity. Fronto has a valuable role to play in the call for a reassessment of the Roman letter-writing voice and identity.

This paper is based on the fourth chapter of my doctoral thesis (2004) on the correspondence of Fronto. I would like to thank the anonymous readers, and the organizers and participants of the Manchester conference on ancient letters for their thoughtful and helpful comments on an earlier draft of this paper. Special thanks also to John Henderson and Ruth Morello.

[1] Foucault (1988) 55.   [2] Willis (1955) 235.

In this study I focus on one strand of subject-matter in the correspondence between Fronto and his pupil, emperor-in-the-making Marcus Aurelius, namely the recurring narrative of sickness and health that features in over eighty of their extant letters with a particular emphasis on the ailments of the former. Fronto has been scorned by his critics for the most part, on account of such neuroses, although some recent studies of the 'Second Sophistic' have picked up on them as corroborative evidence for the 'notorious preoccupation with the body' said to characterize this era.[3] The tendency of some somatic scholarship has been to write Fronto's correspondence seamlessly into a narrative of what is regarded as the 'acceptability' of talking about one's health problems with 'friends' in second-century society.[4]

There is no disputing that concern between correspondents over the question of each other's health is nothing new to ancient epistolography.[5] Pliny and Libanius, for example, two other ancient letter-writers who claim emperors as pen-pals, are certainly familiar with the convention.[6] But neither of these correspondences can hold a candle to Fronto's for sheer volume of output and detail on the subject.[7] The pressing question, therefore, is whether Fronto and Marcus Aurelius' letters should be regarded as simply *reflecting* the trend of *their* age to open up about one's state of health, or whether there is something more pointed, more calculated about such an epistolary narrative. This, let it be said, in a correspondence in which

---

[3] Gleason (1995) xx. On Fronto's 'hypochondria', Whitehorne (1977) inventories the relevant letters; see also Grant (1994) 86, and Bowersock (1969) 72, one of the few critics to recognize that Fronto's letters are something 'quite new to epistolography' in this regard.

[4] See, for example, Swain (1996) 106.

[5] See Hoffer in this volume, on the 'striking overlap between epistolary health and political indigestion' in the letters of Cicero.

[6] For such letters to their imperial correspondents, see, for example, Pliny, *Ep.* 10. 5, 8, 11, 17A (with 18); Libanius, *Ep.* 23 in Bradbury (2004) and *Ep.* 38 and 98.8 in Norman (1992). The canonical letter collections of antiquity, such as those of Cicero, Pliny, and Seneca, all concern themselves at some point or other with the subject of sickness and health. The *consolatio* letter, commiserating the recipient on the death of a friend or relative, was one of the major categories of the genre, according to epistolary guidebooks, for example pseudo-Demetrius, *Epistolary Types* 5: see Malherbe (1988) 35.

[7] For a statistical profile of the correspondences' 'health' obsession, see Freisenbruch (2004) 146 and n. 454.

the special, exclusive nature of *this* tutor and *this* pupil's (epistolary) relationship is constantly reiterated and closely and jealously guarded. This is a central tenet of my reading of Fronto's correspondence as a whole, which I view as a unique epistolary pact between a tutor and a Caesar who co-operate (and compete) in a delicate balancing-act between different power-sharing roles—*magister, discipulus, Caesar, amicus*. Against the background of this complex interfusion of different roles and voices, I shall show how Fronto's epistolary narrative of sickness and health is in fact intimately bound into the teacher's discourse of authority over his pupil, that Fronto's pedagogical prerogative lingers over *all* areas of his discourse with his royal pupil(s).[8]

There are two connected questions we need to investigate in this case study. First, what is it like for Fronto to exchange such information with an emperor of Rome in the making? Throughout their correspondence, Fronto shows himself to be a man acutely aware of the 'right' way to speak and to write. From the letter traditionally assumed to be the earliest of our extant collection, Fronto sets out his stall as guardian of the young Marcus Aurelius' education, staking his claim to be considered arbiter of the correct deployment of words:

haud sciam an utile sit demonstrare, quanta difficultas, quam scrupulosa et anxia cura in uerbis probandis adhibenda sit...

I rather think it might be useful to demonstrate how much difficulty there is, how much scrupulous and anxious care must be brought to bear in the appraisal of words.   (*Ad M. Caes.* 4.3.4)[9]

The entire corpus of letters to Marcus Aurelius from that point on will serve, quite literally, as a correspondence course in how to be a good wordsmith, a good emperor, a good pupil. Why does Fronto choose to set an example by portraying himself as a body in such pain, straying so far from the path established by other epistolary models?[10] The question of what information is being allocated, to

---

[8] The correspondence also contains several letters exchanged between Fronto and Lucius Verus, Marcus Aurelius' adoptive brother and co-regent.

[9] The text used is van den Hout's Teubner edition of 1988, now generally accepted as the authoritative version.

[10] See also Ebbeler in this volume on subversions of epistolary etiquette between correspondents of unequal status.

whom and by whom, is central to the power dynamics of any correspondence. What is at stake for Fronto and Marcus in such exchange of detailed information about their digestive tracts and bodily functions? This is our first consideration.

My second interrelated concern is specifically to question the *epistolary* significance of such an exchange, a factor that tends to be passed over by critics who typically adopt a cherry-picking attitude to the letters, raiding them for snippets of corroborative evidence for studies on friendship, patronage, rhetoric, and so on. But the medium through which this exchange of information is relayed must not be occluded. No other genre or category of writing has the confrontation between 'private' and 'public' more at its heart, the dilemma of how much of one's 'self' to put on the line. This is significant, since the content of some of these 'neurotic' letters of Fronto has convinced some of his editors that they could never have been intended for publication.[11] Such thinking blinkers itself to the way that narratives of the 'public' and the 'private' are inextricably intertwined in the discourse of imperial Roman (letter-writing) society. Letters are not written by accident, and there is nothing accidental in Fronto's choice to paint such an epistolary self-portrait of himself.[12] In this correspondence, Fronto is revealed as the centre of a community of letter-writers, in which the issue of who you write to, what you write to them about, and how you write to them, enacts your position in the competitive hierarchy of Antonine society. *Every* letter here makes a statement about one's participation in a broader (epistolary) community, and Fronto loses no opportunity to advertise his role as savvy leader of the Roman literary *ton*. This leads me back to my original question: to what extent are Fronto and Marcus Aurelius, *magister* and *discipulus*, claiming for themselves an exclusive and privileged level of communication *outside* this community, via this epistolary dialogue of sickness and health? Do these letters show them 'fitting in' or 'opting out'?

[11] On the publication debate over Fronto's correspondence, see Freisenbruch (2004) 23–30.

[12] See Henderson (1982), a pioneering study on letters as self-portraits.

II

Since the earliest scholarship on his correspondence, the 'neurotic' aspect of Fronto's epistolary personality has generally been treated with disdain:

the overall impression that we get from Fronto's letters on the subject of his illnesses is a most unattractive one, and this impression—of a selfish creature ready to complain to anyone foolish enough to listen—can be supported by figures as well as facts.[13]

There is an indisputably heavy concentration on the subject in his letters, summarized by Scarborough in his standard work on Roman medicine.[14] An extensive variety of illnesses, afflictions, and general threats to the well-being of the two main correspondents are catalogued. Fronto is afflicted at one time or another, across the twenty years or so that apparently divide the earliest from the later letters, by ailments from sleeplessness to arm pain, knee pain, foot pain, shoulder pain, elbow pain, groin pain (on both sides!), diarrhoea, a sore throat, crippled hands, a cough, finger pain, rheumatism, pain in his eyes, heartache, grief, depression, and other unspecified instances of ill health.[15] Marcus Aurelius seems less afflicted, but includes the following amongst his sufferings: a cold or chill, chest pain, tiredness, trouble breathing, and discomfort while walking. But significantly, on several occasions, what ails him is that his own health, so he avers, is adversely affected by news of his tutor's illness. This is one of the defining themes of Fronto and Marcus Aurelius' shared narrative of sickness and health—the way they insist on the health of one, directly and tangibly impacting on the health of the other.[16] Sometimes this is expressed in terms of mental distress, but sometimes too, as I will show presently, this discourse of concern suggests that even the letter recipient's physical

[13] Whitehorne (1977) 416.
[14] See Scarborough (1969) 104–5.
[15] In extracts from Aulus Gellius' *Noctes Atticae*, Fronto's ailment is described as *pedibus aegrum* (*Noct. Att.* 2.26; 19.10).
[16] A letter from Libanius to Julian echoes such a motif in their 4th-cent. correspondence: see Bradbury (2004) *Ep.* 23.

Annelise Freisenbruch

health may be affected. The letter will be shown to act as an almost infectious (or inoculatory) extension of one's self.[17]

Despite the well-documented difficulties of transmission, Fronto's fractured and mangled correspondence affords us precious glimpses of mutual epistolary exchange at work.[18] I begin this overview of Fronto and Marcus' diseased dialogue with an example of such an exchange. The two inquire after each other's health, and report back on their own in the process, highlighting their reciprocity in the act, the need to feel each other's pain, as seen in the pupil's avowal that his tutor's health directly impacts on his own.

Domino meo
quomodo manseris, domine, scire cupio. ego ceruicum dolore arreptus sum. uale, domine. dominam saluta.

I desire to know how you have passed the night, my lord. I have been seized by neck pain. Farewell my lord. Greetings to my lady.   (*Ad M. Caes.* 5.27)

Magistro meo sal.
noctem sine febri uideor transmisisse; cibum non inuitus cepi, nunc ago leuissime. nox quid ferat, cognoscemus. sed, mi magister, ceruicum dolore te arreptum, quo animo didicerim, profecto ex tua proxima sollicitudine metiris.
vale mi iucundissime magister. mater mea salutat te.

I seem to have passed the night without fever. I have eaten without reluctance, now I do very well. What the night brings—we shall see. But, my teacher, you may certainly ascertain, based on your own recent anxiety, how I felt, on learning that you had been seized by neck-pain. Farewell, most delightful teacher. My mother sends greetings to you.   (*Ad M. Caes.* 5.28)

Domino meo
ceruicum, domine, dolore graui sum correptus, de pede dolor decessit. uale, domine optime, dominam saluta.

I am in the grip of serious neck-pain, though the pain in my foot has subsided. Farewell, excellent lord. Greetings to my lady.   (*Ad M. Caes.* 5.29)

---

[17] Hoffer, in this volume, also makes the point that there is often an elision of bodily and mental health in epistolary discourse.

[18] See ch. 1 of Freisenbruch (2004) for an overview of the development of scholarship on the Fronto palimpsest, including Angelo Mai's treatment of the 19th-cent. codex, and the various attempts to reconstruct the letters.

MAGISTRO MEO SAL.

ceruicum dolores si tertia quoque die remiserint, erit quod meam redeun-
tem ualetudinem maiorem in modum adiuuet, mi magister. laui et hodie et
ambulaui paulum, cibi paulo plus sumpsi nondum tamen libente stomacho.
uale mi iucundissime magister. mater mea te salutat.

If the pains in your neck have receded, even two days hence, it will be the
thing that most assists my own recovery, my teacher; I have washed and had
a little walk today, I have eaten a little more food, although not yet with a
settled stomach. Farewell, my most delightful teacher. My mother sends you
greetings.   (*Ad M. Caes.* 5.30)

MAGISTRO MEO SAL.

quom tibi etiamtum ceruices doluerint, quom mihei scriberes, non possum
aequo animo ferre neque sane volo aut debeo. ego autem iuuantibus uotum
tuum deis laui hodie et cibi quantum sat erat cepi; uino etiam libenter usus
sum. uale, mi iucundissime magister. mater mea te salutat.

I cannot, do not desire to, and should not bear with equanimity the notion
that you were writing to me at the same time as your neck was giving you
pain. But with the gods helping your prayer, I have washed, and eaten a
sufficient amount of food; I have also taken wine freely. Farewell, my most
delightful teacher. My mother sends you greetings.   (*Ad M. Caes.* 5.31)

DOMINO MEO

dolores quidem ceruicum nihil remiserunt, sed animo bene fuit, quom te
balneo et uino libenter usum cognoui. uale, domine. dominam saluta.

The pains in my neck have not receded, but I cheered up when I learnt that
you had had a bath and taken wine freely. Farewell, my lord. Greetings to my
lady.   (Ad M. Caes. 5.32)

In this chain of letters, Fronto and Marcus Aurelius depend on each
other to validate the other's state of health. Moreover, the *rescriptum*
has the power to act as a panacea (or perhaps, a placebo?), a therapeutic effect we will see at work again shortly. To paraphrase one
critic, these letters demonstrate that one cannot be ill on one's own.[19]
Fronto makes frequent claims to the effect that all aspects of his own
well-being are intricately tied up with that of his pupil, and that
Marcus is even his sole reason for living. But he also warns his
protégé that his love is conditional on Marcus' *eloquentia*—in other
words, on his application to his studies, a clause that is critical to
their entire epistolary contract:

[19] Taylor (1989) 36: 'one cannot be a self on one's own'.

fateor enim, quod res est, unam solam posse causam incidere, qua causa claudat aliquantum amor erga te meus: si eloquentiam neglegas.

For I confess, the fact of the matter is, that there is only one reason why my love for you might falter: if you were to neglect *eloquentia*. (*De Orationibus* 2)

Powering the mechanics of any pedagogical discourse is competition, but in this (epistolary) discourse, we have a particularly complex rivalry for status, which has been finessed by the majority of critics who have neglected to perceive the power politics operating within this correspondence. Fronto's love for his pupil comes with conditions: it will last just so long as his pupil continues to be a credit to him. Even when bemoaning his poor state of health, Fronto's magisterial role *infects* his letters to Marcus, a role he never loses an opportunity to advertise:

quaecumque mihi precatus es, omnia in tua salute locata sunt. mihi sanitas, bona ualetudo, laetitia, res prosperae meae ibi sunt, cum tu corpore, animo, rumore tam incolumi uteris, tam carus patri, tam dulcis matri, tum sanctus uxori, tam fratri bonus ac benignus. haec sunt quae me cum hac ualetudine tamen cupientem uitae faciunt:

All things whatsoever that you have prayed for on my behalf are invested in your well-being. I have good health, mental and physical, happiness, and prosperity, as long as you enjoy so sound a body, mind and reputation, as long as you are so dear to your father, so sweet to your mother, so saintly to your wife, so good and kind to your brother. These are the things which make me want to live, in spite of this health of mine. (*Ad M. Caes.* 5.48)

This letter links Fronto and Marcus Aurelius' co-dependency in terms of their state of health, with Fronto's success (or failure) as Marcus Aurelius' pedagogical mentor. Marcus Aurelius is Fronto's claim-to-fame, and he never forgets it. Significantly, in his royal pupil's epistolary persona at least, Fronto has the perfect accomplice to collude in his self-aggrandizing promotion of his personal legacy as a *sponsor* of emperors. Marcus Aurelius, the *discipulus*, writes on a number of occasions of his own health being adversely affected by hearing of the ill-health of Fronto, his tutor. In the previous letters his distress seems confined to mental disquiet, but in this next example, his anxiety assumes a physical aspect:

ludis tu quidem, at mihi peramplam anxietatem et summam aegritudinem, dolorem et ignem flagrantissimum litteris his tuis misisti, ne cenare, ne dormire, ne denique studere libeat...uale mi magister, cuius salus meam salutem inlibatam et incolumem facit.

You may banter, but with your last letter you have sent considerable anxiety and great suffering, not to mention the most burning pain and fever, to the point that I can take no pleasure in eating, sleeping or even studying ...Farewell, my teacher, whose health makes my health unimpaired and secure. (*Ad M. Caes.* 5.22)

This is one of a number of letters in which the young prince writes that just the reading of a letter reporting Fronto's poor health is enough to induce symptoms of pain in Marcus Aurelius himself.[20] Once again, the language of pain becomes intertwined with a language of learning. *uerum tu orationis hodiernae tuae habeas aliquod solacium*—'but you will have some solace in your speech today'— Marcus points out to his teacher, the line engaging slightly with a Senecan idea of the link between the suffering body and self-knowledge.[21] But in the same letter Fronto's pupil rather subverts the notion that learning might be recuperative, since the news of Fronto's illness has apparently rendered study on his own part impossible: *ne denique studere libeat.* I will return to this theme later.

III

At this point, I want to highlight the multiplicity of epistolary role-playing that occurs in this correspondence. When we talk about Fronto and Marcus Aurelius corresponding, just *who* do we mean by those two individuals? Do we have a teacher writing to his pupil? An emperor writing to his subject? A 'friend' writing to another 'friend'? These two letter-writers self-consciously contest generic categories of *amicitia* and *imperium* at Rome, taking pains to stress

[20] For further examples, see *Ad M. Caes.* 5. 24, 5. 62 and (in a letter from Fronto's other royal correspondent, Marcus Aurelius' co-regent Lucius Verus) *Ad Verum Imp.* 1. 9. See also *De Nepote Amisso* 1. 1 where Marcus writes of being directly affected when Fronto suffers bereavement at the death of his grandson.

[21] See Edwards (1999) 253.

that they write to each other differently than they do to their other correspondents.[22] This has implications for the exploration of the nature of epistolarity across different letter-collections from antiquity, which is the target of this volume as a whole. For while it is of course imperative to locate letters from antiquity, particularly those such as Fronto's under-studied correspondence, within a community of practice, I suggest that we should also press the specific issues generated by particular letter-collections.[23] My concern within this limited case-study is to investigate the extent to which Fronto and Marcus Aurelius play out their correspondence according to a ready-made set of rules, and in whose favour their own claims to have a unique letter-writing arrangement actually worked. More simply, who has the power here, and how do the shifting epistolary personae they create for themselves affect that question?

First, Marcus Aurelius' professed concern for Fronto is not limited to the solicitude of a pupil towards his tutor. Teacher and pupil often scrutinize their own (epistolary) characterization of their relationship, parading it against definitions of *amicitia*. In the following letter, for example, we see how Marcus' anxiety is tied up with such running commentary on the definition of their 'friendship'. Marcus laments that he may not deserve to be called *amicus*, in his failure to attend the bedside of an ill Fronto:

quid ego ista mea fortuna satis dixerim uel quomodo istam necessitatem meam durissimam condigne incusauero, quae me istic ita animo anxio tantaque sollicitudine praepedito alligatum attinet neque me sinit ad meum Frontonem, ad meam pulcherrimam animam confestim percurrere, praesertim in huiusmodi eius ualetudine propius uidere, manus tenere, ipsum denique illum pedem, quantum sine incommodo fieri possit, adtrectare sensim, in balneo fouere, ingredienti manum subicere? et tu me amicum uocas, qui non abruptis omnibus cursu concitato peruolo?

What can I say that does justice to my misfortune, how shall I properly rail against that most cruel circumstance which keeps me detained here, with a heart so anxious and shackled with worry, and does not allow me to hasten

---

[22] See *Ad Verum Imp.* 1. 1–2, where categories of *amicitia* and *officium* are explicitly tested.

[23] The recent letters anthology by Trapp (2003), while clearly sympathetic to and self-aware of both the positives and pitfalls in 'sorting' letters into neat categories, perpetuates the practice nevertheless.

at once to my Fronto, to my most beautiful soul, to come and see you close up especially when you are ill in this way, to hold your hands, and then, as far as possible without detriment, to gently rub the foot itself, to foment it in the bath, to provide support with my hand as you step in? And you call me a friend, when I do not fly to you at full speed, having cast everything else aside?   (*Ad M. Caes.* 1.2.1)

The restorative power of letters is then seen to immediate effect in what appears to be Fronto's *rescriptum*, identifiable in the teacher's gratitude for his pupil's wish to fly to his side:

tu, Caesar, Frontonem istum tuum sine fine amas, uix ut tibi homini facundissimo uerba sufficiant ad expromendum amorem tuum et beniuolentiam declarandam. quid, oro te, | fortunatius, quid me uno beatius esse potest, ad quem tu tam fraglantes litteras mittis? quin etiam, quod est amatorum proprium, currere ad me uis et uolare ... o me beatum! ore tuo me diis commendatum! putasne ullus dolor penetrare sciat corpus aut animum meum prae tanto gaudio? ... neque doleo iam quicquam neque aegre fero: uigeo, ualeo, exulto ... [24]

You, Caesar, love this Fronto of yours without limit, to the point that even a man so eloquent as you has scarcely the words to disclose your love and declare your friendship. I ask you, who can be luckier, more blessed than I to whom you send such fragrant letters? What is more, in a manner appropriate to lovers, you want to run, to fly to me ... Oh I am blessed! I am commended to the gods by your lips. Do you think any suffering can penetrate my body or mind at the expense of such great joy? ... I neither suffer nor endure pain any longer: I thrive, I am strong, I rejoice ...   (*Ad M. Caes.* 1. 3.1–2)

In writing his letter, Marcus has written a *prescription* for Fronto's poor state of health. Just the receiving of it is enough to rid his *magister* of pain.

At the same time, this letter affords Fronto an invaluable opportunity to self-advertise. In the same highly self-congratulatory letter, he goes on to muse on the reasons for the *amicitia* and also the *amor* between himself and young Caesar, ventriloquizing on behalf of his pupil to the effect that it would be impossible for him to love

---

[24] The discourse of *amor* intertwines with *amicitia* throughout Roman culture (e.g. Catullus 50 or 96). But I have chosen not to investigate the putative 'eroticism' of Fronto's leters with Marcus Aurelius. Professor Amy Richlin is engaged in research on this dimension of the correspondence.

Marcus Aurelius more than he loves Fronto.[25] He then ends the
letter: *finis igitur sit epistulae. ualeo reuera multo quam opinabar
commodius*—'So let my letter end. I am really feeling much
better than I imagined'. In the act of writing his reply, and going
over Marcus' letter again, Fronto's illness suddenly clears up. Once
again, the letter, which can be catching, is seen by these latest
examples to be therapeutic:

igitur dum tu iacebis, et mihi animus supinus erit, quomque tu dis iuuantibus bene stabis, et meus animus bene constabit, qui nunc torretur ardentissimo desiderio tuo. uale, anima Caesaris tui, amici tui, discipuli tui.

Therefore, while you are laid low, my spirits will also be low, and when, with
the help of the gods, you stand upright again, my spirit will also stand firm,
which right now is inflamed with most ardent longing for you. Farewell,
spirit of your Caesar, your friend, your pupil.   (*Ad M. Caes.* 3.20)

The valediction of this particular letter serves, in my view, as the
line of axis for this correspondence as a whole. For the variety of
power roles shared and highlighted between Caesar and *magister* in
their correspondence complicates any simple delineation of their
relationship along lines of 'friendship', 'duty', and so on. Is it the
solicitude of an emperor that Marcus Aurelius feels here, the concern
of a friend, or the anxiety of a pupil? (How) does this affect the levels
of obligation in writing? This is an important theme of epistolarity.
When one writes a letter, expressing concern over the health of the
recipient, how many times have we written that letter before, what
measure of formality, of duty, is latent in the gesture? Fronto and his
pupil frequently claim that their letters to each other are generated by
amor, rather than the *officium* that *compels* them to write to others.[26]
Yet the complexity of roles present in their self-constructed relationship to each other dictates that a whole series of agendas must
necessarily be at stake in these letters of sickness and health. But
whose agenda wins out, if any? Do these letters sharing their bodies
with each other serve as the great leveller in their (epistolary) relationship, an illustration of their unique 'friendship' that rejects
classification?

---

[25] See *Ad M. Caes.* 1. 3.11.   [26] See n. 19.

IV

This leads me back to the main point I want to make, namely to reiterate that the narrative of illness in Fronto and Marcus Aurelius' letters is in fact interwoven with the *pedagogical* narrative of the correspondence. Their letters are both teaching aid and tonic.[27] This volume of essays is at one level all about demonstrating how letters are always used at Rome to teach people how to *belong*. As Morello shows, Roman epistolography constructs an 'in-crowd', who lay down the rules of the right way to write literary letters, and thus, the right way to live, the right way to be a good Roman.[28]

But Fronto has a very special investment in having Marcus Aurelius (and his other royal pupil, Lucius Verus) play along with him in their own game. As we have already seen, the message that Marcus Aurelius is Fronto's legacy to the world, and that his state of health is invested not just in his pupil's *amicitia* and *amor*, but also in that pupil's *eloquentia*, is reiterated on several occasions.[29] The same kind of narrative can be found in a letter from Fronto to Lucius Verus, in which he claims to be cheered by the news that his pupil desires his teacher to send him something to read:

fatigatum me ualetudine diutina et praeter solitum graui ac grauissimis etiam luctibus paene continuis adflictum (nam in paucissimis mensibus et uxorem carissimam et nepotem trimulum amisi), sed his plerisque me malis perculsum, releuatum | tamen aliquantum fateor, quod te meminisse nostri et quaedam nostra desiderasse cognoui.

Although I am exhausted from long-standing ill-health, more serious than usual, and afflicted by almost constant and most oppressive sorrows (for in the space of just a few months I have lost a most beloved wife and a 3-year-old grandson), yet, though stricken with these many evils, I confess, however, that I was somewhat consoled when I found out that you remembered me and hankered after something of mine.   (*Ad Verum Imp.* 1.8)

---

[27] See Morrison in this volume on the 'interaction between didacticism and epistolarity' in Horace's *Epistles* 1.

[28] See Morello in this volume.

[29] Compare *Ad Verum Imp.* 1. 3 and 2. 1: Fronto makes clear that he regards Lucius' real achievement as his *eloquentia*. See also Libanius, *Ep.* 30 in Norman (1992).

This letter represents the dying embers of Fronto's life as suddenly revived by a reminder of his role as *magister* to two young would-be emperors. Pride is restored, Fronto's services are needed again, the young pupils remember their old teacher!

In the final section of this paper, I will develop this theme to demonstrate how the issue of handwriting, in terms of when the letter-writer writes in his own hand, or employs another, does not merely reflect the health of the writer, but is also an eagerly scrutinized barometer of credibility and recognition for the recipient. Fronto in particular rebukes his pupil when he does not write in his own hand, and in one letter, which I cannot discuss here, rejoices where his legacy is authenticated by being recorded in the emperor's own handwriting.[30]

But where one does not write in one's own hand, one needs to make the excuse of ill-health to escape censure. Illness as an *excuse* for evading other business is a prominent feature of Fronto and Marcus' 'neurotic' epistolary discourse. For example, at one point, Fronto explains his inability to attend the birthday of one of the emperor's children, on account of his poor health.[31] As we saw earlier, illness can also be used as an excuse by the *discipulus* to justify the neglect of his studies. But it is not his own illness that hinders his learning, but that of his *magister*:

egone ut studeam, cum tu doleas, praesertim cum mea causa doleas? non me omnibus incommodis sponte ipse adflictem? merito hercule. quis enim tibi alius dolorem genus, quem scribis nocte proxuma auctum, quis alius eum suscitauit nisi Centum Cellae, ne me dicam? quid igitur faciam, qui nec te uideo et tanto angore | discrucior? adde eo quod, etiamsi libeat studere, iudicia prohibent, quae, ut dicunt qui sciunt, dies totos eximunt…sed reuera illa res maxime mihi animum a studiis depulit, quod, dum nimium litteras amo, tibi incommodus apud Portum fui, ut res ostendit. itaque ualeant omnes Porci et Tulli et Crispi, dum tu ualeas et te uel sine libris firmum tamen uideam.

Can it be that I am to study, while you are in pain, especially when I am the reason you are in pain? Shall I not torment myself with every punishment, of my own free will? I deserve it, by Hercules. For who else revived the pain of your knee, which you write worsened last night, if not Centumcellae, not to

30 *Ad M. Caes.* 1. 7.2–4.   31 *Ad M. Caes.* 5. 57.1–2.

mention my own part? What therefore shall I do, I who do not see you, and am tortured by terrible anguish? On top of that, even if I wanted to study, the courts prohibit it, a state of affairs which, so those in the know say, takes up whole days.... But in truth the thing which most distracted my mind from my studies was that, because I love literature too much, I caused you injury at the Harbour, as the matter proved. Therefore, farewell to all Catos, Ciceros and Sallusts, until you are well, and I see you thriving, though without books. (*Ad M. Caes.* 5.74)

In a skilful display of work-avoidance, Marcus declares that he cannot possibly study while his *magister* is in pain, particularly when it was his own fondness for his studies that he claims caused his master's illness in the first place. Away with books! The illness of the master provides the pupil with a sugar-coated excuse for neglecting his studies. Marcus excuses the quality of his work again on the same grounds in another letter:

ego adeo perscripsi (tu mitte aliud quod scribam), sed librarius meus non praesto fuit, qui transcriberet. scripsi autem non ex mea sententia, nam et festinaui et tua ista ualetudo aliquantu|lum detriuit mihi;

I have finished the writing (so send me something else to write) but my scribe was not at hand to copy it. But I did not write according to my wishes, for I was in a rush, and the state of your health wore me out somewhat. (*Ad M. Caes.* 5.41)

There is an acute self-consciousness in the pupil's epistolary posturing, a careful calculation of the right thing to say to placate his *magister*. These letters are models of carefully pitched decorum, demonstrating this pupil's keen self-awareness of his role as *discipulus*.

The point I re-emphasize, therefore, is how the sickness and health letters between Fronto and Marcus actually manifest their pedagogical contract. The following letter from Fronto to Lucius Verus, the most detailed exposition on how to cure illness in the whole correspondence, will illustrate the point further:

sed acceptis litteris tuis ea re iam primum bona spes mihi ostentata est, quod tua manu scripseras; deinde quod post abstinentiam tridui et sanguinem satis strenue et prompte demissum liberatum esse te periculo inpendentis ualetudinis nuntiabas. respiraui igitur et reualui et apud omnis foculos, aras, lucos sacros, arbores sacratas (nam rure agebam) supplicaui. et nunc expecto cognoscere ex tuis litteris, quantum mediei isti dies promoverint ad uires reficiendas. enimuero nunc maiore multo cura diligentiaque opus est, ut paulatim temet compleas, nec properes ad detrimenta uirium resarcienda. nam id quidem omnium opinione compertum et traditum est sanguinem, ubi abundet, incursim detrahendum, postea pedetemptim esse reparandum.

But when I received your letter, hope was offered first of all by the fact that you had written with your own hand; then because you announced that after three days of abstinence and enough blood having been vigorously and quickly let, you were free from the danger of impending ill-health. So I breathed once more and I regained my strength and I prayed at all the hearths, altars, sacred groves and consecrated trees—for I was ruralizing. And now I am waiting to find out from your letters how much the intervening days have helped to restore your strength. For now there is need of much more care and conscientiousness, so that you may recharge yourself gradually, and not rush to patch up your depleted strength. For it is an established truth, universally accepted and hallowed by tradition, that when blood overflows it must be let quickly and afterwards it must be replenished cautiously.   (*Ad Verum Imp.* 1.5)

Once again, the theme of one's own health being actually dependent on another's is repeated, and of the arrival of a letter serving as a kind of chicken soup for the soul. *respiraui . . . et reualui*, Fronto writes on learning of Lucius' improved condition, and refers to Marcus Aurelius' state of health being dependent on his brother, at the end of the letter. But at the same time, Fronto, who has claimed mastery of *eloquentia* in his teaching of Marcus and Lucius throughout their correspondence, portraying himself as one armed with the full knowledge to wield the rapier of rhetoric in a way that the young pretender who is *semidoctus*, would be wise not to attempt, now lays claim to some knowledge of medicine in (*magisteri*al) words. He advises Lucius on how to get better, not, it must be said, claiming any originality for his method, but drawing on *omnium opinione*. The language of health he uses here is taken from recognized medical method and language, even though Fronto's pioneering use of 'new words' is an obsession of scholarship on Fronto.[32]

---

[32] *Ad M. Caes.* 5. 30. See Holford-Strevens (1976). See also Hoffer in this volume on Cicero's use of *stomachus*, a term also found in Fronto (*Ad M. Caes.* 5. 30) in an unusual piece of medical phraseology: *libente stomacho* (see van den Hout (1999) n. 74, 7–8.)

But that is not a cue for complacency. Throughout their correspondence, Fronto asserts his status as an arbiter of the correct usage of words, and claims the right to pass judgement on the *eloquentia* of Caesar. He *patronizes* his pupil, praising him for seeking out unusual words, yet warns him that sometimes this dangerous business is best left to the experts.[33] The voice of the *magister* (or should we say *doctor*?) is threaded through his letters. Marcus and Fronto never cease playing the roles of *discipulus* and *magister*, even while describing the symptoms of their latest complaint:

inde salutato patre meo aqua mulsa sorbenda usque ad gulam et reiectanda 'fauces fovi' potius quam dicerem 'gargarissaui', nam est ad Nouium, credo, et alibi.

Having greeted my father, I swallowed honey-water as far as my gullet, then forced it back up, thus 'soothing my throat' I would say, rather than 'gargling', though I believe it is found in Novius, for instance, and elsewhere. (*Ad M. Caes.* 4.6)

This extract in particular demonstrates the self-consciousness of the letters between Fronto, tutor, and Marcus Aurelius, pupil, as they self-reflexively analyse their own construction, pondering over the appropriateness of this word here, that word there. The 'right' words must be used even while one is ill, for there is no time when one may forget one's studies.[34]

V

As promised, I return finally to the importance of the autograph in these letters of sickness and health, in terms of the epistolary dramatization of the relationship between tutor and his pupil-emperor. According to standard accounts of Roman letter-writing practice, the done thing was to dictate letters to a secretary *ab epistulis*, and certainly this was the usual custom of emperors. Marcus writes to

---

[33] On the patronage of pedagogy in Fronto and Marcus Aurelius' correspondence, see ch. 3 of Freisenbruch (2004).

[34] See the poorly transmitted *Ad Amicos* 1. 13: Fronto's knowledge of both the Greek and Latin names for the spine apparently proves of no comfort.

Fronto at one point that he is out of breath from having just dictated thirty letters, and Pliny's letters exchanged with Trajan are universally assumed to have been dictated.[35] But in Fronto and Marcus Aurelius' correspondence, letters that are *not* handwritten have to be accounted for. This applies to *both* master and pupil. Failure to produce an autographed missive is usually explained away by poor health, as we see in the following two extracts from Fronto to Marcus:

me quoque tussicula uexat et manus dexterae dolor, mediocris quidem, sed qui a rescribenda longiore epistula inpedierit; dictaui igitur.

A slight cough is troubling me too, and a pain in my right hand, only moderate, but it is still such as to prevent me from writing back a longer letter; so I have dictated it.　(*Ad Ant. Imp.* 1.2.10)

ne mihi suscenseas, quod non mea manu tibi rescripserim, praesertim cum a te tua manu scriptas litteras acceperim. digitis admodum inualidis nunc utor et detractantibus; tum haec epistula multum uerborum ingerebat, mea autem dextera manus hac tempestate paucarum litterarum.

Do not hold a grudge against me because I did not write to you with my own hand, especially when I received a letter from you in your own hand. I have somewhat feeble and refusing fingers at the moment; this missive heaps up a mass of words, but my right hand at present can only manage a few letters.　(*De Bello Parthico* 11)

In this last letter, Fronto apologizes for not writing in his own hand, even though Marcus did write to him in *his* handwriting, exposing once more the potential for self-aggrandizement in the reciprocity of the letter-form. Marcus too excuses himself for not writing in his own hand, here on the grounds that he is shaky after his evening bath:

mea manu non scripsi, quia uesperi loto tremebat etiam manus.

I did not write to you with my own hand, because it was still trembling after my evening bath.　(*De Nepote Amisso* 1)

Handwriting physically reflects the condition of the correspondents. In a kind of textual metempsychosis, it does not merely describe one's physical or mental affliction, it directly testifies to it. Earlier, in

---

[35] See Millar (1977) 213–28 on letter-writing practices of Roman emperors. On the dictation of Trajan's letters to Pliny, see Peter (1965) 123; Sherwin-White (1966) 536–46 and Williams (1990) 16–17.

a letter from Fronto to Lucius Verus, we saw Fronto's relief in the fact that his pupil had written in his own hand, indicating that his health was on the mend (*Ad Verum Imp.* 1. 5). Below, Marcus alludes to the fact that his physical state is mirrored in his handwriting:

ego inpraesentiarum sic me habeo, ut uel hinc aestimatu facile sit tibi, quod haec precaria manu scribo.

For the present, I am in a state that it will be easy for you to assess, from the fact that I write this with an unsteady hand.   (*Ad M. Caes.* 4.8.1)

In epistolary literature, ink is regularly metaphorized, explicitly or implicitly, as life's blood.[36] Earlier I explored how Fronto and Marcus Aurelius' letters were represented as impacting *physically* on their recipients. Here, Marcus Aurelius' condition, through his handwriting, is almost palpable. The handwritten, material status of letters has always been a jealously guarded signifier of the person(ality) of the writer imprinted on the page, as though writing in one's own hand removed all possible barriers between the soul of the sender and of the recipient.

Rosenmeyer points to how writers of fictional letters apologize for shaky handwriting or for tears spilt on the page, or worry that they may not make the next post.[37] These physical marks of the writer are needed, demanded, to convince the recipient (be it specified addressee or eavesdropping reader) of their 'authenticity', or perhaps, 'sincerity'. The materiality of letters as a substitute for physicality, has long been a theme of epistolary writing. As Altman says, 'epistolary discourse is the language of the "as if" present...; epistolary language, which is the language of absence, makes present by make-believe'.[38] The smudged teardrop on the page, the trace of scent on the paper, these are trademark epistolary devices to carry, unmediated, something 'personal' of the writer to the sender. In their letters of sickness and health, Fronto and Marcus Aurelius make a concerted effort to overturn that boundary between absence and presence, to assert their physical presence in each other's orbit, to the extent that their own health can be measured by, and is interchangeable with, the health of the other.

---

[36] Altman (1982) 149.   [37] Rosenmeyer (2001*a*) 22.
[38] Altman (1982) 140.

But in the process of this assertion, as seen in their epistolary posing and bartering over the right to receive letters with each other's personal autograph, these supposedly 'frivolous' epistles show up the carefully contrived image-consciousness of this correspondence. I do not mean to deny altogether the significance of the 'genuine' voice in letter-writing, but rather to contest its provision of a 'reflection of the writer's soul', and to point instead to the role of this topos as a conceit within epistolary politesse. For it is this 'sincerity' of voice, as reciprocated and authenticated between Fronto and Marcus Aurelius, that provides Fronto with so much fuel for self-promotion in the mutually constituted record of his pedagogical contract with *Caesar*. These letters of sickness and health tread the line between what should be counted 'private' and 'public', between 'spontaneity' and 'strategem' in letter-writing. As Rosenmeyer writes, 'whenever one writes a letter, one automatically constructs a self, an occasion, a version of the truth'.[39] Who you write to, and what you write to them about, says everything about you, at Rome, and in other letter-writing eras.

VI

In conclusion, the scope of the epistolary communications in his correspondence as a whole empowers Fronto to play expert 'letter-writer' at Rome, demonstrating his ability to adapt to the constraints of Roman epistolary decorum, to write to the 'right' people, for the 'right' reasons, and in the 'right' way. But as the letters I have cited demonstrate, this neglected correspondence is an epistolary handbook in itself. It displays an acute self-awareness of epistolary templates and conventions and pays lip-service to them wherever appopriate. At the same time, this diseased dialogue offers Fronto carte blanche to stage an *improvisation* of his role as *magister* and epistolary confidant to Caesar. Fronto offers up a masterclass, to Marcus Aurelius and to us, in how to write, in how to *teach*. Bearing in mind Marcus Aurelius' terse acknowledgement of his former

---

[39] Rosenmeyer (2001*a*) 5.

rhetoric teacher in the foreword to the *Meditations*, people like to ask, how good a teacher *was* Fronto?[40] The question should perhaps rather be, how good a student was Marcus Aurelius? Whatever one decides (it may depend on one's own pedagogical model?), there can be no question that Fronto and Marcus Aurelius' correspondence improvises its own take on epistolary rule-making and -breaking for pupils of Roman epistolography.

[40] Marcus Aurelius, *Meditations* 1. 11.

11

Alciphron's Epistolarity

Jason König

1. EPISTOLARITY AND PRECARIOUS ASPIRATION

The world of Alciphron's *Letters* is a world of longing and loss, a world of fragile happiness and comic disillusionment. There are four books: *Letters from Fishermen, Farmers, Parasites, and Courtesans.* Each of those four groups reveals through its letters its own desires and sufferings, its own extravagant dreams and bathetic failures. Two themes (as far as they can be separated) are particularly prominent:[1] precarious or failed aspiration to material gain, love, or physical comfort; and precarious or failed aspiration to social advancement or role-swapping. The second of those preoccupations leads to an impression of interconnection between the different parts of the work, in the many letters where characters express their desire to cross from membership of one group to another.[2] The unrealistic character of the characters' dreams is matched by the inaccessibility and unreality of Alciphron's world for its readers. The work was written (probably) at some time in the late second or third century AD; or at any rate it is influenced by and has much in common with

---

I am very grateful to Jon Hesk for comments on a draft of this chapter, and for the seminar paper where I heard about Alciphron for the first time.

[1] One or other of them, sometimes both, appears in the majority of the letters in Books 1–3; Book 4 is rather different, as we shall see.

[2] See Section 5, below, for examples.

the sophistic literature of that period,³ for example in the way it looks
back to an imagined landscape of Classical Attica, drawing heavily
on material from New Comedy and a whole range of other sources.⁴
It purports to provide us with an authentic glimpse of the social
underbelly of Hellenic culture. The speakers are the low-class workers
and pleasure-providers of the Greek world, the suppliers of the elite
symposium.⁵ And yet the work is also clearly based on the rhetorical
exercise of *ethopoieia*, the exercise of fabricating speeches in the
persona of a particular type of character.⁶ Moreover, the text draws
attention to that rhetorical character, flaunting its own artificiality,⁷
predictably enough for anyone familiar with stylized representations
of the countryside in sophistic Greek literature,⁸ and with the traditions of rustic narrative inherited from Theocritus.

The aim of this chapter is to ask how far the text's epistolary form
works to intensify its thematic obsessions. My concern is thus primarily with formal issues; the task of analysing the politics of Alciphron's writing seems to me to be still an urgent one, but it will not
be my main aim here.⁹ My starting-point is the work of Janet Altman,
who has influentially discussed the intertwining of form and content
for the epistolary novels of modern European literature.¹⁰ Letters, she

---

³ On Alciphron's close relationship with other texts of the Second Sophistic,
especially the work of Lucian, see (amongst many others) Schmitz (2005), esp. 87–8;
Rosenmeyer (2001*a*) 256–7; Anderson (1997) 2194–9; Santini (1995); see also
Baldwin (1982), who dates the text, for different reasons, to the first decade of the
3rd cent. or earlier.

⁴ On Alciphron's allusions to Classical texts, especially New Comedy, see
(amongst many others) Rosenmeyer (2001*a*), esp. 256–8; Ozanam (1999); Anderson
(1997), esp. 2190–3; Ruiz García (1988); Gratwick (1979); Vieillefond (1979).

⁵ On the prominence of the symposium in Alciphron, see Ozanam (1999) 11;
Ruiz García (1988) 148–51; Longo (1985) esp. 10.

⁶ On *ethopoieia* and its influence on Alciphron, see Rosenmeyer (2001*a*) 259–63;
Ureña (1993); cf. Stirewalt (1993) 20–4 and Stowers (1986) 32–5 for letter-writing as a
school exercise and a basis for rhetorical training; see also Reed (1997), who argues that
rhetorical conventions had strong influence on ancient epistolary practice and theory.

⁷ See Schmitz (2005).

⁸ For examples of sophistic versions of the countryside, see Longus, *Daphnis and
Chloe* (with Saïd (1987) on the fascination of the Greek novelists with rustic settings);
Philostratus, *Heroicus* (with Whitmarsh (2001) 103–5).

⁹ For recent work on the gender politics of Book 4, see n. 33, below; on the
relation between the work's representation of class structures and the social structures
of Alciphron's contemporary world, see Longo (1985).

¹⁰ Altman (1982).

has argued, bring connection between writer and addressee, but also remind us constantly of the intervening distance. Letter writing promises sincerity, personal access to the real voice of the letter-writer, and yet at the same time the epistolary persona is always artificial, always fabricated. The narrative content of the texts she discusses is often paralleled and shaped, she suggests, by these characteristic formal qualities of epistolary communication:

In numerous instances the basic formal and functional characteristics of the letter, far from being merely ornamental, significantly influence the way meaning is consciously and unconsciously constructed by writers and readers of epistolary works.[11]

In that sense, Altman argues, letters provide powerful vehicles for—amongst other things—romantic fiction, which tends to emphasize the oscillation between separation and reunion, between intimacy and disillusionment.[12]

Alciphron's text fits Altman's formulation closely, although the task of demonstrating its relevance is not as easy as might initially seem to be the case. If we approach Alciphron's work with Altman's conclusions in mind it should come as no surprise that Alciphron has chosen the letter form, with all its connotations of insufficient and precarious communication, as the ideal vehicle for opening up to us these landscapes of frustrated desire; or, vice versa, that he gravitates towards the theme of frustrated desire as an ideal means of conveying his conception of epistolary form. The problem is that it is very hard to ground that impression in detailed analysis of the text, largely because Alciphron's characters very rarely discuss in explicit terms the advantages or disadvantages of their own chosen means of communication. The heroines of Ovid's *Heroides* often express anxiety about the potential of the letter form to miscarry, or to distort their intended meanings.[13] Many of the heroes and heroines of Altman's epistolary worlds do the same.[14] Alciphron's characters, by contrast, are for the most part blithely unaware of any such possibility. It is hard

---

[11] Altman (1982) 4.

[12] See esp. Altman (1982) 13–46.

[13] See Altman (1982) 13, citing *Heroides* 18.1–2; other obvious examples include 3.1–4, 5.1, 7.3–6, 11.1–2.

[14] See Altman (1982) 13–46 for many examples.

to find any single instance in Alciphron's work where the letter form is explicitly stated to be a contributing factor towards the precariousness of the characters' communications and aspirations.[15]

My argument here, however, is that the work's epistolarity does nevertheless form a central plank of Alciphron's thematic technique. The epistolary form of the work has often been treated dismissively, as nothing more than a convenient frame for (what is characterized as) his elegant but unoriginal game of patching together literary allusions.[16] More recently Patricia Rosenmeyer's work has gone a long way towards reversing those assumptions.[17] She sets Alciphron within the context of a long tradition of Greek epistolary writing. And she draws out systematically the omnipresent themes of material and social aspiration which I have already mentioned.[18] What she stops short of doing is to take the further step of linking the two, of exploring the ways in which theme and form work together. That is the further step I wish to take in this chapter. I look first at some of the anxious epistolary personas which were so common to real-life letters of request and supplication in the ancient world, as a point of comparison for Alciphron. I then move on to look at the way in which he interweaves theme and epistolary form in three specific areas of his writing: first, in his pointedly uneven use of unanswered letters; secondly, in the distinctively epistolary rhythms of request and answering refusal which run through his text; and thirdly, in his exploitation of these texts' main epistolary markers, the names of writer and addressee which stand at the beginning of each of them.

[15] Rosenmeyer (2001a) 298–307 discusses the way in which the texts of Book 4, unlike the other three books, draw attention self-consciously to their own status as letters, but worries about the possibility of non-delivery or lack of clarity are not thematized heavily even in this more self-conscious part of the text.

[16] e.g. see Ussher (1987) 99: 'Their one concession to epistolary form is the curt prescript'.

[17] Rosenmeyer (2001a) 255–307; see also Rosenmeyer (1994) on epistolary fiction more generally, especially the epistolary novel of Chion of Herakleia.

[18] See esp. Rosenmeyer (2001a) 277–85 on 'complaints and escapism' and 285–91 on role-swapping; for the latter, cf. Longo (1985) 11–14 on movements between the country and the city and vice versa.

2. REQUEST AND ANXIETY IN THE LETTERS
OF OXYRHYNCHUS

Letters in the ancient world were vehicles for bringing connection and control across geographical space (they were also sometimes a more attractive way of conversing even for people near enough to talk in person, as Owen Hodkinson shows for Alciphron in this volume). That idea is prominent within a range of ancient theoretical statements about the power of epistolary communication; it is also clear in countless examples of real communication where we see letter writers proclaiming their own closeness to their addressees on paper.[19] At the same time, however, ancient letter writing is also often acutely aware of the difficulties of communicating across space.[20] For every example of ancient letter writers expressing confidence in their ability to communicate we find counter-examples— often within the same letters—of anxiety about the possibility of miscarriage and ineffective communication. Even the most confident of ancient epistolary pronouncements often show an awareness of the gulf they must cross. These trends are especially prominent in letters which send requests or advice, for example in the thousands of private papyrus letters which survive from Hellenistic and Roman Egypt. For these letters the anxious exercise of control over geographical space is a recurring hallmark. I am interested in them here above all as a point of comparison with Alciphron.[21] I want to suggest that Alciphron parodies some of their commonest features; it seems hardly surprising that he might have gravitated towards these kinds of letters as models in seeking an appropriate vehicle for the anxious voices of his characters. I will also argue, however, that in many ways he resists the example they offer him, and that he prefers to find his

---

[19] For ancient statements of letters as substitutes for conversation, see, for example, Demetrius, *On Style* 223 or Seneca, *Ep.* 75.1 (both of these texts translated in Malherbe (1988) (although see Edwards (1997) for the point that Seneca's self, as presented in the letters, is made up of many different, contradictory voices)); Ussher (1988) 1574–5.

[20] For some examples, see Ussher (1988) 1576.

[21] Cf. Hutchinson in this volume for broader discussion of relations between documentary and literary letter-writing.

own very different ways of articulating the links between the letter
form and his favourite themes of precarious aspiration.

Most commonly, the papyrus letters are written as covering notes
to accompany gifts, in order to guarantee that none of the material in
carriage has gone astray on its journey. Often the writers in turn
request gifts or supplies from their addressees, asking them to send
fish or grain, or to arrange for the supply of articles of clothing or
equipment. In other cases the concern is not so much with specific
items of property as with attempts to give commands at a distance,
sometimes directly to the addressee, sometimes by asking the
addressee to pass on messages or instructions. Elsewhere writers are
very much aware of the division of the world by geographical
boundaries, especially the boundary between city and country,
which must have loomed large for Hellenistic and Roman Egypt, as
for most other ancient regions. We see writers anticipating planned
journeys, or asking their addressees to visit or come home. Many
complain about the failure of their addressees to write, or worry
about losing touch.[22] And in a very high number of them there is a
pointed awareness of the difficulties of epistolary communication,
signalled, for example, through repetitive restatement of instructions, often accompanied by formulaic use of pleas and exhortations.
All of these themes are ubiquitous in the *Oxyrhynchus Papyri* collection and others; in fact it is hard to find any private letter from these
collections which does not follow one or other of these patterns.
Those characteristics are matched by similar features in letters
usually categorized at a higher level of sophistication. Cicero's *Letters
to Atticus* is a good example. His repeated demands to Atticus about
the statues he has ordered, in the opening letters of the collection,
and his anxious requests for information about the progress of his
order,[23] are paralleled by Cicero's requests for news and advice in the

---

[22] For an account of some of the recurring features of these texts, see Stirewalt
(1993) 10–11 and 14–15, drawing on Koskenniemi (1956); for the influence of
handbooks of epistolary style on letters of this kind, see Rosenmeyer (2001a) 32–3;
Turner (1968) 130.

[23] There are requests for Atticus to send statues or information about Cicero's
statue order in the following letters (in chronological order): *Att.* 1.6, 1.7, 1.8, 1.9,
1.10, 1.11, 1.3, 1.4; these letters are discussed by Marvin (1993) 161–7, with translations in an appendix (180–4).

later part, as the country slides into civil war. Throughout the collection Cicero's requests are threaded through with complaints about Atticus' failure to reply, and expressions of anxiety about the many hindrances which stand in the way of successful epistolary communication, anxieties which become particularly acute as the collection goes on, in times of increasing political and military turmoil.[24] Cicero matches the heroines of the *Heroides* in his self-consciousness about the potential of the letter form both to facilitate and obstruct long-distance communication.

There is space here only for one pair of examples, both from the Egyptian papyrus letters. In *P.Oxy.* 937, written probably in the third century AD, we see a speaker who is concerned about his possessions, as so many of Alciphron's characters are:

κἂν νῦν οὖν παραγγέλλω σοι, ὦ κυρία μου ἀδελφή, ἵνα παραβάλῃς πρὸς τῇ πλατείᾳ τοῦ θεάτρου καὶ μάθῃς περὶ τῆς φιάλης τῆς λιθίνης ἐν τῷ πλοίῳ καὶ παραγγείλῃς πᾶσι τοῖς ἐκεῖ, Φιλοκύρῳ καὶ Ζωσίμῳ, παρατηρεῖσθαι αὐτὴν μὴ δόξῃ αὐτῷ τῷ Ἀγατείνῳ λαβῆσαι τὴν φιάλην . . . πέμψον τὸν μαφόρτην σου καὶ τὸ κεράμιον τοῦ γάρους καὶ δικότυλον ἐλαίου χρηστοῦ . . . δέξε δὲ γ σακκούδια παρὰ τοῦ Ἀντινοέως τοῦ σοι τὰ γράμματα διδόντος.

So now I urge you, dear sister, to go over to the street of the theatre and to find out about the stone bowl in the boat and to tell all of them there, Philokyros and Zosimos to keep an eye on it, in case Agateinos himself decides to take the bowl... Send your cloak and the jar of fish-sauce, and a double-measure of good olive-oil... You will receive three bags from the man from Antinoöpolis who is the carrier of this letter.

The letter mentions a succession of different items to be safeguarded or exchanged. It is shot through with a sense of intimacy and closeness, a sense that these matters have been discussed already in

[24] Of the statue letters referred to above, 1.6, 1.9, and 1.3 contain rebukes to Atticus for not writing often enough or fully enough (balanced by praise in 1.10 and 1.11 for the invigorating effect when Atticus' letters do get through); 1.9 and 1.10 explain that the nature of epistolary communication has forced Cicero to write more briefly than he would like (in 1.9 because of the fear that their private conversation will be overseen by strangers; in 1.10 because of the need to write quickly in order to send the letter with a departing messenger); cf. Hutchinson (1998) 18 for brief comment on the striking frequency, in letters between Cicero and his correspondents, of 'excuses that the author, or complaints that the recipient, has not written more regularly or punctually'; Beard (2002) on 'longing, travel and the desire to meet' as dominant themes in book 3 of the *Letters to Atticus*.

a whole string of letters preceding this one. And yet combined with that is a sense of the precariousness of this act of communication, and the precariousness of the possessions which it is meant to safeguard. That precariousness is signalled through the mention of Agateinos' machinations, and the need to pass that warning on to others. The mention of Philokyros and Zosimos by name, qualifying the more general phrase 'all of them there', suggests a desire to control by specifying, instead of leaving the precise details of the safeguarding of the bowl to the addressee's discretion.

P.Oxy. 929, from roughly the same date, is similar:

καλῶς ποιήσεις ἀπαιτήσας Τιθόιν τὸν ναυτικὸν δύμα καροίνου χιτῶνος ἐν ᾧ λίνον καὶ λέντιον τριβακόν, καὶ ἔρια, ταῦτα δὲ πάντα συνενῆι εἰς τὸν χιτῶνα τὸν καροῖνον καὶ ἐσφραγίσθη γῇ λευκῇ, καὶ σὺν τούτῳ ἄλλα δύματα πάντα, ὡς εἶναι ἐπὶ τὸ αὐτὸ ἀριθμῷ ἕξ, ἀποκαταστῆσαί μοι εἰς Ὀξυρυγχείτην ἐξ ὧν ἔσχον τὰ προκείμενα πάντα. διὸ γράφω σοι, ἀδελφέ, ἵν᾽ εἰ ἀλλότριά ἐστιν ἴδῃς, ἐρεῖς δέ μοι ἐν τάχει περὶ τούτου.

Please ask Tithois the sailor for my garment—a brown tunic, in which was a linen cloth, a worn-out towel and some wool. All these things were inside the brown tunic, and it was sealed with white clay. Along with this, please return all the other garments, numbering six in total in addition to the one mentioned. Return them to me in the Oxyrhynchite nome where I bought all the aforementioned items. I write to you therefore, my brother, to ask you to see if they are in someone else's possession. Please tell me quickly about this.

Here again we see how the letter communicates across physical boundaries, in this case bridging between different regions. And once again, the letter is veined with anxiety about loss. The writer is tenacious. He lists everything repetitively to make absolutely sure, but at the same time his anxiety about the difficulty of straight-forward communication often bursts through. 'Please let me know quickly about this', he says, in the closing lines of the text, as if telling anything 'quickly' in a letter, with its inevitable delay between writing and reading, can ever be possible. In the sentence before that his anxiety is even plainer: 'I write', he says, 'to see if they are in someone else's possession'. In including that reminder he repeats the request he has already made in the first part of the letter, where he asked his brother to approach the sailor Tithois, but he speaks now in a much vaguer, more anxious tone, as if worried that they may not be where he thinks they are, that he cannot exercise control through his letter as well as he had hoped.

What relevance do these texts have for our understanding of Alciphron's work? In some cases, all in Books 1 and 2, it is clear that Alciphron is parodying these idioms of rustic correspondence, overlaying them rather incongruously with sophistic or quasi-philosophical material.[25] In 1.7, for instance, a fisherman, Thalassos, writes to another fisherman Pontios:

ἔπεμψά σοι ψῆτταν καὶ σανδάλιον καὶ κεστρέα καὶ κήρυκας πέντε καὶ τριάκοντα, σὺ δέ μοι τῶν ἐρετμῶν δύο πέμψον, ἐπειδὴ τἀμὰ κατέαγεν.

I sent you a turbot, a sole, a mullet and thirty-five shellfish. Please send me a pair of oars in return, since mine are broken.

Here the obsession with movement and exchange of material goods which we find in the papyrus letters is reproduced. However, it is also combined with more erudite preoccupations. In the context of Alciphron's overtly sophistic writing, it is hard not to see a learned voice hiding behind the list of fish, which follows the obsession with piscological listing which we find in Athenaeus, *Deipnosophists* books 7–8, or in Oppian's *Halieutica*. The passage which follows is also playfully erudite. Here the writer ingeniously justifies his own request with a rephrasing of the maxim familiar from Plato and Euripides that 'friends hold everything in common' (κοινὰ τὰ τῶν φίλων).[26] There are similar request letters in 1.17, 2.3, 2.12, 2.39. Like so many of the Egyptian letters, most of them do introduce a note of urgency by repeating their requests in a slightly different form in the closing lines; but once again, as for 1.7, that repetition in all cases takes the form of erudite and epigrammatic use of proverbial language.[27] Other letters follow the standard technique, familiar from the Oxyrhynchus papyri as from countless other sources, of sending a letter together with a gift in order to make sure it does not miscarry.[28]

[25] In that sense Alciphron self-consciously maintains the gap between literary and non-literary writing discussed by Hutchinson in this volume.

[26] e.g. see Euripides, *Orestes* 735, Plato, *Phaedrus* 279c; on the erudite, gnomic character of this ending, see Anderson (1997) 2200.

[27] e.g. in 2.3, the writer quotes from Hesiod, *Works and Days* 350; in 2.12 the writer uses the proverbial phrase κοινὰ τὰ τῶν φίλων, discussed above, in full.

[28] In addition to the examples listed below, see also 2.20.

In 2.27, for example, we hear of an extravagant gift of twenty-five birds for the pot, the result of an unexpectedly large catch, and in 2.29 a gift of two piglets which the writer cannot afford to feed. Here again, however, both letters end in erudite and pointedly non-rustic fashion with concisely crafted, gnomic praise of the ideals of rustic friendship. The first half of 2.27 gives us a description of the catching of the birds with lime which draws on the conventions of ekphrasis, in its description of the 'beautiful sight' ($\theta \acute{\epsilon} \alpha \mu \alpha \ \acute{\eta} \delta \acute{\upsilon}$) of the birds stuck to the branches, and also echoes the fantasy novelistic picture of bird-hunting in the snow in Longus, *Daphnis and Chloe* 3.6 and 3.10.

Alciphron thus signals his awareness of the genres of real-life ancient letter writing which were concerned with transmission of requests and exercise of other kinds of control; he also mimics some of their anxiously repetitive exhortation. One might argue that he uses his repeated parody of these conventions of real-life request letters to hint at the relevance for the collection as a whole of the rhetoric of anxiety they characteristically contain. Ultimately, however, it is the differences between Alciphron and the papyrus letter-writers which this comparison reveals most clearly. The vast majority of the papyrus texts do not go beyond the basic exercise of request and enquiry I have described here. In that sense they fall into a relatively small number of the categories of letters listed by ancient epistolary theorists. Alciphron's letters cover a much wider range of types.[29] The papyrus texts, no doubt like the majority of non-fictional letters in the ancient world, are primarily concerned with making interventions in urgent current situations, passing on instructions, shoring up relationships, offering advice. Alciphron supplements that kind of intervening text with a large number of retrospective letters, which look back to past pleasures and disappointments, rather than giving their main attention to manufacturing or avoiding them in the immediate future. The letter writers of Oxyrhynchus, like the heroines of Ovid's *Heroides* I mentioned earlier, worry constantly about the capacity of the letter form to

[29] For examples of the categorization of letters by epistolary theorists, see ps.-Demetrius, *Epistolary Types* (esp. 11 for the 'supplicatory type' and 12 for the 'enquiring type'), and ps.-Libanius, *Epistolary Styles* (esp. 7 and 54 for the 'requesting style' and 35 and 82 on the 'enquiring style') (both translated in Malherbe (1988)); see also Reed (1997) 172–86.

achieve the things required of it. Alciphron's heroes and heroines set themselves apart from that model conspicuously. In the work as a whole, they tend to oscillate between an acute awareness of the precariousness and disappointment of their aspirations and an absurdly hopeful lack of awareness of those things. One might expect the first of those states of mind to lead them at least sometimes to question the effectiveness of their own acts of writing; but for some reason the letter form is always treated with naïve optimism. They prefer to give their attention to the more reflective activities of story-telling and philosophizing, rather than being dragged into petty worries about the miscarrying of communication. Even where they do repeat their requests—a gesture which in the papyrus letters usually signals urgency—that repetition, as we have seen, tends to be taken as an opportunity for display of gnomic, literary ingenuity which detracts from any sense of anxiety which might have existed in the first half of the letter. Their voices are remarkably unaware of the precariousness of their own attempts at epistolary image projection.

How should one explain that difference? Does it mean that Alciphron is actually much less interested in the precariousness of epistolary communication than the vast majority of his contemporaries, who show such a vivid awareness of it in their day-to-day practices of letter writing? I want to suggest in what follows that if anything the opposite is the case. If Alciphron chooses to make his characters unaware of the fragility of their own acts of epistolary communication—in line with their absurd lack of self-awareness in so many other areas of their lives—that does not mean that he is himself unaware of the capacity of the letter form to convey a sense of incomplete and fragile communication.

3. UNANSWERED LETTERS IN BOOKS 3 AND 4

How, then, does Alciphron exploit the letter form within the detailed texture of his own writing? At first sight one of the most obvious reasons for associating the letter form with failed or fragile communication, and for seeing it as a natural vehicle for the thematization of other kinds of fragile aspiration, is simply that letters do not always get replies. The vast majority of letters in Alciphron's collection are one-way letters. We are left with no indication of whether they ever reached their destination, whether they ever attained the results they aim for.[30] It would clearly be wrong to read too much into that fact, given that the vast majority of ancient letter collections are similarly dominated by one-way letters. Alciphron's readers would not necessarily have expected a coherent dialogue between successive texts, and it therefore seems wrong to read any particular significance into that absence.[31] And yet I want to suggest here that we cannot dismiss the unanswered nature of these texts quite so easily as that, simply because of the way in which Alciphron distributes his letter replies between the different books. Book 4, the book of courtesans' letters, has more replies, more sustained communication than any of the others; it is also the book whose letter-writers go furthest towards escaping from the typically Alciphronic oscillation between hopeless desire and disillusionment. Conversely, Book 3, the *Letters of Parasites*, is the only book where letter replies are completely absent; and the parasites themselves are correspondingly the characters most prone of all to unrealistic fantasy. This patterning suggests some self-consciousness on Alciphron's part about the capacity of unanswered letters to enhance an impression of disappointment and precarious aspiration, at least within the context of a collection where letter replies are not evenly distributed.

The point can be illustrated relatively briefly for Book 3.[32] There, the total absence of sustained communication is particularly appropriate to parasites, whose obsession with their stomachs is so all-consuming that it shuts out any but the most temporary and self-serving alliances. Admittedly we do see many of these parasites longing for a different lifestyle in their letters. These are the spaces where they dream of a more productive, co-operative lifestyle, where they offer encouragement and entertainment to their colleagues off-duty. But the lack of replies—inviting as it does a comparison

---

[30] For an excellent short account of the carefully manufactured atmosphere of fragmentariness in the work, see Reardon (1971) 180–5; cf. Ozanam (1999) 23.

[31] Rosenmeyer (2001a) 260–1 even suggests that Alciphron goes beyond the usual limits of *ethopoieia* by introducing occasional sets of paired letters.

[32] See Longo (1985) 33 on the isolation of the parasites, contrasting this with the sense of a mini-community in Book 4; Rosenmeyer (2001a) 272 makes the point that the letters of Book 3 'rarely even sustain the fiction of an addressee or a letter context'.

with the greater connectedness of other books—hints at the failure of
these abortive attempts at sincere, unparasitical friendship. Moreover
that epistolary isolation is matched by the way in which their words
miscarry in other forms throughout the book. There are very few
examples of parasites communicating verbally with their hosts—
their communication is on the level of theatrical jesting only—and
when they do, it is usually with unintended consequences, which are
unlikely to make us optimistic for the success of their attempts at
written connection. In 3.2, for example, the letter writer tells how he
has been sent with instructions to persuade a courtesan to come to
dinner, and has had boiling water poured on top of him for his pains.
In 3.21, we hear that the writer's drunken insulting of his host's
foster-father has led to reduced payment. In 3.33, a parasite tells
how he informed on the infidelity of his host's wife, only to be
disbelieved, with hints that there will be ominous consequences.

Book 4 is very different. Of the four books of Alciphron's work,
this is the one which has attracted most comment. A number of
critics have felt that Alciphron gives a specially privileged position to
feminine viewpoint and female independence in the voices of his
courtesans, in making them the most self-reliant and materially
prosperous of his four groups.[33] Certainly this is a book very different from the others in its impression of sustained communication.[34]
Many of the letters are immediately followed by replies. We hear pairs
of courtesans exchanging gossip about the anxieties and pleasures of
their relationships, and writing to their lovers, whose replies Alciphron sometimes also includes, as if to make it clear that the courtesans are able to communicate not only with each other but also
with the outside world of the Athenian elite. Not only that, but many
of the correspondents communicate with more than one addressee.
At times Alciphron comes close to offering a novelistic treatment of a
single story, developing over several letters and involving a range of
recurring characters.[35] Bacchis, for example, is the recipient of letter

[33] e.g. see Rosenmeyer (2001*b*) on Alciphron's extension of the tendency to
present the historical Phryne as a figure able to manipulate her own image and
male response to it.
[34] See Rosenmeyer (2001*a*) 272–4 on the greater connectedness of Book 4.
[35] e.g. see Anderson (1997) 2202–3 on the letters between Menander and Glykera
(*Letters* 4.18 and 4.19) as a kind of 'miniature romantic novel' (2203).

4.2; she then proceeds to write to three separate correspondents in turn on related matters, first the orator Hypereides, then her fellow-courtesans Phryne and Myrrhina. The subject matter of the letters is also more consistently optimistic: conflict and threatened loss are regularly overcome by epistolary negotiation. Moreover the fact that many of the characters in this book are historical figures—the poet Menander, the orator Hypereides, mentioned above, the famous courtesans Phryne and Glykera—contributes further to a sense of greater connectedness. They, unlike the marginal characters of Books 1–3, have been saved from oblivion. Admittedly the courtesans' communication is not always successful. Even here, the ghosts of those earlier books have a haunting presence, and there are moments where Alciphron slips back into a more disjointed mode, catapulting us back into the world of precariousness and loss which is so familiar from our encounter with the fishermen and farmers and parasites. It is as though the courtesans, however successful their ploys for escaping from the margins of society, are always in danger of being dragged back. In 4.10, for example, where Myrrhina complains that her lover Diphilus has deserted her, it is hard not to be reminded of the unhappy separations and hopeless loves of the fishermen and farmers in Book 1–2. But for the most part the distinction holds. The world of the courtesans is less affected than the other books by an atmosphere of evanescence and precariousness, and one of the ways in which Alciphron signals that change is to render it through a more continuous, less disjointed arrangement of successive letters.

4. NARRATIVE PATTERNING IN EPISTOLARY COLLECTIONS

We have seen, then, that one of the ways in which letters can act as convenient vehicles for the portrayal of failed aspiration is through their capacity to go unanswered. One of the other ways in which they can do this is through their capacity to prompt answering letters of refusal and rebuttal. This too is a feature Alciphron exploits. Books 1 and 2 have a total of five pairs of letters and one triplet out of a total of 61 letters overall.[36] In all six of these cases the answering letters contain refusal of the advice or request offered in the original letter, in most cases expressed in highly insulting language.[37] That repeated pattern of refusal might lead us to expect that the likely response to all of the other letters of the collection would be equally negative if Alciphron had provided it, although admittedly many of the other letters of these two books are not the kind of letters which explicitly invite replies. This seems to be a world where the ideals of sharing and friendship which the farmers and fishermen so often refer to in making requests, as we saw in Section 2, are rarely carried out in practice.

I also want, however, to go beyond that simple point about Alciphron's sporadic use of paired letters to suggest that the rhythms of refusal and rebuttal work their way into the texture of the collection even when there is no explicit interaction between successive texts. One of the consequences of putting unanswered letters together in a collection, at least for Alciphron, seems to be that the reader is prompted to construct a narrative from them, though always a narrative which contains striking disjunctions between its different parts.[38] Repeatedly the narrative patterns which emerge from Alciphron's text are patterns of seesawing between contradictory assertions.[39] Repeatedly, if we accept the challenge to read the collection consecutively, the claims made in one letter are contradicted in the next. The expectation that request will be followed by refusal in any letter which gets a response from its original addressee is echoed

[36] The groups are 1.11 and 1.12; 1.17, 1.18, and 1.19; 1.21 and 1.22; 2.6 and 2.7; 2.15 and 2.16; 2.24 and 2.25.

[37] Cf. Hodkinson in this volume for discussion of some of these pairs.

[38] Cf. Morrison in this volume on the implied narrative of Horace's progress in his *Epistles*; and Beard (2002) on the way in which the traditional (i.e. non-chronological) arrangement of Cicero's letters prompts us to see thematic continuity and narrative logic within particular books; cf. Sharrock (2000) for more general discussion of the impulses towards seeing unity and linearity which are central to the experience of reading, but also the constant presence of other ways of reading which work to disrupt those impulses.

[39] Cf. Altman (1982) 167–84 on the way in which the discontinuity of modern European epistolary novels stands in tension with narrative threads which invite us as readers to see continuity; esp. 179–81 on the way in which a range of writers show a fascination with antiphonal rhythms within this kind of 'epistolary mosaic', through juxtaposition of letters of contrasting tone.

repeatedly in more abstract terms even within ostensibly uncon-
nected texts. That argument needs to be made cautiously, given the
insecurity of the text's manuscript tradition.[40] The letters have come
down to us arranged in many different patterns within different
manuscripts, and the currently established order is a consequence
of the editorial choices of an unidentifiable number of successive
editors. And yet for two reasons the argument seems to me to stand:
first of all, because Alciphron has introduced such a high degree of
thematic interconnection into these many different letter texts that
links of this type would have the potential to emerge however the
work was arranged; and secondly, because the editor or editors
responsible have patterned the text in a way which is highly sensitive
to that potential, as I aim to show in what follows, responding to
Alciphron's work in a way which may not exactly match the form of
the work as it was originally circulated, but which is clearly consistent
with some of its underlying conceptions. The collection hints repeatedly at patterns of oscillation between success and failure, hope and
despair; and it gives those oscillations a specifically epistolary inflection by interspersing pairs of connected letters, in all of which the
second letter gives a negative response to or version of its predecessor. These connected pairs act as models for the more abstract kinds
of rebuttal between successive letters which we see elsewhere in the
collection.

In order to exemplify those features I here look briefly at the
opening letters of Book 1. For Alciphron's fishermen, the oscillation
between abundance and shortage, hope and despair is given a distinctively piscatorial character. That effect comes partly from the fact
that the fisherman holds such an ambiguous position in Graeco-
Roman thought. The fisherman is the collector of the greatest of all
culinary luxuries, but also paradoxically a representative of the greatest poverty. He stands on the very margins of society, forced to the
sea because the land refuses to produce, and facing enormous risk.[41]
These contradictory images of fishing—which oscillate between

---

[40] See Schmitz (2005) 88–9 for a summary account of the manuscript tradition,
and 89 n. 8 for criticism of Rosenmeyer's attempt to view the opening letters of each
book as programmatic when the original order of publication is uncertain.
[41] See Purcell (1995).

extravagance and lack—are mirrored by the oscillation between dreams of prosperity (sometimes temporarily attained) and threat of starvation which pervade the stories the characters tell. In addition, fish are the archetypal elusive prey, slipping out of reach whenever the nets come close to them, just like so many of the other objects of desire in the lives Book 1 reveals to us. The scene of large catches of fish which slip away at the last moment is one which is repeated several times in the book.[42] It offers a recurring metaphor for the elusiveness of prosperity which these letter-writers experience in other areas of their lives too.

Book 1 opens with a rare success story. A fisherman writes to his friend about a three-day storm, and then the enormous catch of fish which followed it. The storm, first of all, is described with the language of ekphrasis.[43] The winds, we hear

καὶ λάβρως κατὰ τοῦ πελάγους ἐπέπνεον ἐκ τῶν ἀκρωτηρίων οἱ βορεῖς, καὶ ἐπεφρίκει μὲν ὁ πόντος μελαινόμενος, τοῦ ὕδατος δὲ ἀφρὸς ἐξηνθήκει, πανταχοῦ τῆς θαλάσσης ἐπ᾽ ἀλλήλων ἐπικλωμένων τῶν κυμάτων—τὰ μὲν γὰρ ταῖς πέτραις προσηράσσετο, τὰ δὲ εἴσω ἀνοιδοῦντα ἐρρήγνυντο.

. . . blew violently down upon the sea from the headlands, the sea turned black and bristled, foam blossomed out of the sea water, everywhere in the sea the waves broke against each other, some of them dashing against the rocks, others swelling up from inside the water and bursting into spray. . .   (1.1.1)

The landscape is fixed here like a work of art. The sea becomes a solid surface, like the surface of a painting or a sculpture, through the word 'bristled' (ἐπεφρίκει). The foam 'blossoms' like a flower, an image which suggests the transformative powers of art to bring beauty out of danger. And there is a sense of balance and order arising out of chaos in the 'some. . . others' clause (τὰ μέν . . . τὰ δέ). Here we have an immediate reminder that these are sophistic fishermen. We also have a sense that the writer is attempting to capture the beauty of the storm to fix it in textual form for his addressee, even as the memory slips

[42] e.g. 1.13 and 1.20, discussed further in n. 47, below.
[43] For an example of a storm as a subject of ekphrasis, see Webb (2000) 223 on Sopater Rhetor; see also Rosenmeyer (2001a) 268–9 on the sense of a double audience in this letter, and the way in which Alciphron allows the sophistic preoccupation with detailed, journalistic description to overshadow the purported function of communication between friends.

away.[44] We then hear of the fishermen's good fortune. They pull in nets which are bulging with fish. The fish-sellers are waiting for them. The memory of the sight fills him with emotion as he writes: φεῦ τῆς εὐοψίας, ὅσον ἰχθύων ἐξειλκύσαμεν ('Oh, what an abundance of seafood, what a great number of fish we dragged up') (1.1.4).[45] They even have enough to feed their wives and children, not just for one day, but even for several days, in case the storm comes back. And yet there are also hints in that detail that this writer will very soon be looking back to this plenty nostalgically, hints that the bad weather and the hunger will all too soon return. Even this most contented of all the fishermen's letters is inscribed with a feeling of loss and nostalgia, of ungraspable riches in the past. Letters have the capacity to introduce shifts of focalization between the writer in the present, and his or her former self at the time of the events being narrated.[46] This opening letter of Alciphron's collection at first sight seems to resist that possibility: the writer's pleasure in the catch is still keenly felt, just as it was at the time. There seems to be no sense of disillusionment, no sense of ironic commentary on the instabilities of human fortune. In that sense this letter is very different from most of those which will come later (although there is throughout the collection a scattering of other contented letter-writers like this one). And yet even here there is just a hint in these closing lines that the writer is aware of how his future self may look back on this time nostalgically, even bitterly, even if he is revelling for now in a rare opportunity to keep those feelings of pessimism at bay.

That suggestion of bitterness and anxiety bursts out more openly in the very beginning of the letter which follows. Here the sense of plenty is reversed:

Μάτην ἡμῖν τὰ πάντα πονεῖται, ὦ Κύρτων, δι' ἡμέρας μὲν ὑπὸ τῆς εἵλης φλεγομένοις νύκτωρ δὲ ὑπὸ λαμπάσι τὸν βυθὸν ἀποξύουσι, καὶ τὸ λεγόμενον δὴ τοῦτο εἰς τὸν τῶν Δαναΐδων τοὺς ἀμφορέας ἐκχέομεν πίθον· οὕτως ἄπρακτα καὶ ἀνήνυτα διαμοχθοῦμεν.

---

[44] Ekphrasis, as theorized by the rhetoricians of the Roman Empire, was the technique of bringing scenes from the past to life, imbuing them with 'vividness' (*enargeia*); at the same time, however, it often had the capacity to undermine its own sense of the presence of the past, drawing attention to its own evanescence and artificiality: see Webb (2000), esp. 225, on Athenaeus, *Deipnosophists*, book 5.

[45] The use of φεῦ + genitive gives a stylized, quasi-tragic feel to the writer's language, enhancing the impression that this is a sophisticated, allusive quality to his retelling of past pleasures and pains.

[46] Cf. Bray (2003).

All of our work is for nothing, Kyrton. By day we are burnt by the heat of the sun, and at night we scrape at the abyss by torchlight, emptying our amphorae into the jar of the Danaids, as the saying goes. That's how unprofitable and endless our labour is.   (1.2.1)

Here the labour of the Danaids is equated with the work of the fishermen, which is thus characterized as futile, in contrast with the fruitful harvests of 1.1. There may even be an implied parallel between the leakiness associated with the vessels of the Danaids and the leakiness and ineffectiveness of the fishermen's nets, which repeatedly come up empty, unlike the bulging nets of the previous letter. In addition, the sun has become the fishermen's enemy, again, in contrast with the opening letter, where it is described as the bringer of pleasant warmth and the herald of prosperous fishing after the storm. And the image of 'scraping' or 'combing' (ἀποξύουσι) the sea picks up on the description of the bristling of the storm in letter one. It casts fishing as a painful process, a painstaking, human attempt to stir up the waters, in contrast with the effortless and (in Alciphron's description) beautiful violence of the storm. From there the writer goes on to lament his hunger, due to the loss of a fellow-worker, who has been enticed away by some independent fishermen, leaving the others to be further exploited by a cruel master, complaining, with the language of parasitical resentment, that their master gets all the fish and the coins, while they cannot even fill their stomachs. In these first two letters we see two very different sides to the process of supplying the elite symposium. In 1.1 the fish-buyers are benefactors, waiting at the harbour to give the fishermen their longed-for payment after the bumper catch, and even leaving food for the fishermen's families. But in 1.2—and indeed in many later letters, where the positive catch of 1.1 is an important reference point, to be undermined and contradicted[47]—the story is very different. The fishermen toil to supply delicacies to the city: it is an order for sponges and sea-wool, used to dye the robe of a rich young woman

---

[47] e.g. 1.13, where a fisherman mortgages his boat in order to finance the mending of his net for a projected haul of fish which fails to materialize, and where the opening word of the letter, εὐοψία ('abundance of seafood') signals not plenty, as it does in 1.1, but instead dangerous illusions of plenty; and in 1.20, where a bulging net turns out to contain a dead camel, rather than a large catch of fish.

from the city, which has driven the writer's co-worker to desert. That
sense of balance between these two letters reminds us again of the
ordering hand of sophistic artifice which lies behind the whole text,
much like the balanced clauses in the description of the storm.
Arguing for both sides of the same case was a common sophistic
entertainment. Here we have a rhetorical exercise of praise for the
fisherman's career in 1.1 balanced by the diametrically opposite
exercise in 1.2. But it is also an effect which is particularly appropriate to the letter form: the rhythms of letter and response here find
ghostly echoes in the elusive balancing structures of the book as a
whole, in their oscillation between profit and loss. That is not to say
that the movement from request to rebuttal is an inherent feature of
epistolary communication. But it does seem to be an essential characteristic in the world of Books 1–3, where replies, in the few cases
where Alciphron gives them to us, are always in the negative, as we
have seen.

That sense of balance is then matched in letters 1.3 and 1.4. In 1.3,
as so often in Alciphron, we find a character who longs to become
something he is not, longs to jump over the boundaries which
separate these four books (more on that motif in the next section).
The writer is a fisherman, informing his wife of his desire that they
should become farmers. He bases his argument on both experience
and learning (πείρᾳ καὶ διδασκαλίᾳ), the former partial (he knows the
hardship and danger of the sea, admittedly, but his judgement of the
land seems to be at second hand); and the latter very cursory, based
on one snippet of poetry he has picked up from his travels to Athens.
He describes how he once overheard a philosopher—ἑνὸς τῶν ἐν τῇ
Ποικίλῃ διατριβόντων ἀνυποδήτων καὶ ἐνεροχρώτων ('one of the
corpse-like and barefooted men who spend their time in the Porch'),
hardly a reliable witness to the nourishing power of the Attic soil, we
might think—quoting from Aratos' *Phainomena* about the folly of
going to sea: ὀλίγον δὲ διὰ ξύλον ἄϊδ᾽ ἐρύκει ('It is only a thin plank that
wards off Hades'). That tiny extract seems to be all the letter-writer can
remember, and its uncontextualized brevity surely prompts us to
question his judgement. And indeed, this writer's judgement about
the relative safety of the land and the sea is challenged a number
of times in what follows, for example in 2.4, where a farmer decides
to take to the sea, in disgust at the hardships of working on the land.

But the most conspicuous reversal comes in the very next letter, 1.4. There Kymothoos writes to his wife Tritonis, who has been attending festivals in the city. The letter-writer denounces the land in an attempt to get her to give up this habit: ἡμῖν δὲ οἷς βίος ἐν ὕδασι, θάνατος ἡ γῆ καθάπερ τοῖς ἰχθύσιν ἥκιστα δυναμένοις ἀναπνεῖν τὸν ἀέρα ('for us, who have our livelihood from the water, the land brings death, just as it does to the fish who are entirely unable to breathe air') (1.4.2). The immediate reversal of the longings of 1.3 introduces an impression of instability, an impression that the hierarchies between different habitats, which Alciphron's letter-writers embrace so vehemently, are unstable or illusory and only likely to lead to eventual disillusionment. Letters 1.3 and 1.4 thus dovetail together, in much the same way as the first two letters of the collection. Once again, the rhythms of assertion and rebuttal are ingrained even in pairs of letters which do not have any explicit correspondence with each other.

5. EPISTOLARY NAMING

I have argued, then, that the spectre of unanswered letters and the rhythms of epistolary refusal haunt Alciphron's text, and make a sustained contribution to its atmosphere of frustrated aspiration. My final point is that that thematic emphasis is also enhanced by the only explicit marker these letters carry of their epistolary identity, that is the pair of names, identifying writer and addressee, which each one of them is headed with. It was, of course, standard practice for private letters in both Greek and Latin to be headed in these terms. Seeing the name of writer and addressee at the beginning of a text was precisely the thing which guaranteed that text's epistolary identity.[48] Alciphron, however, uses that convention in particularly pointed ways. Almost without exception, in Books 1–3, the names he chooses are absurdly unrealistic, and absurdly appropriate to habitats of their bearers: thus fishermen have names connected with the sea and with seafood; parasites have names which signal their obsession

---

[48] Cf. Rees in this volume.

with particular types of food or their mania for the customs of the symposium. One of the functions of these names is to signal ostentatiously the sophistic unreality of Alciphron's characters.[49] More importantly for the purposes of this chapter, they contribute to the idea that these characters are rooted in their own environments, however strong their expressed desire to escape.[50] Over and over again the opening epistolary markers signal to us the hopelessness of the writer's aspirations even before the letter has begun. Here again, then, Alciphron's portrayal of disappointed fantasy is ingrained specifically within his use of the letter format. The opening name should be the thing which guarantees that we are hearing the real voice of the letter writer, speaking almost miraculously across geographical space; but in Alciphron's hands it does the opposite, parading his characters' artificiality and geographical boundedness.

In 1.3, for example, as we have already seen, a fisherman tries to persuade his wife that they should take up a life of farming. Their watery names (Glaukos and Galateia) suggest that the sea is their natural element. Glaukos is the name of a sea-god,[51] an epithet of the sea ('blue-green'), and a type of fish. Galateia was the nymph loved by the Cyclops Polyphemus in Theocritus, *Idylls* 6 and 11, and separated from him in part by his ugliness, but also by her reluctance to cross the boundary between sea and land. By giving this name to the fisherman's wife, Alciphron hints at the difficulty he may have in persuading her to make the move. In 2.32, a parasite named Gnathon ('Jaws') writes asking for a post as a farm labourer, and his name immediately signals his incongruity with the rustic letters of the rest of the book. In 3.5, Oinopniktes ('Wine-Choker') writes to Kotylobrochthisos ('Cup-Guzzler') about a plan to abduct a courtesan, in the hope that their master will be pleased and will reward them by calling them 'friends' rather than 'parasites', but their names point to the illusory nature of that hope.

---

[49] See Schmitz (2005) 98–9.

[50] See Schmitz (2005) 100; on Alciphron's use of names, see also Ureña (1993); Anderson (1997) 2201–2.

[51] e.g. see Plato, *Republic* 611c–d.

Elsewhere, the letter-writer's name not only signals the unchanging nature of his or her identity, but also takes on a particularly pointed significance from the events described within the letter itself. In 3.25, for example, we hear a typically indignant lament:

Ἡράκλεις, ὅσα ὑπέστην πράγματα ῥύμματι καὶ νίτρῳ Χαλαστραίῳ χθιζινοῦ ζωμοῦ τοὐμοὶ περιχυθέντος τὴν γλισχρότητα ἀποκαθαίρων. καὶ οὐχ οὕτω με ἔδακνεν ἡ ὕβρις ὅσον τὸ διάφορον τοῦ ὑβρίζοντος. ἐγὼ μὲν γὰρ Ἀνθεμίωνος υἱὸς τοῦ πλουσιωτάτου τῶν Ἀθήνησι καὶ Ἀξιοθέας τῆς κατὰ γένος ἐκ Μεγακλέους ὡρμημένης, ὁ δὲ ταῦθ' ἡμᾶς ἐργαζόμενος πατρὸς μὲν ἀσήμου μητρὸς δὲ βαρβάρου, Σκυθίδος οἶμαι ἢ Κολχίδος ἐν νεομηνίᾳ ἐωνημένης.

By Herakles, what great trouble I had in cleaning off the stickiness of the soup which was thrown over me yesterday with soap and Chalastraian soda. It is not so much the insult which bites at me, but the difference between my own position and the position of the man who insulted me. For I am the son of Anthemion the richest man in Athens and Axiothea, who came from the line of Megakles; but the man who did this to me is the son of a non-entity of a father and a barbarian mother—a Scythian or Kolchian slave, I think, bought on the first day of the month.

The speaker has lost not only his bodily dignity, but also, it turns out, his identity, having been forced to take on the name of Skordosphrantes ('Garlic-Sniffer') in place of his given name of Polybius. The name which appears at the head of the letter is thus particularly humiliating here because of what it replaces. The speaker's decision to sign himself as Skordosphrantes is a tacit acknowledgement that his old name is useless for the purposes of identification, that he has no prospect of reversing the journey from prosperity to parasitism. 3.19 is a similarly pointed example. There a parasite called Autokletos ('Gate-Crasher') writes to his friend Hetoimaristos ('Ready-for-Breakfast'), describing a birthday party given by a host with social pretensions for his daughter; the climax of the description is a scornful description of the drunken misbehaviour of the philosophers who were present. Here, the writer's name once again implies the inevitability of his parasitical nature. In this case, however, it also hints at his pretensions to higher things. He is a 'gate-crasher' into the category of elite identity, in the sense that he claims superiority over the philosophers who attend the party; and it perhaps also suggests pretensions to independence, if we take it to mean 'self-called', as if this is a speaker who claims to have control over his own self-definition, in contrast with the letter-writer of 3.25. The heading of this letter thus seems to be a rare example for Alciphron of epistolary naming implying the potential for empowerment rather than humiliation. Even here, however, the speaker's self-righteous adoption of an elitist tone of moral superiority is undermined in the closing sentences of the letter, where it turns out, in a final twist, that he is criticizing the philosophers not for their drunkenness and immorality, but distracting attention from himself and his fellow entertainers. His parasitical nature, his ultimate inability to throw off a parasitical perspective, reveals itself in the end, making it clear that his appropriation of a stance of social and moral superiority is only a very temporary act of 'gatecrashing' into styles of elite self-representation.

6. POSTSCRIPT

I have argued, then, that Alciphron's use of letters is very far from being an arbitrary and inert frame for his fictional world. Instead, it is an inextricable part of his thematic conception, enhancing the obsession with frustrated aspiration which he returns to so often. I have pointed to his artfully varied use of unanswered letters; his manipulation of the see-saw rhythms of epistolary rebuttal; and finally his exploitation of the comic potential of the conventions of epistolary naming. I wish, as a final postscript, to raise one other area in which we might see links between form and theme within Alciphron's works, and that is in its obsession with artificiality. I have discussed only in passing, in the opening paragraph of the chapter, the arguments recently made by Thomas Schmitz that Alciphron's work is distinguished above all by the way in which it flaunts its own unrealistic, sophistic character, foregrounding the allusiveness and imaginary status of its own version of classical Attica even as it allows its readers to indulge the fantasy of having an authentic glimpse back in time. What Schmitz misses is the further point that Alciphron repeatedly presents us with striking similarities between these processes of sophistic imagination and the many examples of unrealistic dreaming we see within the world of the letters. It seems to me hard to avoid the conclusion that Alciphron means us to draw a connection between the artificial fantasies of himself and his sophistic readers, and the evanescent fantasy visions which his characters themselves construct. The act of imagining a way of life different from one's own which so many of the characters indulge in is also the basis for the exercise of *ethopoieia* which Alciphron himself is engaged in.[52] In that sense, the work's many portrayals of extravagant acts of imagination, in the fantasies of its four main groups of characters, potentially have self-reflexive implications for the acts of imagination which Alciphron's readers necessarily themselves engage in. Self-consciousness about the way in which sophistic visions of the past are always fabricated and illusory and fantastical, always just out of reach, and yet all the more attractive for their elusiveness—just as the fantasies of Alciphron's characters are—has recently come to be viewed as one of the hallmarks of the sophistic literature of the Roman Empire.[53] By that standard, the characters of Alciphron's work are themselves sophistic figures, and their dreams are comical equivalents of sophistic imaginings.

Not only that, but the arguments of Janet Altman which I referred to at the very beginning of this chapter might once again lead us to expect that the letter form would be a particularly powerful vehicle for such an enterprise, given the way letters so often stand halfway between sincerity and artificiality, purporting to offer us unmediated access to the authentic voice of the letter writer, while at the same time always relying on the projection of a more or less self-consciously fabricated epistolary persona. Those tensions between sincerity and fabrication may be particularly apparent for the ancient world, which held ideals of epistolary connection across space— already discussed in Section 2—in tension with the idea of epistolary personas and formulae as things which could be taught in school exercises, and manipulated for entertainment in rhetorical exercises of *ethopoieia*.[54] There is no space here to explore further the degree to

---

[52] e.g. in the contrasting views of the life of the farmer in the fishermen's letters of 1.3 and 1.4 discussed in Section 4, above; or in the many letters where urban characters imagine or live out their fantasies of life in the country: e.g. 1.15, 2.32, 3.34, 4.13, 4.16.

[53] e.g. see Porter (2001).   [54] Cf. Rosenmeyer (1994) 147.

which Alciphron points up that link between letter form and sophistic fabrication within the texture of his work, or the degree to which he draws his readers' attention to the possibility of a self-reflexive link between parasitical and sophistic imagination. But it seems to me that it may provide one starting-point for thinking through the difficult question of why Alciphron could have expected his readers to care about this work, or to engage with it. By this argument one of the pleasures it offers is to give the reader a set of images for thinking through his or her engagement with the enterprise of sophistic creation.[55] And if that is right, it means that Alciphron is exploiting the letter form not only for its capacity to act as a powerful vehicle for the theme of desire and frustration, aspiration and disillusionment, but also because of its capacity to encapsulate the obsessions with fabrication and artifice which lay at the heart of the sophistic enterprise.

---

[55] For alternative views of the parasite as a powerful image for thinking through processes of social and intellectual interaction in both Greek and Latin literature, see Whitmarsh (2000); Damon (1997).

12

Better than Speech: Some Advantages of the Letter in the Second Sophistic

Owen Hodkinson

GENRE

Scholarship on Greek epistolary literature has until recently been scarce, in part due to the questionable authenticity of many of the corpora contained in *Epistolographi Graeci*.[1] However, with the renewed interest in epistolary literature, both more broadly and within Classics, has come much fretting over the issue of genre: (to what extent) is genre a useful analytical tool? And specifically in the case of literary letters: *is* there such a genre, or are these texts of so many and such different forms and functions that their 'epistolary' features—formulaic greetings and the like—constitute no more than a superficial epistolary *mode* or *style* imposed upon a variety of genres? Or to consider the question from another angle: is the epistolary genre by nature a broad and capacious one, capable of including everything from treatises through limited (auto-) biography to love-letters? In this section I shall suggest some ways of

I am grateful to the editors, and to Ewen Bowie, Jaś Elsner, Jason König, and Chris Pelling for comments on versions of this paper; to the organizers and participants of the Ancient Letters conference in Manchester for their comments; to William Fitzgerald and Simon Goldhill for inviting me to give a version of this paper as part of an epistolary-themed seminar series at Cambridge, and to the audience there for the discussion.

[1] Hercher (1873).

thinking about the epistolary genre and its development in Greek
literature, as an introduction to my study of some particular examples
from 'Second Sophistic'[2] epistolographers who built upon and added
to these developments.

The first suggestion is this: if any literary form follows the Cairn-
sian model of the formation of genres—that is, that genres are
functional in origin[3]—the literary letter must. It seems obvious
that no writer would invent letters attributed to real or fictional
characters (whether quoted within historical or other narratives, or
circulating independently), before the use of letters in 'real life' is
established and familiar to some potential readers.[4] If this obvious
point is rather trivial, it might be refined using the Russian formalist
concept of the 'canonization' of non-literary forms: 'While literature's innovatory thrust may draw strength from the past, it as often
moves laterally and turns to popular culture for its devices. This
[idea] gave rise to Shklovskij's law of the "canonization of the junior
branch." '[5] In the current context, this means that the inventor of
literary epistles must turn to *real* letters (in combination with other
literary genres) as models. It may be that letters quoted by historians,
and possibly genuine letters published along with an author's other
works or in a letter collection, were intermediaries in this process; or
perhaps the historians' 'quoted' letters bear the same relation to 'real'
letters as do their speeches,[6] in which case *these* letters might be our

---

[2] A problematic term, often applied too broadly to *any* Imperial Greek literature; but
still convenient shorthand, and applicable to the authors I am concerned with here.

[3] Cairns (1972) advances this theory for poetic genres; cf. Fowler (1982) 152, who
notes that it works for some genres but not others.

[4] Note that the earliest extant literary letters are those 'quoted' by the historians,
and that we have extant earlier real letters, the earliest being *SEG* 26. 845. 3 (text 1 in
Trapp (2003)), around 500 BC.

[5] Fowler (1982) 158. Cf. Erlich (1955) 227. Fowler notes the influence of such
ideas upon Todorov's dictum that 'a new genre is always a transformation of one or
several old genres' (Todorov (1976) 161), rightly adding the qualification that 'either
we have to expand "genre" to include nonliterary forms, or else we must allow for
extraliterary transplant as a separate means of innovation'.

[6] A contentious issue, of course, with a massive bibliography (cf. Marincola (2001)
77 with n. 77 for orientation on the debate on Thucydides' speeches; 42–3 with n. 106
for Herodotus: I am grateful to Emily Baragwanath for these references). Most would
now allow Thucydides some invention in his speeches, if only in the sense that they
are paraphrases or summaries of the speeches Thucydides (or his sources) recounts
from memory, and many would go much further.

first 'literary letters'. However this may be, literary epistles must draw on distinct and recognizable features of real letters in order to count as such; and indeed there clearly were certain conventions and common themes of epistolography which could be adapted for this purpose[7] (such as formulae identifying the sender and addressee). Once the first literary epistle is published, and increasingly thereafter, epistolographers can read and use as models both literary *and* real letters, consciously employing and adapting established conventions in order to be recognizably epistolary. The picture is completed by the epistolary theorists and handbooks, each influenced by and influencing the composition of real and literary letters. The epistolary is thus a distinct kind of literature with its own rules and conventions (typical themes as well as formal elements), which both varied from one producer to another and developed different branches over time.

Of course, the co-extension of real and literary epistles over the centuries has complicated the picture more than if a non-literary form had been 'canonized' and then ceased to exist beyond its literary extension. As it is, the changing and increasingly common uses of real letters (and the growing tradition of literary epistles) gave rise to an increasingly varied and popular literary form. So, if there was such a thing in the ancient world as a 'real' letter, which could serve a great many functions, vary greatly in length and in its use of epistolary conventions, and potentially include within it other types of writing, then there was a corresponding and similarly varied genre of literary epistles. To return to my initial question, therefore, I prefer to think of the literary letter as belonging to a capacious genre, which can *contain* writing of other genres just as a real letter can include extended meditations or treatises. This is not merely a matter of terminology: it is a very different position to the one which holds that 'epistle' is too broad a category to be thought of usefully as a genre. I would rather seek epistolary motifs in texts with an epistolary 'form' or 'frame', and use epistolary theory *as well as* modes of criticism specific to other genres with which they combine, than dismiss every overlong epistle as a treatise with 'Dear sir' and 'Yours sincerely' tacked on (although admittedly this *is* sometimes the case). Letters

---

[7] Trapp (2003) 34–42.

are naturally capacious, but they are also suited to and suggestive of certain themes and modes of expression: for instance letters of recommendation were an essential part of travel and hospitality in the ancient world, so that such letters can often be found in collections of literary epistles.[8]

However one classes letters, epistolographers of the empire undeniably had a huge corpus of Greek letters from which to draw inspiration;[9] a substantial portion of this survives, albeit largely neglected since Bentley demonstrated the spuriousness of many collections attributed to historical figures.[10] The case for genuineness has now plausibly been made for some letters, for instance, among the corpora of Isocrates and Demosthenes.[11] But for a study of letters as literature, the question of authenticity is not so important (although it would help us to date some letters precisely): far more important is to recognize that many later authors either treat such collections as genuine or do not consider the question of authenticity.[12] These letters were available to, *and read by* later authors;[13] and sometimes alluded to and self-consciously used as models of epistolary style, as Cicero and Pliny were by later Latin epistolographers.[14] Greek epistolographers of the empire were therefore writing within a long-established tradition, and could exploit its motifs and formal conventions just as writers in other genres.

---

[8] Cf. Trapp, loc. cit. with texts 26–30. The themes which are particularly apt for epistolary literature are not necessarily inherent in the concept of a letter, then, but contingent upon culture-specific uses of the letter.

[9] In addition to whichever of the letters in Hercher (1873) are earlier, the number of letters available at that time is attested by the many books of letters Diogenes Laertius attributes to his subjects in *Vitae Philosophorum*.

[10] Bentley (1697).

[11] Isocrates: van Hook (1945); Demosthenes: Goldstein (1968).

[12] Wohl (1998) raises interesting questions concerning what is at stake in the question of epistolary authenticity: *seeming* authenticity is of course often at the heart of the appeal of literary letters, but this does not mean that the question of *actual* authenticity (often insoluble anyway) is particularly important for the development and the reading of the genre, still less that it should determine whether spurious letters are read at all.

[13] e.g. the notoriously spurious Platonic *Epistles* were read as genuine up until the 5th cent. AD: Wohl (1998) 60 n. 1; 71, with n. 25.

[14] Cf. Demetrius, *On Style* 223–35, and Philostratus of Lemnos, *On Letters* (Kayser (1871) 2: 257–8), for Greek models of epistolary style; Julius Victor, *Ars Rhetorica* 27 for Cicero as Latin model.

I shall now turn from the genre of individual literary epistles to suggest that the epistolary *collection* might itself be considered as a distinct 'genre' or kind of literature. If there are any genuine letters in the collections, say, of Isocrates, Demosthenes, or Plato, it is certain in each case that there are (also) spurious letters added later. Manuscript traditions and papyrus evidence suggest that letters were sometimes published alongside an author's other works, sometimes in separate epistolary collections; by the first century AD there is evidence for epistolary volumes containing letters attributed to several writers, so that letters are not just being read as an appendix to an author's larger works.[15] Later, spurious additions to a collection of genuine letters are examples of epistolographic composition *for* a collection; in such cases, attempts are made to imitate the author's style, but also to make the letter cohere within the collection through its theme or by filling in a gap in the chronology of the existing letters.[16] This process might have been an intermediate stage before the creation of entirely spurious epistolary collections, in which coherence might be obtained by such internal similarities and chronological sequences.

Once fictional epistolary collections are being written *qua* collections, there is scope for development in a variety of directions, for example by varying the number and persona(s) of supposed letter-writers (one, a pair of correspondents, or more; the supposed author as epistolographer, or fictional or mythical characters), and by varying the form and coherence of the collection—narrative, dialogue, or something more miscellaneous. At this stage in its development, it is worth considering the epistolary collection as analogous to the poetic book—that is, as a macro-unit of composition; a kind of literature in which the author can experiment with miniature correspondences, personas, chronological and thematic relations and intratextual allusion. The term 'collection' is in this sense potentially misleading,

---

[15] e.g. for Plato's *Epistles* appended to his other works cf. Wohl (1998) 60 n. 1; Smith (1990) 35–41 for papyri and the dual MS transmission of the Hippocratic *Epistles* through the Hippocratic corpus on the one hand and epistolographic collections on the other: 'The two lines of transmission for the Hippocratic letters existed separately from at least the first century A.D.' (p. 38). Cf. also Düring's (1951) introduction for transmission of literary epistles.

[16] e.g. Hippocratic *Epp.* 1–2 were probably composed later than *Epp.* 3 ff., 'rather cleverly, as an introduction to [them]' (Smith (1990) 18).

since it could imply a later activity applied to 'ready-made' letters: epistolary *book* is a better term.[17]

The potential development of the book of 'bespoke' letters in many directions was realized by Greek authors of the empire and possibly earlier. The different strands include epistolary novels (*Chion, Themistocles*);[18] more varied books such as the letters of Brutus or the Socratics, which do not form a coherent narrative thread but nevertheless contain sketches of moments in a life, or *sententiae*; the book of Philostratus, mainly love letters with a few on more disparate themes, written as if from the author himself—that is, creating a (more or less) coherent authorial persona; and the letters of Aelian and Alciphron, written as from fictional characters, often one-off but sometimes in corresponding pairs. It is upon these last two that the remainder of this chapter will focus, in order to illustrate a particular aspect of such epistolary literature. They are roughly contemporary, and are clearly related somehow by literary imitation,[19] so that it makes sense to treat them together; and both individually and together (along with Philostratus) they represent the most varied and sophisticated use of the 'epistolary book' genre in the non-novelistic fictional strand of its development.

ADVANTAGES

Well they said if I wrote the perfect letter
That I would have a chance

('I'll Sail this Ship Alone', The Beautiful South)

[17] And of course there are books of verse epistles by Horace and Ovid to be taken into account: these may well have influenced writers of Latin prose literary epistles, and possibly also Greek authors (either directly or indirectly). Cf. Morrison in this volume on significant ordering, and Fitzgerald in this volume on a coherent epistolary book (Pliny's seventh).

[18] On the applicability of the term to these works, and for an analysis of modes of communication within the latter including the issue of the (dis-) advantages of epistolarity, cf. Hodkinson (2006).

[19] It is impossible to prove who imitated whom, given that there is no evidence for the date of Alciphron other than supposed literary imitations by or of him: cf. Hunter (1983) 6–15 for an appropriately inconclusive survey of the connections between him, Longus, Lucian, and Aelian.

'Real' letters are normally motivated by the writer's separation from the addressee, and scholarship on epistolarity has recognized the importance of this distance also in fictional letters, both as imparting verisimilitude and as an epistolary motif.[20] The letter is thus characterized as an unsatisfactory form of communication: inferior to dialogue, necessitated by distance, not chosen.[21] Writing a letter can, however, sometimes be a positive choice, and fictional epistolographers can also exploit this fact. Taking examples from fictional letters in which there seems to be no obstacle to verbal communication, I shall argue that they do not constitute lapses in verisimilitude on the author's part; rather, such letters add variety to the imagined situations of their letter-writers, allowing the reader to reconstruct possible motives for writing where none is mentioned. The authors thus illustrate some potential advantages of the letter over verbal communication.

Within the Greek epistolary tradition, there are precedents for referring to the advantages of letters, which will illustrate the idea. So many letters make a point of disparaging the epistolary medium, comparing it unfavourably to oration or dialogue, that this becomes a motif of literary letters. Isocrates' first epistle, addressed to the tyrant Dionysius, is a classic case: 'I know, to be sure, that it makes a great difference for those trying to give advice that they do not do so by letter, but go in person...'[22] (*Οἶδα μὲν οὖν ὅτι τοῖς συμβουλεύειν ἐπιχειροῦσιν πολὺ διαφέρει μὴ διὰ γραμμάτων ποιεῖσθαι τὴν συνουσίαν ἀλλ' αὐτοὺς πλησιάσαντας...*); the letter then goes on to list many disadvantages of epistolarity (*Ep.* 1.2–3). But this letter in fact enables Isocrates to 'speak' his mind without fear of reprisal (1.4 ff.):

πολλὰς ἐλπίδας ἔχω φανήσεσθαι λέγοντας ἡμᾶς τι τῶν δεόντων· ἡγοῦμαι γὰρ ἁπάσας ἀφέντα ⟨σε⟩ τὰς δυσχερείας τὰς προειρημένας αὐταῖς ταῖς πράξεσιν προσέξειν τὸν νοῦν. (1.3)

I have great hope that I shall prove to be saying something useful; for I think that you will let the aforementioned difficulties [of the epistolary medium] pass and turn your mind to the content itself.

---

[20] e.g. Trapp (2003) 38–42.
[21] Cf. König in this volume for such anxieties in real letters.
[22] All translations are my own.

Indeed, words for 'speaking' and 'listening' recur throughout the
letter: it thus attempts to *hide* its epistolary form, breaking free
from generic constraints (such as the opening formula 'Isocrates to
Dionysius, greetings (χαίρειν)') to contain within the body of the
letter a treatise (marked as such by its length and language),[23]
masquerading as a personally delivered oration bravely advising a
tyrant. But of course Isocrates is not actually present: he is hiding
behind a letter, written from a safe distance—if, that is, the letter was
ever sent, which is doubtful. Another example is Plato's third epistle,
in which he says that he was afraid to speak his mind to the tyrant:

κἀγὼ τὸ μετὰ ταῦτα ὃ ἐπῄει μοι εἰπεῖν οὐκ εἶπον, φοβούμενος μὴ σμικροῦ
ῥήματος ἕνεκα τὸν ἔκπλουν ὃν ποσεδόκων, μή μοι στενὸς γίγνοιτο ἀντ'
εὐρυχωρίας ... (319c)

But I did not say what it occurred to me to say after this, since I was afraid
that because of a short saying the homeward voyage I was expecting might
be closed off instead of an open passage...

He then goes on to say what was on his mind when he was there in
person with Dionysius. These examples from among the earlier
Greek letter collections show that the self-conscious examination of
epistolarity and its disadvantages were already a theme of epistolary
literature; this was well established by the time of Aelian and Alciphron, thus giving them a literary convention to play with.

The first example of this is a letter by Alciphron from a fisherman's
daughter to her mother:

Οὐκέτ' εἰμὶ ἐν ἐμαυτῇ, ὦ μῆτερ, οὐδὲ ἀνέχομαι γήμασθαι ᾧ με κατεγγυήσειν
ἐπηγγείλατο ἔναγχος ὁ πατήρ, τῷ Μηθυμναίῳ μειρακίῳ τῷ παιδὶ τοῦ
κυβερνήτου, ἐξ ὅτου τὸν ἀστικὸν ἔφηβον ἐθεασάμην ...
... ἢ τούτῳ μιγήσομαι ἢ τὴν Λεσβίαν μιμησαμένη Σαπφὼ οὐκ ἀπὸ τῆς
Λευκάδος πέτρας, ἀλλ' ἀπὸ τῶν Πειραϊκῶν προβόλων ἐμαυτὴν εἰς τὸ
κλυδώνιον ὤσω. (*Ep.* 1.11)

I am no longer myself, mother, and I cannot bear to marry the boy to whom
father recently promised to betroth me, the captain's son from Methymna,
since I saw the *ephebe* from the city...

---

[23] In fact it seems to be an introduction to be added to a longer (more generally
addressed?) treatise, breaking off without any proper conclusion: cf. van Hook's
(1945) introduction to this letter.

... either I will have this man, or, imitating Lesbian Sappho I shall throw myself into the surf, not from the Leucadian cliff but from the promontory of Peiraeus.

The first question that comes to mind is where we are to imagine Glaucippe at the time of writing. Why should an unmarried Greek girl write to her mother (with whom she surely lives)? She might be supposed to be staying with a relative, or attending a festival (such as the Oschophoria at which she saw her young guardsman), but even then her mother would be likely to accompany her; and no such separation from the home is mentioned, as it is in letters where this is the case. Another possible explanation is Alciphron's incompetence: perhaps the letter was conceived without real consideration of the imagined situation from which it is supposed to arise—this would constitute a lapse in verisimilitude. Before dismissing Alciphron's ability in this manner, however, I would prefer to look for other motivations for Glaucippe's letter.[24]

One reason for writing a letter is to express a sentiment or report a fact which one either *could* not, or would *rather* not, say in person. That is to say, rather than being motivated by absence, a letter can be used deliberately to *ensure* this absence at the crucial moment. The distance thus created might be desirable if, for example, it bears bad news, especially if what it reports might be blamed upon the sender. In the case of Glaucippe's letter, the disobedient sentiments and petulant threats might, if expressed face-to-face, earn her a scolding, or worse—as the responding letter (to which I shall return) suggests. Perhaps we might imagine Glaucippe writing her letter at home and leaving it for her mother to find—she might then set out for the Peiraeus, or hide out of sight of the house, in order to make her threat seem real or to avoid the confrontation it will provoke.

Another motivation for epistolary communication is the opportunity it gives for the writer to be 'heard' out, an opportunity which the presence of hearers, paradoxically, might deny. Letters are frequently employed to persuade the addressee of something,[25] and this

---

[24] Cf. Rosenmeyer (2001*a*) 306–7 for a defence of Alciphron and epistolary literature against the charge of 'artificiality' and on Alciphron's verisimilitude.

[25] Cf. Rosenmeyer (2001*a*) 263 'Letters by nature are conventional, clever, and written to have a particular effect on their readers.'

is no exception. Glaucippe's letter is a rhetorical set piece, arguing for her marriage to the guardsman on several fronts: the duration of her desire; his beauty (at length and in great detail); and finally, a threat to throw herself into the sea if she is denied. The influence of oratory is palpable in this and other letters of the 'Second Sophistic' (indeed, part of their charm is the incongruity of eloquent rustics so prevalent in literature of the period)[26]. As Rosenmeyer says, letters can 'persuade and manipulate just as an orator does, but in writing'.[27] The 'but' is crucial, however: a text is *fixed*, and a letter-writer can take advantage of this to produce an unbroken stream of rhetoric, ensuring his motives are not misunderstood—in short, attempting to get a proper 'hearing', without argument or interruption.[28] This is the other side to the same coin which Isocrates presents as a *dis*advantage in *Ep.* 1.

Glaucippe, on attempting to deliver her message to her mother orally, would not get past the first sentence without being silenced by a reproach similar to the beginning of the response: 'You are mad, dear daughter, and truly out of your mind' (Μέμηνας, ὦ θυγάτριον, καὶ ἀληθῶς ἐξέστης, 1.12.1). As it is, she is not merely scolded and silenced, because she has gone and left the letter in her place, forcing her mother at least to read what she has to say and to recognize that she is in earnest. The fact that letters give a voice to those who would otherwise not be heard (out) is one of the attractions of the epistolary form, and one exploited particularly by Aelian and Alciphron: it allows authors to explore the sentiments of a further range of fictional types, and to write the speeches their real counterparts could never give. This quality means that letters persuade their addressees, not '*just as* an orator does', but (potentially) even better;

---

[26] Cf. e.g. Aelian's *Letters*; Longus; Dio's *Euboean Oration*. Cf. Whitmarsh (2001) 100–8, with further references, on the polarity 'rustic' vs. 'educated' as a literary topos in this era.

[27] (2001*a*) 263–4.

[28] Of course, it is still only an *attempt* at being heard out: as an anonymous reader for the Press points out, the writer still depends on the reader actually reading the letter through to the end. However, a letter is an object in the reader's hands and a fixed text, and while a reader might interrupt her reading and perhaps remark aloud on its contents, this will not have the same effect as it would on a speech: there is always the possibility, which I would suggest is taken up more often than not by real readers of letters, of completing the reading.

while for the external reader, the literary letter can be a self-reflexive form which highlights and *performs* the differences between oral and written communication, as I have argued at greater length elsewhere.[29]

Aelian exploits this potential in the correspondence between Callipides and Cnemon, four letters based largely on Menander's *Dyscolus*.[30] Callipides writes to Cnemon to complain of his antisocial behaviour, including 'hurl[ing] clods of earth and wild pears' at him (βάλλεις γοῦν ἡμᾶς ταῖς βώλοις καὶ ταῖς ἀχράσι, *Ep.* 13). As with Glaucippe's letter, it is not distance which prevents Callipides confronting his neighbour in person: the reader is left to infer that, as in the play, it is the threat of violence or rebukes which prompts Callipides to write, in order to get his message across without being attacked. To an extent, the ploy succeeds—he manages to get two replies and thereby engage the misanthrope in (written) conversation, which he could not achieve in person. The shifting of the comic situation from its oral, dialogic genre to the written, epistolary form[31] thus has consequences for the actions of its characters: Aelian explores the potentials and limitations of epistolary communication through this shift.

For Cnemon, the advantage of writing is that he can avoid other people:

Ἔδει μὲν μηδὲν ἀποκρίνασθαι· ἐπεὶ δὲ εἶ περίεργος καὶ βιάζῃ με ἄκοντά σοι προδιαλέγεσθαι, τοῦτο γοῦν κεκέρδαγκα τὸ δι' ἀγγέλων σοι λαλεῖν, ἀλλὰ μὴ πρὸς αὐτόν σε. (*Ep.* 14)

I didn't have to reply at all; but since you are a busybody, and force me against my will to enter into dialogue with you, at least I have the advantage of speaking to you through messengers and not in your presence.

There is nothing preventing Cnemon talking to his neighbour, but his misanthropy is such that he chooses to write a letter instead. This reverses the common epistolary convention of referring to the letter as inferior to face-to-face communication, and it suits the misanthrope. After Callipides tries again to reason with him, Cnemon uses his second reply 'in order to rebuke you and vent some of my bile

---

[29] Hodkinson (2006).　　[30] *Epp.* 13–16; cf. Thyresson (1964).

[31] Regarded by ancient epistolary theorists as comparable to dialogue: Demetrius, *On style* 223, quoting an Artemon who edited Aristotle's letters.

upon you' ('Ἵνα σοι καὶ λοιδορήσωμαι ταῦτ' ἀντεπιστέλλω καὶ ἀφῶ τι τῆς ὀργῆς ἐς σέ, *Ep.* 16). In this correspondence, both parties exploit the letter's capacity for facilitating full and uninterrupted expression of opinions. For the external reader, the pleasure is in the representation of two opposing viewpoints as rationally justifiable, including (almost paradoxically) the position of a misanthrope. Unlike Menander's *dyscolus*, who is forced to join in the conventional celebrations which end the play, Aelian's Cnemon is free from such dramatic conventions, and so free to have the last word, concluding the correspondence, in character: 'Not by making sacrifices will you become my friend, nor by any other means' (ἐμοὶ δὲ μήτε θύων εἴης φίλος μήτε ἄλλως, *Ep.* 16).

Another feature of letters which can make them the choice method of communication rather than an inferior alternative is their importance: they are often used to convey crucial or secret information, whether political, military, or personal. The choice of a letter over an oral message even at a distance was not automatic, so that the use of the epistolary medium can alert the addressee to the significance of the message: the writer wants to ensure that his exact words reach the recipient, or that they reach *only* the intended recipient.[32] Where there is *no* distance or other obstacle to verbal communication, the extra effort of writing a letter adds to the significance of its message, emphasizing the writer's earnestness. Glaucippe's letter may be read as an attempt by a child—not normally listened to or taken seriously—both to be 'heard' and to show her mother that she really is determined to get her man or else carry out her threat.

Connected with the extra effort of composing a letter is the time it requires; the lack of immediacy of epistolary communication is another reason that it is characterized as inferior to speech, the time lapse between writing and reading sometimes rendering its contents untrue or irrelevant.[33] There is another side to this coin,

[32] Cf. e.g. Hdt. 3.126–8 with Rosenmeyer (2001a) 50–1 for the significance of letters; op. cit. 70 for the authority of a letter as authentication token added to oral discourse (in the context of drama).

[33] Cf. Trapp (2003) 36–7 on the epistolary time-lag; Rosenmeyer (2001a) 70 for the staging of this aspect of letters by Euripides (e.g. in *IA* 'Agamemnon frantically tries to undo an earlier letter by penning a separate postscript, but cannot escape his own prior words once they have reached their addressee').

however: the letter's lack of immediacy implies not only time for the writer to reflect clearly on a past event or ongoing situation (away from the 'heat of the moment') but also allows the recipient to do likewise and give a rational response. Letters such as those of Glaucippe or Callipides may seem to their writer to show their considered opinion, and to merit more consideration by that very fact. The reasonable tone of Callipides' first letter seems to contain a confidence that, given the opportunity to see things from his point of view, Cnemon cannot fail to heed his 'friendly advice':

ἀλλ', ὦ βέλτιστε Κνήμων, τὸ σκαιὸν τοῦ τρόπου κατάλυσον, μηδέ σε ὁ θυμὸς
ἐς λήθην προαγέτω, μὴ καὶ μανεὶς σεαυτὸν λάθῃς· ταῦτά σοι φίλα παρὰ φίλου
παραγγέλματα ἔστω καὶ ἴαμα τοῦ τρόπου.   (*Ep.* 13)

But, my good Cnemon, away with this awkward manner, and don't let your temper lead you to forget yourself, or you might go mad without noticing it. Let this be friendly advice from a friend for you, and mend your ways.

In this case, the external reader knows Cnemon's likely response from familiarity with the Menandrian plot upon which the situation is based. In the case of Glaucippe, or the fisherman who asks another for an abandoned net (Alciphron, *Ep.* 1.17: see below), the reader is less sure—indeed there is no reason to assume that there will even be a responding letter, as most of the letters of Aelian and Alciphron stand alone, the reader left to imagine the possible response.[34]

DISADVANTAGES

> Well they said if I wrote the perfect letter
> That I would have a chance
> Well I wrote it, and you burnt it
> And now do I have a chance anyway?
>
> ('I'll Sail this Ship Alone', The Beautiful South)

---

[34] Cf. Rosenmeyer (2001*a*) 306–7 (summarizing her chapter on Alciphron): 'These letters … invite a response, offer [the reader] the chance to try his or her hand at *ethopoieia*.'

I have chosen as examples the rarer cases of letters with responses—
responses which demonstrate the failure of the first writers' rhetoric—
not to undermine my own arguments about the advantages of the
letter, but to make a further point about books such as those of
Aelian and Alciphron. Part of the appeal of 'stand-alone' letters may
be that the external reader can use his or her imagination to reconstruct from a single, one-sided document the situation from which it
arose, and its sequels. A reader accustomed to being so exercised by a
book of letters will react in the same way to a letter *with* a response—
the existence of which, on the first reading, will be unknown.[35] The
reader can thus be swayed by, or react against, the rhetoric of each
letter, only to find in some cases that a ready-made response is
provided. I would like now to consider briefly the effect of responding letters in the context of books which contain mostly single letters.

Both Alciphron and Aelian, writing in the 'Second Sophistic', are
authors of their time: their letters are masterful miniatures of rhetoric,
making the epistolary form seem ideal for persuasion and manipulation. I have argued that sometimes, rather than being enforced by
physical distance between writer and recipient, the decision to write a
letter can be made deliberately in order to *create* an artificial distance
between them at the crucial moment of revelation. Authors of fictional
letters can exploit awareness of this function of letters by making their
characters also aware of it. Thus Glaucippe or Callipides both make a
very good case for themselves, if their letters are taken in isolation from
the responses (and from the intertexts of the latter).[36]

[35] Cf. König in this volume on Alciphron's paired letters, and on the possible
effects of the state of his MSS upon any such discussion. König also discusses other
significant ordering within a sequence of letters which are 'stand-alone' (i.e. are not
connected by forming a correspondence and therefore a narrative).

[36] It is true, as König says (in this volume), that Alciphron's letters do not deal so
explicitly with the advantages and disadvantages of epistolarity as many real and other
literary letters do; I would, of course, agree with him that this is due to his characters' 'lack
of self-awareness' rather than any lack on Alciphron's part. I would emphasize, however,
Glaucippe's (blinkered) awareness of the *possibilities* of epistolary communication, in
other worlds than that of her own, ordinary life—it is merely that, wrapped up in her
Sappho-fuelled fantasies, she does not also see the very real pitfalls, which are realized with
her mother's response. In the other pairs I discuss it will emerge that a lack of awareness of
the addressee's character, and consequent likely response, is even more of a problem.
These letters therefore illustrate the often self-centred nature of epistolary activity, allowing a writer to come up with a solution which makes perfect sense to her/him on her/his
own, in isolation from the very person with whom the solution must be negotiated.

However, the responses show that there is a further 'distance' between the correspondents, which means that the rhetoric fails—a difference in character. In these cases, it is the letter-writer's assumptions about the addressee's motivations and sympathies, rather than the rhetoric itself, which is at fault. We have already seen that Cnemon's response to Callipides is true to his misanthropic stereotype: the latter assumes that he will see reason, but in fact Cnemon has his own 'rationale' for throwing clods of earth at people—he hates them. The response of Glaucippe's mother similarly shatters any illusions she may have had, and offers a swift corrective to the external reader who may have been won over by the rhetoric Alciphron has put in her hand:

εἰ γάρ τι τούτων ὁ σὸς πατὴρ πύθοιτο, οὐδὲν διασκεψάμενος οὐδὲ μελλήσας τοῖς ἐναλίοις βορὰν παραρρίψει σε θηρίοις. (*Ep.* 1.12)

If your father hears anything of this, he won't stop to think before throwing you into the sea for fish-fodder.

Charope's letter is to the point and prosaic compared with her daughter's poetic praise of the guardsman: the love-struck girl's dreams are crushed, her suicide threat seemingly exposed as a childish bluff by a parental reproach which wittily threatens to punish her insolence by throwing her into the sea—the very fate she threatened to bring upon herself. Charope threatens to show Glaucippe's letter to her father, or else to tell him about it, which would violate the epistolarity of this little scene: the letter was also supposed to guarantee confidentiality—for mother's eyes only—but mother is not playing by the rules. For the external reader, this is part of the game with paired letters: the fictional letter-writers are granted awareness of the advantages of distance and epistolary communication (along with a rhetorical training to make any Greek-speaker proud!); but by making them and the external reader unaware of the distance between the characters' outlooks or personalities, the authors can illustrate the advantages and disadvantages of the letter in two easy steps. And of course such breaches of privacy are always a risk with letters, and this disadvantage is therefore a common theme of epistolary literature. The external reader can be convinced by one letter, and then shown in the next how its effectiveness relied on their detachment from the fictitious situation and the isolation of the letter from its context. With these paired letters, then, unlike the single ones, although readers *are* given 'an opportunity to write themselves into the correspondence',[37] the opportunity is withdrawn as soon as the response is read: in this game, the reader can never be other than *outside* the correspondence. Indeed, the notional privacy of letters is central to the literary reader's enjoyment of them—a kind of 'eavesdropping' experience.

This game of paired letters can be seen as in essence a game of competing genres or literary registers: each letter draws upon a particular genre, and its rhetoric is thus sustained by the mode of 'logic' peculiar to that genre. The letter's capaciousness as a genre is thus exploited here: it can be made to perform, and therefore to contain, a range of literary genres in its own form;[38] and the epistolary book as compositional unit also lends itself well to the creation of a series of letters performing several contrasting genres in succession. To return to Glaucippe's letter: the girl writing about her beloved in poetic and cultured language[39] belongs in the tradition of lyric poetry, and particularly Sappho, to whom she explicitly compares herself in threatening suicide.[40] Read within the tradition of lyric and particularly Sapphic poetry, as we are encouraged to do, the letter's rhetoric makes sense: why should a girl in love not behave like this? Of course, the context of the collection may cast some doubts, but it is only when Glaucippe reads the response that she is placed firmly back in the prosaic and commonsensical world of her parents; while the external reader is abruptly shifted from lyric to comic (a parent rebuking a child, in a conversational or low register: this is clearly reminiscent of New Comedy, upon which Alciphron draws heavily).[41] A similar shift occurs with the letter of Encymon, a fisherman asking a colleague for an abandoned fishing-net:

---

[37] Rosenmeyer (2001*a*) 307.

[38] I owe some of this formulation to Jaś Elsner.

[39] Costa (2001) ad loc. notes imagery borrowed from Meleager (*AP* 5.156) and a phrase recalling Euphorion (fr. 87 Powell); Benner and Fobes (1949) 63 n. find a possible source for one phrase in a pentameter preserved in *EM* s.v. Ἀργαφίης.

[40] Note the reference to Methymna at the beginning of the letter—the Lesbian references may be indicators of the literary tradition against and within which the letter is to be read (*pace* Costa (2001) ad loc.).

[41] Cf. Benner and Fobes (1949) 16–18 with further bibliography.

Ἡρόμην ἰδὼν ἐπὶ τῆς ᾐόνος τῆς ἐν Σουνίῳ παλαιὸν καὶ τετρυχωμένον δίκτυον,
ὅτου εἴη καὶ τίνα τρόπον οὐκ ἐξ ὄγκου μόνον ἀποσχισθέν, ἤδη δὲ καὶ ὑπὸ
χρόνου παλαιότητος διερρωγὸς ἀποκέοιτο...
... αἰτῶ οὖν σε τὸ τῇ φθορᾷ καὶ τῷ χρόνῳ μὴ σόν. σὺ δ᾽ ᾧ παντελῶς ἀπώλειαν
προσένειμας, ἥκιστα ζημιούμενος, ἕτοιμος ἔσο πρὸς τὴν δόσιν.   (*Ep.* 1.17)

When I saw an old and worn fishing-net on the beach at Sunium, I asked
whose it was, and how it came to be abandoned there, not only torn apart by
its heavy load, but also by now fallen to pieces through the passing of much
time...
...Therefore I am asking you for what is not yours, through ruin and the
passing of time. Since you are in no way being deprived of what you have
given up completely to ruin, be ready to give it away.

The letter's rhetoric builds up a series of logical arguments to the
seemingly reasonable conclusion that the abandoned net, unwanted
by its owner, may as well be made use of by one who does want it. It is
in the mode of forensic oratory, and in legal-sounding language, and
the external reader, taking it as such, can be swayed by arguments
which might prevail in such a context. However, the nature of
Halictypus' response is not one the reader expects: it is not so
much the refusal that is a surprise, but the shift of generic tradition.
Rather than a carefully argued response of similar stylistic and
rhetorical quality, it is an outburst of reproach and abuse, accompanied by flat, unargued refusal:

τίς γάρ σοι τῶν ἐμῶν φροντίς; τί δὲ τὸ παρ᾽ ἐμοῦ ῥᾳθυμίας ἠξιωμένον κτῆμα
σὸν εἶναι νομίζεις;   (*Ep.* 1.18)

What concern do you have with my property? And why do you think a
possession which I value little is yours?

The response, like that of Glaucippe's mother, brings the readers
(internal and external alike) back down to earth and lowers the
register. The following letter is even more blunt—here it is in full:
'I didn't ask for what you possess, but what you don't possess. Since
you don't want another to have what you don't have, keep what you
don't have!' (Οὐκ ᾔτησά σε ἃ ἔχεις, ἀλλ᾽ ἃ μὴ ἔχεις. ἐπεὶ δὲ οὐ βούλει ἃ
μὴ ἔχεις ἕτερον ἔχειν, ἔχε ἃ μὴ ἔχεις, 1.19). This sequence, especially
the short, sharp responses, seen together and in order on the page,
resemble nothing so much as an extract from a dialogue—or indeed,
from a New Comic play. It is this play with shifting literary traditions

within a sequence of letters which gives an otherwise potentially simple rhetorical game of arguing both sides its wit.

CONCLUSION

We have seen that the traditionally disadvantaged status of the letter as a form of communication is meditated upon within literary letters in the Greek epistolary tradition, and becomes a recognizable topos of the genre; it thus constitutes a conventional aspect of epistolary literature which later writers in the tradition have recourse to and, as in my examples, which they can reverse in order to explore the advantages of epistolarity. The letter could in some (real) situations have advantages over oral communication, and authors of literarary letter-books can vary their imagined contexts by, for instance, having the fictional writers exploit its potential for creating distance, rather than being forced to write by physical distance. But the sequences of letters we have seen employ a more complex strategy, in which distance of a different kind—of points of view in the case of internal writers and readers, and of literary traditions for the external reader—is created between corresponding letters. This play of genres in Aelian and Alciphron exploits the capaciousness of the letter as a form of writing and of literature. It also employs the potential of the letter-book as a unit of composition—after the model of the poetic book—much more fully than books of letters collected subsequent to their writing,[42] or which grow over time.[43]

---

[42] Of course authors or editors putting together such a collection can go some way towards this (cf. Fitzgerald in this volume on the links between letters within bk. 7 of Pliny; cf. Cicero's *Fam.* bk. 13, with Rees in this volume, as a coherent unit created by editing rather composition); but short of inventing responses, or altering existing ones, they cannot create the same kind of carefully composed correspondences.

[43] i.e. by the addition of (further) spurious letters to an earlier core in cases such as the Platonic epistles.

13

Mixed Messages: The Play of Epistolary Codes in Two Late Antique Latin Correspondences

Jennifer Ebbeler

By the end of the first century BC, letter exchange was widely practised in elite Roman society. Participation in letter exchange—a practice closely related to other forms of text exchange—was an essential means by which aristocratic Romans advertised and negotiated social status *domi et foris*.[1] Caesar used his correspondence with Cicero to negotiate his position vis-à-vis the Senatorial class during his rise to power.[2] Cicero and his *amici* exchanged letters of consolation in a 'cooperative competition' designed to encourage the speedy return of the bereaved recipient to his social and literary obligations.[3] Several essays in this volume, particularly those of Henderson, Morello, and Freisenbruch, likewise consider the function of specific letter exchanges in the complicated competition for status that was an essential

My thanks to Ruth Morello, Andrew Morrison, and Roy Gibson for organizing a stimulating conference on Ancient Letters at Manchester in July 2004; and to Ruth and Andrew for their exceptionally diligent efforts in putting this volume together and seeing it through the shoals of publication. I am equally grateful to Jim O'Donnell, *dominus illustris*, for his incisive comments on an earlier draft of this essay; and to the two anonymous readers for OUP, whose observations improved the argument.

[1] See e.g. the illuminating studies of Habinek (1998) and Woolf (2003).

[2] White (2003) 68–95. See Ebbeler (2003) 3–19 for observations on Caesar's place in the tradition of late republican letter-writing.

[3] Wilcox (2005) 237–56. In this volume, Freisenbruch makes a similar argument about the inherently competitive nature of the correspondence of Fronto and Marcus Aurelius as they seek to position themselves in Antonine Rome.

component of aristocratic life in late republican and imperial Rome. Through the exchange and publication of letters, elite Romans created and advertised social norms to which their peers (and those who aspired to be their peers) were expected to adhere.

At the same time, the practice itself was governed by a clearly articulated set of rules: write back frequently, maintain confidentiality when it was expected, use an appropriate tone, avoid excessive length, and so forth.[4] If an epistolary relationship was to proceed smoothly, it was imperative that each correspondent play by the rules and, especially, perform his prescribed part (e.g. student, teacher, doctor, patient, father, son). Correspondents generally adopted conventional personae, which they could then manipulate to particular ends.[5]

This essay considers two celebrated epistolary relationships from the fourth century AD: the famously dysfunctional correspondence of Augustine and Jerome; and the reputedly bitter final years of Ausonius' correspondence with his former pupil Paulinus. In both of these exchanges, epistolary codes are cleverly manipulated to remarkable rhetorical effect; and any explication of what went wrong (or right) in these complicated letter exchanges requires close attention to the 'rules' of the epistolary game. In the case of Augustine and Jerome, I will suggest, the discernible hostilities in the correspondence arise because Augustine deliberately refuses to play the *iuuenis* to Jerome's *senex* and instead represents himself as Jerome's exegetical equal. In the case of Ausonius and Paulinus, on the other hand, it is precisely through their careful adherence to the codes of father–son letters that we see evidence for a persistent *amicitia* despite apparent tensions. Though the epistolary transcript of their relationship breaks off before these tensions are satisfactorily resolved, this is more likely due to factors other than a fundamental religious incompatibility.

---

[4] Malherbe (1988) extracts many of these 'rules' as they are expressed in the letters of various classical and late antique epistolographers.

[5] See Freisenbruch's essay in this volume. She makes a compelling argument for reading the 'narrative of sickness' in the correspondence of Fronto and Marcus Aurelius as intimately connected to the authority of a teacher over his student. When Fronto and Marcus by turns play the part of doctor and patient, argues Freisenbruch, they are enacting a 'unique epistolary pact between a tutor and a Caesar who co-operate (and compete) in a delicate balancing-act between different power-sharing roles—*magister, discipulus, Caesar, amicus*'. Morrison makes a similar argument when he suggests that Horace manipulates the didactic resonances of the epistolary genre to speak in an authoritative voice.

PIETAS ET PATERNITAS: AUSONIUS AND PAULINUS

By the time Ausonius and Paulinus wrote the letters that survive for us as their correspondence, they had already enjoyed a decades-long association that began when Paulinus' father sent him to study under Ausonius in Bordeaux sometime in the 350s AD.[6] Although Ausonius left for Trier in 366/367 when Paulinus was probably no more than 14 or 15, the two kept in contact and Ausonius seems to have exercised his connections with the court on Paulinus' behalf in the 370s. By 383, Ausonius had stepped down from the political stage and retired to Bordeaux; Paulinus had also returned home from Italy and was enjoying the leisured life of an educated aristocrat, writing poetry, managing his estate, and cultivating *amicitia*.

In this same period Paulinus married a Spanish woman, Therasia, and began his drift towards a more committed form of Christianity (though it is not possible to pin down the exact nature of Therasia's influence on Paulinus).[7] In 389 Paulinus and Therasia left Bordeaux for Spain; while in Spain, Paulinus fortified his ascetic convictions and became what Charles Witke has dubbed a 'cultural Christian', that is, an exceptionally devout Christian. Unlike most men of his generation, whose pre-baptismal life bore a strong resemblance to their post-baptismal life (if they were even baptized before they took to their deathbed), Paulinus embraced the Christian ideals of his Gallic countryman Martin of Tours and eventually made his way to Nola, in Campania, to establish his version of a monastic community.

The extant correspondence of Ausonius and Paulinus consists of seven letters authored by Ausonius and two (possibly three, depending on the editor) by Paulinus.[8] There is substantial difficulty in

[6] Trout (1999) 28–52.

[7] Trout (1999) 68–77 offers the compelling suggestion that Ausonius' misogynist attacks on Therasia (he calls her a Tanaquil, among other things) are motivated by his concerns that she is leading Paulinus into association with the heretical Priscillianists in Spain. Having witnessed the violence Priscillian caused in Bordeaux in the 380s—a violence that resulted in the deaths of Priscillian and many of his adherents— Ausonius may be afraid for the life of his dear student and friend. On the Priscillianist movement, see also Burrus (1995).

[8] I follow Green's edition and numbering for the letters of Ausonius. His edition includes a concordance to the earlier editions of Peiper and von Hartel. For the numbering of Paulinus' letters, I cite both Green and von Hartel.

establishing a secure chronology for the correspondence, especially for Paulinus' responses to Ausonius.[9] Typically, this correspondence has been read as the textual artefact of a relationship fractured by Paulinus' deep commitment to Christian asceticism and Ausonius' persistent 'pagan' tendencies.[10] But, following Michael Roberts's more optimistic reading of Paulinus' final epistolary poem, I will suggest that there is no clear-cut evidence for a serious break in the friendship.[11] To be sure, the correspondence is not free from tension; but there is nothing to suggest that these tensions were fatal to the letter exchange. Paulinus, in fact, made every effort to reconcile his old, classical education and life devoted to the *cursus honorum* to his new life as a Christian.

Before Paulinus' departure for Spain in 389, by all appearances he and Ausonius enjoyed the kind of playful correspondence that was typical between a teacher and his successful former student. In the earliest extant letter of the exchange (*Ep.* 17), Ausonius addresses Paulinus as *filius* in the salutation (*Ausonius Pontio Paulino filio*). He offers his critique of a hexameter poem Paulinus had sent to him and sends his own beginnings of a hexameter poem for Paulinus' critique. Forty years Paulinus' senior, Ausonius treats his former pupil as a talented junior colleague whose intellectual judgement he respects.[12]

Part of what makes this relationship work is Paulinus' willingness to play son to Ausonius' father. Like letters of consolation or recommendation, father–son letters and their permutations (e.g.

---

[9] The chronology proposed by Fabre (1948) has not been seriously challenged, though this is largely because there is a serious lack of external corroborating evidence. It is important, I think, to recognize that our sense of an established chronological sequence for this exchange rests on shaky ground.

[10] For the widely accepted argument that Paulinus broke with Ausonius on religious grounds, see Frend (1974) 110 and Conybeare (2000) 157. Witke (1971) 6 urges caution: 'it would be wrong to think that conversion to Christianity was responsible. Paulinus was baptized and ordained in 393, three or four years after he went to Barcelona and only shortly before Ausonius' death.' See also Matthews (1975) 150 for evidence that Ausonius' close family members opted for asceticism without falling out of favour.

[11] Roberts (1985) 271–3.

[12] Salzman (forthcoming) points out that the bond between Symmachus and his father—one specifically designed for public consumption—was also defined by their shared literary interests. This suggests the obvious point that there was tremendous slippage between the father–son and teacher–student relationship in the ancient world.

student–teacher; doctor–patient) appear to have been a widely practised epistolary sub-genre in classical and late antique epistolography.
The 'father', literal and metaphorical, dispenses wisdom, moral
exhortation, and cultural tradition to his correspondent. The 'son'
is expected to be a cipher, asking for and eagerly receiving fatherly
advice. Examples of this dynamic from classical antiquity include the
letters the Elder Cato sent to his son while the youth performed his
military service (Plut. *Vit. Cat. Mai.* 20.2–21). In a fascinating twist,
the exceptionally virtuous Cornelia plays the role of father to her son
Gaius Gracchus following her husband's death.[13] Cicero seems to
exploit these epistolary codes in his *De Officiis*, a three-book epistolary treatise addressed to his son Marcus.[14] Likewise, the childless
Pliny studiously portrays himself as what John Henderson has
termed a 'proxy patriarch' at various points in his correspondence.[15]
Evidence for the continuity of the father–son letter type into the
fourth century AD appears in the collection of the Roman senator
Symmachus, who preserves several letters sent to him by his own
father together with his responses.[16]

From the first extant letter of his correspondence with Ausonius,
the younger Paulinus employs paternal language to figure himself as

[13] The fragments of the letter attributed to Cornelia are transmitted in the margins
of a manuscript of Cornelius Nepos' *Vitae*. Its authenticity is questionable, but the
witnesses of both Cicero (*Brut.* 211) and Quintilian (*Inst.* 1.1.6) suggest that some
letters from Cornelia to Gaius were in circulation by the 1st cent. AD. Both Tac. *Dial.*
28 and Plut. *Vit. C. Gracch.* 1 describe Cornelia's role in the education of her sons in
terms reminiscent of Cato's involvement in his own son's education, as Plutarch
depicted it.

[14] Cicero sent this lengthy exhortation to Marcus in Athens in an attempt to
correct his young son's habits of wine, women, and song. It is worth observing that
Cicero alludes to a letter of Cato to his son as precedent for his text and, I would
argue, thereby casts himself as a father not just to his own son but to the youth of
Rome. Four centuries later Cicero's text would be the model for Ambrose, the Bishop
of Milan, as he figured himself as the episcopal father to his spiritual sons, that is, the
clergy of Milan and northern Italy. See also Gibson and Morrison's comments on this
text in the Introduction to this volume. To my mind, they overestimate the importance of formal markers in determining the epistolarity of a text; and underestimate
the extent to which Cicero manipulates epistolary conventions in the *De Officiis*.

[15] Henderson (2003) 67. See also Hoffer (1999) 93–110 for his insightful discussion of Pliny's engagement with paternity in *Ep.* 1.8. Bernstein (forthcoming) has
made a similar point about several letters from book 8.

[16] See Salzman (forthcoming) for an incisive reading of Symmachus' correspondence with his father.

Ausonius' son. This is clearly illustrated in a poem Paulinus sent to Ausonius (two lines of which Ausonius then quotes back to Paulinus in his response):

liquido adiurare possum nullum tibi ad poeticam facundiam Romanae iuuentutis aequari. certe ita mihi uideri. si erro, pater sum, fer me et noli exigere iudicium obstante pietate.... accessit tibi ad artem poeticam mellea adulatio. Quid enim aliud agunt:

> audax Icario qui fecit nomina ponto
> et qui Chalcidicas moderate enauit ad arces

nisi tu uegetam et sublimem alacritatem tuam temeritatem uoces, me uero, et consultum et quem filius debeat imitari, salutari prudentia praeditum dicas? (*Ep.* 17.30–41)

I can absolutely swear that for fluency in verse none of our Roman youths is your equal. At any rate, that is my opinion. If I am wrong, I am your father, bear with me and do not force from me a verdict which my natural feelings reject... Your skill in poetry has the additional attraction of delicious flattery. For what else do these lines:

> He who daringly made a name for the Icarian sea and he who, in control of himself, sailed to the Chalcidian citadels

mean except that you call your own active and soaring liveliness rashness but affirm that I, being both wary and one whom a son ought to imitate, am endowed with a healthy sense of caution?

Ausonius is particularly pleased that Paulinus, in comparing himself to the rash Icarus and Ausonius to the skilful Daedalus, has also acknowledged Ausonius' figurative role as his father. He is flattered to play the older, wiser man to Paulinus' rash but adventurous child.

In three other letters dating to roughly the same period, the good-natured tone of the relationship is very much in evidence. In the first of these (*Ep.* 18), composed in elegiac couplets, Ausonius wishes Paulinus a long and healthy life. He acknowledges the superiority of Paulinus' genealogy and poetic skill, but reminds him: *longaeuae tantum superamus honore senectae* ('I am victorious only in the rank of longevity'). In the second letter (*Ep.* 19), he thanks Paulinus for the gift of oil and fish sauce, praises the young man's devotion to him (*Ep.* 19.11–13: *o melle dulcior, o gratiarum uenustate festiuior, o ab omnibus patrio stringende complexu*), and encloses a witty iambic poem; in the third (*Ep.* 20), he asks Paulinus to let his profligate estate manager Philo stay with him. In these early letters we see a typical display of late Roman epistolary *amicitia* (albeit one resolutely shaped by paternal rhetoric), rife with learned allusions to Classical Latin poetry.

The relative chronology of the letters dated by editors to Paulinus' time in Spain (389–94) is unclear; but it is apparent that, in tone and metre, they represent a distinctive second phase in the letter exchange.[17] The playful tone of the early letters is replaced by tense frustration as Ausonius repeatedly tries to elicit a response from Paulinus. Whereas we have no sense of Paulinus' responses to Ausonius' letters before 389, this second group of letters preserves the echo of Paulinus' voice in dialogue with Ausonius.

The first two letters from this second phase reveal to the reader an increasingly impatient Ausonius irritated by his correspondent's persistent refusal to follow epistolary decorum and write back. In *Ep.* 21, Ausonius cites numerous examples of 'natural' dialogism: enemies in battle greet each other; rocks echo; streams murmur; musical instrument clang. Response, Ausonius implies, is part of the natural order and Paulinus' silence is unnatural (*nil mutum natura dedit*). Ausonius wholly abandons paternal rhetoric and focuses all of his energy on persuading Paulinus to resume the letter exchange. In *Ep.* 22, Ausonius revives the theme of epistolary silence and reminds Paulinus that, like a father, he can exercise a sort of *patria potestas* (6–7): *anne pudet, si quis tibi iure paterno | uiuat amicus adhuc maneasque obnoxius heres?* ('or does it shame you if a living friend claims a paternal right over you while you remain the submissive heir?'). He offers Paulinus advice for writing secret letters and recounts to him the example of Philomela, who communicated through weaving after Tereus ripped out her tongue; and Cydippe, who wrote a love letter to Acontius on an apple. He suggests that Paulinus write coded letters in milk. Finally, after accusing Paulinus' wife Therasia of being a Tanaquil, he once again reminds Paulinus of the terms of their relationship:

---

[17] See above, n. 9. Green (1991) 648 may be a bit optimistic when he claims that 'in spite of... conflicting testimony, and the hesitation of some critics (notably Villani and Prete), it is not difficult to establish the true order'.

> tu contemne alios nec dedignare parentem
> affari uerbis. ego sum tuus altor et ille
> praeceptor, primus ueterum largitor honorum,
> primus in Aonidum qui te collegia duxi.   (32–5)

Scorn others, but don't think you are above speaking to your father.
I fostered you, I am your tutor, the first bestower of ancient offices, and
the first to introduce you into the guild of the Muses.

Ausonius reminds Paulinus of his debts and of the roles that he is
expected to play: son, student, and client. We also see hints of
eroticism in this letter. Paulinus is a Philomela, a Cydippe, an elegiac
mistress sending off secret love letters; Therasia is Ausonius' erotic
rival, the husband-figure who is keeping him from his beloved.[18]
From Ausonius' perspective, the problems with the correspondence
are epistolary silence and physical absence. Ausonius has simply been
denied access to Paulinus, either by normal postal problems or a
demanding wife who has taken him off to Spain and is now encouraging her husband to cut old ties.

   In his final letter (*Ep.* 24), a now desperate Ausonius trades
paternal rhetoric for the erotically charged language of classical
Roman *amicitia*. He invokes the marital metaphor of the yoke and
accuses Paulinus of refusing it:

> Discutimus, Pauline, iugum quod nota fouebat
> temperies, leue quod positu et uenerabile iunctis
> tractabat paribus Concordia mitis habenis   (1–3)
>
> .   .   .   .
>
> et mansit, dum laeta fides nec cura laborat
> officii seruare uices, sed sponte feruntur
> incustoditum sibi continuantia cursum.   (12–14)[19]

We are shaking off the yoke, Paulinus, that was once made easy by a tried and
true restraint, a yoke lightly laid and venerable for those it joined, which
gentle Concord drew with equal reins … And it remained while there was
happy trust and it took no effort to maintain the dutiful exchange of letters;
these duties flowed freely, preserving intact their unguarded course.

---

[18] For a detailed reading of the erotic character of this letter exchange, see Knight
(forthcoming).
[19] Most editors print Green's *Epp.* 23–4 as a single letter. For a defence of his
editorial decision, see Green (1991) 654–6.

In an epistolary context the yoke could also refer to the dialogue, oral or written, between two interlocutors (cf. August. *Ep.* 72.3). So long as letters could be sent with little effort, accuses Ausonius, Paulinus pulled his weight. But as soon as some effort was demanded, Paulinus shirked his epistolary duties (*uices officii*). Ausonius encourages his correspondent to resume the yoke, naming him a *consors*, *sodalis*, and *amicus*; he likens him to a limb of his body. He compares their relationship to those of Theseus and Peirithous; Euryalus and Nisus; Orestes and Pylades; and Scipio and Laelius. Finally, he blames Spain herself for Paulinus' epistolary shortcomings:

> quid queror eoique insector crimina monstri?
> occidui me ripa Tagi, me Punica laedit
> Barcino, me bimaris iuga ninguida Pyrenaei.   (59–61)

Why do I moan and groan about the criminal deeds of that Eastern monster?[20] The banks of western Tagus, Punic Barcelona wounded me, the snowy ridges of the sea-joining Pyrenees harmed me.

Despite his apparent distress, Ausonius still has the presence of mind to offer his correspondent a clever wordplay on *iugum*. While the letter opened with the accusation that Paulinus had shaken off the yoke of letter-exchange, Ausonius now uses *iugum* in its transferred sense to refer to the heights of the Pyrenees mountains that are to blame for Paulinus' silence. For nearly forty more lines, Ausonius laments the geographical distance that separates them before concluding with a detailed description of an imaginary visit from Paulinus as he journeys through various Spanish towns home to Bordeaux (111–24).[21] This dreamlike scene ends with a famous Virgilian line (*Ecl.* 8.108): *credimus? an qui amant ipsi sibi somnia fingunt?* ('Can I believe it, or do lovers fashion dreams in their own minds?'). This is no mere tag line displaying Ausonius' familiarity with classical literature. As Paulinus undoubtedly recalled from his classical education, this line came at the end of an erotically charged love song performed by the shepherd Alphesiboeus (impersonating a woman) in an attempt to bring her beloved Daphnis home from

---

[20] The 'eastern monster' is the goddess of vengeance, Nemesis.
[21] Mratschek (2002) 196 points out that this imaginary journey followed exactly an old Roman road between Spain and Bordeaux.

the city. In turn, Alphesiboeus' song is modelled on the erotic incantation of the witch Simaetha in Theocritus, *Idyll* 2. By casting Paulinus in the role of the faithless beloved, Ausonius sends him a clear message: come home now. If filial piety does not compel you, then perhaps love will.

When Paulinus finally does respond to Ausonius' letters, he claims (not unreasonably) that there was a lengthy postal delay.[22] He is perplexed by Ausonius' critical tone, albeit one moderated by fatherly affection:

> Quarta redit duris haec iam messoribus aestas
>   et totiens cano bruma gelu riguit,
> ex quo nulla tuo mihi littera uenit ab ore,
>   nulla tua uidi scripta notata manu,
> ante salutifero felix quam charta libello
>   dona negata diu multiplicata daret.   (10.1–6)
>
>   .   .   .   .
>
> dulcia multimodis quaedam sub amara querellis
>   anxia censurae miscuerat pietas.
> Sed mihi mite patris plus quam censoris acerbum
>   sedit et e blandis aspera penso animo.   (9–12)[23]

The fourth summer has now returned for the hard-working reapers, and the same numbers of times has the winter grown frigid with hoary frost since a letter came to me from your mouth; since I saw writings written with your hand; before your page, auspicious because it carries a greeting, gave me the gifts many times over which had long been denied.... Troubled affection has mixed with criticism things sweet though somewhat soured with manifold complaints. But in me rests the gentleness of a father rather than the harshness of a critic and in my mind I weigh out the harsh words from the sweet.

Paulinus refutes Ausonius' charges in a lengthy, carefully argued letter prefaced with an elegiac poem that takes pains to assure Ausonius that he values his fatherly criticisms, however wrongheaded they are in this case. Paulinus determinedly reassures Ausonius that Spain and his growing interest in ascetic Christianity need

---

[22] It is worth pointing out that Paulinus also broke off contact with the Bishop of Bordeaux, Delphinus, and his presbyter Amandus during this same period; but the two of them received his silence with far more equanimity than Ausonius, so far as we can tell.

[23] Green prints a slightly different text and punctuation for lines 9–10: *dulcia multa modis, quaedam subamara querellis,* | *anxia censurae, miscuerat pietas.*

not interfere with their relationship. He excuses his lengthy delay in responding by denigrating his literary talents (*Carm.* 10.23–8) and explaining the claims of another father on him:

> nunc alia mentem uis agit, maior deus,
>   aliosque mores postulat
> sibi reposcens ab homine munus suum,
>   uiuamus ut uitae patri.   (10.29–32)

Now another force stirs my mind, a Greater God, who demands another mode of life, claiming for himself from man the gift he gave, that we may live for the Father of Life.

Although Ausonius could claim to exercise *patria potestas* over Paulinus, the demands of the Christian God, the Father of Life, trump those of any mortal father.[24]

If Ausonius insists on framing their relationship as paternal, he must understand that he is not the only father competing for Paulinus' attentions. Throughout this eighty-line iambic poem, Paulinus repeatedly argues that God the Father is all things for him: the light of truth, the path of life, the strength, mind, hand, and power of the Father, and so on. At the same time, Paulinus argues, he is not forgetful of his debt to Ausonius' paternal care and suggests that there is a continuity between his devotion to the Christian God and Ausonius:

> ne quaeso segnem neue peruersum putes
>   nec crimineris impium.
> pietas abesse Christiano qui potest?   (83–5)
>
>   .   .   .   .
>
> hanc cum tenere discimus, possum tibi
>   non exhibere, id est patri,
> cui cuncta sancta iura, cara nomina
>   debere me uoluit deus?
> tibi disciplinas, dignitatem, litteras,
>   linguae, togae, famae decus
> prouectus, altus, institutus debeo,
>   patrone, praeceptor, pater.   (89–96)

24 See Conybeare (2000) 152 for further observations on Paulinus' use of *pater* in this letter poem.

Don't think that I am lazy or that I have turned away from you and don't accuse me of lacking filial piety. How can piety be lacking in a Christian? ... Can I fail to show it towards you, that is towards my father, to whom God has willed that I should owe all sacred duties and names of affection? To you I owe training, offices, learning, my pride of eloquence, of civil rank, of reputation, being by you advanced, fostered, and instructed, my patron, tutor, father.

It is not that this *maior Deus* has replaced Ausonius in Paulinus' life or created an impasse in their decades-long relationship; but rather, that he mediates the friendship and makes it possible for Paulinus to acknowledge Ausonius' position as father, teacher, and patron. On the one hand, Paulinus states his allegiance to a new father, a new teacher; on the other hand, he reaffirms his filial loyalty to Ausonius and continues to play the role of dutiful son and student.

In another letter—or possibly a continuation of his initial defence—Paulinus develops this theme of dual filial loyalty. He continues to acknowledge Ausonius as a father, but refers to God as his *auctor*, his 'highest creator' (*summus genitor*) and suggests:

> quare gratandum magis est tibi, quam queritandum,
> quod tuus ille, tuis studiis et moribus ortus,
> Paulinus, cui te non infitiare parentem,
> nec modo, cum credis peruersum, sic mea uerti
> consilia, ut sim promeritus Christi fore, dum sum
> Ausonii.   (10.147–52)

For this reason you should give thanks instead of complaining because I— your son, offspring of your intellect and character, Paulinus, whose parentage you don't deny even now when you think I'm making a mistake—have so changed my principles that I have gained grace to become the child of Christ while I am the child of Ausonius.

He continues his flattery of Ausonius, calling him *parens uenerandus* and *dominus illustris* while justifying his decision to remain in Spain following a life of committed Christianity.

It emerges from these letters that the source of tension between Ausonius and Paulinus is not especially religious; or related to Paulinus' replacement of the Muses with Christ as his source of poetic inspiration. The aged Ausonius simply wants Paulinus to return to him in Bordeaux, so that the two might again enjoy a face-to-face relationship; and Paulinus refuses to accommodate this request. That is to say, Ausonius' complaints are typical of most epistolary relationships. As Ovid's Penelope wrote to Ulysses (*Her.* 1.2): *nil mihi rescribas attinet: ipse ueni* ('Come in person—don't send a letter!').

In a second letter poem (*Carm.* 11), Paulinus returns to the theme of absence and presence and reassures Ausonius that the yoke of their mutual love will transcend geographic separation.[25] The letter opens with Paulinus' defence against Ausonius' charges of neglected friendship. He also takes Ausonius to task for his earlier comments about his wife's uxorious behaviour and suggests that he is not behaving like a proper father or friend. For his part, says Paulinus, he has never abandoned the yoke of friendship:

> dulcis amicitia aeterno mihi foedere tecum
> et paribus semper redamandi legibus aequa.
> hoc nostra ceruice iugum non scaeua resoluit
> fabula, non terris absentia longa diremit,
> nec perimet, toto licet abstrahar orbe vel aeuo.
> numquam animo diuisus agam. prius ipsa recedet
> corpore uita meo quam uester pectore uultus.   (11.42–8)

Sweet friendship makes us peers through the eternal bond between us and through the equal laws of endless mutual love. This yoke no malicious tale has unloosed from my neck, no long absence from my land has broken it nor ever shall destroy it, though I should be removed from you by the entire span of space and time. Never will I live separate from you in soul. Sooner will life itself depart from my frame than your face from my heart.

The letter ends with a short poem in elegiac couplets celebrating the eternal bond that Ausonius and Paulinus will share across time and space, concluding with the valediction *uale domine illustris* (49–68). This is not an eternal farewell, signalling the end of a decades-long relationship; but rather, Paulinus concluding this reassuring letter with a nod to Ausonius' important guiding role in his life. Far from a rejection of Ausonius and his pagan ways, this valediction re-inscribes Ausonius' position as, like the Christian God, a *dominus* for Paulinus.

---

[25] Green (1991) appendix B 4.

It is, unfortunately, impossible to determine the relative chronology
of Paulinus' responses to Ausonius—and even if we could, the order of
composition does not necessarily reflect the order in which Ausonius
himself received the letters. Still, it is tempting to see Paulinus' *Carm.*
11, with its poignant farewell to Ausonius, as the latest surviving letter
in the exchange.[26] After these three letters, the last of which is conventionally dated to 394, we have no surviving evidence of any relationship between the two, epistolary or otherwise.

This break in the textual record is generally treated as a reflection
of an actual break in the correspondence. Various theories have been
suggested, all of which centre on the assumption that there was some
fundamental religious incompatibility caused by Paulinus' embrace
of a more radical form of Christianity. As Sigrid Mratschek has
convincingly argued, however, Paulinus' new Christian ideals did
not prevent him from cultivating *amicitia* with Christians of varying
degrees of religious commitment into the fifth century.[27] Indeed, she
points out, Augustine liked to send his problem cases to Nola to
experience life in Paulinus' 'monastic' community. It makes little
sense that Paulinus would destroy a decades-old friendship with
Ausonius on the grounds of his 'paganism', only to strike up relationships with others who shared Ausonius' intellectual outlook
(Romanianus' son Licentius is a useful case in point).[28]

In truth, we have no inkling how Ausonius did—or might have—
responded to Paulinus' letters; nor do we have any substantive
evidence that Paulinus did, in fact, reject Ausonius. Certainly, the
correspondence had its tense moments, but this was not an unusual
feature of a lengthy letter exchange, especially one between two correspondents who had known each other for the better part of four
decades. Likewise, given the difficulty and expense of epistolary communication in the late fourth century, it is notable that Paulinus did
write back at least two, possibly three, lengthy letters in response to
Ausonius' complaints. If Paulinus in fact felt that his life had become
incompatible with his muse-loving mentor, why did he bother to send
off even one letter, much less two or three, between 393 and 395?

---

[26] Roberts (1985) 271 n. 1 follows Fabre's chronology and argues against the view
that *Carm.* 10 was the final letter to Ausonius.

[27] Mratschek (2001) 511–53 and (2002) 547–91.

[28] See Mratschek (2002) 164–6.

In the case of Ausonius and Paulinus, the textual record—which is surely fragmentary—does not permit us to draw any firm conclusions about the final stage of the long-term relationship between them.[29] In 395 Paulinus and Therasia left Spain for Nola in southern Italy; we know none of the details of Ausonius' final years, though he seems to have died by 395. By this point, he would have been 85: a long life by any standard, but particularly those of the ancient world. When we take into account the fact that, between 389 and 394, Ausonius was probably an infirm old man whose best days were behind him, his persistent requests for Paulinus to return to Bordeaux, or at least write back, had a certain urgency. It is possible that Ausonius' pleas were motivated by his sense that he did not have long to live. We might even speculate that Paulinus was aware of his former teacher's illness. If so, his elegiac farewell, with the epitaphic *uale domine illustris* is apt.

The correspondence of Ausonius and Paulinus did not, so far as we can tell, disintegrate because of rancour and religious incompatibility; but instead, was probably cut short by the death of Paulinus' lifelong mentor. Indeed, Paulinus reassured Ausonius that the love they shared would transcend the bonds of mortal life. The letter exchange was not without its tensions in the final years; but, by the witness of the letters themselves, the fundamental source of tension was the geographic distance that separated Paulinus from his aged mentor. For his part, Paulinus carefully reassured Ausonius that he remained his *magister*, *pater*, *dominus*, and *patronus* despite their geographic separation and his own deepening allegiance to the Christian God.

LITUM MELLE GLADIUM: AUGUSTINE AND JEROME

Peter Brown has described the epistolary interaction of Augustine and Jerome as an instance of 'two highly-civilized men conducting, with studied courtesy, a singularly rancorous correspondence. They

---

[29] We have exceedingly few letters from either side of what was surely an energetic correspondence. Indeed, Ausonius' repeated and impatient requests for a response suggest that he was accustomed to a steady flow of epistolary traffic from Paulinus when the two were separated.

approach each other with elaborate gestures of Christian humility.
They show their claws, for an instant, in classical allusions, in quotations from the poets which the recipient would complete for himself.
Neither will give an inch.'[30] While Brown ultimately blames Augustine for provoking Jerome, J. N. D. Kelly characterizes his biographical subject as 'morbidly suspicious and ready to take offence'.[31] The
extant correspondence itself leaves no doubt that the 'friendship'
between Augustine and Jerome, at least in its first decade, was
acrimonious. It is not so clear what precisely went wrong. There is
a general tendency to blame Jerome's infamously prickly personality
for the difficulties, but such a conclusion underestimates the extent
to which Jerome's ire was aroused by Augustine's unwillingness to
'play by the rules' in the elite game of letter exchange.

In the first years of the 390s, Augustine experimented with the
steady voice of authority that would become his hallmark as Bishop
of Hippo. He played the teacher advising the student in the early
books of *De Doctrina Christiana*; he made a stab at writing commentaries on the Psalms and several Pauline epistles;[32] he preached a
sermon (*De fide et symbolo*) at the Council of Hippo in 393. He
encouraged Aurelius, the Bishop of Carthage, to put a stop to the
Donatist practice of celebrating orgiastic feasts (*laetitiae*) at martyr
shrines (*Ep.* 22). Probably about 394, Augustine initiated a correspondence with Jerome. He demanded that the famous ascetic and
translator of the Vulgate defend his interpretation of Paul's rebuke of
the older Apostle Peter in Galatians 2: 11–14 (*Ep.* 28).[33] Specifically,
Augustine was troubled by Jerome's claim (taken over from the Greek
commentators, notably Origen) that the two apostles were play-
acting for their audience.[34] Such an interpretation implied that the

---

[30] Brown (2000) 271.   [31] Kelly (1975) 264.

[32] Augustine's work on a commentary on Galatians led him to Jerome's thoroughly Origenist commentary on Galatians, perhaps on the recommendation of
Aurelius, the Bishop of Carthage. See Plumer (2003) 33–53 for additional comments.

[33] See Hennings (1994), Fürst (1999), Conring (2001), and O'Donnell (2005) for
discussions of the correspondence. The epistolary relationship endured, off and on,
until Jerome's death in 420 and produced a total of 18 extant letters. Eleven (six by
Augustine and five by Jerome) date to the decade between 394/5 and 405.

[34] Briefly, Paul criticizes Peter for continuing to adhere to the Mosaic Law even
after its replacement by Grace. Citing evidence of similar behaviour by Paul, Jerome
suggests that, in these early days of Christianity, Peter and Paul both had difficulties
eradicating the rituals of Mosaic Law from the practice of Christianity. Thus,

scriptures contain falsehoods—a slippery slope if there ever was one. This passage had been a crux of Christian scholarship in both the Greek and Latin traditions since at least Clement of Alexandria;[35] and it was the sort of issue on which a young, ambitious Christian could make or break his reputation. Augustine's public announcement that he was a biblical scholar also challenged Jerome's documented view that exegesis was a *scientia* best left to the trained professionals.[36]

When he initiated the correspondence, Augustine was a relative unknown. He had achieved some measure of success in Milan, as a speechwriter for the imperial court on the recommendation of Symmachus; the year before that triumph, spent in Rome, had been disappointing.[37] Following his baptism into Ambrose's church during the Easter holiday of 387, Augustine returned to North Africa without his mother or a clear sense of his future.[38] A series of events, including the deaths of his Neoplatonic friend Nebridius and his son Adeodatus, precipitated his decision to become a priest in the 'Catholic' church at Hippo.[39]

Jerome, on the other hand, was an established scholar and translator with impeccable academic qualifications and wealthy Italian and Gallic patrons who funded his scholarship in the Holy Land.[40] Though Augustine and Jerome were both in Rome in 383–4, their paths apparently did not cross.[41] If Jerome knew anything about Augustine by reputation, it was that he associated with the suspicious community of Manichees, had Neoplatonic leanings, and certainly

theorizes Jerome, Paul understood what Peter was doing, but together they were performing for their audience a kind of one-act play about the superiority of Grace to the Mosaic Law.

[35] See Souter (1924). Plumer (2003) 7–59 discusses its treatment by pre-Augustinian Latin exegetes.

[36] See Vessey (1993*a*) 175–213, esp. 179–85.

[37] Brown (2000) 57–61 summarizes this period in Augustine's biography.

[38] Brown (2000) 139–50.

[39] O'Donnell (2005) 209–19 addresses Augustine's religious identity within North African Christianity.

[40] Kelly (1975) is the standard biographical treatment of Jerome's life and writings, now supplemented by Rebenich (2002).

[41] This is an important reminder that, however small we think the ancient world was, there was little interaction between distinct social circles. This missed opportunity would be repeated in Hippo following the sack of Rome, when Augustine never managed a meeting with Pelagius.

was not an orthodox Christian. Jerome may have heard from his
contacts in Milan that the North African had been baptized into
Ambrose's church, but it is likely that he received this news with a
healthy scepticism. It probably did not help Augustine's case that
shortly after his baptism he returned home to North Africa—a region
whose Donatist schismatics had been a thorn in the Roman imperial
government's side since Constantine. Jerome had his difficulties (e.g.
the Origenist controversy), but in the mid-390s he was a celebrity in
the Catholic Christian community. Augustine had a lot to gain by
establishing an epistolary relationship with Jerome but Jerome would
benefit little, beyond adding Augustine to his roll-call of young men
eager to flaunt a relationship with the famous scholar. As James
O'Donnell remarks, 'Jerome was nothing if not well-, if often acerb-
ically, connected, and by coming into communication with Jerome
Augustine was linking up with a "textual community" of no small
importance.'[42]

While Augustine's initial letter to Jerome has the veneer of civility
and genuine intellectual curiosity, it is impossible to overlook
the audacity that motivated Augustine to challenge Jerome's theological authority.[43] It did not help matters that the correspondence
was apparently plagued by postal problems: waylaid messengers, lost
letters, letters circulating in public before being read by their
addressee, and the like. All of this only added to what J. N. D. Kelly
has characterized as 'Jerome's irascible refusal to be drawn into
discussion'.[44]

Finally, in the early years of the fifth century and after Augustine
had ascended to the office of Bishop, Jerome realized that he could no
longer openly ignore Augustine's demand for a retraction without
appearing to concede victory to his younger rival.[45] He responded,

[42] O'Donnell (1991) 14.

[43] See Brown (2000) 271: 'There is no doubt that Augustine provoked Jerome; and
Jerome, though treating Augustine with more respect than others who had crossed
him, would not resist playing cat and mouse with the younger man.'

[44] Kelly (1975) 263.

[45] August. *Ep.* 40.7: *Quare arripe, obsecro te, ingenuam et uere christianam cum
caritate seueritatem ad illud opus corrigendum atque emendandum et palinodian, ut
dicitur, cane!* ('Wherefore, I beg you, accept my noble and truly Christian criticism,
delivered in a spirit of Christian love, aimed at correcting and improving that work of
yours [i.e. his commentary on Galatians] and sing a palinode, as it is called.') Cf. Cic.
Att. 7.7.1.

but pointedly. Though Jerome was probably only a decade and a half Augustine's senior, he repeatedly figured himself as a wise but tired old man and Augustine, now in his mid-40s, as a disrespectful adolescent:

ceterum optime nouit prudentia tua unumquemque in suo sensu abundare et puerilis esse iactantiae, quod olim adolescentuli facere consueuerant, accusando illustres uiros, suo nomini famam quaerere. (August. *Ep.* 68.2)[46]

But Your Wisdom well knows that everyone abounds in his own opinion and that it is puerile boasting to seek, as young men of old were in the habit of doing, fame for one's own name by finding fault with famous men.

In just one sentence, Jerome imposes a hierarchy on his relationship with Augustine: he is older and, more importantly, famous. Whereas Augustine had attempted to frame the correspondence in terms of Christian fraternity, Jerome pointedly refuses to see Augustine as a spiritual *frater* mutually in pursuit of scriptural understanding. He develops this theme with a barbed literary reference:

superest ut diligas diligentem et in scripturarum campo iuuenis senem non prouoces. nos nostra habuimus tempora et cucurrimus, quantum potuimus. nunc te currente et longa spatia transmittente nobis debetur otium simulque, ut cum uenia et honore tuo dixerim, ne solus mihi de poetis aliquid proposuisse uidearis, memento Daretis et Entelli. (68.2)

It remains for you to show some respect to the one who is respecting you, and, as a young man, not to call out in the battlefield of scriptural interpretation an old man. I had my day in the sun and I ran as much as I could. Now, since you are running and making great strides, I ought to have some peace and quiet; at the same time, that I may speak with your permission and all due respect, don't seem to be the only one to have offered to me a passage from the poets. Remember Dares and Entellus.

The man who wept for Dido certainly would have recognized Jerome's pointed allusion to the famous scene from the funeral games in *Aeneid* 5, when the youthful Dares boasted that he could defeat the older and more experienced Entellus in a boxing contest (5.363–484).[47] Entellus, of course, took up the challenge and soundly defeated his blustering young rival.

---

[46] All passages from the correspondence of Augustine and Jerome are taken from Daur's (2005) CCSL edition.
[47] See also Fürst (1999) 131–9.

The prickly scholar continues to attack the overly ambitious Augustine for using Jerome's reputation to make a name for himself:

> nonnulli familiares mei... suggerebant non simplici a te animo factum, sed laudem atque rumusculos et gloriolam populi requirente, ut de nobis cresceres, ut multi cognoscerent te prouocare me timere, te scribere ut doctum me tacere ut imperitum, et tandem repperisse, qui garrulitati meae modum imponeret.   (August. *Ep.* 72.2)

> Some of my intimates... suggested to me that this had not been done by you in a guileless spirit, but seeking praise and celebrity and some smidgen of glory from other people, so that your reputation might grow at my expense and so that many men might know that you challenged me and that I was afraid of you; that a learned man had written while the ignorant one remained silent, and that finally there was someone who could put an end to my blabbing.

Jerome underscores the contentious tone of the exchange when he compares himself to the famously dilatory Roman general Fabius Cunctator and Augustine to the Carthaginian invader Hannibal:

> sin autem tuam uis uel ostentare uel exercere doctrinam, quaere iuuenes et disertos et nobiles... qui possint et audeant tecum congredi, et in disputatione sanctarum scripturarum iugum cum episcopo ducere! ego quondam miles nunc ueteranus et tuas et aliorum debeo laudare uictorias, non ipse rursus effeto corpore dimicare, ne si me ad scribendum frequenter impuleris illius recorder historiae, quod Hannibalem iuueniliter exsultantem Quintus Maximus patientia sua fregerit.   (72.3)

> But if, however, you wish to display or exercise your learning, seek young men, both eloquent and well-born, the sort who are willing and able to meet you and pull the yoke with a Bishop in debates over the holy scripture. I was once a soldier but now I am retired and I ought to praise your victories and those of other men, not return to battle with my exhausted body. If you should repeatedly force me to write back, I would call to mind the story that Quintus Maximus, through his patience, broke Hannibal's youthful exuberance.

Once again framing their relationship in hierarchical terms, this time using a military metaphor, Jerome advises Augustine to find interlocutors who are his age-mates (*iuuenes*). His advice is cloaked in a transparent ethnic insult: while Jerome plays the part of the noble general who rescued Rome from the Punic invaders, Augustine is identified with the irrationally exuberant Carthaginian general Hannibal who terrorized the Italian and Roman populace during the Punic Wars in the second and third centuries BC. Any reader of the letter, especially the North African Augustine, knew the ending of this particular story.

Less transparent is Jerome's allusion to a passage in Cicero's *De Senectute*, a fictional philosophical conversation between Laelius and Cato in the course of which the advantages (and disadvantages) of old age are analysed. Fabius, as we might expect, is praised as a stellar example of a wise sage who belies his age:

hic et bella gerebat ut adulescens cum plane grandis esset et Hannibalem iuueniliter exultantem patientia sua molliebat.   (*Sen.* 4.10)

He even continued to wage war as if a young man, although he was clearly getting along in years and through his patience he softened Hannibal's youthful exuberance.

Implicit in Jerome's allusion is a threat. While Jerome claims that he is ready to retire from the battlefield, like Fabius he remains a steadfast warrior. If Augustine insists on pushing Jerome into battle, he will find a worthy opponent.

The conclusion of the letter reinforces the image of a juvenile Augustine rashly engaging with an experienced veteran:

prouocas senem, tacentem stimulas, uideris iactare doctrinam. Non est autem aetatis meae putari maliuolum erga eum, cui magis fauorem debeo.   (72.5)

You are challenging an old man to battle, you are pushing the buttons of the one who remains silent, you appear to boast of your learning. But it is not suitable for someone of my age to be thought malevolent towards a man to whom I rather ought to show favour.

In other words, Augustine's inappropriate behaviour has forced Jerome out of his proper role as teacher and mentor. Jerome was prepared to offer Augustine the usual scriptural direction expected of a man in his position; but Augustine's refusal to 'play his part' has disrupted Jerome's expectations. While he does not wish to appear mean-spirited, attacking a too-easy target, Jerome cannot let Augustine's impudence pass without comment. The letter exchange will proceed smoothly only if Augustine retreats into the roles of 'son' and 'student' eager for guidance—a point Jerome makes explicit in his valediction (72.5): *uale, mi amice carissime, aetate fili, dignitate parens* ('Farewell, my dearest friend, my son in age, my father in rank'). Jerome acknowledges Augustine's superior ecclesiastical rank, but insists that Augustine respect his intellectual authority.

His extant correspondence attests that Jerome regularly received letters asking for his interpretation of a particular biblical passage; or for his views on assorted Christian practices. He depended on an international group of supporters to fund his scholarly endeavours. In exchange, he offered them copies of his writings, Latin translations of Greek patristic texts, and opinions on complicated doctrinal issues. Rarely, however, did a correspondent challenge Jerome's self-construction as an impeccable biblical scholar and theological sage moulded in the image of Origen.[48] Each correspondent played his assigned role and the epistolary relationship proceeded smoothly.

When Jerome finally did respond to Augustine's challenge, he did so by pointedly re-inscribing his authority over his younger rival. At the same time, the formal salutations of Jerome's letters identify Augustine as 'father and lord (*pater et dominus*)'—a nod to Augustine's ecclesiastical position as bishop. In terms of ecclesiastical rank, Jerome the presbyter is the son to Augustine's father; but under no circumstances will Jerome concede intellectual authority to Augustine. He repeatedly attempted to force Augustine into the role played by so many of Jerome's other correspondents: the inquisitive student who wants the advice and guidance of the famous Jerome. For his part, Augustine resisted this inscription and staked his claim as Jerome's equal, even superior, in the field of scriptural exegesis. Scholars have long been troubled by the vitriolic tone of Jerome's responses to the superficially good-willed letters of Augustine. Jerome's defensiveness is nevertheless rational when taken as a reaction to Augustine's attempt to usurp his scholarly authority as 'father and teacher' in the broader Christian community.

This essay has argued that letter-exchanges are textualized social performances, carried out in accordance with a scripted set of conventions and coded rhetoric. Correspondents constructed 'faces' for

---

[48] For a discussion of Origen's influence on Jerome's scholarly persona, see Vessey (1993*b*) 135–45.

themselves and each other, whose particularities varied over the course of a correspondence.[49] So long as both correspondents performed according to expectations, the correspondence proceeded apace. If they did not, as we saw in the case of Augustine, the epistolary relationship grew contentious. Scholars are quick to blame Jerome's bad temper for the derailment of the exchange with Augustine; but, as I have argued, Augustine is just as much at fault for failing to adhere to epistolary norms and audaciously challenging Jerome's scholarly authority. In the correspondence of Ausonius and Paulinus, on the other hand, we see that Paulinus conscientiously performed the role of student and son to the very end. To be sure, Ausonius was troubled by Paulinus' apparent silence as well as his absence from Bordeaux. But there is no hard evidence that the relationship was irrevocably fractured by Paulinus' growing commitment to a Christian life and Ausonius' persistent devotion to the classical Muses. More likely, the death of Ausonius may be blamed for the end of the epistolary conversation between two of late antiquity's brightest lights.

---

[49] Ellen Oliensis (1998) has made a similar argument with regard to Horace's construction of authority.

14

St Patrick and the Art of Allusion

Andrew Fear

Some time in the first third of the fifth century AD a slave raid took place on the coast of Ireland under the auspices of one Coroticus, a warlord based in Britain.[1] Coroticus had chosen his time well, arriving when St Patrick was holding a mass baptism of catechumens, and this produced a bumper crop of captives for the raiders. Such attacks were not unusual and there was a set response to them—a request was made to the attacker to agree terms for ransoming those abducted.[2] Patrick sent a priest accompanied by some minor clerics to Coroticus with a now lost letter making precisely this request. But Coroticus was not playing the game: Patrick's request was rebuffed and his envoys roughly handled.[3]

This provoked the saint to reach for the most potent weapon in an ecclesiastic's armoury, excommunication. His target is Coroticus' men—though not their leader—who are to be excommunicated until they do penance and free their captives, but the letter makes it clear that Patrick holds out little hope that such repentance will be forthcoming.

---

[1] Traditionally Coroticus has been seen as a king based at Dumbarton: see Bury (1998) 190–2, but see *contra* Thompson (1999) 126–31.

[2] See Patrick's discussion of this procedure in chapter 15 of his *Epistola*. The best edition of the *epistola* is Howlett (1994). I am indebted to David Howlett and to Four Courts Press for permission to include his text and translation of Patrick's Letter at the end of this paper.

[3] *Epistola* 3.

The method which Patrick uses to make his act of excommunication known is the letter. This letter, known as the *Epistola*, is one of only two authentic works by the saint that have survived, and it falls into a distinct sub-genre of epistolary writing, the Open Letter, where it is made explicit that the intended audience is larger than simply the ostensible addressee in order that the addressee's sins, or more rarely praises, are broadcast as widely as possible. Patrick insists not only that his letter be uncensored and given the greatest possible circulation, but he also actively asks his audience to treat it as a round robin—'I ask earnestly that whoever is a willing servant of God be a carrier of this letter, so that on no account it be suppressed or hidden by anyone, but rather be read before all the people, and in the presence of Coroticus himself.'[4]

Patrick's choice of the open letter as the medium for his attack should come as no surprise, as it neatly kills two birds with one stone. On the one hand, it brings down divine vengeance on his enemies, but as excommunication is a social penalty which requires co-operation if it is to be effective, it also ensures that the rest of the population will know that they ought to shun Coroticus' men and the reasons for doing so. The insistence that the *Epistola* be read in the presence of Coroticus is not merely bravado, though undoubtedly this does play a role, but also a way of undermining Coroticus' authority by reminding his men in his hearing that though their leader may be able to protect them from secular judgement, he is powerless to ward off divine sanctions and their everlasting repercussions.

But if Patrick's choice of genre is understandable, at first sight the content of his *Epistola* is more unexpected. Normally an open letter has a clear and firmly focused target, since after all the intention of the writer is to make his views about the addressee clear to one and all, but Patrick's terms of reference seem to wander back and forth—both Coroticus' men and their chief are addressed, but so perhaps are other groups too—and the *Epistola* also incorporates material which has often been seen as completely irrelevant to, if not positively detracting from, its overall purpose.

---

[4] *Quaeso plurimum ut quicumque famulus Dei promptus fuerit ut sit gerulus litterarum harum, ut nequaquam subtrahatur uel abscondatur a nemine, sed magis potius legatur coram cunctis plebibus et praesente ipso Corotico*, *Epistola*, ch. 21.

There is no doubt that the letter was written in anger, and at times one can almost feel Patrick's quill pushing through the paper. The seeming flaws in the *Epistola* outlined above have therefore sometimes been treated as the products of a raw, impassioned emotional outburst from the heart. Often, too, the excuse of rusticity has been added to that of passion. This is the view of, *inter alios*, Fletcher, who comments, 'He longs, passionately longs, to make himself clear to his readers but has the utmost difficulty in doing so. His Latin is simple, awkward, laborious, sometimes ambiguous, occasionally unintelligible.'[5] It will be argued here that the ambiguity which Fletcher detects is more often the product of deliberate artifice, than of artlessness.

While Patrick insists in the first sentence of the *Epistola* that he is an unlettered man, an *indoctus*—an assertion that is also at the beginning of his other extant work the *Confessio* where he describes himself as a great boor, *rusticissimus*—we need not accept his words as any more than a form of the standard topos of *sermo humilis*. The *Epistola*'s constant quotation of, and allusion to, biblical and patristic literature gives the lie to Patrick's assertion of rusticity, nor does he himself consistently take such a position: at the end of the *Epistola* his claim to set out the word of God in Latin is a claim to literacy and culture.[6] Indeed, it would be a great mistake to see the *Epistola* as the spontaneous rage of a simple cleric. Despite Patrick's protests, which sadly have all too often been taken at face value, his *Epistola* is a highly skilful literary work. The style of chapter 5 where the excommunication is pronounced takes care to copy the phraseology of the *curia* in Rome and throughout the work there is a high degree of linguistic dexterity.[7] This can be seen in chapter 2 where we find the oxymoron *in morte uiuunt* and the continuous and deliberate use of alliteration and assonance for verbal effect, for example, *sanguilentos sanguinare de sanguine innocentium Christianorum* and *danda et tradenda militibus mittenda*.[8]

[5] Fletcher (1997) 82.

[6] *Non mea uerba sed Dei et apostolorum atque prophetarum quod ego Latinum exposui*, 'It is not my words that I have set forth in Latin but those of God, the Apostles, and the Prophets', *Epistola* 20.

[7] Nerney (1949).

[8] 'Blood-stained men blooded in the blood of innocent Christians'; 'to be given, delivered and sent to his soldiers'. For the literary competence of Patrick's style in general see Howlett (1994) and Conneely (1993) 206–14.

This literary craftsmanship should alert us to the possibility of finding similar skills deployed at a higher level in the *Epistola* and we do indeed find larger structural contrasts worked into the text, such as that between the eternal kingdom, *aeterna regna*, of the martyred in chapter 18 and the kingdom of this world, *regnum temporale*, of the raiders in chapter 19. Other literary ploys such as *recusatio* are also to be found.[9]

Moving to a higher level again, the form of the letter itself is a part of Patrick's literary tactics and is used not only because it is apposite to convey his anger, but also because it adds weight to his words. While today the open letter is very much the vehicle of often impotent protest, in Patrick's day the two forms in which it was normally encountered carried a much weightier resonance. These were Imperial Rescripts of the Roman Emperors and the Epistles of the New Testament, both of which spoke to their direct addressees and a wider audience with authority, and the issue of authority, as will be seen, is one with which Patrick is much concerned in the *Epistola*.

Unsurprisingly the more important of these two models for Patrick is the Bible, and the *Epistola* is peppered with biblical and patristic quotations and allusions. These are designed precisely to lend weight to Patrick's words, giving the reader the impression that he is doing no more than what is required by Sacred Scripture.[10] Patrick's procedure of excommunication as outlined in the *Epistola* closely follows the threefold admonition as laid down in the Bible— the sinner is first warned privately, then in the presence of witnesses, then before the church.[11] The excommunication itself is drawn from two of the Epistles: 1 Corinthians and I Timothy. Patrick rounds on Coroticus' men and describes them as neither his fellow-citizens nor those of the 'holy Romans', but rather fellow-citizens of the demons. In part, this is simple abuse, as can be seen from the fact that Patrick describes his addressees as allies of the pagan Irish, Picts, and apostates. However, the phrase is also reminiscent of I Timothy where St Paul declares that he is delivering up Hymenaeus and Alexander to

---

[9] *Epistola* 9.

[10] The allusions are usefully listed in Conneely (1993). For their persuasive purpose, see *Epistola* 20 quoted in n. 6 above.

[11] See Matt. 18: 15–17; cf. Titus 3: 10.

Satan.[12] Abuse therefore is mingled with supernatural authority, against which Coroticus can offer no protection. It is Patrick who through his excommunication changes the status of Coroticus' men, turning them into fellow-citizens of the demons and delivering them up to hell where they will burn forever. Patrick's ban on the faithful taking food and drink with Coroticus' men would have found a strong echo in Celtic society where hospitality was highly valued and no doubt this is why it has a prominent place in the excommunication,[13] but it is again grounded in biblical authority, being found in I Corinthians.[14] The denunciation of Coroticus' men in chapter 8 is full of biblical *exempla* from both the Old and New Testaments, and similarly in chapter 9 their sins are also given biblical parallels.

But how can chapters 10 and 11 be understood? Here Patrick breaks off from his fierce denunciation of Coroticus' men and instead digresses at length on his own life history and role as an evangelist. As Thompson has commented, 'Why on earth should he tell all this to a band of outlaws?'[15] We could add: why on earth should they have been remotely interested or swayed by such personalia? It could be argued that all that is present here is a poor rhetorical gambit by Patrick to engage the sympathy of his wider audience. But the careful literary strategies which we have seen in the *Epistola* should make us cautious in dismissing this central section of the letter as simply an unfortunate and bungling error of composition or from seeing it as a later interpolation on the grounds that it does not seem to fit with the rest of the text.

In fact, Patrick here is not being inept or self-pitying. Instead, he is continuing to play a careful literary game which is meant to justify his actions in terms of ecclesiastical politics. In chapter 10 in his description of the personal sacrifices he has made for Christ he makes his readers aware that he is British and not Irish, 'I am a slave in Christ to a foreign people...'.[16] In chapter 11, paraphrasing a passage found in all four Gospels where Christ finds himself rejected by the

---

[12] I Tim. 1: 20.

[13] For the culture of the feast, see, *inter alia*, *The Mabinogion*, *passim*, and Muirchu, *Vita Sancti Patricii* 19.

[14] I Cor. 5: 11.

[15] Thompson (1999) 139.

[16] *seruus sum in Christo genti exterae*.

people of Galilee, he comments, 'and if my own people do not recognize me, a prophet does not have honour in his own country'.[17] This phrase works on several levels—the biblical paraphrase is a piece of persuasive, one might almost say blasphemous, rhetoric, where Patrick likens his reception among his own people to that experienced by Christ. There is also a note of defiance as Christ presses on regardless of his rejection and so, implies Patrick, will he. But it is what lies beneath the layer of rhetoric that is more interesting. Given what has just been said in the previous chapter, 'my own people', *mei*, must refer to Britons, not the Irish.

The question the reader must then ask is which Britons does Patrick mean? The obvious point of reference is Coroticus' men who are British, something made clear from the second chapter of the *Epistola* where Patrick denies that they are his fellow-citizens, presumably to refute a claim that they themselves did make.

If we accept the slave raiders as the primary target of Patrick's words, we can then see the core of the dilemma that he faced and why he may have wished to direct his words further afield that his ostensible target. As Coroticus and his men were based in Britain, technically Patrick had no right to excommunicate them at all. Rather, they would have fallen under the jurisdiction of the British bishop in whose diocese they lived. Early Church rules were quite clear on this matter, and Pope Callistus had written on the subject a good two hundred years before Patrick's birth, stating, 'Let no one trespass upon the boundaries of another, nor presume to judge or excommunicate one belonging to another's parish; because such judgement or excommunication or condemnation, shall neither be ratified nor have any virtue; since no one shall be bound by the decision of another judge than his own, neither shall he be condemned by such.'[18] The reasoning of the Church had a point, since bishops could, and did, abuse their power abroad for private ends[19] and indeed Patrick's excommunication of Coroticus' men in the

[17] *Et si mei non cognoscunt, 'propheta in patria sua honorem non habet'.* See Matt. 13: 57, Mark 6: 4, Luke 4: 24, John 4: 44.

[18] *Nemo quoque alterius terminos usurpet nec alterius parochianum iudicare aut excommunicare praesumpserit, quia talis iudicatio aut excommunicatio uel damnatio nec rata erit nec uires ullas habebit quoniam nullus alterius iudicis nisi sui sententia tenebitur aut damnabitur, Ep.* 2.3 = *PL* 130: 132–3.

[19] See Gregory the Great, *Ep.* 2.34.

Epistola falls into exactly the type of action beyond a bishop's own diocese that was forbidden by Callistus. It is clear that no action had been taken by the British Church to bring Coroticus to book for his activities. One reason for this may be that many in Britain regarded Patrick's mass-baptisms as potentially corrupt, self-aggrandizing actions by a man who carried no clear authority. In his *Confessio* Patrick furiously denies that he expected cash payments for baptism ('but when I baptized so many thousands of folk, did I look for even half a scruple from any of them?'), and other denials later in the same work show that these were not the only accusations of corruption levelled against him.[20] Whatever the rights and wrongs of such charges, to the saint himself it was clear that he was facing the reverse of the problem foreseen by Pope Callistus and being forced to react to circumstances where bishops had failed to use their powers responsibly at home, either from fear of, indifference to, or positive connivance with wrongdoers. Furious at this inaction, Patrick uses his letter to vent his anger on his fellow-churchmen. His attack is not made directly, perhaps because of the delicacy of his political position, or simply through lack of proof, but rather indirectly by blurring the issue of whom he is addressing in the *Epistola* so that while it could always be seen as dealing solely with Coroticus and his men, other addressees would also naturally occur to his readers' minds.

A prime example of this technique is the way Patrick chooses to deploy the word *mei*, 'my people' in chapter 11. While this could refer to Coroticus' men, that is never explicitly made the case, leaving in the reader's mind the possibility it refers instead to another group of some, or perhaps all, Britons. An obvious possibility, given Patrick's stormy relationship with it, is the British Church— Patrick's fellow compatriots and clergymen, by whom the saint felt himself to have been abandoned and betrayed. Such a feeling in the reader would have been strengthened by the fact that *mei* carries

---

[20] *Forte autem quando baptizaui tot milia hominum sperauerim ab aliquo illorum uel dimidio scriptulae?*, *Confessio* 50. Further issues of corruption are raised in *Confessio* 52–3. Modern doubts about the regularity of Patrick's position stem from the statement of Prosper of Aquitaine, *Chron.* 1307, that the first bishop of Ireland was Palladius, appointed in AD 431, see Macalister (1935) 169–70, and Esposito (1956–7). That there was a long-standing contemporary campaign against the saint can be seen from *Confessio* 26–7.

overtones of a family relationship and Patrick could legitimately be thought of as part of the family of the Church, especially as terms of family address were common within the Church at this time. This impression would have been further intensified by the fact that the saint was the son of a clergyman.[21] Patrick's skilful use of ambiguity therefore turns his *Epistola* from a simple broadside directed at a secular ruler into an act of defiance aimed at corrupt ecclesiastical authority.

Such a reading of the *Epistola* helps explain the inclusion of the personal details found in chapter 10. Patrick is demonstrating what he has sacrificed to become, as he puts it, an exile for the love of God, a *profuga ob amorem Dei*, merely to be cast aside by the Church's hierarchy. Only if we assume Patrick is obeying the standard practice of an open letter and addressing one firmly identified group is this passage irrelevant to his purpose. But Patrick is bending the rules to his advantage. Just as he blurs the referent in his text to suit his purpose, so he also blurs the question of whom exactly he is addressing. Normally the wider audiences of an open letter are simply witnesses to the author's views, but here Patrick makes them the direct addressees of his words. For while it is true that Coroticus' men would be supremely indifferent to Patrick's lost social status, this is much less likely to be the case with Patrick's broader British audience, who would have regarded exile with its subsequent loss of links in society with horror, and it is to them that Patrick is speaking at this point in order to perpetuate his attack on the British Church by underlining the wrongs he has suffered at its hands.

Nor is this the only time in the *Epistola* where Patrick addresses a third party by implication. At the beginning of the letter Patrick makes an immediate claim to authority stating, 'I, Patrick, ... declare that I am a bishop and know for sure that what I am I have received from God.'[22] Stripped of its context, this declaration is nothing unusual and follows an expected pattern: Paul often makes similar assertions at the beginning of his letters.[23] However, the *Epistola* is

---

[21] *Patrem habui Calpornium diaconum*, 'My father was Calpornius the deacon', *Confessio* 1.

[22] *Patricius ... episcopum me esse fateor*.

[23] See, for example, I Cor. 'I Paul called to be an apostle of Jesus Christ by the Will of God ...'.

using this convention for a specific purpose. While Patrick's comments could be read as the mere use of a biblical model to underline his authority to Coroticus' men in an attempt to frighten them into obeying him, we must remember that the saint's authority and episcopate had not gone uncontested in Britain. This is a theme to which Patrick returns much more explicitly in his old age when in his *Confessio* he attacks the 'lordly men of letters' who sneer at him, and asks them the rhetorical question about who they think had established his mission.[24] The answer there, as here, is God himself. In making this ringing assertion of his episcopal power, Patrick is addressing Coroticus' men, but also is directly engaging with his wider audience to persuade them, and in particular to assert to those churchmen in Britain who would deny him his episcopal rights, that he holds episcopal authority direct from God—a useful ally to have, given his breach of ecclesiastical law. The point is reiterated in chapter 6, where Patrick states 'I am not exceeding my authority....'.[25] Many of his contemporaries would have complained that here Patrick protests too much, as in point of fact that is exactly what he does do in the eyes of the law by his act of excommunication, but for Patrick at least, and hopefully for his audience, either willingly or grudgingly, his claim to divine authority saves the day.

Chapter 1 also uses a further standard convention in a similar fashion. Patrick announces his regret at being forced to resort to excommunication, 'I had no wish that something so grim and harsh should pour forth from my mouth.'[26] Again, this could be superficially read as merely a standard topos—the Christian never wishes to act harshly, but is at times compelled to do so—and, no doubt, Patrick would have made such a pious statement in any circumstances. However, given the issue of ecclesiastical authority which is about be raised by his act of excommunication, he is preparing his readers for another message which allows him to take the moral high ground. This is the implication that had the Church in Britain taken steps against Coroticus, Patrick would have had no need to act, but that their inaction and betrayal has forced his hand. In short, Patrick

---

[24] *Dominicati rhetorici, Confessio* 13.
[25] *Non usurpo.*
[26] *Non quod optabam tam dure et tam aspere aliquid ex ore meo effundere.*

is saying if there is any blame to be attached to the excommunication it lies not with him, but with those over the water.

Chapter 12 also shows Patrick's mastery of indirect address. Here the saint bemoans the fact that he is hated and greatly despised.[27] Again, we are never exactly told at whose hands Patrick is suffering these indignities nor to whom he is addressing his grievances at this point. This is deliberate. On one, perhaps superficial, reading, Patrick could be taken as referring to, and rebuking, only Coroticus and his men. However, care is taken to make clear neither those responsible for these actions nor those addressed and it is difficult to resist the thought that Patrick is talking by implication about the British Church, and that the saint's complaints are not addressed to Coroticus' men, but directly to his wider audience.

This tactic of indirect implication culminates in Patrick's impassioned plea in chapter 16: where he apostrophizes the dead victims of the slave raid, saying in a passage which is essentially a cento of biblical quotations 'The wickedness of the wicked has prevailed over us. We have been made, as it were, outcasts. Perhaps they do not believe that we have received one and the same baptism, or have one and the same God as Father. For them it is a disgrace that we are Irish.'[28] Patrick then ends his complaint with one final biblical citation from Malachi to force home his point, 'As it is written, have you not One God? Why have each and every one of you, forsaken his neighbour?'[29] The grammar of this quotation is intriguing, the referents of 'you' are not defined, nor are the earlier 'they' who despise the Irish. Both could be read as referring to Coroticus' men, but as they have already been singled out as allies of the pagan Irish, this seems unlikely.

Again, the British Church seems to be a far more plausible target for Patrick's rhetoric. The strength of the quotation 'each and every one of you' carries the implication that the whole church, not just the odd rogue clergyman, is at fault. But Patrick's point of reference may

[27] *Inuidetur mihi . . . Ualde despicior.*

[28] *'Praeualuit iniquitas iniquorum super nos.' Quasi 'extranei facti sumus'. Forte non credunt 'unum baptismum' percepimus uel 'unum Deum patrem' habemus. Indignum est illis Hiberionaci sumus.*

[29] *Sicut ait: 'Nonne unum Deum habetis?' 'Quid dereliquistis unusquisque proximum suum?',* Mal. 2: 10.

go even wider. 'You' here could also be another direct address to the wider audience of the *Epistola*. In this case, Patrick is implicating the whole British Christian community in its Church's complacency. The chapter does contain a dark hint that there is a strand of racial hostility in Britain towards Irish Christians, who are, it seems, if we are to believe Patrick, not regarded as Christians at all. That such hostility existed should not surprise us, as proselytizing outside of the Roman world was not common at this time or even regarded as desirable: indeed Patrick may have been the first to think that such evangelization was necessary.[30]

As has been seen, Patrick is happy to break the rule that there should be a single addressee for an open letter when it suits his purposes. Along with Coroticus and his men, elements of the wider audience of the open letter, who are normally in this sub-genre mere passive readers, are actively addressed. While in the instance above Patrick may rebuke them directly, more often he slides into address-ing his audience as part of a strategy of 'persuasive inclusion', where the terms of his address are such that his readers cannot but help find themselves not as witnesses, but active partisans in Patrick's quarrel.

The excommunication in chapter 5 of the *Epistola* begins, 'Let every man who fears God know that they are separated from me and from Christ my God...'.[31] The tactic is far from subtle, but in Patrick's position, where the legitimacy of his actions are likely to be queried, it is a useful one. Those of his audience who agree with him are the men 'who fear God', and who would not wish to be so described? By moving out to embrace his wider readership in this way, Patrick has gained the initiative in his battle for legitimate authority, placing on those who disagree with him the onus of formulating a reason why their disagreement does not constitute contempt for God. The same tactic is used in chapter 7, where Patrick enjoins all 'pious men of humble heart'[32] to shun the company of Coroticus' men, and in chapter 13 when the saint asks, 'Which of the saints would not shudder to make merry or feast with such men?',[33]

---

[30] See Fletcher (1997) 86, Thompson (1999) 80–2, and *Confessio* 34, 38.
[31] *resciat omnis homo timens Deum quod a me alieni sunt et a Christo Deo meo.*
[32] *sancti et humiles corde.*
[33] *Quis sanctorum non horreat iocundare uel conuiuium fruere cum talibus.*

going on to describe how their halls are full of plunder taken from Christians and warning that those who deal with evil damn themselves for eternity.

This final rhetorical question not only brings back to the reader's mind the terms of the excommunication found in chapter 5 which is explicitly couched in terms of feasting, but perhaps also suggests that some Christians have been happy to sup with Coroticus. Given Coroticus' high status, it is likely that powerful secular or clerical figures are intended. Once again, Patrick is attacking the British Church at one remove. At the very end of the *Epistola* Patrick deploys this tactic one more time, this time to increase the circulation of his letter, when in chapter 21 he pleads that 'whoever is a willing servant of God' should distribute his letter.[34]

Patrick's failure to follow the normal conventions of the open letter is not therefore a rustic slip; rather, it is a deliberate tactic which manipulates a specific genre and particular incident in a way that gives the saint a far broader range of targets—Coroticus and his slave raiders are among them, but so are the British Church, and perhaps also the British laity. Yet these targets, though forcefully suggested to the reader's mind, are never made explicit. This too is not fortuitous. While unhappy with his mother church, Patrick would not have wished to alienate himself permanently from it. The *Epistola* is designed to allow him both to have his cake and to eat it. The assault on the Church is strident but by making it via allusion and through forceful ambiguities, it never becomes concrete and so could always be denied. If reconciled to the Church, it would not be hard for Patrick to insist that the *Epistola* had only attacked Coroticus and his men. Patrick's ecclesiastical war is thus both real, and yet remains in the shadows. His manipulation of the rules of composition also allows Patrick to recruit troops for his war, as by shifting addressees he implicates his wider audience in his position and finally recruits them as evangelists of his words.

Given this craft, it can be seen that the *Epistola* is not the work of a rustic, but of a turbulent priest well practised in politics and in the verbal machinations which form part of the politician's trade. Patrick's final plea was that the *Epistola* be passed on unaltered. To

[34] *quicumque famulus Dei promptus.*

the end the saint plies his cunning trade. We can take his words as bombast and a demonstration that he is not ashamed or afraid of anything which he has said. But Patrick also knows that any changes, especially ones which ironed out the *Epistola*'s ambiguities, could do nothing but detract from the multiple messages he wished it to convey. While mindful that Christ used the analogy of sending out the apostles as sheep among wolves, an epithet applied to Coroticus' men in the *Epistola*,[35] it is equally clear that Patrick, despite his reputation for disposing of snakes, also took Christ's injunction to exercise a serpent's guile to deal with such predators very much to heart.[36]

[35] See *Epistola* 5.
[36] 'Behold, I send you forth as sheep in the midst of wolves: be ye therefore wise as serpents, and harmless as doves', Matthew 10: 16.

Epistola ad Milites Corotici

Translated by David Howlett

(1) Patricius peccator indoctus scilicet Hiberione constitutus episcopum me esse fateor. Certissime reor a Deo 'accepi id quod sum'. Inter barbaras itaque gentes habito proselitus et profuga ob amorem Dei; testis est ille si ita est. Non quod optabam tam dure et tam aspere aliquid ex ore meo effundere, sed cogor zelo Dei et ueritas Xpisti excitauit, pro dilectione proximorum atque filiorum, pro quibus 'tradidi' patriam et parentes et 'animam meam usque ad mortem'. Si dignus sum uiuo Deo meo docere gentes etsi contempnor aliquibus. (2) Manu mea scripsi atque condidi uerba ista danda et tradenda militibus mittenda Corotici, non dico ciuibus meis neque ciuibus sanctorum Romanorum sed ciuibus daemoniorum ob mala opera ipsorum. Ritu hostili in morte uiuunt, socii Scottorum atque Pictorum apostatarumque, sanguilentos sanguinare de sanguine innocentium Xpistianorum, 'quos' ego innumerum numerum Deo 'genui' atque 'in Xpisto' confirmaui. (3) Postera die qua crismati neophyti in ueste candida—flagrabat in fronte ipsorum dum crudeliter trucidati atque mactati gladio supradictis—misi epistolam cum sancto presbytero quem ego ex infantia docui cum clericis ut nobis aliquid indulgerent de praeda uel de captiuis baptizatis quos ceperunt: cachinnos fecerunt de illis. (4) Idcirco nescio quid magis lugeam: an qui interfecti uel quos ceperunt uel quos grauiter zabulus inlaqueauit. Perenni poena gehennam pariter cum ipso mancipabunt quia utique 'qui facit peccatum seruus est' et 'filius zabuli' nuncupatur. (5) Quapropter resciat omnis homo timens Deum quod a me alieni sunt et a Xpisto Deo meo 'pro quo legationem fungor', patricida, fratricida, 'lupi rapaces deuorantes plebem Domine ut cibum panis', sicut ait 'Iniqui dissipauerunt legem tuam, Domine', quam in supremis temporibus Hiberione optime benigne plantauerat atque instructa erat fauente Deo.

(6) Non usurpo. Partem habeo cum his 'quos aduocauit et praedestinauit' euangelium praedicare in persecutionibus non paruis 'usque ad extremum

terrae', etsi inuidet inimicus per tyrannidem Corotici, qui Deum non uer-
etur nec sacerdotes ipsius, quos elegit et indulsit illis summan diuinam
sublimam potestatem, 'quos ligarent super terram ligatos esse et in caelis'.
(7) Unde ergo quaeso plurimum 'sancti et humiles corde' adulari talibus
non licet 'nec cibum' nec potum 'sumere' cum ipsis nec elemosinas ipsorum
recipi debeat donec crudeliter paenitentiam effusis lacrimis satis Deo faciant
et liberent seruos Dei et ancillas Xpisti baptizatas, pro quibus mortuus est et
crucifixus. (8) 'Dona iniquorum reprobat Altissimus.' 'Qui offert sacrificium
ex substantia pauperum quasi qui uictimat filium in conspectu patris sui.'
'Diuitias' inquit 'quas congregauit iniuste euomentur de uentre eius, trahit
illum angelus mortis, ira draconum mulcabitur, interficiet illum lingua
colubris, comedit autem eum ignis inextinguibilis' ideoque 'Uae qui replent
se quae non sunt sua', uel 'Quid prodest homini ut totum mundum lucretur
et animae suae detrimentum patiatur?' (9) Longum est per singula discutere
uel insinuare, per totam legem carpere testimonia de tali cupiditate. Auaritia
mortale crimen. 'Non concupisces rem proximi tui. Non occides.' Homicida
non potest esse cum Xpisto. 'Qui odit fratrem suum homicida' adscribitur
uel 'Qui non diligit fratrem suum in morte manet'. Quanto magis reus est
qui manus suas coinquinauit in sanguine filiorum Dei, quos nuper 'adqui-
siuit' in ultimis terrae per exhortationem paruitatis nostrae?

   (10) Numquid sine Deo uel 'secundum carnem' Hiberione ueni? Quis me
compulit? 'Alligatus' sum 'Spiritu' ut non uideam aliquem 'de cognatione mea'.
Numquid a me piam misericordiam quod ago erga gentem illam qui me
aliquando ceperunt et deuastauerunt seruos et ancillas domus patris mei?
Ingenuus fui 'secundum carnem'; decurione patre nascor. Uendidi enim
nobilitatem meam—non erubesco neque me paenitet—pro utilitate aliorum;
denique seruus sum in Xpisto genti exterae ob gloriam ineffabilem 'perennis
uitae quae est in Xpisto Iesu Domino nostro'. (11) Et si mei me non cognoscunt
'propheta in patria sua honorem non habet'. Forte non sumus 'ex uno ouili'
neque 'unum Deum patrem' habemus, sicut ait 'Qui non est mecum contra me
est et qui non congregat mecum spargit'. Non conuenit: 'Unus destruit, alter
aedificat.' 'Non quaero quae mea sunt.' Non mea gratia sed Deus 'qui dedit
hanc sollicitudinem in corde meo' ut unus essem de 'uenatoribus siue pisca-
toribus' quos olim Deus 'in nouissimis diebus' ante praenuntiauit. (12) Inuidetur mihi. Quid faciam, Domine? Ualde despicior. Ecce oues tuae circa me
laniantur atque depraedantur et supradictis latrunculis iubente Corotico hostili mente. Longe est a caritate Dei traditor Xpistianorum in manus Scottorum
atque Pictorum. 'Lupi rapaces' deglutierunt gregem Domini, qui utique
Hiberione cum summa diligentia optime crescebat, et filii Scottorum et filiae
regulorum monachi et uirgines Xpisti enumerare nequeo. Quam ob rem
'iniuria iustorum non te placeat'; etiam 'usque ad inferos non placebit'.

(13) Quis sanctorum non horreat iocundare uel conuiuium fruere cum talibus? De spoliis defunctorum Xpistianorum repleuerunt domos suas, de rapinis uiuunt. Nesciunt miseri uenenum letale cibum porrigunt ad amicos et filios suos, sicut Eua non intellexit quod utique mortem tradidit uiro suo. Sic sunt omnes qui male agunt: 'mortem' perennem poenam 'operantur'. (14) Consuetudo Romanorum Gallorum Xpistianorum: mittunt uiros sanctos idoneos ad Francos et ceteras gentes cum tot milia solidorum ad redimendos captiuos baptizatos. Tu potius interficis et uendis illos genti exterae ignoranti Deum; quasi in lupanar tradis 'membra Xpisti'. Qualem spem habes in Deum uel qui te consentit aut qui te communicat uerbis adulationis? Deus iudicabit. Scriptum est enim 'Non solum facientes mala sed etiam consentientes damnandi sunt'. (15) Nescio 'quid dicam' uel 'quid loquar' amplius de defunctis filiorum Dei, quos gladius supra modum dure tetigit. Scriptum est enim 'Flete cum flentibus' et iterum 'Si dolet unum membrum condoleant omnia membra'. Quapropter ecclesia 'plorat et plangit filios' et filias 'suas' quas adhuc gladius nondum interfecit, sed prolongati et exportati in longa terrarum, ubi 'peccatum' manifeste grauiter impudenter 'abundat', ibi uenundati ingenui homines, Xpistiani in seruitute redacti sunt, praesertim indignissimorum pessimorum apostatarumque Pictorum. (16) Idcirco cum tristitia et maerore uociferabo: O speciosissimi atque amantissimi fratres et filii 'quos in Xpisto genui' enumerare nequeo, quid faciam uobis? Non sum dignus Deo neque hominibus subuenire. 'Praeualuit iniquitas iniquorum super nos.' Quasi 'extranei facti sumus'. Forte non credunt 'unum baptismum' percepimus uel 'unum Deum patrem' habemus. Indignum est illis Hiberionaci sumus. Sicut ait 'Nonne unum Deum habetis?' 'Quid dereliquistis unusquisque proximum suum?'

(17) Idcirco doleo pro uobis, doleo, carissimi mihi; sed iterum gaudeo intra meipsum: non gratis 'laboraui' uel peregrinatio mea 'in uacuum' non fuit. Et contigit scelus tam horrendum ineffabile, Deo gratias, creduli baptizati, de saeculo recessistis ad paradisum. Cerno uos: migrare coepistis ubi 'nox non erit' 'neque luctus neque mors amplius', 'sed exultabitis sicut uituli ex uinculis resoluti et conculcabitis iniquos et erunt cinis sub pedibus uestris'. (18) Uos ergo regnabitis cum apostolis et prophetis atque martyribus. Aeterna regna capietis, sicut ipse testatur inquit 'Uenient ab oriente et occidente et recumbent cum Abraham et Isaac et Iacob in regno caelorum. Foris canes et uenefici et homicidae' et 'Mendacibus periuris pars eorum in stagnum ignis aeterni.' Non inmerito ait apostolus 'Ubi iustus uix saluus erit peccator et impius transgressor legis ubi se recognoscet?' (19) Unde enim Coroticus cum suis sceleratissimis, rebellatores Xpisti, ubi se uidebunt, qui mulierculas baptizatas praemia distribuunt ob miserum regnum temporale, quod utique in momento transeat? 'Sicut nubes uel fumus, qui utique uento dispergitur', ita 'peccatores' fraudulenti 'a facie Domini peribunt; iusti

autem epulentur in magna constantia' cum Xpisto 'iudicabunt nationes et' regibus iniquis 'dominabuntur' in saecula saeculorum. Amen. (20) 'Testificor coram Deo et angelis suis' quod ita erit sicut intimauit imperitiae meae. Non mea uerba sed Dei et apostolorum atque prophetarum quod ego Latinum exposui, qui numquam enim mentiti sunt. 'Qui crediderit saluus erit, qui uero non crediderit condempnabitur, Deus locutus est.' (21) Quaeso plurimum ut quicumque famulus Dei promptus fuerit ut sit gerulus litterarum harum, ut nequaquam subtrahatur uel abscondatur a nemine, sed magis potius legatur coram cunctis plebibus et praesente ipso Corotico. Quod si Deus inspirat illos 'ut quandoque Deo resipiscant', ita ut uel sero paeniteant quod tam impie gesserunt—homicida erga fratres Domini—et liberent captiuas baptizatas quas ante ceperunt, ita ut mereantur Deo uiuere et sani efficiantur hic et in aeternum. Pax Patri et Filio et Spiritui Sancto. Amen.

Part I

I, Patrick, a sinner, untaught, to be sure, established in Ireland, profess
   myself to be a bishop.
Most certainly I consider that I have received from God that which I am.
Consequently I dwell among barbarian gentiles
as a sojourner and a refugee because of the love of God.
He is the testifier whether that is so.
Not that I preferred to pour out from my mouth anything so harshly and
   so savagely,
but I am compelled by the zeal of God, and the truth of Christ has roused
   [me] up
for the love of [my] nearest neighbours and sons,
for whom I have handed over my fatherland and parents and my soul up to
   the point of death.
If I am worthy I live for my God to teach gentiles,
even if I am despised by some.
With my own hand I have written and composed these words,
to be given and handed over, dispatched to the soldiers of Coroticus,
I do not say to my fellow citizens, nor to fellow citizens of the holy Romans,
but to fellow citizens of demons because of their evil works.
By hostile behaviour they live in death,
comrades of Scots and Picts and apostates,
bloody men who are bloody with the blood of innocent Christians,
whom I have begotten for God, an innumerable number, and confirmed
   in Christ.

On the day after that on which the new converts in white clothing were anointed with chrism,

it was shining on their brow while they were relentlessly slaughtered and slain with the sword by the abovesaid men,

I dispatched an epistle with a holy presbyter,

whom I have taught from infancy, with clerics,

so that they might concede something to us from the loot or from the baptized captives whom they captured.

They made guffaws about them.

Because of that I do not know what I should lament more,

whether those who were killed, or those whom they captured,

or those whom the devil has oppressively ensnared.

In everlasting punishment they will subject [themselves] to hell equally with him,

because indeed he who commits sin is a slave,

and he is named a son of the devil.

On which account let every man fearing God get to know

that they are estranged from me

and from Christ my God,

for whom I perform an embassy.

Parricide, fratricide, rapacious wolves devouring the folk of the Lord as a meal [lit. 'food'] of bread.

Just as it declares, The unjust have utterly destroyed Your Law, Lord,

which in these last times He had propagated in Ireland most excellently, kindly,

and it had been built up [also 'instructed, taught'] with God favouring it.

Part II

I am not claiming too much.

I have a part

with those whom He has called to [Him]

and predestined to proclaim the Gospel

among not insignificant persecutions

as far as the most remote part of land,

even if the enemy shows his jealousy through the tyranny of Coroticus,

who is not in awe of God nor His priests,

whom He has chosen and conceded to them the highest divine sublime power,

that those whom they may bind on land are bound also in the heavens.

Whence therefore I request most of all, [you] holy and lowly in heart,
that it not be permitted to flatter such men,
to take neither food nor drink with them,
nor should one be obliged for alms of those men to be received
until they perform penance relentlessly enough with tears poured out to
    God
and free the slaves of God and the baptized handmaids of Christ,
for whom He died and was crucified.
The Most High reproves the gifts of unjust men.
He who offers sacrifice from the substance of poor men
[is] as he who makes a victim of a son in the sight of his own father.
The riches, it affirms, which he has gathered unrighteously will be vomited
    out from his belly.
The angel of death drags him away.
By the wrath of dragons he will be mutilated.
The tongue of the serpent will kill him.
Inextinguishable fire, moreover, eats him up.
And therefore, Woe to those who refill themselves with things which are
    not their own,
or, What advantage comes to a man that he should acquire as profit the
    whole world
and suffer the loss of his own soul?
It is long-winded to shake out or make known from single cases,
to pluck from the whole Law testimonials about such greed.
Avarice [is] a mortal crime.
You shall not covet the possession of your neighbour.
You shall not murder.
A homicide cannot be with Christ.
He who hates his own brother is ascribed [or 'assigned to the category of']
    a homicide,
or, He who does not love dearly his own brother remains in death.
How much more guilty is he
who has defiled his own hands in the blood of the sons of God,
whom He has recently acquired in the furthest parts of land through the
    exhortation of our insignificance.

Part III

Can it be that I came to Ireland without God or according to the flesh?
Who compelled me?

I am bound by the Spirit that I should not see anyone from my kindred.

Can it be from myself that I perform a pious act of pity toward that gentile people
who once captured me
and ravaged the slaves and handmaids of my father's house?
I was freeborn according to the flesh.
I am born of a decurion father.
But I have sold my nobility,
I do not blush nor does it cause me regret,
for the advantage of others.
At the last I am a slave in Christ for that remote gentile people
because of the unutterable glory of everlasting life
which is in Christ Jesus our Lord.
If even mine do not recognize me,
a prophet does not have honour in his own fatherland.
Perhaps we are not from one sheepfold,
and we do not have one God as father.
Just as He declares, He who is not with me is against me,
and he who does not gather with me scatters.
It does not come together:
One destroys;
another builds.
I do not seek the things which are mine.
Not by my grace,
but God Who has given this solicitude in my heart,
so that I should be one of the hunters or fishers
whom God foretold once before for the final days.
Jealousy is shown to me.
What shall I do, Lord?
I am especially despised.
Look, Your sheep are torn to pieces around me and looted,
even by the abovesaid wretched little thieves, with Coroticus commanding
from his hostile mind.
Far off from the charity of God is the betrayer of Christians
into the hands of Scots and Picts.
Rapacious wolves have gulped down the flock of the Lord,
which was indeed growing most excellently in Ireland with the highest
loving care.
Both sons and daughters of the petty kings of the Scots
[were] monks and virgins of Christ,
I cannot count out.

For which reason may the injustice done to the righteous not please You,
even as far as the lower depths it will not please.
Which of the holy ones would not be horrified to rejoice
or to enjoy a banquet with such men?
From the spoils of deceased Christians they have refilled their houses.

They live from plunderings.
They do not know, pitiable men, that they offer poison, a lethal food to
   their own friends and sons,
just as Eve did not understand that she certainly handed over death to her
   own husband.
So are all who perform badly;
they work death as an everlasting punishment.
The custom of the Christian Roman Gauls:
they dispatch holy substantial men to the Franks and other gentiles
with so many thousands of solidi for redeeming baptized captives;
you rather kill and sell them to a remote gentile people ignorant of God,

as if you are handing over into a brothel [lit. 'house of she-wolves'] the
   members of Christ.
What hope do you have in God,
or anyone who agrees with you,
or who communicates with you in words of flattery?
God will judge.
For it is written, Not only those committing bad deeds,
but also those agreeing with [them] are to be condemned.
I do not know what I shall say
or what I shall speak further
about the deceased
of the sons of God
whom the sword has touched harshly beyond measure.
For it is written, Weep with those weeping,
and again, If one member grieves
all members should grieve together.
On which account the Church cries and bewails
its own sons and daughters
whom so far the sword has not yet killed,
but removed afar and deported to far-off places of lands
where sin openly, oppressively, impudently abounds;
there freeborn men are given for sale;
Christians are reduced to slavery,
particularly among the most unworthy worst apostates and Picts.

Because of that I shall raise my voice with sadness and mourning.
O most beautiful and most beloved brothers and sons whom I have
  begotten in Christ,
I cannot count out,
what shall I do for you?
I am not worthy to come to the support of God nor men.
The injustice of unjust men has prevailed over us,
as if we have been made remote outsiders.
Perhaps they do not believe we have received one baptism
or we have one God as father.
It is scandalous [lit. 'unworthy'] to them that we are Irish.
Just as it declares, Do you not have one God?
Why have you abandoned, each one of you, his own neighbour?

Part IIII

Because of that I grieve for you,
I grieve, dearest to me,
but again I rejoice within myself.
Not for free have I laboured,
or my exile has not been in vain.
And the shameful deed, so horrendous, unutterable, has befallen so that,
thanks be to God, as baptized faithful men
you have departed from this age to paradise.
I perceive you clearly,
you have begun to journey where there will not be night nor lament nor
  death any more,
but you will exult just as calves freed from chains,
and you will trample down the unjust underfoot,
and they will be dust under your feet.
You therefore will reign with apostles and prophets and martyrs,

you will capture eternal realms.
Just as He Himself testifies,
He affirms,
They will come from the rising and the setting [*i.e.* from east and west],
  and they will lie back with Abraham and Isaac and Jacob in the realm of
  the heavens.
Outside dogs and makers of poison and homicides,
and their portion with lying perjurers in the pool of eternal fire.

Not undeservedly the apostle declares, Where the righteous man will
   scarcely be saved,
where will the sinner and impious transgressor of the Law recognize
   himself?
Whence, then, Coroticus with his most shameful men,
rebels against Christ, where will they see themselves,
they who distribute baptized little women as prizes
because of a pitiable temporal realm
which may indeed pass away in a moment?
Just as a cloud or smoke, which indeed is dispersed by the wind,
so fraudulent sinners will perish from the face of the Lord.
But the righteous will feast in great constancy with Christ.
They will judge nations, and they will lord it over unjust rulers
for ages of ages. Amen.
I bear testimony before God and His angels that it will be so, just as He
   has intimated to my unlearnedness.
Not my words,
but God's and the apostles' and prophets',
which I have set out in Latin,
who, however, have never lied.
He who will have believed will be saved,
but he who will not have believed will be condemned.
God has spoken.
I request most of all that any servant of God will have been quick to
   respond,
that he may be bearer of this letter,
that it by no means be stolen,
or that it be hidden by no one,
but much rather that it be read before all folk,
even Coroticus himself being present.
Which if God inspires them that whenever they return to their senses for
   God,
or so that they may repent [even] late what they have done so impiously,
homicide against the brothers of the Lord,
and they may free baptized captive women whom they captured before,
so that they may deserve to live for God
and be made sane
here and for eternity.
Peace to the Father and to the Son and to the Holy Spirit. Amen.

Bibliography

ABEL, K. (1981), 'Das Problem der Faktizität der senecanischen Korrespondenz', *Hermes* 109: 472–99.

ACOSTA-HUGHES, B. (2002), *Polyeideia: The Iambi of Callimachus and the Archaic Iambic Tradition* (Berkeley, Los Angeles, London).

ADAMS, J. N. (1995), *Pelagonius and Latin Veterinary Terminology in the Roman Empire* (Leiden).

—— (2003), *Bilingualism and the Latin Language* (Cambridge).

ALBRECHT, M. VON (2003), *Cicero's Style: A Synopsis* (*Mnemosyne* Suppl. 245; Leiden).

ALTMAN, J. G. (1982), *Epistolarity: Approaches to a Form* (Columbus, Ohio).

ANDERSON, G. (1997), 'Alciphron's Miniatures', *ANRW* 2.34.3: 2188–2206.

ANDERSON, W. S. (1963), *Essays on Roman Satire* (Princeton).

ANDREWS, R. (1992) (ed.), *Rebirth of Rhetoric: Essays in Language, Culture and Education* (London and New York).

ARMSTRONG, D. (1993), 'The Addressees of the *Ars poetica*', in A. Schiesaro, P. Mitsis, J. S. Clay (eds.), *Mega Nepios* (Pisa): 185–230.

—— (2004), 'Horace's *Epistles* 1 and Philodemus', in D. Armstrong, J. Fish, P. A. Johnston, M. B. Skinner (eds.), *Vergil, Philodemus and the Augustans* (Austin, Tex.): 267–98.

ARRIGHETTI, G. (1973) (ed.), *Epicuro: Opere* (2nd edn., Turin).

BAGNALL, R. S., and CRIBIORE, R. (2006), *Women's Letters from Ancient Egypt: 300 BC–AD 800* (Ann Arbor).

BALDWIN, B. (1982), 'The Date of Alciphron', *Hermes* 110: 523–4.

BARNES, J. (1997), *Logic and the Imperial Stoa* (Leiden).

BARTSCH, S. (1994), *Actors in the Audience: Theatricality and Doublespeak from Nero to Hadrian* (Cambridge, Mass.).

BEARD, M. (2002), 'Ciceronian Correspondences', in T. P. Wiseman (ed.), *Classics in Progress* (Oxford): 103–44.

BECCARIA, A. (1956), *I Codici di medicina del periodo presalernitano (secoli ix, x e xi)* (Rome).

BENNER, A. R., and FOBES, F. H. (1949) (eds.), *Aelian, Alciphron, Philostratus: The Letters* (Cambridge, Mass.).

BENTLEY, R. (1697), *A Dissertation upon the Epistles of Phalaris, Themistocles, Socrates, Euripides and the Fables of Aesop* (London).

Bérenger-Badel, A. (2000), 'Les Critères de compétence dans les lettres de recommendation de Fronton et de Pline le Jeune', *Revue des études latines* 78: 164–79.

Bernstein, N. (forthcoming), 'Each Man's Father Served as his Teacher: Ancestral Emulation and Fictive Kinship in Pliny's *Letters*'.

Bing, P. (2000), 'Text or Performance/Text and Performance', in R. Pretagostini (ed.), *La letteratura ellenistica* (Rome): 139–48.

Boscherini, S. (2000), 'La dottrina medica comunicata *per epistulam*. Struttura e storia di un genere', in Pigeaud and Pigeaud: 1–11.

Bowersock, G. (1969), *Greek Sophists in the Roman Empire* (New York).

Bowman, A. K., Thomas, J. D., and Adams, J. N. (1994) (eds. and comm.), *The Vindolanda Writing-Tablets (Tabulae Vindolandenses II)* (London).

Bowra, C. M. (1964), *Pindar* (Oxford).

Bradbury, S. (2004), *Selected Letters of Libanius: From the Age of Constantius and Julian* (Liverpool).

Bray, J. (2003), *The Epistolary Novel. Representations of Consciousness* (London).

Brémond, É., and Mathieu, G. (1962) (eds.), *Isocrate: Discours*, vol. 4 (Paris).

Brown, P. R. L. (2000), *Augustine of Hippo* (rev. edn., Berkeley and Los Angeles).

Buffa Giolito, M. F. (2000), '*Topoi* della tradizione letteraria in tre prefazioni di testi medici latine', in Pigeaud and Pigeaud: 13–31.

Bundy, E. L. (1962), *Studia Pindarica* (Berkeley).

Burrus, V. (1995), *The Making of a Heretic* (Berkeley and Los Angeles).

Burton, R. W. B. (1962), *Pindar's Pythian Odes* (Oxford).

Bury, J. B. (1998), *The Life of St. Patrick and his Place in History* (London).

Cairns, F. (1972), *Generic Composition in Greek and Roman Poetry* (Edinburgh).

Cancik, H. (1967), *Untersuchungen zu Senecas Epistulae Morales* (Hildesheim).

Cancik-Lindemaier, H. (1998), 'Seneca's Collection of Epistles', in A. Yarbo Collins (ed.), *Ancient and Modern Perspectives on the Bible and Culture: Essays in Honour of Hans Dieter Betz* (Atlanta): 88–109.

Carey, C. (1981), *A Commentary on Five Odes of Pindar* (New York).

Carey, J. (2005), *What Good are the Arts?* (London).

Castillo, C. (1974), 'La epístola como género literario de la antigüedad a la edad media latina', *Estudios Clásicos* 18: 427–42.

Chapa, J. (1998), *Letters of Condolence in Greek Papyri* (Florence).

CLAY, J. S. (1993), 'The Education of Perses: From "Mega Nepios" to "Dion Genos" and Back', in A. Schiesaro, P. Mitsis, J. S. Clay (eds.), *Mega Nepios* (Pisa): 23–33.

COLEMAN, R. (1974), 'Seneca's Epistolary Style', *Classical Quarterly* 24: 276–89.

CONNEELY, D. (1993), *The Letters of Saint Patrick* (An Sagart).

CONRING, B. (2001), *Hieronymus als Briefschreiber* (Tübingen).

CONYBEARE, C. (2000), *Paulinus Noster: Self and Symbols in the Letters of Paulinus of Nola* (Oxford).

CORBEILL, A. (1996), *Controlling Laughter: Political Humor in the Late Roman Republic* (Princeton).

COSTA, C. D. N. (2001) (ed.), *Greek Fictional Letters* (Oxford).

COTTON, H. (1981), *Documentary Letters of Recommendation in Latin from the Roman Empire* (Beiträge zur klassischen Philologie 132; Königstein).

—— (1985), '*Mirificum genus commendationis:* Cicero and the Latin Letter of Recommendation', *AJP* 106: 328–34.

CRIBIORE, R. (1996), *Writers, Teachers, and Students in Graeco-Roman Egypt* (American Studies in Papyrology 36; Atlanta).

—— (2001), *Gymnastics of the Mind: Greek Education in Hellenistic and Roman Egypt* (Princeton).

CUGUSI, P. (1983), *Evoluzione e forme dell'epistolografia latina nella tarda repubblica e nei primi due secoli dell'impero, con cenni sull'epistolografia preciceroniana* (Rome).

—— (1992) (ed. and comm.), *Corpus epistularum Latinarum papyris tabulis ostracis servatarum*, 2 vols. (Florence).

CUMONT, F. (1926), 'Le Sage Bothros ou le phylarque Arétas?', *Revue de philologie* 50: 13–33.

D'ALESSIO, G. B. (2004), 'Past Future and Present Past: Temporal Deixis in Greek Archaic Lyric', *Arethusa* 37.3: 267–94.

DAMON, C. (1997), *The Mask of the Parasite: A Pathology of Roman Patronage* (Ann Arbor).

DAUR, K. (2005), *Sancti Aurelii Augustini Epistulae*, vols. I–II (Turnhout).

DE MEO, C. (1986), *Lingue tecniche del latino* (2nd edn., Bologna).

DE PRETIS, A. (2002), *'Epistolarity' in the First Book of Horace's Epistles* (Piscataway, NJ).

—— (2003), ' "Insincerity", "Facts", and "Epistolarity": Approaches to Pliny's Letters to Calpurnia', *Arethusa* 36: 127–46.

DEISSMANN, A. (1923), *Licht von Osten: Das Neue Testament und die neuentdeckten Texte der hellenistisch-römischen Welt* (Tübingen).

DERRIDA, J. (1987), *The Post Card* (trans. A. Bass; Chicago).

DRACHMANN, A. B. (1891), *Moderne Pindarfortolkning* (Copenhagen).

DUNKEL, G. E. (2000), 'Remarks on Code-Switching in Cicero's Letters to Atticus', *Museum Helveticum* 57: 122–9.

DÜRING, I. (1951) (ed.), *Chion of Heraclea: A Novel in Letters* (Göteborg).

DYCK, A. (1996), *Cicero's De Officiis* (Ann Arbor).

DZIATZKO, K. (1897), 'Brief', *Pauly's Real Encyclopädie der classischen Altertumswissenschaft* 3: 836–43.

EBBELER, J. (2003), 'Caesar's Letters and the Ideology of Literary History', *Helios* 30.1: 3–19.

EDMUNDS, L. (1982), 'The Roman Invitation Poem: What is it? Where did it Come From?' *American Journal of Philology* 103: 184–8.

EDWARDS, C. (1997), 'Self-Scrutiny and Self-Transformation in Seneca's *Letters*', *Greece and Rome* 44: 23–38.

—— (1999), 'The Suffering Body: Philosophy and Pain in Seneca's Letters', in J. L. Porter (ed.), *Constructions of the Classical Body* (Ann Arbor): 252–68.

ENGELS, L. J., and HOFMANN, H. (1997) (eds.), *Neues Handbuch der Literaturwissenschaft*, 4: *Spätantike* (Wiesbaden).

ENOS, T., and BROWN, S. C. (1993) (eds.), *Defining the New Rhetorics* (Newbury Park, London, New Delhi).

ERLICH, V. (1955), *Russian Formalism: History-Doctrine* (The Hague).

ERSKINE, A. (2003), 'Cicero and the Shaping of Hellenistic Philosophy', *Hermathena* 175: 5–15.

ESPOSITO, M. (1956–7), 'The Patrician Problem and a Possible Solution', *Irish Historical Studies* 10: 131–55.

FABRE, P. (1948), *Essai sur la chronologie de l'œuvre de saint Paulin de Nole* (Paris).

—— (1949), *Saint Paulin de Nole et l'amitié chrétienne* (Paris).

FANTHAM, E. (1996), *Roman Literary Culture* (Baltimore).

FARNELL, L. R. (1930), *The Works of Pindar*, 3 vols. (London).

FARRELL, J. (1991), *Virgil's Georgics and the Traditions of Ancient Epic* (Oxford).

FEENEY, D. (2004), 'Interpreting Sacrificial Ritual in Roman Poetry: Disciplines and their Models', in A. Barchiesi, J. Rüpke, S. Stephens, *Rituals in Ink: A Conference on Religion and Literary Production in Ancient Rome held at Stanford University in February 2002* (Wiesbaden): 1–21.

FERRI, R. (1993), *Il dispiaceri di un epicureo* (Pisa).

FINK, R. O. (1971), *Roman Military Records on Papyrus* (Case Western Reserve University).

FISCHER, K.-D. (1989), 'Medizinische Literatur', R. Herzog and P. L. Schmidt, eds. *Handbuch der lateinischen Literatur der Antike, Vol. I: Die archaischer Literatur von den Anfängen bis Sullas Tod*, Munich. 5: §§511–14 (pp. 74–83).

—— (2000), *Bibliographie des textes médicaux latins: Antiquité et haut Moyen Âge. Premier supplément, 1986–1999* (Saint-Étienne).

—— (2002), 'Die pseudohippokratische *Epistula de uirginibus*. Bemerkungen zu ihrer Textüberlieferung und zu ihrem Vokabular', *Les Études Classiques* 70: 101–22.

—— (2005), 'De epistulis XVIII et XVIIII codicis Bruxellensis 3701', in A. Ferraces Rodríguez (ed.), *Isidorus medicus. Isidoro de Sevilla y los textos de medicina* (La Coruña): 263–9.

—— (forthcoming *a*), 'Marcellus', R. Herzog and P. L. Schmidt, eds. *Handbuch der lateinischen Literatur der Antike, Vol. I: Die archaischer Literatur von den Anfängen bis Sullas Tod*, Munich. 6: §608. 1.

—— (forthcoming *b*), 'Pseudo-Hippocrates, Epistulae', R. Herzog and P. L. Schmidt, eds. *Handbuch der lateinischen Literatur der Antike, Vol. I: Die archaischer Literatur von den Anfängen bis Sullas Tod*, Munich. 6: §608. 3.

—— and VON STADEN, H. (1996), 'Ein angeblicher Brief des Herophilos an König Antiochos, aus einer Brüsseler Handschrift erstmals herausgegeben', *Sudhoffs Archiv* 80: 86–98.

FLAMMINI, G. (1990), 'La *praefatio* ai *Matheseos libri* di Firmico Materno', in Santini and Scivoletto: I. 67–115.

FLETCHER, R. (1997), *The Conversion of Europe* (London).

FÖGEN, T. (2002), 'Metasprachliche Reflexionen antiker Autoren zu den Charakteristika von Fachtexten und Fachsprachen', in Horster and Reitz: 31–60.

FOUCAULT, M. (1988), *The Care of the Self: The History of Sexuality*, vol. 3 (= (1984), *Histoire de sexualité*, iii: *Le Souci de soi*) (Harmondsworth).

—— (2001*a*), *Fearless Speech* (ed. J. Pearson; Cambridge, Mass.).

—— (2001*b*), *L'Herméneutique du sujet: Cours au Collège de France 1981–1982* (Paris).

FOWLER, A. (1982), *Kinds of Literature: An Introduction to the Theory of Genres and Modes* (Oxford).

FOWLER, D. P. (2000), 'The Didactic Plot', in M. Depew, D. Obbink (eds.), *Matrices of Genre* (Cambridge, Mass., and London): 205–20.

FRAENKEL, H. (1957), *Horace* (Oxford).

FREISENBRUCH, A. G. (2004), 'The Correspondence of Marcus Cornelius Fronto', Ph.D. thesis (Cambridge).

FREND, W. H. C. (1974), 'The Two Worlds of Paulinus of Nola', in J. W. Binns (ed.), *Latin Literature of the Fourth Century* (London and Boston): 100–33.

FUHRMANN, M. (1974) (ed.), *Neues Handbuch der Literaturwissenschaft*, 3: *Römische Literatur* (Frankfurt am Main).

FURLEY, D. (1970), 'Variations on Themes from Empedocles in Lucretius' Proem', *Bulletin of the Institute of Classical Studies* 17: 55–64.

FÜRST, A. (1999), *Augustins Briefwechsel mit Hieronymus* (Münster).

GALE, M. R. (1994), *Myth and Poetry in Lucretius* (Cambridge).

—— (2000), *Virgil on the Nature of Things* (Cambridge).

GALLAGHER, C., and GREENBLATT, S. (2000), *Practicing New Historicism* (Chicago).

GAMBERINI, F. (1983), *Stylistic Theory and Practice in the Younger Pliny* (Hildesheim).

GANTZ, T. (1978), 'Pindar's Second Pythian: The Myth of Ixion', *Hermes* 106: 14–26.

GEERAERTS, D., and GRONDELAERS, S. (1995), 'Looking Back at Anger: Cultural Traditions and Metaphorical Patterns', in J. Taylor and R. E. MacLaury (eds.), *Language and the Construal of the World* (Berlin): 153–80.

GENTILI, B. (1988), *Poetry and its Public in Ancient Greece* (trans. A. T. Cole; Baltimore and London).

GIBSON, R. K. (1997), 'Didactic Poetry as a "Popular" Form: A Study of Imperatival Expressions in Latin Didactic Verse and Prose', in C. Atherton (ed.), *Form and Content in Didactic Poetry* (Bari): 67–98.

GIGANTE, M. (1995), *Philodemus in Italy* (Ann Arbor).

—— (1999), *Kepas e Peripatos* (Naples).

—— (2000), 'Seneca, ein Nachfolger Philodems?', in M. Erler (ed.), *Epikureismus in der späten Republik und der Kaiserzeit* (Stuttgart): 32–41.

GLÄSER, R. (1990), *Fachtextsorten im Englischen* (Tübingen).

GLEASON, M. W. (1995), *Making Men: Sophists and Self-Presentation in Ancient Rome* (Princeton).

GOLDSTEIN, J. A. (1968), *The Letters of Demosthenes* (New York).

GONIS, N. (1997), 'Troubled Fields: CPR VII 52 Revisited', *Tyche* 12: 47–50.

GORDON, P. (1996), *Epicurus in Lycia* (Ann Arbor).

GOW, A. S. F. (1952), *Theocritus*, 2 vols. (2nd edn., Cambridge).

GOWERS, E. (1993), *The Loaded Table: Representations of Food in Roman Literature* (Oxford).

GRANT, M. (1994), *The Antonines: The Roman Empire in Transition* (London).

GRATWICK, A. (1979), 'Sundials, Parasites, and Girls from Boeotia', *Classical Quarterly* 29: 308–23.

GRAVER, M. (1996), 'Therapeutic Reading and Seneca's Moral Epistles', Ph.D. thesis (Brown).

GREEN, R. P. H. (1991), *The Works of Ausonius* (Oxford).

GRIFFIN, M. T. (1992), *Seneca: A Philosopher in Politics* (2nd ed., Oxford).

—— and ATKINS, E. M. (1991), *Cicero: On Duties* (Cambridge).

GUILLEMIN, A. M. (1929), *Pline et le vie littéraire de son temps* (Paris).

GUMMERE, R. M. (1917), *Seneca: Epistulae Morales* (London and Cambridge, Mass.).

GUNDERSON, E. (1997), 'Catullus, Pliny and Love Letters', *Transactions of the American Philological Association* 127: 201–32.

HABINEK, T. N. (1998), *The Politics of Latin Literature: Writing, Identity, and Empire in Ancient Rome* (Princeton).

HACHMANN, E. (1995), *Die Führung des Lesers in Senecas* Epistulae Morales (Münster).

HAIGHT, E. E. (1948), '*Epistula item quaevis non magna poema est*: A Fresh Approach to Horace's First Book of Epistles', *Studies in Philology* 45: 525–40.

HAMILTON, P. (1996), *Historicism* (London).

HARDIE, P. (2002), *Ovid's Poetics of Illusion* (Cambridge).

HARRISON, S. J. (1995), 'Poetry, Philosophy and Letter-Writing in Horace, *Epistles* 1', in D. Innes, H. Hine, C. B. R. Pelling (eds.), *Ethics and Rhetoric* (Oxford): 47–61.

HARVEY, A. E. (1955), 'The Classification of Greek Lyric Poetry', *Classical Quarterly* 5: 157–75.

HEATH, M. (2004), *Menander: A Rhetor in Context* (Oxford).

HEINIMANN, F. (1955), 'Diokles von Karystos und der prophylaktische Brief an König Antigonos', *Museum Helveticum* 12: 158–72.

HEINZE, R. (1919), 'Horazens Buch der Briefe', *Neue Jahrbücher für das klassische Altertum* 43: 305–15.

HENDERSON, J. (1982), 'Pliny's Letters: A Portrait of the Artist as a Figure of Style', *Omnibus* 4: 31–2.

—— (2002), *Pliny's Statue: The Letters, Self Portraiture & Classical Art* (Exeter).

HENNINGS, R. (1994), *Der Briefwechsel zwischen Augustinus und Hieronymus und ihr Streit um des alten Testaments und die Auslegung von Gal. 2.11–14* (Leiden).

HERCHER, R. (1866) (ed.), *Claudii Aeliani de natura animalium libri xvii, varia historia, epistolae, fragmenta*, vol. 2 (Leipzig).

—— (1873) (ed.), *Epistolographi Graeci* (Paris).

HERINGTON, C. J. (1985), *Poetry into Drama* (Berkeley and London).

HICKS, R. D. (1931), *Diogenes Laertius: Lives of Eminent Philosophers*, vol. 2 (rev. edn., London).

HODKINSON, O. D. (2006), '"Novels in the Greek letter": Inversions of the Written-Oral Hierarchy in the *Briefroman* "Themistocles"', in V. Rimell (ed.), *Orality and Representation in the Ancient Novels* (Ancient Narrative Supplementum 5; Groningen).

HOFFER, S. E. (1999), *The Anxieties of Pliny the Younger* (Atlanta).

HOLFORD-STREVENS, L. (1976), 'Elocutio novella', *Classical Quarterly* 26: 140–1.

HOLLIS, A. S. (1977), *Ovid Ars Amatoria 1* (Oxford).

HOLZBERG, N. (1994), 'Der griechische Briefroman: Versuch einer Gattungs-stypologie', in N. Holzberg (ed.), *Der griechische Briefroman: Gattungs-typologie und Textanalyse* (Tübingen): 1–52.

HORSFALL, N. (1979), 'Horace: Sermones 3?', *Liverpool Classical Monthly* 4: 117–19.

HORSTER, M., and REITZ, C. (2002) (eds.), *Antike Fachschriftsteller: Litera-rischer Diskurs und sozialer Kontext* (Akten der Tagung an der Universität Rostock, November 2001) (Stuttgart).

HOWALD, E., and SIGERIST, H. E. (1927) (eds.), *Antonii Musae De herba uettonica liber, Pseudoapulei Herbarius, Anonymi De taxone liber, Sexti Placiti Liber medicinae ex animalibus*, etc. (Corpus medicorum Latinorum 4; Leipzig and Berlin).

HOWLETT, D. H. (1994), *The Book of Letters of Saint Patrick the Bishop* (Dublin).

HUME, D. (1757), 'Of the Standard of Taste', in E. F. Miller (ed.), *Essays Moral, Political, Literary* (Indianapolis, 1987).

HUNTER, R. L. (1983), *A Study of Daphnis & Chloe* (Cambridge).

—— (1999), *Theocritus: A Selection* (Cambridge).

HUTCHINSON, G. O. (1988), *Hellenistic Poetry* (Oxford).

—— (1989), review of M. Gronewald, *et al., Kölner Papyri (P. Köln)* VI, *Classical Review* 39: 356–8.

—— (1998), *Cicero's Correspondence: A Literary Study* (Oxford).

—— (2001), *Greek Lyric Poetry: A Commentary on Selected Larger Pieces* (Oxford).

INWOOD, B. (1995), 'Seneca in his Philosophical Milieu', *Harvard Studies in Classical Philology* 97: 63–76.

—— (2002), 'God and Human Knowledge in Seneca's *Natural Questions*', in D. Frede and A. Laks (eds.), *Traditions of Theology: Studies in Hellenistic Theology, its Background and Aftermath* (Leiden): 119–57.

—— (2005), *Reading Seneca* (Oxford).

JACQUES, X., and VAN OOTEGHEM, J. (1967), *Indexe de Pline le Jeune* (Naumur).

JANSON, T. (1964), *Latin Prose Prefaces: Studies in Literary Conventions* (Stockholm).

JOHNSON, W. R. (1993), *Horace and the Dialectic of Freedom* (Ithaca, NY, and London).

KASTER, R. A. (2001), 'The Dynamics of *fastidium* and the Ideology of Disgust', *TAPA* 131: 143–89.

—— (2003), '*Invidia*, νέμεσις, φθόνος, and the Roman Emotional Economy', in D. Konstan and K. Rutter (eds.), *Envy, Spite and Jealousy: The Rivalrous Emotions in Ancient Greece* (Edinburgh): 253–76.

KAYSER, C. L. (1871) (ed.), *Flavii Philostrati Opera*, 2 vols. (Leipzig).

KELLY, J. N. D. (1975), *Jerome: His Life, Writings, and Controversies* (New York).

KERKHECKER, A. (1999), *Callimachus' Book of* Iambi (Oxford).

KEYES, C. W. (1935), 'The Greek Letter of Introduction', *American Journal of Philology* 56: 28–44.

KIM, C.-H. (1972), *Form and Structure of the Familiar Greek Letter of Recommendation* (Missoula, Mont.).

KIND, F. E. (1930), 'Marcellus (58)', *Pauly's Real Encyclopädie der classischen Altertumswissenschaft* 14. 2: 1498–1503.

KLEIJWEGT, M. (1971), *Ancient Youth* (Amsterdam).

KNIGHT, G. (forthcoming), 'Friendship and Erotics in the Late Antique Verse Epistle: Ausonius and Paulinus Revisited'.

KOSKENNIEMI, H. (1956), *Studien zur Idee und Phraseologie des Griechischen Briefes bis 400 n. Chr.* (Helsinki).

KROON, C. (1995), *Discourse Particles in Latin: A Study of* nam, enim, autem, vero *and* at (Amsterdam).

KULLMANN, W., and ALTHOFF, J. (1993) (eds.), *Vermittlung und Tradierung von Wissen in der griechischen Kultur* (Tübingen).

—— —— and ASPER, M. (1998) (eds.), *Gattungen wissenschaftlicher Literatur in der Antike* (Tübingen).

LANA, I. (1991), 'Le "Lettere a Lucilio nella letteratura epistolare"' in P. Grimal (ed.), *Sénèque et la prose latine* (Fondation Hardt, Entretiens XXXVI; Geneva): 253–311.

LANGSLOW, D. R. (2000*a*), *Medical Latin in the Roman Empire* (Oxford).

—— (2000*b*), 'Latin Discourse Particles, "Medical Latin" and "Classical Latin"', *Mnemosyne* 53: 537–60.

—— (2005), '"Langues réduites au lexique"?—the Languages of Latin Technical Prose', in T. Reinhardt, M. Lapidge, and J. N. Adams (eds.), *Aspects of the Language of Latin Prose* (Proceedings of the British Academy 129; Oxford): 287–302.

LEACH, E. W. (2003), '*Otium* as *luxuria*: Economy of Status in the Younger Pliny's *Letters*', *Arethusa* 36.2: 147–65.

LEEMAN, A. D. (1951), 'The Epistolary Form of Sen. *Ep.* 102', *Mnemosyne* 4: 175–81.

—— (1953), 'Seneca's "Moralis Philosophia" and his Epistles', *Mnemosyne* 6: 307–13.

LeMOINE, F. (1991), 'Parental Gifts: Father-Son Dedications and Dialogues in Roman Didactic Literature', *Illinois Classical Studies* 16: 337–66.

LENGEN, R. (2002), *Form und Funktion der aristotelischen Pragmatie: Die Kommunikation mit dem Rezipienten* (Stuttgart).

LIEBS, D. (1974), 'Die juristische Literatur', in Fuhrmann: 195–208.

LONG, A. A. (1986), *Hellenistic Philosophy: Stoics, Sceptics and Epicureans* (2nd edn., London).

—— (1988), 'Socrates in Hellenistic Philosophy', *Classical Quarterly* 38: 150–71.

LONGO, O. (1985), 'Alcifrone: lo spazio del piacere', in E. Avezzu (ed.), *Alcifrone: Lettere di parassiti e di cortigiane* (Venice): 9–41.

LUCK, G. (1961), 'Brief und Epistel in der Antike', *Das Altertum* 7: 77–84.

LUDOLPH, M. (1997), *Epistolographie und Selbstdarstellung: Untersuchungen zu den 'Paradebriefen' Plinius des Juengeren* (Munich).

MACALISTER, R. A. S. (1935), *Ancient Ireland* (London).

McGANN, M. (1969), *Studies in Horace's First Book of Epistles* (Brussels).

McGING, B. (1995), *Greek Papyri from Dublin (P. Dub.)* (Bonn).

MACKENDRICK, P. (1989), *The Philosophical Books of Cicero* (London).

MACKINNEY, L. C. (1943), 'An Unpublished Treatise on Medicine and Magic from the Age of Charlemagne', *Speculum* 18: 494–6.

MACLEOD, C. (1979), 'The Poetry of Ethics: Horace, *Epistles* 1', *Journal of Roman Studies* 69: 16–27.

MAGGIULLI, G. (1997), 'Lo pseudo-Apuleio di Marcello', *Serta antiqua et mediaevalia* 1: 211–24.

MALHERBE, A. (1977), *The Cynic Epistles: A Study Edition* (Missoula, Mont.).

—— (1988) (ed.), *Ancient Epistolary Theorists* (Atlanta).

MARINCOLA, J. (2001), *Greek Historians* (Greece and Rome New Surveys in the Classics 31; Oxford).

MARTINDALE, C. (2005), *Latin Poetry and the Judgement of Taste* (Oxford).

MARVIN, M. (1993), 'Copying in Roman Sculpture: The Replica Series', in E. d'Ambra (ed.), *Roman Art in Context* (Englewood Cliffs, NJ): 161–88.

MATTHEWS, J. (1975), *Western Aristocracies and Imperial Court* AD *364–425* (Oxford).

MAURACH, G. (1970), *Der Bau von Senecas Epistulae Morales* (Heidelberg).

——— (1991), *Seneca: Leben und Werk* (Darmstadt; 2nd edn. 1996).

MAVROUDIS, A., and FISCHER, K.-D. (2005), 'Überlegungen zu einem Corpus der medizinischen Briefe des Altertums und des Frühmittelalters' (unpubl.).

MAYER, R. (1986), 'Horace *Epistles* 1 and Philosophy', *American Journal of Philology* 107: 55–73.

——— (1994), *Horace: Epistles 1* (Cambridge).

——— (1995), 'Horace's *Moyen de Parvenir*', in S. J. Harrison (ed.), *Homage to Horace* (Oxford): 279–95.

——— (2003), 'Pliny and *Gloria Dicendi*', *Arethusa* 36: 227–34.

MAZZOLI, G. (1989), 'Le "Epistulae Morales ad Lucilium" di Seneca: Valore letterario e filosofico', *ANRW* 2.36.3: 1833–77.

MEISSNER, B. (1999), *Die technologische Fachliteratur der Antike: Struktur, Überlieferung und Wirkung technischen Wissens in der Antike (ca. 400 v. Chr.–ca. 500 n. Chr.)* (Berlin).

MILLAR, F. (1977), *The Emperor in the Roman World: 31 BC–AD 337* (London).

MITSIS, P. (1993), 'Committing Philosophy on the Reader: Didactic Coercion and Reader Autonomy in *De Rerum Natura*', in A. Schiesaro, P. Mitsis, J. S. Clay (eds.), *Mega Nepios* (Pisa): 111–28.

MOLES, J. (1985), 'Cynicism in Horace, *Epistles* 1', *Proceedings of the Liverpool Latin seminar* 5: 33–60.

——— (2002), 'Poetry, Philosophy, Politics and Play', in A. J. Woodman, D. C. Feeney (eds.), *Traditions and Contexts in the Poetry of Horace* (Cambridge): 141–57.

MOMIGLIANO, A. (1933), 'Una lettera a Claudio e una lettera ad Antigono Gonata', *Athenaeum* 11: 128–35.

MORELLO, R. (2003), 'Pliny and the Art of Saying Nothing', *Arethusa* 36.2: 187–209.

MORETTI, F. (1988), *Signs Taken for Wonders: Essays in the Sociology of Literary Forms* (2nd edn., London and New York).

MORRISON, A. D. (2006), 'Advice and Abuse: Horace, *Epistles* 1 and the Iambic Tradition', *Materiali e discussioni per l'analisi dei testi classici* 56: 29–61.

MRATSCHEK, S. (2001), '*Multis enim notissima est sanctitas loci*: Paulinus and the Gradual Rise of Nola as a Center of Christian Hospitality', *Journal of Early Christian Studies* 9.4: 511–53.

——— (2002), *Der Briefwechsel des Paulinus von Nola: Kommunikation und soziale Kontakte zwischen christlichen Intellektuellen* (Göttingen).

MUTSCHMANN, H. (1915), 'Seneca und Epikur', *Hermes* 50: 321–56.

NELSON, A. (1932), 'Zur pseudohippokratischen Epistula ad Antiochum regem', in A. Nelson (ed.), *Symbolae philologicae O. A. Danielsson octogenario dicatae* (Uppsala): 203–17.

NERNEY, D. S. (1949), 'A Study of St. Patrick's Sources', *Irish Ecclesiastical Record* 71: 97–110, 265–80.

NORDEN, E. (1905), 'Die Composition und Literaturgattung der Horazischen *Epistula ad Pisones*', *Hermes* 40: 481–528.

NORMAN, A. F. (1992) (ed.), *Libanius: Autobiography and Selected Letters*, 2 vols. (Cambridge, Mass.).

ODER, E., and HOPPE, C. (1924–7), *Corpus Hippiatricorum Graecorum*, 2 vols. (Leipzig).

O'DONNELL, J. J. (1991), 'The Authority of Augustine', *Augustinian Studies* 22: 7–35.

—— (2005), *Augustine: A New Biography* (New York).

OLIENSIS, E. (1998), *Horace and the Rhetoric of Authority* (Cambridge).

OPSOMER, C., and HALLEUX, R. (1985), 'La Lettre d'Hippocrate à Mécène et la lettre d'Hippocrate à Antiochus', in I. Mazzini and F. Fusco (eds.), *I Testi di medicina latini antichi: Problemi filologici e storici* (Rome): 339–64.

OZANAM, A.-M. (1999), *Alciphron*: Lettres de pêcheurs, de paysans, de parasites et d'hétaïres (Paris).

PANI, M. (1992), *Potere e valori a Roma fra Augusto e Traiano* (Bari).

PAOLUCCI, P. (2000), 'Epistolografia medica e retorica epistolare: Per un'analisi formale dell'Epistula Anthimi de observatione ciborum ad Theudericum regem Francorum', in Pigeaud and Pigeaud: 241–9.

PARSONS, P. J. (1980), 'Background: The Papyrus Letter', in J. Veremans and F. Decreus (eds.), *Acta Colloquii Didactici Classici Octavi* (Didactica Classica Gandensia 20; Gent): 3–19.

PAVIS D'ESCURAC, H. (1992), 'Pline le Jeune et les lettres de recommandation', in E. Frézouls (ed.), *La Mobilité sociale dans le monde romain* (Strasbourg): 55–69.

PETER, H. (1901), *Der Brief in der römischen Literatur* (Leipzig; repr. Hildesheim, 1965).

PIGEAUD, A., and PIGEAUD, J. (2000) (eds.), *Les Textes médicaux latins comme littérature* (Actes du VIᵉ colloque international sur les textes médicaux latins du 1ᵉʳ au 3 septembre 1998 à Nantes) (Nantes).

PIGEAUD, J. (1981), *La Maladie de l'âme: Étude sur la relation de l'âme et du corps dans la tradition médico-philosophique antique* (Paris).

PINKSTER, H. (1995), 'Notes on the Syntax of Celsus', in P. J. van der Eijk, H. F. J. Horstmanshoff, and P. H. Schrijvers (eds.), *Ancient Medicine in its Socio-Cultural Context*, 2 vols. (Amsterdam): II. 555–66.

Bibliography 361

PLANTERA, A. (1977–8), 'Osservazioni sulle commendatizie latine da Cicerone a Frontone', *Annali della Facoltà di Magistero dell'Università di Cagliari*, NS 2: 5–36.

PLUMER, E. (2003), *Augustine's Commentary on Galatians* (Oxford).

PORTER, J. (2001), 'Ideals and Ruins: Pausanias, Longinus, and the Second Sophistic', in S. E. Alcock, J. Cherry, and J. Elsner (eds.), *Pausanias: Travel and Memory in Roman Greece* (Oxford): 63–92.

POWELL, J. U. (1970), *Collectanea Alexandrina* (Oxford).

PURCELL, N. (1995), 'Eating Fish: The Paradoxes of Seafood', in J. Wilkins, D. Harvey, and M. Dobson (eds.), *Food in Antiquity* (Exeter): 132–49.

RACE, W. H. (1997), *Pindar*, 2 vols. (Cambridge, Mass., and London).

RADICE, B. (1963), *The Letters of the Younger Pliny* (Harmondsworth).

REA, J. (1986), 'A Letter of Condolence: CPR VI 81 Revised', *Zeitschrift für Papyrologie und Epigraphik* 62: 75–8.

—— (1993), 'A Student's Letter to his Father: P Oxy. XVIII 2190 Revised', *Zeitschrift für Papyrologie und Epigraphik* 99: 75–88.

REARDON, B. P. (1971), *Courants littéraires grecs des IIe et IIIe siècles après J-C* (Paris).

REBENICH, S. (2002), *Jerome* (New York).

REED, J. T. (1997), 'The Epistle', in S. Porter (ed.), *Handbook of Classical Rhetoric in the Hellenistic Period (330 BC–AD400)* (London): 171–93.

REYNOLDS, L. D. (1965), *The Medieval Tradition of Seneca's Letters* (Oxford).

RHYS ROBERTS, W. (1902) (ed.), *Demetrius On Style* (Cambridge).

ROBERTS, M. (1985), 'Paulinus Poem 11, Virgil's First Eclogue, and the Limits of *Amicitia*', *Transactions of the American Philological Association* 115: 271–82.

ROELCKE, T. (1999), *Fachsprachen* (Berlin).

RÖMER, F. (1987), 'Zum Vorwort des Scribonius Largus', *Wiener Studien* 100: 125–32.

—— (1990), 'Sulla prefazione di Scribonio Largo', in Santini and Scivoletto: I. 339–54.

ROSENMEYER, P. (1994), 'The Epistolary Novel', in J. Morgan and R. Stoneman (eds.), *Greek Fiction: The Greek Novel in Context* (London): 146–65.

—— (2001a), *Ancient Epistolary Fictions: The Letter in Greek Literature* (Cambridge).

—— (2001b), '(In)versions of Pygmalion: The Statue Talks Back', in L. McClure and A. Lardinois (eds.), *Making Silence Speak: Women's Voices in Ancient Greek Literature and Society* (Princeton): 240–60.

ROUSE, W. H. D., and SMITH, M. F. (1992), *Lucretius: De Rerum Natura* (rev. edn., London).

Rudd, N. (1979), '"Epistles" and "Sermones"', *Liverpool Classical Monthly* 4: 147.

Ruiz García, E. (1988), *Teofrasto, Caracteres: Alcifrón, Cartas de pesca- dores, campesinos, parásitos y cortesanas* (Madrid).

Russell, D. A., and Winterbottom, M. (1972) (eds.), *Ancient Literary Criticism: The Principal Texts in New Translations* (Oxford).

Rutherford, R. (1995), *The Art of Plato* (London).

Sabbah, G., Corsetti, P.-P., and Fischer, K.-D. (1987), *Bibliographie des textes médicaux latins: Antiquité et haut Moyen Âge* (Saint-Étienne).

Saïd, S. (1987), 'La Société rurale dans le roman grec ou la campagne vue de la ville', in E. Frézouls (ed.), *Sociétés urbaines, sociétés rurales dans l'Asie Mineure et la Syrie hellénistiques et romaines* (Strasbourg): 149–71 (trans. in S. Swain (ed.), *Oxford Readings in the Greek Novel* (Oxford, 1999): 83–107).

Salzman, M. (forthcoming), 'Symmachus and his Father: Patriarchy and Patrimony in the Late Roman Senatorial Elite'.

Santini, C. (1990), 'Le *praefationes* dei gromatici', in Santini and Scivoletto: i. 137–48.

—— and Scivoletto, N. I. (1990–2) (eds.), *Prefazioni, prologhi, proemi di opere tecnico-scientifiche latine*, i–ii (Rome).

——, —— and Zurli, L. (1998) (eds.), *Prefazioni, prologhi, proemi di opere tecnico-scientifiche latine*, iii (Rome).

Santini, L. (1995), 'Tra filosofi e parassiti: l'epistola III.19 di Alcifrone e i modelli lucianei', *Atene e Roma* 40: 58–71.

Scarborough, J. (1969), *Roman Medicine* (London).

Schepers, M. A. (1905) (ed.), *Alciphronis rhetoris epistularum libri iv* (Leip- zig).

Scherer, V. (1976), *Die Epistula de ratione ventris vel viscerum: ein Beitrag zur Geschichte des Galenismus im frühen Mittelalter*, Diss. med. dent. (Freie Universität, Berlin).

Schmalzbauer, G. (1974), 'Medizinisch-diätetisches über die Podagra aus spätbyzantinischer Zeit', *Jb. d. österr. Byzant.* 23: 229–43.

Schmidt, P. L. (1972), 'Catos Epistula ad M. filium und die Anfänge der römischen Briefliteratur', *Hermes* 100: 568–76.

—— (1974), 'Cicero und die republikanische Kunstprosa', in Fuhrmann: 147–79.

—— (1997), 'Brief', *Der Neue Pauly* 2: 771–5.

Schmitz, T. A. (2002), *Moderne Literaturtheorie und antike Texte* (Darm- stadt).

—— (2005), 'Alciphron's Letters as a Sophistic Text', in B. Borg (ed.), *Paideia: The World of the Second Sophistic* (Berlin): 87–104.

SCHNEIDER, J. (1954), 'Brief', *Rivista di archeologia cristiana* 2: 564–85.

SCHÖNEGG, B. (1999), *Senecas epistulae morales als philosophische Kunstwerk* (Bern).

SCHUBERT, P. (1995), 'Philostrate et les sophistes d'Alexandrie', *Mnemosyne* 48: 178–88.

SCHULZE, C. (2005), 'Von wem stammt der Brief an Pullius Natalis?', *Hermes* 133: 486–95.

SEDLEY, D. (1998), *Lucretius and the Transformation of Greek Wisdom* (Cambridge).

SEGOLONI, M. P. (1990), 'L'Epistola dedicatoria e l'appendice in versi del *De medicamentis* di Marcello', in Santini and Scivoletto: I. 367–79.

SELDEN, D. L. (1994), 'Genre of Genre', in J. Tatum (ed.), *The Search for the Ancient Novel* (Baltimore): 39–64.

SETAIOLI, A. (1988), *Seneca e i Greci* (Bologna).

SHACKLETON BAILEY, D. R. (1965–70), *Cicero's letters to Atticus*, 7 vols. (Cambridge).

—— (1977), *Cicero Epistulae Ad Familiares* II (Cambridge).

SHARROCK, A. R. (2000), 'Intratextuality: Texts, Parts and (W)holes in Theory', in A. R. Sharrock and H. Morales (eds.), *Intratextuality: Greek and Roman Textual Relations* (Oxford): 1–39.

—— (2003), review of Volk (2002), *Classical Philology* 98: 306–9.

SHELTON, J.-A. (1987), 'Pliny's Letter 3.11: Rhetoric and Autobiography', *Classica et Mediaevalia* 38: 121–39.

—— (1990), 'Pliny the Younger and the Ideal Wife', *Classica et Mediaevalia* 41: 163–86.

SHERWIN-WHITE, A. N. (1966), *The Letters of Pliny: A Historical and Social Commentary* (Oxford).

SMITH, W. D. (1990), *Hippocrates: Pseudepigraphic Writings (Letters—Embassy—Speech from the Altar—Decree) edited and translated with an introduction* (Leiden).

SOUTER, A. (1924), *Earliest Latin Commentaries on the Epistles of St. Paul* (Oxford).

STADEN, H. VON (1989), *Herophilus: The Art of Medicine in Early Alexandria* (Cambridge).

STIREWALT, M. L. (1993), *Studies in Ancient Greek Epistolography* (Atlanta).

STOFFREGEN, M. (1977), *Eine frühmittelalterliche lateinische Übersetzung des byzantinischen Puls- und Urintraktats des Alexandros*, Diss. med. (Freie Universität, Berlin).

STOWERS, S. K. (1986), *Letter Writing in Greco-Roman Antiquity* (Philadelphia).

SUERBAUM, W. (2002a), 'M. Porcius Cato (Censorius)', R. Herzog and P. L. Schmidt, eds. *Handbuch der lateinischen Literatur der Antike, Vol. I: Die archaischer Literatur von den Anfängen bis Sullas Tod*, Munich. 1: §162 (pp. 380–418).

—— (2002b), 'Cornelia, die Mutter der Gracchen', R. Herzog and P. L. Schmidt, eds. *Handbuch der lateinischen Literatur der Antike, Vol. I: Die archaischer Literatur von den Anfängen bis Sullas Tod*, Munich. 1: §174 (pp. 456–8).

SWAIN, S. (1996), *Hellenism and Empire: Language, Classicism and Power in the Greek World, AD 50–250* (Oxford).

—— (2002), 'Bilingualism in Cicero?', in J. N. Adams, M. Janse, and S. Swain (eds.), *Bilingualism in Ancient Society: Language Contact and the Written Text* (Oxford): 128–67.

SYKUTRIS, J. (1931), 'Epistolographie', *Pauly's Real Encyclopädie der classischen Altertumswissenschaft* Suppl. 5: 185–220.

TAYLOR, C. (1989), *Sources of the Self: The Making of Modern Identity* (Cambridge).

TEICHERT, D. (1990), 'Der Philosoph als Briefschreiber', in G. Gabriel and C. Schildknecht (eds.), *Literarische Formen der Philosophie* (Stuttgart): 62–72.

THESLEFF, H. (1965), *The Pythagorean Texts of the Hellenistic Period* (Åbo).

THOMAS, B. (1991), *The New Historicism and Other Old-Fashioned Topics* (Princeton).

THOMPSON, E. A. (1999), *Who was Saint Patrick?* (Bury St. Edmunds).

THYRESSON, I. L. (1964), 'Quatre lettres de Claude Élien inspirées par le Dyskolos de Ménandre', *Eranos* 62: 7–35.

TODOROV, T. (1976), 'The Origin of Genres', *New Literary History* 8: 159–70.

TOMLIN, R. S. (1998), 'Roman Manuscripts from Carlisle: The Ink-Written Tablets', *Britannia* 29: 31–84.

TOOHEY, P. (1996), *Epic Lessons* (London).

TRAPP, M. B. (2003), *Greek and Latin Letters: An Anthology with Translation* (Cambridge).

TROUT, D. (1999), *Paulinus of Nola: Life, Letters, and Poems* (Berkeley and Los Angeles).

TURNER, E. G. (1968), *Greek Papyri: An Introduction* (Oxford).

—— (1975), 'Oxyrhynchus and Rome', *Harvard Studies in Classical Philology* 79: 1–24.

UREÑA, J. (1993), 'La carta ficticia griega: los nombres de personajes y el uso del encabezamiento en Alcifrón, Aristéneto y Teofilacto', *Emerita* 61: 267–98.

Ussher, R.(1987), 'Love, Letter, Novel: Alciphron and "Chion"', *Hermathena* 143: 99–106.

—— (1988), 'Letter Writing', in M. Grant and R. Kitzinger (eds.), *Civilization of the Ancient Mediterranean*, vol. 3 (New York): 1573–82.

van den Hout, M. P. J. (1999), *A Commentary on the Letters of M. Cornelius Fronto* (Leiden).

van der Eijk, P. J. (2000–1), *Diocles of Carystus: A Collection of the Fragments with Translation and Commentary*, vol. 1: *Text and Translation*; vol. 2: *Commentary* (Leiden).

van Hook, L. (1945) (ed.), *Isocrates*, vol. 3 (Cambridge, Mass.).

Vessey, M. (1993*a*), 'Conference and Confession: Literary Pragmatics in Augustine's *Apologia Contra Hieronymum*', *Journal of Early Christian Studies* 1: 175–213.

—— (1993*b*), 'Jerome's Origen: The Making of a Christian Literary *Persona*', *SP* 28: 135–45.

Vieillefond, J.-R. (1979), 'L'Invention chez Alciphron', *Revue des études grecques* 92: 120–40.

Volk, K. (2002), *The Poetics of Latin Didactic* (Oxford).

Waterfield, R., and Tredennick, H. (1990), *Xenophon: Conversations of Socrates* (London).

Webb, R. (2000), 'Picturing the Past: Uses of Ekphrasis in the *Deipnosophistae* and Other Works of the Second Sophistic', in D. Braund and J. Wilkins (eds.), *Athenaeus and his World: Reading Greek Culture in the Roman Empire* (Exeter): 218–26.

Weichert, V. (1910) (ed.), *Demetrii et Libanii quae feruntur 'Typoi epistolikoi' et 'Epistolimaioi characteres'* (Leipzig).

Wenskus, O. (2001), 'Wie schreibt man einer Dame? Zum Problem der Sprachwahl in der römischen Epistolographie', *Wiener Studien* 114: 215–32.

White, J. L. (1986), *Light from Ancient Letters* (Philadelphia).

White, P. (2003), 'Tactics in Caesar's Correspondence with Cicero', *Papers of the Langford Latin Seminar* 11: 68–95.

Whitehorne, J. E. G. (1977), 'Was Marcus Aurelius a Hypochondriac?', *Latomus* 36: 413–21.

Whitmarsh, T. (2000), 'The Politics and Poetics of Parasitism', in D. Braund and J. Wilkins (eds.), *Athenaeus and his World: Reading Greek Culture in the Roman Empire* (Exeter): 304–15.

Wilamowitz-Moellendorff, U. von (1922), *Pindaros* (Berlin).

—— (2001), *Greek Literature and the Roman Empire: The Politics of Imitation* (Oxford).

WIEDEMANN, W. (1976), *Untersuchungen zu dem frühmittelalterlichen medizinischen Briefbuch des Codex Bruxellensis 3701–15*, Diss. med. dent. (Freie Universität, Berlin).

WILCOX, A. (2005), 'Sympathetic Rivals: Consolation in Cicero's Letters', *American Journal of Philology* 126.2: 237–56.

WILDBERGER, J. (2003), *Seneca und die Stoa*, I: *Der Platz des Menschen in der Welt* Diss. (Frankfurt am Main).

WILLIAMS, W. (1990) (ed.), *Pliny the Younger: Correspondence with Trajan from Bithynia* (Warminster).

WILLIS, J. (1955), review of M. P. J. van den Hout (1954) (ed.), *M. Cornelii Frontonis epistulae, Journal of Roman Studies* 45: 235–6.

WILSON, M. (1987), 'Seneca's Epistles to Lucilius: A Revaluation', *Ramus* 16: 102–21.

—— (2001), 'Seneca's Epistles Reclassified', in S. J. Harrison (ed.), *Texts, Ideas and the Classics* (Oxford): 164–87.

WINTER, B. W. (2002), *Philo and Paul among the Sophists: Alexandrian and Corinthian Responses to a Julio-Claudian Movement* (2nd edn., Grand Rapids, Mich.).

WITKE, C. (1971), 'Ausonius's Correspondence with Paulinus of Nola', in *Numen Litterarum: The Old and the New in Latin Poetry from Constantine to Gregory the Great* (Leiden and Cologne): 3–51.

WITTGENSTEIN, L. (1967), *Philosophical Investigations* (transl. G. E. M. Anscombe; Oxford).

WOHL, V. (1998), 'Plato avant la lettre: Authenticity in Plato's Epistles', *Ramus* 27: 60–93.

WOODBURY, L. (1968), 'Pindar and the Mercenary Muse: *Isthm*. 2:1–13', *Transactions of the American Philological Association* 99: 527–42.

WOOLF, G. (2003), 'The City of Letters', in C. Edwards and G.Woolf (eds.), *Rome the Cosmopolis* (Cambridge): 203–21.

WRAY, D. (2001), *Catullus and the Poetics of Roman Manhood* (Cambridge).

YOUNG, D. C. (1968), *Three Odes of Pindar* (Leiden).

—— (1983), 'Pindar's Pythians 2 and 3', *Harvard Studies in Classical Philology* 87: 31–48.

ZELZER, M. (1994/5), 'Der Brief in der Spätantike', *Wiener Studien* 107/8: 541–51.

—— (1997), 'Die Briefliteratur', in Engels and Hofmann: 321–53.

ZURLI, L. (1990), 'Cinque *epistulae de tuenda ualetudine*', in Santini and Scivoletto: I. 381–97.

Index Locorum

General Index

Printed and bound by CPI Group (UK) Ltd, Croydon, CR0 4YY